The Christian Faith

The Christian Faith

An Introduction to Christian Thought

Dallas M. Roark

BAKER BOOK HOUSE
Grand Rapids, Michigan

*This work is lovingly dedicated
to my wife, Elaine, who contributed to its
finish in many ways, and
to my children, Lyman and Dalaine, without
whose interruptions it would have
been finished sooner*

086491

Scripture quotations are from the Revised
Standard Version

DEWEY DECIMAL CLASSIFICATION NUMBER: 230
Library of Congress catalog card number: 69–14369
Printed in the United States of America
4.Je68 KSP

Contents

Preface

I set out initially to write this work for the serious junior or senior who is interested in knowing something of the range of Christian thought. As the work progressed it appeared that it might serve also as a preliminary survey for the seminary student who would then turn to more extensive works on various rubrics of systematic theology.

There are a number of people who deserve some word of appreciation for their service over the years. Several student secretaries have helped in typing and research of books. My first student secretary was Miss Jo Ella Tweedy (now Mrs. Ronny Turner) who was followed by Judy Sato, Johenne Hamby, and Mary Gilbert. Last of all was Susie Penner who typed the various drafts.

I wish to thank Dr. William Seiler, chairman of the Division of Social Science, Kansas State Teachers College, for reducing my teaching load the fall semester of 1967 during the finishing stages of this work.

A word of appreciation should be given to my former colleagues, Ivyloy Bishop and Fred Howard, for their inspiration and encouragement.

As this goes to press I hope that I have been fair and as objective as possible. Theology cannot survive without these two qualities.

I. Why Believe in God?

There are only three kinds of persons: those who serve God having found Him; others who are occupied in seeking Him, not having found Him; while the remainder live without seeking Him, and without having found Him. The first are reasonable and happy, the last are foolish and unhappy; those between are unhappy and reasonable.

Blaise Pascal, *Pensées*

Seeing God everywhere and all things upheld by Him is not a matter of sanctity, but of plain sanity, because God is everywhere and all things are upheld by Him. What we do about it may be sanctity; but merely seeing it is sanity. To overlook God's presence is not simply to be irreligious: it is a kind of insanity.

F. J. Sheed, *Theology and Sanity*

That there exists in the human mind, and indeed by natural instinct, some sense of Deity, we hold to be beyond dispute, since God himself, to prevent any man from pretending ignorance, has endued all men with some idea of his Godhead, the memory of which he constantly renews and occasionally enlarges, that all to a man, being aware that there is a God, and that he is their Maker, may be condemned by their own conscience when they neither worship him nor consecrate their lives to his service. . . .there is no nation so barbarous, no race so brutish, as not to be imbued with the conviction that there is a God.

John Calvin, *The Institutes of the Christian Religion*

It cannot be denied that man is usually religious. Whether this is good or bad can be debated, but that the culture of mankind is saturated with religious influences cannot be denied. The study of the great religions of the world points up the fact that man has be-

1

lieved in many gods. It seems evident that man in all ages and places has given obedience to something he calls "god."

Why man has come to believe in God can be boiled down to two different explanations—naturalistic and theistic. The naturalistic explanation may take many forms but essentially it is this: religion is born out of man's mind, heart, and life. Thus, religion is a creation or projection of man's needs. The theistic explanation is that religion arose because of God's self-revelation to man, and worship is essentially born of a relationship initiated by the Divine.

The variations of the naturalistic view are many. Religion is wishful thinking and is the result of a world of fantasy. Man becomes persuaded of the reality of his thought and a religion soon arises. Again, religion has been explained in terms of fear. The gods are "hypostasized terrors of the mind which cannot come to terms with a world so full of baffling perplexity and suffering. Just as the child, when it is afraid in the dark, 'sees' all kinds of terrifying forms, so man in his fear of life 'sees' himself surrounded by divine powers, which are partly friendly and helpful and partly menacing." [1]

David Hume (1711–76) explained the origin of religion along these lines. Ludwig Feuerbach (1804–72) set forth an idea essentially the same in which God is the projection of man's thought. He wrote, "The heart is itself the existence of God, the existence of immortality." [2] "God is first with himself in man; in man first begins religion, providence." [3] The difference between Feuerbach and Freud (1856–1939) lies in the fact that Feuerbach pronounced religion as good, whereas Freud regarded it as an illusion that was psychologically unhealthy. But for both, the gods are nothing more than projected wishes.

Wherever one begins, whether it be with William James (1842–1910) and a consciousness of an "objective presence," [4] with Schleiermacher (1768–1834) and the "surrender" to the Universe,[5] or

---

[1] Emil Brunner, *Revelation and Reason,* trans. Olive Wyon (Philadelphia: Westminster Press, 1946), p. 239.

[2] *The Essence of Christianity,* trans. George Eliot (New York: Harpers), p. 285.

[3] *Ibid.,* p. 300.

[4] *The Varieties of Religious Experience* (New York: Collier Books, 1961), p. 62.

[5] Friedrich Schleiermacher, *On Religion* (New York: Harper Torchbook), p. 58.

some mystical understanding of religion as in Rudolf Otto,[6] one must be careful not to equate religion in general, whether as a product of the human mind, imagination or emotion, with the second concept relating to the origin of religion.

Certain writers distinguish between the idea of religion and Christianity. Emil Brunner says, "The Christian faith, faith in the God revealed in Jesus Christ, is not 'one of the religions of the world.' "[7] It is true that for the sake of survey one includes Christianity as one of the great religions of the world, but the nature of Christianity sets it apart from the other religions of the world. The distinction is seen in the persons of the founders. Christianity is founded upon the person of Jesus Christ who is said to be the God-man. The religions of the world have been founded by men who claimed nothing more than religious insight into life and its problems. Regardless of whether one agrees with the distinction, it is significant. It gives the departure point for a theistic view of religion's origin. Christianity thus is not regarded as anthropocentric "religion"; that is, it did not originate in man's mind.

Although various explanations have been given for the origin of religion, there is a prior question to be raised. Why should one believe in God at all? In general, people do not deeply consider reasons for their believing in God. The search for reasons is often left to the philosophers and theologians who have argued both for and against the existence of God. Thus the history of human thought has presented a number of approaches to this question. We shall consider them under their appropriate headings.

Rational Arguments for the Existence of God

Before dealing with the arguments some preliminary comments must be made concerning the so-called "proofs." The proofs do not "prove" in the sense that one adds up a sum in arithmetic. Instead, the arguments fit into the category of probability. "There is no argument known to us which, as an argument, leads to more than a probable (highly probable) conclusion."[8] If one were to argue con-

---

[6] *The Idea of the Holy* (New York: Oxford University Press, 1958); cf. Brunner, *op. cit.,* pp. 252–56.

[7] Brunner, *op. cit.,* p. 258.

[8] J. Oliver Buswell, Jr., *A Systematic Theology of the Christian Religion* (Grand Rapids: Zondervan, 1962), I, 72.

cerning the rising of the sun tomorrow morning, the basis for the argument would be on the past experience that it has done so for as long as man has observed it, and the probability is that it will happen again tomorrow. This is an inductive argument based on an observed fact. "The theistic arguments are no exception to the rule that *all* inductive arguments about what exists are probability arguments. This is as far as the arguments, qua arguments, claim to go." [9]

One other comment is in order. Although the arguments only infer that God is—and is a reasonable explanation of the things that exist—the arguments are often attacked for their lack of consistence in reasoning, or the evidence has counterevidence opposing it, as in the argument from design. These attacks are misdirected. The real problem is that God is *inferred* from the argument and nobody can be happy with only an *inferred* God. But this is not to conclude that the arguments have no valid use. We will return to this after the arguments have been sketched.

Cosmological Argument

The cosmological argument is based in its variations on the fact that there is a cosmos, a world. One of its more familiar forms was in the order that Thomas Aquinas (1225–74) used.

> It is certain . . . that . . . some things are in motion. Now whatever is moved is moved by another, for nothing can be moved except it is in potentiality to that towards which it is moved. . . . If that by which it is moved be itself moved, then this also must needs be moved by another, and that by another again. But this cannot go on to infinity, because then there would be no first mover. . . . Therefore it is necessary to arrive at a first mover, moved by no other; and this everyone understands to be God.[10]

A basic objection against this argument is summed up in the child's question, "Who made God?" The theist seems to be resolving this problem in a mystery by believing in God who is self-existent. He pushes the matter one step further back than the atheist who is content to rest the issue in the universe as it stands. The difference in stance seems to be where one wants to stop in the argument and what mystery he prefers. The theist in his belief in God attempts

---

[9] *Ibid.*

[10] *Introduction to Saint Thomas Aquinas,* ed. Anton C. Pegis (New York: The Modern Library, 1948), p. 25.

to incorporate the aspect of intelligence in the world as its adequate cause, whereas for the atheist, intelligence grows up within the structure of nature.

J. O. Buswell maintains that the argument should be restructured as follows: "If motion does now exist, then either motion must have been eternally actual or potential, or on the other hand, motion must have arisen from nothing. Among the various hypotheses it is most probable that the God of the Bible existed eternally as the potential Originator of motion."[11]

The first part of the argument, "If something now exists, (1) something must be eternal unless (2) something comes from nothing,"[12] must be considered. The real issue is to determine what is eternal, since something does exist, or we are faced with the alternative that something comes from nothing. The latter alternative, that something comes from nothing, seems to have had its supporters. Fred Hoyle is the leading proponent of the continuous creation theory (steady state).[13] Hoyle has set forth the theory that hydrogen atoms are coming into existence without a cause and new galaxies arise as the universe expands. In this sense one could say that something comes from nothing.

However, the evidence seems to be going the other way and lending support to the theory that something other than the universe may be eternal. First, the study of quasars (quasi-stellar sources which are on the farthest reaches of known space where, according to Hoyle, there should be nothing as yet) support the fact that the number of quasars was larger when the earth was younger and they seem to have disappeared as the universe evolved. Furthermore, quasars are slowing down, a fact not explainable in the steady-state theory.[14]

Second, the second law of thermodynamics or the law of entropy points up the fact that the universe is running down. This law is expressed in the example that heat passes into a cold state but the reverse is not true. Radioactive minerals lend further support to the law of entropy. Radioactive materials that lose their radioactivity at a steady rate are used to determine the beginning age of the universe.

---

11 Buswell, *op. cit.*, p. 79.
12 *Ibid.*, p. 82.
13 *The Nature of the Universe* (New York: Harpers, 1950); *Frontiers of Astronomy* (New York: Harpers, 1955).
14 *Time*, March 11, 1966, pp. 81–84.

This may be concluded if in fact the universe is running down. If one were to conclude with some philosophers that it never had a beginning in the first place, it has had all eternity to run down and it perhaps should be completely run down. This however is not the case. Science points seemingly to a beginning point, thus one may conclude that the universe is not eternal.

What then is eternal? The restructured argument points in the direction of a Being who created the world but who is not identical with it. Something is now because Something is eternal. It is not enough to stop and declare Nature to be the ultimate. One must move beyond the material, which appears to be finite, to the eternal.

Another form of the cosmological argument is called the argument from efficient cause. Aquinas wrote: "In the world of sensible things we find there is an order of efficient causes. There is no case known . . . in which a thing is found to be the efficient cause of itself . . . if in efficient causes it is possible to go on to infinity, there will be no first efficient cause, neither will there be an ultimate effect. . . . Therefore, it is necessary to admit a first efficient cause, to which everyone gives the name of God." [15]

The same objections are raised here as in the first argument of Aquinas. A similar reconstruction is suggested by Buswell for the argument: "If there now does exist a chain of causality, then either it is itself eternal as a chain, or it originated in an eternal potential cause, or it originated from nothing. The God of the Bible is then shown to be the most probable eternal potential cause." [16]

Also included in the cosmological argument category is the one based on contingency. This argument is more widely preferred by modern Roman Catholic theologians than the other arguments. A modern version is the following:

First of all . . . we know that there are at least some beings in the world which do not contain in themselves the reason for their existence. . . . Now, secondly, the world is simply the real or imagined totality or aggregate of individual objects, none of which contain in themselves alone the reason for their existence. . . . Therefore . . . since objects or events exist, and since no object of experience contains within itself the reason of its existence, this reason, the totality of objects, must have a reason external to itself. That reason must be an existent

---

[15] *Introduction to Saint Thomas Aquinas*, pp. 25–26.
[16] Buswell, *op. cit.*, p. 79.

being. . . . So . . . in order to explain existence, we must come to a being which contains within itself the reason for its own existence, that is to say, which cannot not-exist.[17]

Sympathetic critics would advocate a similar reconstruction as follows: "If anything does now exist, then either something must be eternal, or something not eternal must have come from nothing." One must proceed then to show that there is something eternal and that the eternal God is the most reasonable of the probable hypotheses.

Teleological Argument

This argument is based upon purpose, or teleology, in the world. Sometimes called the argument *from* design, it would be better named as the argument *to* design, or a Designer. Possibly more popular than some of the other arguments, it has appealed to scientific knowledge for its support. Aquinas wrote: "We see that things which lack knowledge, such as natural bodies, act for an end. . . . Hence it is plain that they achieve their end, not fortuitously, but designedly. Now whatever lacks knowledge cannot move toward an end, unless it be directed by some being endowed with knowledge and intelligence. . . . Therefore some intelligent being exists by whom all natural things are directed to their end, and this being we call God." [18]

The development of this argument includes such diverse unique examples as the snowflake, or the water crystal, or the amazing structure of the eye. However, instead of a few small items, one must develop the argument in the direction of a cosmic teleology. It is not enough to speak of the snowflake, but one must go on to speak of the seeming design of man's habitation whirling through space, turning on its axis at one thousand miles per hour. A speed of one hundred miles per hour would make the nights too long and the days too hot so that the earth would alternately freeze and burn. The earth's proximity to the sun is such that it is at the right distance to secure enough heat but not overheat. The proximity of the moon to the earth is such that it keeps the oceans from inundating the land mass twice a day. A thinner atmosphere would allow meteors to bombard the earth

---

[17] John Hick (ed.), *The Existence of God* (New York: The Macmillan Co., 1964), pp. 168–169.

[18] *Introduction to Saint Thomas Aquinas*, p. 27.

rather than burn out in the sky. In many ways, the earth appears to be designed for life.

The greatest objection to the argument from design is that it does not include a basic tenet in the argument which is an affirmation of Christian faith; namely, the world in which we live is a "fallen" or sinful world. Thus, the problem of evil is one of the greatest objections to the argument.[19] In the world of the creatures it is argued that one beast devouring another for survival and food is a natural evil. The problem of evil in terms of sickness and disease is another feature. How does evil fit into purpose? In the matter of waste, what can be said for the desert or cragged mountains?

How does one reconcile the existence of evil with the goodness of God? Faced with the propositions that God is good and also all powerful, some have concluded that either God is not good or he is not all powerful, or both, because of the presence of evil in the world. Some, like Edgar Brightman, have argued that a finite god is struggling with evil and will eventually defeat it.

From the Christian perspective these are not the only alternatives. God is good, but he only does what he wills. "All-powerfulness" is used to imply that God should abolish evil immediately if he is able. This is not a biblical view of God. Can it be that God has willed something else, something that involves a cosmic risk, something that will give rise to evil? Is not freedom a neglected concept? Although the problem of evil is difficult to understand, even with the rich concept of freedom, it is all the more difficult to understand without it. The limitation of the teleological argument is that it does not give room, or a basis, for understanding aberrations from teleology or goodness due to freedom. "The meaning of evil is linked with freedom. Without it, no theodicy is possible." [20]

Freedom is the presupposition of evil and sin. Freedom as a concept must be large enough to involve the world as we experience it in life's heartaches.[21] Such a "fallenness" of the creation and man

---

[19] John Stuart Mill, *Nature and Utility of Religion* (New York: Bobbs-Merrill Co., 1958), pp. 19–27. Mill has a violent attack upon religion based upon the evil in nature.

[20] Nicolai Berdyaev, *Christian Existentialism* (New York: Harper Torch-books, 1965), p. 189.

[21] The space trilogy by C. S. Lewis develops a cosmic view of evil not only in the world but in nature to some degree. See his *Out of the Silent Planet, Perelandra,* and *That Hideous Strength,* all by Macmillan.

is presupposed in the Scriptures (cf. Rom. 8; Gen. 1–3). The bondage of the creation under the power of demonic freedom may serve as a means of understanding evil or dysteleological facts in the world. Without freedom this sin would not be possible. Without sin some suffering of man would be unintelligible.

While freedom is necessary to explain the appearance of evil in the cosmic sense, and this is implied in the existence of the devil, freedom does not mean that man and evil are without limitations. On the other hand, because sin and evil are evident in the world, one must not conclude that man is as sinful and the world is as filled with evil as is possible.

In conclusion, while the teleological argument does not recognize the existence of evil, the Christian faith affirms it as a basic problem of man and the world in a purposeful world. But the purposefulness of it is not the sole item in existence. While some things point to purpose, not everything does. The limitation of the argument for design may be seen in the statement of Pascal: "Nature has some perfections to show that she is the image of God, and some defects to show that she is only His image." [22]

The Argument from Ontology

The ontological argument goes back to Anselm of Canterbury (1033–1109). The argument is expressed succinctly in the words, God is that being "than which nothing greater can be conceived." [23] This argument can be summed up in three short statements: Man has an idea of a perfect being; existence is an attribute of perfection; therefore, a perfect being must exist. Although this is a logical conclusion, the second premise is not necessarily a true one. One could conceive of a perfect idea of a centaur, but the idea is not its real existence. Anselm's reply to this is that the case of God is a special one. Other concepts do not have the quality of existence, even though they might be perfect; but God is unique and one can be justified in passing from concepts in thought to existence in reality.

Although Anselm's argument has been attacked for the weakness mentioned above, some writers see in Anselm's work another line of reasoning. Norman Malcolm is widely known for his defense of

[22] Blaise Pascal, *Pensées* (New York: Modern Library, 1941), p. 190.
[23] St. Anselm, *Proslogium*, trans. Sidney N. Deane (La Salle, Ill.: Open Court Publishing Co., 1959), p. 7.

Anselm. He maintains that Anselm really offered two different proofs, although Anselm himself made no such distinction in his work. Malcolm develops his argument, maintaining that Anselm states, "[a] being whose nonexistence is logically impossible is 'greater' than a being whose nonexistence is logically possible (and therefore that a being greater than which cannot be conceived must be one whose nonexistence is logically impossible.)" [24]

Instead of only speaking of existence as implied in perfection, Malcolm emphasizes the qualifying term "necessary existence as a perfection." Thus, a necessary existing being is greater than if it does not necessarily exist. Within the definition of God as eternal, one logically sees the necessity of his being. Malcolm summarizes the argument as follows:

If God, a being greater than which cannot be conceived, does not exist then He cannot *come* into existence. For if He did He would either have been *caused* to come into existence or have *happened* to come into existence, and in either case He would be a limited being, which by our conception of Him He is not. Since He cannot come into existence, if He does not exist His existence is impossible. If He does exist He cannot have come into existence (for the reasons given), nor can He cease to exist, for nothing could cause Him to cease to exist nor could it just happen that He ceased to exist. So if God exists His existence is necessary. Thus God's existence is either impossible or necessary. It can be the former only if the concept of such a being is self-contradictory or in some way logically absurd. Assuming that this is not so, it follows that He necessarily exists.[25]

Besides Anselm, there have been others who have dealt with the ontological argument. René Descartes (1596–1650) set forth both a deductive and inductive form of it. The inductive form is more interesting. He wrote, "The existence of God is demonstrated *a posteriori* from this alone that his idea is in us." [26] Descartes argued that we have an idea of the sky because there is something outside of the mind making an impression upon it. We conclude that the sky is doing it. Likewise, there must be an adequate cause of our idea of God. Thus, one may conclude that God exists.

[24] Hick, *op. cit.*, p. 52.
[25] *Ibid.*, p. 56.
[26] *The Meditations and Selections from the Principles of Philosophy*, trans. John Veitch (LaSalle: Open Court Publishing Co., reprint 1946), p. 220.

The argument of Descartes may be applied to the idea that man has that God is holy love. This is something new to the world. From where did man receive this idea? The conclusion is that this new concept must come from God and not from man.

The Moral Argument

The moral argument has assumed a number of forms. Immanuel Kant (1724–1804) argued from the standpoint that man possesses a sense of "oughtness" or duty to pursue the highest good. Because one is commanded to pursue the *summum bonum,* morality or happiness or the holy, or the highest good, one must be able to and free to do so. But because one does not achieve it in this life, although one makes great progress, there is the moral necessity of a future life where this goal must be realized. But as the basis for immortality, or life beyond the grave, it is "morally necessary to assume the existence of God." [27]

A similar statement begins with the correlation that should exist between goodness and happiness, which is often negative. The morally good man should always be happy while the immoral man should be unhappy. Therefore, it is argued that God must exist to uphold justice in the universe, purity of motives as a standard of living, and bring ultimate happiness to the deserving.

Hastings Rashdall (1858–1924) has given an interesting version of the argument based on morality. Drawing an analogy from other areas of knowledge, one may suppose that there is a standard of truth, although people's ideas about it may vary all the way to falsehood. However, this does not cast doubt about the truth and its existence, whatever it may be. Thus he wrote: "We say that the Moral Law has a real existence, that there is such a thing as an absolute Morality, that there is something absolutely true or false in ethical judgement, whether we or any number of human beings at any given time actually think so or not. Such a belief is distinctly implied in what we mean by Morality." [28]

Thus obviously a moral idea does not exist in material things or in any one individual. He concludes that "an absolute moral idea can

---

27 Immanuel Kant, *Critique of Practical Reason,* trans. Lewis Beck (New York: Bobbs-Merrill, 1956), p. 130.

28 Hick, *op. cit.,* pp. 148–149.

exist only in a Mind from which all Reality is derived." [29] Therefore, "objective Morality implies the belief in God." [30]

The moral argument labors under the difficulty of an almost universal relativism in ethics and morality. However, the statistical report, based on what people *are doing,* does not negate the standard of what *ought to be.* Even in very primitive societies where morality seems to have disappeared, there is yet a basic moral standard. Although a society may think it good to steal, murder, rob, and lie to other groups, it does not permit the same action against members of its own group by members of its own group. There is a limit to relativity.

On the other hand, it must not be concluded that a known universal ethical standard would result in everyone's living up to it. The phenomenon of sin declares that people do not live according to what they do know.

The Argument from Personal Experience

This argument proceeds on the fact that men believe in God because they experience him. Some men believe because of intellectual reasons only, but others believe because of personal experience or encounter. Elton Trueblood has written, "The fact that a great many people, representing a great many civilizations and a great many centuries, and including large numbers of those generally accounted the best and wisest of mankind, have reported direct religious experiences is one of the most significant facts about our world." [31]

In this sense the religious person stresses empirical or pragmatic approaches. Gabriel Marcel wrote that "the mystics are perhaps the only thoroughgoing empiricists in the history of philosophy." [32] This implies that the religious person has an interchange with a fact (or better, a person) that is not measured by the five senses. Verification of experience is appealed to in terms of changed lives in the present life and fuller verification after death.

A. E. Taylor gives a variation on the argument. In music or art there is something "objective" that brings forth a response. There may be various interpretations of aesthetic experience, but the better

[29] *Ibid.,* p. 150.

[30] *Ibid.*

[31] *Philosophy of Religion* (New York: Harpers, 1957), p. 145.

[32] *Royce's Metaphysics,* trans. V. and G. Ringer (Chicago: Henry Regnery Co., 1956), p. 12.

interpretations are made by the "experts." We are not justified, however, in arguing that there is no beauty in the world because we do not recognize it, nor are we led to reason that every man's experience of beauty is to be trusted. Although all can react to the "presence of beauty," the expert is more able to interpret the "presence" than others.

In relating this to God, one might argue that there is something that is calling forth a response in man. In worship one responds to God in religious experience. God is the "given" or "the presence," and men respond according to their sensitivity to him. Because some men do not respond or "see" him, one is not justified in concluding that God does not exist. Although there are possibilities of aberrations and being led astray, the overwhelming repetition of religious experience throughout the ages lends support to the argument.

One objection to the argument of religious experience comes in the matter of the "who" of the experience. Can one be sure that it is God and not the devil he encounters? The answer seems to be that the moral transformation in the life of the person conforms to the nature of the person encountered. The aspect of a changed life for good could hardly be attributed to the demonic.

The usefulness of the religious experience argument involves the possibility of directing others to the same experience. This is no basic problem, for within Christianity, as a single example, directions are given for becoming a Christian; i.e., repent (or turn from sin) and trust (or commit one's life to) God on the basis of his promise in the gospel.

The Argument from Practical Use

A pragmatic test of truth is its workability. From the standpoint of God, there is a workability about belief in him. Religious belief and commitment mean the difference between a life that is meaningless and one that is filled with purpose and zest for living. "Atheism . . . has had little staying power. It has tended to take some of the morale and drive out of life and often leads to pessimism, cynicism, and a sense of futility." [33] It is obviously true that what one believes about the existence of God, that is, whether he accepts it or not, makes a big difference in the manner in which he conducts his life.

---

[33] Harold H. Titus, *Living Issues in Philosophy* (New York: American Book Co., 1964), p. 439.

Existential Approaches

Blaise Pascal (1623–62) outlined some of the issues men face in considering God's existence. "If there is a God," he wrote, "He is infinitely incomprehensible, since having neither parts nor limits, He has no affinity to us. We are then incapable of knowing either what He is or if He is." He then explains that Christians "profess a religion for which they cannot give a reason. They declare, in expounding it to the world, that it is a foolishness," [34] and then the world complains when they do not prove it! The underlying assumption for the above is the Christian assertion that God is hidden. It is for this reason that he cannot be proved or disproved. Yet, the paradox is that the Christian is called upon to prove something he cannot, says Pascal.

The issue of God's existence is not something about which one can be indifferent. Man *must* wrestle with the question of whether God is or is not! To which side will he incline? "Reason can decide nothing here. There is an infinite chaos which separated us. A game is being played at the extremity of this infinite distance where heads or tails will turn up. What will you wager? According to reason you can do neither the one thing nor the other; according to reason you can defend neither of the propositions." [35]

There is no possibility of neutrality. One must wager on the question, for it is not optional. The wager is set forth in the following terms:

If I bet that God is:
1. And he is, then I have gained all. Remember the stakes involve eternity.
2. And he is not, then I have lost nothing. (There is the possibility of gain if a good, moral, and "godly" life is valued more than an "immoral" one.

---

[34] Pascal, *op. cit.*, p. 80.

[35] *Ibid.*, p. 81. One should understand the role that Pascal gives to reason. He is not an unreasonable man, but reason must be put in its place. Pascal admits only that the final question is not determined on the basis of reason alone. "I lay it down as a fact that there never has been a complete sceptic. Nature sustains our feeble reason, and prevents it raving to this extent" (*ibid.*, p. 143). There are two extremes which are impossible: to be a complete dogmatist and a complete skeptic, for "nature confutes the sceptics, and reason confutes the dogmatists." Later he comments, "Know then, proud man, what a paradox you are to yourself. Humble yourself, weak reason; be silent, foolish nature; learn that man infinitely transcends man, and learn from your Master your true condition of which you are ignorant. Hear God" (*ibid.*).

If I bet God is not:
   1. And he is, then I have everything to lose including everlasting happiness.
   2. And he is not, then nothing is lost except the possibility of temporal happiness if through this conclusion one finds no meaning to life.
Therefore, if the odds are a billion to one, the reasonable man, the sensible man would bet his life on God.[36]

It is obviously wrong to conclude that one becomes a believer for the sake of "fire insurance." But Pascal did believe that by following the way by which others believed, one would come to faith. Pascal anticipated the theory of feeling and will, later taught by a Danish physiologist, Lange, and an American, William James.

It is the theory that the outward expression of any emotion leads to the experiencing of that emotion itself, and also to the ideas with which the emotion is associated. It is quite wrong to speak, in this regard of *auto-suggestion*. . . . If a man of good will expresses in practice the deeds and gestures which normally proceed from religious experience, there is opened in him a channel for the grace of God. There is thus provided a bridge between intellectual assent and actual experience of God.[37]

The wager is designed, therefore, to put certain common facts into perspective. The truth is that man will love either God or himself, the idol. There is a certain monstrosity about self-love and man has not been created for such. Pascal would have agreed with Luther that man is going to worship something, but it is only a question of whom or what? God or an idol? Although the wager does not prove the existence of God, it grants that there is basis for believing in God. There are enough evidences and it is of such a kind that "it cannot be said that it is unreasonable to believe them."[38] The evidence is sufficient, but it cannot be the basis for decision; man must wager.

One objection that is often raised against the wager is that one must make some side bets on the various gods. How do you know the right one? Can you make the wrong bet? Pascal dealt with this issue in terms of the criteria for the true religion. Using an inductive method of observation, he set forth a number of propositions con-

[36] *Ibid.,* p. 81.
[37] Emile Cailliet, *Pascal, The Emergence of Genius* (New York: Harpers, 1945), p. 107.
[38] Pascal, *op. cit.,* p. 185.

cerning what the true religion should be like. These will be dealt
with in a following chapter. At this point, one can say for Pascal
that the real issue is Christianity or atheism, and none other. On the
basis of the criteria for the true religion, the side bets are ruled out.
Man must place his bet on the existence of God, who has revealed
himself in the Judeo-Christian tradition.

Another important man in the existential approach was Sören
Kierkegaard (1813–55). Kierkegaard has been called the father of
the existential movement. Like Pascal, he concluded that reason is
not supreme and cannot solve some of the issues of life. Concerning
God's existence, S. K. did not presume to prove it. He did point
up some of the difficulties in believing in God. The problems are in
man. God's existence is assumed by S. K., but man does not believe
in God for the simple reason that he rebels against all authority. He
is unwilling to obey and hence insubordination is seen at every turn.
The real problem is not due to intellectual doubt but rebellion. This
is the personal confession of Kierkegaard in his *Journals.*

In his *Philosophical Fragments* he treats the matter differently.
Skepticism is not a result of a lack of evidence or facts.

The Greek sceptic did not doubt by virtue of his knowledge, but by an
act of will (refusal to give assent . . .). From this it follows that doubt
can be overcome only by a free act, an act of will, as every Greek
sceptic would understand as soon as he had understood himself. But he
did not wish to overcome his scepticism, precisely because he willed to
doubt. For this he will have to assume the responsibility; but let us not
impute to him the stupidity of supposing that doubt is necessary.[39]

The real answer concerning God's existence is to leave off proving
and take the leap of faith. God will be there catching you.[40] You
can't prove God, but you can experience him. One does not give
reasons for loving someone, but he experiences love. Kierkegaard
used the analogy of a boat run aground in the mud: "It is almost
impossible to float it again because it is impossible to punt, no punt-
poles can touch bottom so that one can push against it. And so the
whole generation is stuck in the mud banks of reason; and no one
grieves over it, there is only self-satisfaction and conceit, which always

---

[39] Sören Kierkegaard, *Philosophical Fragments,* trans. David F. Swanson
(Princeton: Princeton University Press, 1936), pp. 67–68.
[40] *Ibid.,* p. 34.

follow on reason and the sins of reason. Oh, the sins of passion and of the heart, how much nearer to salvation than the sins of reason." [41]

Kierkegaard begins with the Teacher (God), who gives the learner true knowledge of himself and makes him a new creature. The leap of faith is climactic for the moment and the future. The disciple "who is born anew owes nothing to any man, but everything to his divine Teacher." [42]

The Christological Assertion

The line of reasoning is as follows. There once lived a man who claimed to be of the nature of God, equal with God, who spoke of God in intimate terms that no one else dared use. He disclosed the fact that God is love and seeks to redeem men. The account speaks of his miraculous birth; his deeds, such as healing the blind and maimed, raising the dead, and doing what no other person had ever done. Living among a fanatically strict monotheistic people who did not believe that every man is a part of God, or has a spark of divinity, he was condemned to death for his claims of equality with God and messianic claims. Had he simply died, it would be the death story of a misguided man who possibly had the quirks of a genius. But the claim is also made that he arose from the dead, was seen by as many as five hundred people at one time, and on numerous other occasions. Jesus is the person who claimed equality with God, identified in a unique way with him as Son, and maintained that his main purpose for existence among men was to declare that God seeks to redeem them.

This assertion is based on the following considerations. First, it is related to the fulfilment of a messianic prophecy declared centuries beforehand among the Jewish people. Second, it is maintained that the records of the life of Jesus were written down within a few years of his death and resurrection and not within centuries, as is the case of other religious leaders such as Buddha and Confucius. Thus, it is argued that the accounts were known even by the enemies of Jesus and evidence could have been set forth to the contrary were this the case. Instead, it is maintained that Jesus' opponents were convinced that something unusual happened, but they were content to regard

---

[41] Alexander Dru (ed.), *The Journals of Kierkegaard*, (New York: Harpers, 1959), p. 214.

[42] *Philosophical Fragments*, p. 14.

his work and person as demonic. Third, it is averred that within his lifetime his monotheistic disciples acknowledged him to be the Messiah and the Son of God.

The alternatives have been placed in the following ways:

A man who was merely a man and said the sort of things Jesus said would not be a great moral teacher. He would either be a lunatic—on a level with the man who says he is a poached egg—or else he would be the Devil of Hell. You must make your choice. Either this man was, and is, the Son of God: or else a madman or something worse. You can shut Him up for a fool, you can spit at Him and kill Him as a demon; or you can fall at his feet and call Him Lord and God. But let us not come with any patronizing nonsense about His being a great human teacher. He has not left that open to us. He did not intend to.[43]

Objections have been raised in every generation to the christological assertion. Of recent, it has been proposed that the life of Jesus was an extended masquerade on the part of a person who became possessed with the idea that he was the Messiah. The masquerade was cut short when the soldier pierced his side to see whether he was dead or not, and the puncture killed him. Such reconstructions are not new, as the work of Albert Schweitzer has shown.[44]

But there is a deeper issue that must be considered, and that is the question of records. Basically all that one can know of the life of Jesus is found in the New Testament. Can one trust the witness of the records? Unless one does, there is no way of even attempting to reconstruct a viewpoint to refute the viewpoint of the records. More fundamental are the problems centering around motives. Why would Jesus come to conclude that he was the foretold Messiah? Why would the disciples fabricate such a story of his resurrection when the accounts themselves admit that all of the disciples fled and were completely discouraged with the tragic turn of events? What of the resurrection?

Another problem is posed in the fact that there are always people who appear now and then maintaining themselves as God. How is Jesus any different? A defense of his claim would include the difference of his being a Hebrew where a Messiah was prophesied. He

---

[43] C. S. Lewis, *Mere Christianity* (New York: The Macmillan Co., 1960), p. 41.
[44] *The Quest of the Historical Jesus,* trans. W. Montgomery (London: Adam and Charles Black, 1948).

would also be different in his person and works. It would not be difficult to point up the moral problems of these claimants; whereas, it is maintained that Jesus was free of sin.

The greatest issue centers around the matter of two things: for the non-Jew, there is the pressing issue of naturalism versus supernaturalism. If naturalism is the full story of life, then the assertion is sheer myth. If naturalism is not the complete story then the possibility of theism raises its head again and within this concept is hidden the fact that the Creator might conceivably be interested in his world to redeem it. The other issue centers around the question that is of vital interest to the Hebrew. Was Jesus the promised Messiah or not?

These questions must not be answered before a full examination of the materials is made. In this, one must consider the claim, the personal portrait of Jesus, the motives of the writers, and the possibility of self-communication of God if he exists.

The Approach of the Bible

In the last few pages, we have been considering materials not strictly based on reasons or conclusions drawn from observation of natural phenomena. It has served as a transition to the approach of the Bible.

The Bible nowhere attempts to justify the existence of God. The existence of God is presupposed in the first verse of the Bible. Genesis 1:1 implies the creativity, sustenance, and upholding power of God. A similar presupposition is stated in Hebrews 11:6, where the necessity of faith is the prerequisite for coming to know God.

An empirical suggestion is given in John 7:17: "If any man's will is to do his will, he shall know whether the teaching is from God or whether I am speaking on my own authority." The book of Psalms contains further statements concerning experiential verification: Psalm 50:15 says, "Call upon me in the day of trouble; I will deliver you, and you shall glorify me." Psalm 145:18 declares, "The Lord is near to all who call upon him, to all who call upon him in truth." Jeremiah offers further challenges: "Call to me and I will answer you, and will tell you great and hidden things which you have not known" (33:3). The empirical approach as it relates to these verses is not without prerequisites. Faith *is* required and there is no guarantee that God will reveal himself to a person without faith.

The Bible gives another type of approach in its overall context. The history of Israel points up the fact of deliverance. The Bible sets forth a view of history in which God has been at work in the descendants of Abraham. The religious, historical, and geographical development of ancient Israel is such that the existence of the Sovereign God is presupposed. This line of argument is expressed in the story related by Karl Barth.

Frederick the Great once asked his personal physician Zimmermann of Brugg in Aargau: "Zimmermann, can you name me a single proof of the existence of God?" And Zimmermann replied, "Your Majesty, the Jews." By that he meant that if one wanted to ask for a proof of God, for something visible and tangible, that no one could contest, which is unfolded before the eyes of all men, then we should have to turn to the Jews. Quite simply, there they are to the present day. Hundreds of little nations in the Near East have disappeared, all other Semitic tribes of that time have dissolved and disappeared in the huge sea of nations; and this one tiny nation has maintained itself. . . . In fact, if the question of a proof of God is raised, one need merely point to this simple historical fact. For in the person of the Jew there stands a witness before our eyes, the witness of God's covenant with Abraham, Isaac, and Jacob and in that way with us all.[45]

As interesting as this is, there may be problems with it. It may be possible to improvise another explanation for the existence of the Jews. Nevertheless, the existence of the Jews is remarkable, and it does seem that a strange providence has been at work among them.

Another type of beginning point for belief in God contained in the Bible is miracles. Among older theologians, many things were proved by the use of miracles. In modern times, miracles have met with less acceptance among theologians. Yet in the Bible, there is significance in miracles. A basic presupposition of the biblical miracle is the closeness of God, but the Hebrews were prohibited the use of images and representations. Consequently, there was always the danger of the idea of God's becoming a far-off, impersonal being who was disinterested in his people. The miracle in the Old Testament points up God's concern and nearness.

However, the miracle in the Old Testament had certain limitations. The miracle did not necessarily validate the truth of a statement made by a man. Instead, the miracle only gave the right to be heard

---

[45] *Dogmatics in Outline* (New York: Harpers, 1959), p. 75.

and then the listener assented or dissented to the message according to whether it corresponded with the Torah. The Bible recognizes the possibility of false miracles, or signs produced for the sake of exhorting the people to serve false gods.

In the New Testament, the four Gospels accord the signs and miracles of Jesus with some content of evidence. Jesus defended himself and his authority from God in the Fourth Gospel by commenting, "Unless you see signs and wonders you will not believe" (John 4:48). The conclusion of Nicodemus, as well as others in the days of Jesus, was that "no one can do these signs that you do, unless God is with him" (John 3:2). Even the enemies of Jesus did not deny that the blind had their sight restored, the deaf could hear, and the dead were raised. However, they interpreted all of these acts as demonic in nature rather than divine.

The most significant miracle from which all others have their meaning is the resurrection.[46] Paul speaks of Jesus as being the Son of God "in power according to the Spirit of holiness by his resurrection from the dead" (Rom. 1:4). Indeed it can be argued that if Jesus was the kind of person he declared himself to be, then it would be very unusual if miracles did not take place.

There is another direction that the Bible records concerning God's existence. The creation is said to reveal something of God's existence. The letter to the Romans declares, "For what can be known about God is plain . . . because God has shown it. . . . Ever since the creation of the world his invisible nature, namely, his eternal power and deity, has been clearly perceived in the things that have been made" (1:19–20). The same letter speaks of a primitive revelation in that "although they knew God they did not honor him as God" (v. 21). A conclusion is reached that man knew God's decrees but he did not practice them (v. 32). These are references to a revelation in the past.

The biblical viewpoint is not as though a man were trying to prove the existence of something that does not exist, or that he has never heard of; instead, it begins with the declaration that God has declared himself in times past. The revelatory activity of God reached its climax in the declaration of himself through his Son—Jesus, the Christ. He *has* spoken in a decisive way. The book of Hebrews declares the superiority and finality of the revelation in the Son. In

---

[46] A stimulating work on miracles is the work by C. S. Lewis, *Miracles* (New York: Macmillan, 1947).

essence, God has spoken in many ways in the past, "but in these last days he has spoken to us by a Son" (1:2). The very obvious point is that God has spoken in a meaningful way, which makes his message one that is relevant to the needs of mankind.

Concerning revelation as a possibility, Carnell wrote, "Although few really think about it, no cogent philosophic argument can be introduced to preclude the possibility of revelation." [47] Ultimately we have to conclude that we cannot really know anything about God unless God reveals it of himself. What *I* think about God is not very important to anyone else, and I ought to be duly surprised if anyone attaches real importance to what I think of him. If God exists, however, it becomes very important what anyone thinks of him. Without a sure word from God himself, no one has any assurance that our thoughts of him correspond to his true nature. The witnesses of the apostolic period and the writers of the New Testament have preserved a word of the historic revelation, which is the foundation of the Christian faith.

As we conclude this chapter, there are certain implications that need to be drawn.

First, although it is not possible to prove the existence of God, there are arguments that suggest the probability of his existence. In this sense, one might speak of the arguments as pointers, signs, hints, or "testimony" to God's existence. It is not thus unreasonable to believe that a Supreme Being exists. The accumulative effect of the various arguments for God's existence is significant, however.

Concerning evidence, Joseph Butler (1692–1752) wrote, "Probable proofs by being added, not only increase the evidence, but multiply it." [48] Some theologians attack the arguments with an attitude suggesting that it is unreasonable to believe in God at all. What they really want to point up is the inadequacy of the "proofs" as proof. While their mode of expressing their doubt about the usefulness of the arguments is not the best, these theologians find real depth of meaning in the words of Pascal, "The heart has its reasons, which reason does not know." [49] The heart of man grasps for God. If man

---

[47] E. J. Carnell, *An Introduction to Christian Apologetics* (Grand Rapids: Wm. B. Eerdmans Publishing Co., 1948), p. 175.

[48] *The Analogy of Religion, Natural and Revealed* (J. M. Dent, Everyman Library), p. 217.

[49] *Op. cit.*, p. 95.

does not worship the true God he speaks of the abstract Beauty, or Goodness, or Nature, or elevates himself as the absolute.

Second, there are dangers that befall the use of arguments for God's existence. One does not meet God at the end of the argument. It is possible that being religious and believing in a God can be a substitute for knowing the basic proposition of theology. Unless God reveals himself, we cannot know him in a meaningful redemptive sense. Biblical theology rests upon this proposition. Unless God has spoken, we are yet in the dark in our knowledge about him as well as yet being in our sins. It is not enough to accept the intellectual truth that God exists. The essence of faith is commitment to a person, not a proposition. Certainly there are propositions about the Person we need, but a proposition without the Person is meaningless. This is the sense in which Pascal's statement is to be understood: that the god of the philosophers is not the God of Abraham, Isaac, and Jacob. The god of the philosophers may be nothing more than an abstract or concluding argument for his existence, which is unexperienced, while the God of the patriarchs was known as the self-revealing God.

Third, a man's life and destiny depend upon his answer to the question of whether God is or is not. If God has revealed himself in times past, then the responsibility of man to learn about him is great. It is not a matter merely of trying to escape from judgment but a matter of learning the meaning of life as well as what life really is.

Fourth, "belief in God enables man to explain what otherwise is unexplained or is explained in a less satisfactory manner. From this point of view, it satisfies an intellectual demand." [50] There are problems in not believing in him.

Fifth, belief in God seems to be a necessary item for mental health and stability of the person. This is a problem concerning idolatry in its modern forms. When the "idol"—career, money, house, home, ambition—is swept away, the world collapses around the person. It is important to know the living God, who is not perishable, and to establish one's life in the Absolute, which cannot be swept away.

Sixth, belief in God implies absoluteness in the moral realm, whereby man may judge himself and thereby check his human tendency to pride or egotism. At the same time, theism is the system that grounds ethics in a transcendent source.

---

[50] Titus, *op. cit.*, p. 442.

Finally, life can be lived without relation to God, but it is generally true that ultimately life is purposeless and a mockery without God. Without the fact of God, one feels that life is as a tale told by an idiot. There is a deep longing in the heart of man for God—a longing expressed in the words of Augustine: "Thou hast made us for thyself and we are restless until we rest in thee."

II. Why Christianity of All Religions?

Do not, then, let us serve the creature rather than the Creator, or become vain in our thoughts. That is the rule of perfect religion.

Augustine, *Of True Religion*

For myself, I confess that so soon as the Christian religion reveals the principle that human nature is corrupt and fallen from God, that opens my eyes to see everywhere the mark of this truth: for nature is such that she testifies everywhere, both within man and without him, to a lost God and a corrupt nature.

Pascal, *Pensées*

The way of the good and blessed life is to be found entirely in the true religion wherein one God is worshipped and acknowledged with purest piety to be the beginning of all existing things, originating, perfecting and containing the universe.

Augustine, *Of True Religion*

With the world shrinking in size and non-Christian religions making great missionary efforts, one can well question any exclusive claims of Christianity. Are there any good reasons for being a Christian as opposed to being a Buddhist or Muslim? [1] Many people take a casual look at religion and conclude that religions in general are all the same. Some are blasé and say with the people of Java that "all religions are ultimately one." [2] Or, they assent to the statement that "there is a bit of truth in all religions." [3] Others may remark that all

---

[1] Hendrik Kraemer, *Why Christianity of All Religions?* (Philadelphia: Westminster Press, 1962). The title of the chapter is adopted from Kraemer as well as part of the discussion that follows.

[2] Kraemer, *The Christian Message in a Non-Christian World* (Grand Rapids: Kregel Publications, 1963), p. 200.

[3] *Why Christianity of All Religions?*, p. 6.

religions are supposed to lead to the same place. Still others argue that so many people in intense devotion have as much right as Christianity to claim that their way of worship is valid.

If one, in rebuttal to these general remarks, poses a narrow view concerning world religions, he is charged with being narrow, dogmatic, or provincial; but the charges are often made in ignorance of the facts and are the result of naïve thinking. Men tend to ignore both sides of the question; they have emphasized the glories of the great religions but often have remained ignorant of the dark sides. There is real truth in Kraemer's assertion that "the only people that maintain that it all boils down to the same things are those who have never taken the trouble to find out what 'it all' is." [4]

When one turns to review the contributions of some writers in this area, one is similarly confronted with diverse viewpoints. Many are the followers of Toynbee, who said:

I think it is possible for us, while holding that our own convictions are true and right, to recognize that, in some measure, all the higher religions are also revelations of what is true and right. They also come from God and each present some facet of God's truth. They may and do differ in content and degree of revelation that has been given to mankind through them. They may also differ to the extent that this revelation has been translated by their followers in the practice, both in the individual practice and social practice. But we should recognize that they too are light radiating from the same source from which our own religion derives its own spiritual light. This must be so if God is the God of all men, and is also another name for love.[5]

On this basis, therefore, Toynbee says, "We ought also, I should say, to try to purge our Christianity of the traditional Christian belief that Christianity is unique. This is not just a Western Christian belief; it is intrinsic to Christianity itself." [6] In this conclusion, Toynbee approvingly quotes Symmachus, " 'It is impossible that so great a mystery should be approached by one road only.' " [7]

There are many who follow Toynbee's line of reasoning. There is much that is attractive about it, for Toynbee is interested in appealing for tolerance, forbearance, and respect; and doing away with religious

---

[4] *Ibid.*, p. 13.
[5] Arnold Toynbee, *Christianity Among the Religions of the World* (New York: Charles Scribner's Sons, 1957), pp. 99–100.
[6] *Ibid.*, pp. 95–96.
[7] *Ibid.*, p. 112.

bigotry. Does not Christianity in its biblical content have concern for these problems?

Toynbee is not without his critics, however. Kraemer charges that Toynbee has ignored the real issue: the truth question.[8] It is at the issue of truth that Kraemer makes one of his important contributions, for he draws a hard distinction between the trueness of a religion and its value or function.

From the standpoint of function, value, and religious experience, one may argue for a bighearted approach. If one grants that all religions fill some need in human psychology, one may argue that all religions are revelations of God in various cultures. This is to stress their practical or functional value. The question of truth is not necessarily an issue here. A counterfeit dollar will serve a practical value as long as the genuineness or truthfulness of the matter is not a question. Essentially, there is nothing new or modern about the value of religions in fulfilling a human need. This is as old as Hinduism and as modern as a Hegel or Schleiermacher and their descendants.

The popularity of religion in general shows something of its functional role. When religions are evaluated on a functional basis, then all religions become relative. But it is just a short step from the relativity of all religions to the irrelevancy of all religions.[9] When one compares Christianity with the non-Christian religions along the line of value and function, one can acknowledge that

the non-Christian religions can just as well as Christianity show up an impressive record of psychological, cultural and other values, and it is wholly dependent on one's fundamental axioms of life whether one considers these non-Christian achievements of higher value for mankind than the Christian. The weakness of the value-argument in relation to the problem of ultimate and authoritative truth is still more patent if one remembers that from the standpoint of relative cultural value fictions and even lies have been extraordinarily valuable and successful.[10]

Since one cannot judge the ultimate truthfulness of a religion from its functional value, then some other approach must be considered. When a Christian confronts a Buddhist or Hindu, or some other adherent of a world religion, there must be some type of common ground for discussion.

---

[8] *Why Christianity of All Religions?* p. 46.
[9] Kraemer, *The Christian Message in a Non-Christian World*, p. 14.
[10] *Ibid.*, pp. 106–7.

It is of little value to quote the Christian Bible to a man who rejects its authority. It is possible for adherents of various world religions to indict Christianity from a similar stance. A Muslim, for example, would speak of the incompleteness of Christianity.

Where can one begin in discussing the question of a true religion? If this question is to be taken seriously, it must demand one presupposition. The presupposition is that the classical beginning of faith is important, and is determinative, regardless of how the faith evolves away from the founder. The faith must be judged from the standpoint of the founder's teaching and practice. In this sense do we speak of classical Christian faith, classical Buddhist faith, and so on.

Criteria of a True Religion

If the discussion of a true religion is to be meaningful, it must have an objective starting point. In a sense it must parallel the scientific method. We cannot start with a given factor, although we may arrive with one in the end. The starting point must be one that all people can have and assume.

Such a system of beginning was proposed by Blaise Pascal, the French scientific and religious genius of the seventeenth century. Pascal attempted to put forth certain propositions, based in part on observation and in part on reason, which would help one to discover the true religion if it existed. Although Pascal never finished his proposed work, his fragmented thoughts (*Pensées*) have become one of the classics of world literature. Pascal's approach has a feature common to all men: each man may look, observe, and draw conclusions from where he is. It is really an inductive method.[11] Pascal maintains that for a religion to be true, it must give an adequate and satisfactory answer to the following criteria.

1. *The true religion teaches the hiddenness of God.*—It is quite evident that if God is, he is not perceived by sensory perception. God is not an object that has been analyzed in the laboratory. If God exists, he exists in some hidden state or form; for we cannot see him.

---

[11] Should it be argued that Pascal's approach is prejudicial because he belonged to the Christian tradition, then it must be remembered that these principles are not a product of the Christian faith. Whether these principles are true or false depends not on whether one is a Christian or not. They deal with facts that can be discussed in the context of any religion. These are questions that are common to all men, and can be verified from the experience of all men.

Concerning this, Pascal wrote, "God being thus hidden every religion which does not affirm that God is hidden is not true and every religion which does not give the reason of it, is not instructive." [12] The hiddenness of God, or to use the Latin phrase, *Deus absconditus,* is a basic beginning point for dialogue among religious traditions.

In applying this principle, one may begin with pantheistic religious systems. A popular definition of pantheism is that "all things or beings are modes, attributes, or appearances of one single reality of Being; hence nature and God are believed to be identical." [13]

Man as the observer cannot conclude from his examination of reality that nature and God are identical. To be a pantheist, one must bring something with his observation; namely, the faith that God and Nature are one. He will not get this out of nature alone. Pantheism applied to man's existence means that man is part of the divine essence. Man is a spark of divinity. But again, this is not something we know by observation, by sight, touch, or self-knowledge. It may be the grossest perversion of self-knowledge. All that the senses will approve are two alternatives: God is hidden, or God is not! [14]

Pantheisms are dangerous because man is led to have an overoptimistic view concerning his own nature. Pantheism is caught up in trying to explain evil away or it is logically blamed on God. Kraemer charges that the result of pantheism, as in parts of Hinduism, is "that God or the divine never really exists." [15] The only thing that one really experiences is human consciousness which is regarded as a mirage at best. But paradoxically, those religions which identify man with God in some pantheistic form are those that stand in abhorrence of a true incarnation, in which God assumes human flesh.[16]

In a negative way, this principle of Pascal is seen in the classical

---

[12] Pascal, *Pensées*, p. 191.

[13] Van Harvey, *Handbook of Theological Terms* (New York: The Macmillan Co., 1964), p. 173.

[14] In asserting such a radical alternative, reference must be made to the first chapter and the "proofs" for the existence of God. The knowledge that one may gain in the arguments is a knowledge for the most part based on "effects" or works of God. It is not the kind of knowledge that will give direction to life nor even intimate that God may love or redeem man.

[15] *The Christian Message in a Non-Christian World,* p. 162.

[16] The avatar of Hinduism is quite different from the incarnation of Christianity, for the incarnation means that God assumed true human flesh. The avatar is a "mythological personification of a god conceived for a practical purpose, while the real divine is the attributeless and actionless pure essence" (*Ibid.,* pp. 370–71).

teachings of Buddha and Confucius as we know them. Neither of these founders was interested in discussing the existence of God. For all practical purposes, Gautama and Confucius were nontheists. In due time, not only were the founders apotheosized, but other gods were added.

Gautama cannot be said to have received a "divine revelation." What happened was that he came to see a basic truth about the nature of suffering, the reason for it, and the possibility of escaping from it. It is an insight about the way to happiness as one views happiness as the escape from desire.

Confucius taught nothing more than an ancient form of humanism. He declared that "absorption in the study of the supernatural is most harmful." [17] In true humanist style, Confucius "explained evil as human selfishness, delusion and incapability. When a pupil asked him about death and service of the spirits, he replied, 'Till you have learnt to serve men, how can you serve the ghosts? . . . Till you know about the living, how are you to know about the dead?' " [18]

The irony is that both Gautama and Confucius, who had little to say about whether God exists or not, were declared to be gods by their later followers.

In the case of Islam, the deity is hidden but there is no explanation as to why he is hidden, which relates to the second part of Pascal's proposition. The Qur'an does not know of the holy God who has hidden himself because of man's sinfulness. Islam is a moralistic, rationalistic form of religion emphasizing the works of righteousness as a means of acceptability before God. Kraemer says that it is a "legalistic religion in which everything hangs upon the efforts of the believer and on whether he fulfils the requirements of the Divine Law. Thus it is, so to say, a religion permeated by a form—a somewhat inflected form—of self-deliverance, self-justification and self-sanctification with, in the end, no firm and settled basis for it." [19]

The hiddenness of God demands that a radically new concept of God be in evidence as the explanation. The concept of God must not be a construction of human thought, for man cannot ferret out

[17] Lionel Giles, *The Sayings of Confucius* (London: John Murray, 1917), p. 94.
[18] Edward J. Jurji, *The Christian Interpretation of Religion* (New York: The Macmillan Co., 1952), p. 183.
[19] *Why Christianity of All Religions?* p. 105.

that which is hidden as the hidden relates to God. The concept of *Deus absconditus* is closely related with the reason for its hiddenness. For Pascal the explanation of God's hiddenness is in man's sin. Where sin is not taken seriously, identification of man with the divine comes easy. Where sin is a grave, serious act against the divine, an ethical act and an ethical deviation, then it is not possible to identify man with God. The qualitative difference between God and man must be stressed. For the most part, the religious traditions of the world fail to take seriously the concept of sin.[20] Brunner declares, "The counterpart of unhistorical religion, religion without a mediator, is the failure to recognize the radical character of the guilt of sin. It is an attempt to create a relationship with God which takes no account of the fact of Guilt." [21]

In the concept of the hidden God, one cannot conclude from observation that God is holy or that he is love. This is a message that has to come from God to man; it has not originated with man.

The message that God is Love is something wholly new in the world. We perceive this if we try to apply the statement to the divinities of the various religions of the world: Wotan is Love, Zeus, Jupiter, Brahma, Ahura Mazda, Vishnu, Allah, is Love. All these combinations are wholly impossible. Even the God of Plato, who is the principle of all Good, is not Love. Plato would have met the statement "God is Love" with a bewildered shake of the head." [22]

Brunner continues to say that it is possible to find a "gracious" God in some of the religions of the world, "but the fact that God is Love, and thus that love is the very essence of the Nature of God, is never explicitly said anywhere, and still less is it revealed in divine self-surrender. The God of the *Bhakti* religion, which is often regarded as parallel to the Christian Faith, is 'essentially—in his relation to the World—wholly uninterested.' " [23]

---

[20] Note Jurji's comment on Islam, which ignores the idea of a redeemer "largely because Islam knew nothing of original sin and its founders and interpreters were oblivious to the problem of evil and sidestepped the need of the soul for forgiveness, a personal Saviour, and prayer as an eventful intercourse with the Eternal" (*op. cit.,* p. 256).

[21] Emil Brunner, *The Christian Doctrine of the Church, Faith and the Consummation,* trans. David Cairns and T. H. L. Parker (Philadelphia: Westminster Press, 1962), p. 7.

[22] Brunner, *Christian Doctrine of God,* trans. Olive Wyon (Philadelphia: Westminster Press), p. 183.

[23] *Ibid.,* p. 200.

In conclusion to this section, we must affirm the hiddenness of God. If God is thus hidden, we must know the reason for it. This means that if we are to know of God and what he is like, this knowledge will not be found in any other way than for God to speak. Because God is hidden, we must reject those approaches to religious life that equate man with God. If God is hidden, the reason for his hiddenness will be given by God and will not be discoverable by man alone. A crucial question that enters here is: Has God spoken in a clear way concerning these things? This will be answered later.

2. *The true religion must explain the misery of man.*—Pascal wrote, "That a religion may be true, it must have knowledge of our nature. It ought to know its greatness and littleness, and the reason of both" (*Pensée 433*) In *Pensée 493*, he wrote, "The true religion teaches our duties; our weaknesses, our pride, and lust; and the remedies, humility, and mortification." Pascal's insight into the nature of man is one that can naturally grow out of an inductive observation. He wrote of man, "What a novelty! What a monster, what a chaos, what a contradiction, what a prodigy! Judge of all things, inbecile worm of the earth; depositary of truth, a sink of uncertainty and error; the pride and refuse of the universe!" (*Pensée 434*, p. 143).

What best accounts for the misery of man? Pascal's answer is found in the meaningful little word "sin." We have said that sin as a concept is lacking in much of the religious thought of the world. Misunderstanding can arise here if we are not careful. In many religions, depending upon their orientation, sin is not understood in ethical terms. Sin is a nonethical impediment that keeps one from achieving union with the world soul. In the thought of Hindus, for example, sin would be the continuing erroneous thought about the actual existence of individuality. This sin is not ethical but a matter of knowledge. In this sense, sin may be defined as maya, or illusion. A similar situation prevails in Christian Science in America. Sin is erroneous thinking.

With reference to sin, as seen in certain forms of bhakti, Kraemer declares, "Sin in these religions is not the result of self-centered and misdirected human will that opposes the will of the God of holiness and righteousness, but an impediment for the realization of that fellowship of the soul with Ishvara, in which salvation consists." [24]

---

[24] *The Christian Message in a Non-Christian World*, p. 172.

As one probes more deeply into the real nature of religious expression, he sees that sin is generally regarded as really insignificant and many religions are really means of "self-redemption, self-justification, and self-sanctification" [25]—concepts that basically ignore sin.

Following the clue of Pascal, one may conclude that there is only one adequate concept to explain the misery of man as one can observe man's problems, and that is sin as a wilful rebellion against a holy God. The sinfulness of man has caused man to pervert his religious worship. He has turned from the Creator to the creatures and reveres a cow, while his children starve from protein deficiency. He has taken food from his starving babies to give to an idol that does not consume it. His famine is not due to his ignorance of modern technology alone; his religion, with its inadequate definition of and emphasis on sin, can explain much of his misery.

In concluding this section, we must say that these two propositions go together. A serious definition of sin is the explanation of why God is hidden. He is hidden in his relationship to men for two reasons: first, he is holy, and his nature is against the whole fabric of sin; second, his hiddenness is for man's protection. If the holiness of God were revealed against man in his sin, he could not survive. His grace and love toward man provides the reason for his withdrawing himself from man's presence.

3. The true religion must teach how man can know God who is hidden, or give the remedy for his alienation and misery.—Pascal declared, "The true religion, then, must teach us to worship Him only, and to love Him only. But we find ourselves unable to worship what we know not, and to love any other object but ourselves, the religion which instructs us in these duties must instruct us also of this inability, and teach us also the remedies for it" *(Pensée 489).*

In Pensée 546, [Pascal] said, "We know God only by Jesus Christ. Without this mediator all communion with God is taken away: through Jesus Christ we know God. . . . In Him then, and through Him, we know God. Apart from Him, and without the Scripture, without original sin, without a necessary mediator promised, and come, we cannot absolutely prove God, nor teach right doctrine and right morality. . . . Jesus Christ is then the true God of man. But we know at the same time

---

[25] Kraemer, *Why Christianity of All Religions?* p. 94.

our wretchedness; for this God is none other than the Saviour of our
wretchedness. So we can only know God well by knowing our iniquities."

In Pensée 555, he wrote, "All who seek God without Jesus Christ, and
who rest in nature, either find no light to satisfy them, or come to form
for themselves a means of knowing God and serving Him without a
mediator.

The basic idea involved here is the necessity of a mediator. Men
in their religious traditions often either ignore the existence of God,
or make religion a way of life and human achievement to "buy" God
off, or assume that one can enter into communion with God by some
mystical experience that ignores God's holiness. In all of these attempts to enter into a relationship with God, the first two propositions
are ignored. God does not need man's proud religious activities, nor
will he be united in mystical experience with presumptuous, sinful
men. The god who accepts such is not a holy god.

However, if God is truly hidden as is true to observation and experience, then it is impossible for men to find him by searching. God
must come to man but God has no basic reason for the Incarnation.
Man in his wretchedness and sin cannot enter into the presence of a
holy God.

The necessity of a mediator is pointed up by Sören Kierkegaard
in his little book *Philosophical Fragments*. He told the story of a king
who fell in love with a humble maiden. He was a mighty king; every
nation feared his wrath. But the king was anxious, like all men, when
it came to getting the right girl to be his wife. The thought that entered his kingly mind was this: Would she be able to summon confidence enough never to remember what the king wished, only to
forget that he was a king and that she was a humble maiden? The
king was anxious lest she reflect upon this and let it rob her of happiness. If the marriage was unequal, the beauty of their love would
be lost.

A number of alternatives could be suggested to the king. First,
he could elevate the maiden to his side and forget the inequality.
But there was always the possible thought coming into the maiden's
heart that after all she was a commoner and he was a king. Such a
marriage could be consummated, but love would never be maintained on a basis of equality.

Second, as an alternative, should someone suggest that the king
could expose her to all his majesty, pomp, and glory and she would

fall down and worship him and be humbled by the fact that so great a favor was being bestowed upon her. To this the king would undoubtedly demand the execution of the person suggesting this as high treason against his beloved. The king could not enter into a relationship such as this. Such was the kingly dilemma.

The solution comes in the third alternative. The king should descend and thereby give up his throne to become a commoner for the purpose of loving the maiden as an equal.

Kierkegaard applies this story to the relation of God with man. God could have elevated man into his presence and transfigured him to fill his life with joy for eternity. But the king, knowing the human heart, would not stand for this, for it would end only in self-deception. To this Sören Kierkegaard says, "No one is so terribly deceived as he who does not suspect it." [26] On the other hand, God could have brought worship from man, "causing him to forget himself over divine apparition." [27] Such a procedure would not have pleased man, nor would it have pleased the king, "who desired not his own glorification but the maiden's." This is an impossible alternative because of God's holiness.

Regarding this, Sören Kierkegaard said, "There once lived a people who had a profound understanding of the divine. This people thought that no man could see God and live—Who grasps this contradiction of sorrow: not to reveal oneself is the death of love, to reveal oneself is the death of the beloved!" [28] The holiness of God revealed to sinful man would have meant his destruction. It is for this reason that God is hidden.

The third alternative for bringing reconciliation or union between God and man is the same as for the king. "Since we have found that the union could not be brought about by the elevation it must be attempted by a descent. . . . In order that the union may be brought about, God must therefore become the equal of such a one and so he will appear in the lives of the humblest but the humblest is one who must serve others and God will therefore appear in the form of a servant." [29]

Both Kierkegaard and Pascal support the idea that only Christian-

---

26 *Philosophical Fragments,* p. 22.
27 *Ibid.,* p. 22.
28 *Ibid.,* p. 23.
29 *Ibid.,* p. 24.

ity offers a mediator. Gautama, Confucius, Muhammad,[30] and others
made no claim to being anything more than men with religious insight.

Before concluding this section, a reference should be made to
Judaism, Christianity, and Islam. Judaism is to be regarded as a
"true religion" only as far as it goes, or is true to itself. The last of
the Old Testament prophets appeared in John the Baptist calling
Israel to a decision. With John the Baptist, the Old Testament sees
itself coming to fulfilment. Old Testament Judaism speaks of a coming Messiah; the prophet John the Baptist declared Jesus to be the
fulfilment of the ancient prophecies. It is questionable whether Judaism can be regarded as a continuation of the Old Testament religion,
especially since the authoritative influence of the Talmud has shaped
postbiblical religious life.

Islam poses a particular problem with reference to Christianity
and the matter of being the final successor to Judaism and Christianity. Islam claims that it stands in the line of the prophets and
the biblical revelation of Judaism and Christianity. Inasmuch as
Islam bases its historical religious background on the Old and the
New Testament to some degree, it undercuts the support it seeks in
appealing to the Bible. If Islam is to acknowledge some truthfulness
in Christianity as its antecedent, it must reckon with the claim of
Christian faith that the revelation of God in Christ was final. This
finality in Christ eliminates any other coming prophet such as Muhammad. The epistle of Hebrews speaks with finality about God's
last word, his highest word, coming in his Son. Islam cannot therefore be regarded as an extension, culmination, or completion of the
Judeo-Christian tradition.

The Uniqueness of Christ

Pursuing the line of Pascal's argument, one may conclude that
Christianity alone gives the best answer to the three questions: Why
is God hidden? Why is man in misery? How can man know God? If

---

[30] "Islam's doctrine of God knows nothing of a Mediator, and Koranic
Christology, though paying reverence to Jesus as man and messenger of God
and as the Word and Spirit of Allah, forswears nevertheless the Incarnation and
hence renders void the redemptive purpose of God. Indeed, this is the parting
of the road between Islam and Christianity" (Jurji, op. cit., p. 247).

we can say that Jesus Christ is the mediator, then there are some things about his person that are important. In these he was unique as a founder, as opposed to other founders.[31]

The Incarnation is a necessity for the act of redemption. Human experience has shown, when viewed honestly, that man is incapable of redeeming himself. Anything less than God as Redeemer is to make a mockery of the idea. P. T. Forsyth once said, in stressing the place of the Incarnation, "A half-god cannot redeem what it took a whole God to make." Nowhere in the other living religions of the world is there a claim on the part of a founder that he was the Son of God in the unique sense of the word. This claim remains alone to Jesus Christ.

It is sometimes argued that the Christian faith is unique in relation to the sublime sayings of Jesus. This proves nothing. It has been shown by Claude Montefiore, the Jewish scholar, that Jesus said little that was new and different from the thought of Judaism. The only thing that he found that was quite distinctive was the picture of the Divine Shepherd going out into the wilderness to seek a lost sheep. This is only a fragment of the truth of the uniqueness of Christian faith. The uniqueness of Jesus is not in what he said but in what he did. The founders of the world religions proposed ways of self-deliverance, self-sanctification, and self-realization. Jesus Christ, on the other hand, did for man something man could not do for himself. It is for this reason that there is a gospel, a good news, and it is the news of something that *happened* in Jerusalem at a given point in history. The event that took place was redemption of man in the person of Jesus Christ. His life, death, and resurrection are the redemptive events. He *alone* gave his life as an atonement for alienated mankind.

There is only one statement that has to be made concerning all the founders of the living religions: they died and were buried! The stories of their lives end there. The word concerning Christ is different. He came forth from the grave, was raised up, and ascended to the Father. Without the resurrection, one could only conclude that Jesus was a great teacher, perhaps a second Moses, but with the resurrection he is declared to be the Son of God. On this Barth says:

---

31 Uniqueness is not an argument for truthfulness, necessarily. All religions are unique. However, the founders of other religions have more in common with one another than with Jesus.

The knowledge which the Apostles acquired on the basis of Christ's Resurrection, the conclusion of which is the Ascension of Christ, is essentially this basic knowledge that the reconciliation which took place in Jesus Christ is not some casual story, but that in this work of God's grace we have to do with the word of God's omnipotence, that here an ultimate and supreme thing comes into action, behind which there is no other reality.[32]

While it is evident that one cannot become a Christian on a purely reasonable basis, Christian faith alone gives adequate answers to the questions of the mind concerning the facts of observation and existence. The founder of the Christian faith possesses a uniqueness that cannot be duplicated or rivaled in the founders of other religions. We conclude with Pascal that "the knowledge of God without that of man's misery causes pride. The knowledge of man's misery without that of God causes despair. The knowledge of Jesus Christ constitutes the middle course, because in Him we find both God and (the answers to) our misery" (*Pensée 526*).

Pascal's line of thought has a close relation to the beginning of Christian faith. Where individuals and movements have deviated from the pattern as set forth in the Scriptures they stand under the criticism of the Founder Jesus Christ. There is no justification for development away from the person of Jesus Christ.

The Exclusiveness of the Gospel

Pascal's propositions can lead to the conclusion that Christian faith alone gives the best answers to the observable experience of man. At the same time, the New Testament is written on the assumption that the final revelation of God has taken place. In contrast to Judaism and the Old Testament, the revelation of God in his Son is declared to be the greatest expression of himself to man (Heb. 1:1–3). Jesus Christ is said to be a better mediator of the covenant than Moses (Heb. 9:15), a better high priest than Melchizedek (Heb. 7:1–28), and a better sacrifice than that offered by the Levitical priesthood (Heb. 8–9). These references imply the completion or fulfilment of Judaism.

In the preaching of Paul to the townspeople of Athens, he declared the Creator who has been the unknown God among heathen people. All other representations in gold, silver, and stone are due to man's corrupt way of thinking (Acts 17:29). The preaching of Peter in

---

[32] *Op. cit.*, p. 126.

Jerusalem was to the intent that "there is no other name under heaven given among men by which we must be saved" (Acts 4:12). The New Testament viewpoint is identical on exclusiveness with that of Isaiah (45:21–22): "There is no other god besides me, a righteous God and a Savior; there is none besides me. Turn to me and be saved, all the ends of the earth! For I am God, and there is no other."

Not only is there an exclusive viewpoint expressed in the New Testament, but other religions are "forms" denying the power of godliness (2 Tim. 3:5). Originators of new religions or religious concepts apart from the apostolic gospel are liken unto gangrene eating away the true flesh (2 Tim. 2:17). The followers of such "strange new religions" are foretold in 1 Timothy 4:1–2. Anything contrary to Christ is anathema (Col. 2:8; Gal. 1:8).

It is very obvious that Christianity does make exclusive claims to being the only right way of knowing God. One may not like it or agree with it, but the claim is there. A man of Christian faith may not like it, but he is not at liberty to change it for the sake of sentimentality. We may not like two plus two being four, but there are certain facts that we cannot change by nature of the universe.

With an exclusive attitude on the one hand and different religious viewpoints on the other, what is one to say to it all? Can we conclude with Schleiermacher that there is an "essence of religion" which is common to all religions and which manifests itself in different forms? Or is Brunner correct in saying, "It is impossible to be a Christian— in the New Testament sense—and at the same time to accept the view that there is a universal 'essence of religion' of which Christianity has a predominant share. The Christian revelation and these 'relative' theories of religion are mutually exclusive." [33]

We must certainly agree with W. C. Smith in declaring that "from now on any serious intellectual statement of the Christian faith must include, if it is to serve its purpose among men, some sort of doctrine of other religions." [34] We now turn our efforts to this consideration.

W. C. Smith and the Identity of "Faith"

In a recent effort to deal with Christian faith and the faiths of other men, or religious persons, W. C. Smith sets forth the thesis that the word "religion" means something different from what the founders of the so-called religions had in mind. In other words, a

---

[33] *Revelation and Reason*, p. 220.
[34] *The Faith of Other Men* (New York: Mentor Books, 1965), p. 121.

religion is a doctrinal system rather than an attitude or a way of life. He traced the rise and evolution of the term from antiquity to the present. In Christianity, for example, the key word in its initial stages was "faith," or a way of apprehending the transcendent, whereas, through the centuries the term "religion" grew up. The English term "religion" has had no equivalent in many languages until some word is borrowed to convey this idea. The distinction Smith makes can be seen from the two standpoints of the observer and the participant. "The participant is concerned with God; the observer has been concerned with 'religion.' " [35] Therefore, from the participant's standpoint, there is nothing known as "religion"; there are only religious persons who are involved in some way with the transcendent by "faith." [36]

It has been because of the emphasis on "religion" that a question of rightness has arisen. When the term religion is discarded and faith regained in viewing other men's worship, then the rightness of one theological system against another is not an issue. W. C. Smith predicts that "a time will come, perhaps fairly soon, when men will see rather that if the Christian revelation is valid, then it follows from this very fact that other men's faith is genuine, is the form through which God encounters those other men, and saves them." [37]

Why does Smith argue this way? Some answers are available in the two works referred to. First, there is the matter of peace. It is imperative that we construct a world of order, or mankind will perish.[38] The world in which we live must be a shared world; it is a world of different faiths, different values, and different cultures. We *must* get along with one another. Smith argues that if there must be competition between religious traditions, let them compete in the area of reconciliation, of bringing men together.

Second, Smith is motivated by a problem that has largely been

---

[35] Wilfred Cantwell Smith, *The Meaning and End of Religion* (New York: Mentor Books, 1963), p. 119.

[36] *The Meaning and End of Religion* (New York: Mentor Books, 1964), p. 172. "There is no generic Christian faith; no 'Buddhist faith,' no 'Hindu faith,' no 'Jewish faith.' There is only my faith, and yours, and that of my Shinto friend, of my particular Jewish neighbor. We are all persons, clustered with mundane labels, but so far as transcendence is concerned, encountering it each directly, personally, if at all. In the eyes of God each of us is a person, not a type."

[37] *The Faith of Other Men*, p. 85.

[38] *Ibid.*, p. 92.

ignored in theology but which is exceedingly thorny to the Christian who is sensitive to justice and yet maintains a view that the Christian faith only is true. What do you do about people who have never heard the name of Christ? [39] This problem is acute not only for the present time, when millions are ignorant of Jesus Christ, but it is also a problem for the vast civilizations before the time of Christ. Are these people condemned to hell for their ignorance? Smith seems motivated to find some alternative to condemning vast numbers to judgment.

In attempting to set forth an alternative, Smith argues that truth is the truth of God regardless of where one finds it. In fact he says, "Truth is God." [40] Thus using the Muslims as an example he says, "The first step that a Christian or a Jew must take if he is to understand Muslims is to recognize that when the Muslim speaks of 'God' or 'Judgment' or 'Creation' or the like, he is talking about the same things as those to which a Christian also refers. . . . Yet the second step is to discover that he is talking and thinking about them in a different way." [41]

As a background for accepting the above statement, Smith maintains that Christians do not know everything about God. They know him in a unique way, but the Buddhists, Muslims, and others know him also in a unique, though not a comprehensive, way. The Christian speaks of the transitoriness of this world, and the Hindu does the same. Both express the same truth from a different viewpoint.

Smith does not accept the possibility of eclecticism, or the amalgamation of religions. This would be unfair to each tradition as well as muddle the truth of each, or ignore the truths not incorporated into the eclecticism. Instead, he declares: "A truly Christian attitude to outsiders must involve both the validity of Christian orthodoxy *and* an acceptance of men of other orthodoxies as one's brothers—in one's own eyes, and in the eyes of God. In this, the image says to me, as in all ultimate matters, truth lies not in an either/or, but in a both/and." [42]

In another context Smith cautiously says,

I rather feel that the final doctrine on this matter may perhaps run along

[39] See Addenda at the end of this chapter for a discussion of this question.
[40] *The Faith of Other Men,* p. 81.
[41] *Ibid.,* p. 79.
[42] *Ibid.,* p. 74.

the lines of affirming that a Buddhist is saved, or a Hindu or a Muslim, or whosoever, is saved, and is saved only, because God is the kind of God whom Jesus Christ has revealed Him to be. . . . But because God is what He is, because He is what Christ has shown him to be, *therefore,* other men *do* live in His presence. Also, therefore we (as Christians) know this to be so.[43]

By way of evaluation, the position of Smith rests upon certain assumptions that others may find it difficult to accept. The first assumption is the developmental nature of religious traditions. Smith prefers the term "cumulative tradition" as the objective material that is studied. Cumulative tradition means "the entire mass of overt objective data that constitutes the historical deposit, as it were, of the past religious life of the community in question: temples, scriptures, theological systems, dance patterns, legal and other social institutions, conventions, moral codes, myths, and so forth; anything that can be and is transmitted from one person, one generation, to another, and that a historian can observe." [44]

Thus the responses of the followers of the founders of religious traditions is as important as the founders themselves.[45] Smith thus rejects what can be called the "essence" of religion that one gets to when accretions are peeled off. There is no ideal Buddhism, Christianity, or Hinduism.

It is apparent that one must agree with Smith that religion *has* developed. But can we say that religion *should* develop? The idea of development has been so influential in other disciplines that we assume it is all good. Development can be regressive. Smith's own thesis testifies to that; namely, an evolution from "faith" to "religion." While he rejects this development as a good thing, we raise the question: why not go further and reject the developmental principle altogether? In other words, why not return to the founders and stress the things that were taught by them? Smith does not do this, however. The probability of world religions' doing this is almost nil, but if truth is at stake, it must be considered.

This leads us to the second assumption which is closely related to the first. Smith debunks what has been called the "cult of the origins," or the theory that the "earliest form of religion or of a

---

43 *Ibid.,* p. 126–27.
44 *The Meaning and End of Religion,* p. 141.
45 *Ibid.,* p. 113.

particular religion is somehow the true form, with all subsequent development an aberration." [46] It would seem that in this one there is a serious problem in Smith's thesis. On the one hand, he wants to recover "faith" as the essence of religion, and he defines it as "my present awareness of eternity." [47] In this the term "faith" may be applied to any religious person. On the other hand, development is of paramount importance in the study of religious persons and we must accept them for what they are today.

For Smith there cannot be an ideal in faith or in the essence of what a religion should be.[48] This raises the serious question of what it is to have faith. How may we know there is Christian faith unless we return to the testimony documents in the New Testament? Can we ever know what Christian faith should be without the original meaning? Was this not the principle in operation in the Reformation of Luther and Calvin?

One might push the argument further and say with Emil Brunner, who rejected the principle of development and emphasized the "origins" of Christianity, that the real trouble in Christianity in general arose out of the developmental perversions of the church—idea and faith.[49] How does one recover the meaning of the church and faith? By evolving further? Or by returning to the founder's meaning? If there is to be any constancy in Christian faith it must come by means of faith in Christ. If we throw out the importance of the beginning point as the standard and example, there is nothing to keep faith from developing into "unfaith."

It would seem that the idea of "origins" as rejected by Smith is really the only tenable one. What gives one the right to refer to himself as Christian if one has evolved so far in his thinking to be anti-Christian? The founder of the religion is the one who professes the deepest understanding of a religious insight. If this has been embodied in writing—in which it is in most cases—it would be better to come to grips with these insights in terms of the original expressions than to follow a secondhand report, regardless of how good it is, much less one that has been contaminated with trappings from

---

[46] *Ibid.*, p. 134.
[47] *Ibid.*, p. 173.
[48] *Ibid.*, p. 172.
[49] Cf. *The Misunderstanding of the Church* (Philadelphia: Westminster Press, 1953).

who knows where for hundreds of years. Furthermore, can we trust the expressions of succeeding generations to keep the insight from contamination? The vast erudition shown by Smith demonstrates that we cannot. Faith did become corrupted. There is no way of recapturing the fresh insights of a religious tradition without going back to the founders.

At this point, Smith raises a serious point. Hinduism knows no recorded founder as is true of other religions. There is also a problem of history in distinguishing between legend and fact in the material relating the biographical facts of Buddha, Confucius, Zoroaster, Muhammad, and others. This may seem precarious, but would it not be better to attempt a recovery of the "true" insight rather than to be content with a garbled, or possibly legendized, account? If we are to accept the developmental principle in religion, what are we to say about the multiplication of deities as in the religious tradition of China, where an outright fabrication of a deity takes place? [50]

What of those who worshiped faithfully such an unreal deity? Does it make little difference who is worshiped as long as one worships? Are we to give less attention to deciding which gods we worship than we give to buying a car or trading for some article for hunting?

In conclusion, regarding Smith's positions, he decries the conceit expressed in claiming that one true religion only exists. The Christian, however, is not the only one guilty of this. The missionary zeal of Islam and Buddhism embody it. However, if one knows the truth—regardless of what it is—there is no basis for arrogance. It is alien to Christian faith to be arrogant. To speak the truth in love is the *only* meaningful alternative.

Morever, there is an existential involvement in the issue in question: if all men worship with the same quality of faith which Smith sketches, then certainly the missionary movement as traditionally conceived is dead. On the other hand, if there is truth in the "one-religion-only" concept, it becomes imperative that Christians, or whoever possesses the true way, declare it widely and openly.

---

[50] Emperor Chen Tsung in A.D. 1005 was defeated by the Tartars. He lost not only "face" but territory to them. His adviser Wang Ch'in-jo advised the emperor to fabricate a revelation from heaven. The result: a deity was proclaimed, named Yü Huang who was elevated to supremacy, and widespread response on the part of the people followed. (Cf. Noss, *Man's Religions*, pp. 364–65.)

Paul and "God Is Not Without a Witness"

The viewpoint of Smith is certainly attractive, but it raises problems. Can one conclude in favor of a related view and do so within the context of the Scriptures? Smith does not develop this beyond saying that the "exclusive" viewpoint has been dominant in Christian faith but that it is not the only one. He refers to Clement of Alexandria and a more liberal strand developing after that.

There are men who seek to develop a solution to the problem of relationship between Christian faith and other world religions on the basis of certain Scripture texts.

First, one might begin with a statement like that found in Romans 1–2. God has not left himself without a witness, "for what can be known about God is plain to them, because God has shown it to them" (1:19). Since the beginning of creation—presumably of man —God's power and deity have "been clearly perceived in the things that have been made" (v. 20). One might further add the words in Romans 2: "When Gentiles who have not the law do by nature what the law requires, they are a law to themselves, even though they do not have the law. They show that what the law requires is written on their hearts" (vv. 14–15).

On the basis of the foregoing, one might argue that much of the insight that is common to Christianity and other world religions might be accounted for. The insight in Buddhism that the world is transient may be compared to the Christian statement that the "world and its lust shall pass away, but he that doeth the will of God abides forever" (1 John 2:17). A similar truth could be expressed in the quotation of the non-Christian poets that Paul refers to in his address to the Athenians (Acts 17). Paul agrees with the insight of the pagan poet who wrote that in God we live and move and have our being (v. 28).

The common insights growing out of man's religious heritage, such as the prohibition against killing, the concern and care for one's own family, and other ethical concerns, could be accounted for on the basis of God's witness of himself.

A second principle comes into play in this line of argument. Man tends to corrupt his faith and relationship to God. This corruption is a second generation movement. Smith's thesis that faith becomes religion is sound as it relates to the second generation's reception of a founder's faith. This is why a return to the original deposit is necessary for each generation. Faith in the Christian movement became

the "assent to intellectual acceptance" of truth in the second generation and thereafter of Christianity. The Puritans emphasized conversion in the early days in America. The second generation got by
with acceptance of the theology as true. The third generation changed
the structure of Puritanism. The Quakers have had difficulty trans-
mitting the "experience" to their children. Numerous instances can
point up the corruption of faith.

Paul pointed this up long ago. Men have known the true God,
but "they did not honor him as God or give thanks to him, but they
became futile in their thinking and their senseless minds were dark-
ened" (Rom. 1:21). They claimed to be wise, but really were foolish.
To make their aberration worse they "exchanged the glory of the
immortal God for images resembling mortal man or birds or animals
or reptiles" (v. 23). In their exchange of truth for a lie, they "worshiped and served the creature rather than the Creator" (v. 25).

A third principle supporting the "exclusive" viewpoint is related
to God's reaction to the knowledge man has had of God. Three times
the passage in Romans speaks of the people's being "given up" (Rom.
1:24,26,28) to go their own way into moral, intellectual, and spiritual
sin. The words of judgment make it difficult to conclude that God
regards the worship of the idolater with indifference.

A final principle may be found also. The book of Romans traces
an argument that concludes in the inability of any man to redeem
himself either without the law or under it. In the third chapter (vv.
19–20) the conclusion of the section is reached: The "whole world
may be held accountable to God." Immediately thereafter is introduced the righteousness from God—the gift which is bestowed—
that a man receives in faith. Certainly it is a gift to the obedient who
receive it. Can it be a gift to all people? Some theologians argue
thus on the basis of chapter 5 (vv. 17–18), where a parallel exists
between the death of Christ and the fall into sin by the first man,
Adam. A further implication would be found in Romans 11:32,
where "God has consigned all men to disobedience, that he may have
mercy upon all."

It is easy on the basis of the above passages to speak of man's departure into sin, and it is also easy to see how man has universally
taken to sin. But it is not easy to justify the universal redemption of
man on the basis of the Scriptures. However, if one could speak of
a confrontation with God for every man the matter might be resolved.

John Wesley attempted to build such a viewpoint based on John 1:9: "The true light that enlightens every man was coming into the world." Wesley argued that every man shall not come to the point of death without a moment of truth, a moment in which he is personally confronted with the decision that determines his eternal destiny.

This viewpoint has been expressed in a different way by Thomas Aquinas.

It belongs to Divine Providence to provide each man with what is necessary for salvation, as long as man himself does not raise obstacles. For if a man who has been brought up amongst the beasts of the forest were to follow the lead of natural reason in seeking good and avoiding evil, we ought to consider it certain that God would either make known to him by interior inspiration the truths which must necessarily be believed, or send someone to preach the faith to him as he sent Peter to Cornelius.[51]

While the above line of argumentation can be supported by the Scriptures, it must be balanced out with the statements in the New Testament that there is one God and there is "one mediator between God and men, the man Christ Jesus" (1 Tim. 2:5). It was the apostolic preaching that declared, "There is salvation in no one else, for there is no other name under heaven given among men by which we must be saved" (Acts 4:12).

Thus joining the two lines of thought in tension, one could say that if men anywhere are to be redeemed their redemption must come through Jesus Christ. If God so chooses to work beyond the normal pattern set forth in the New Testament that is his business. The New Testament stresses the righteousness of God in redemption. Where judgment is declared, it is also a righteous judgment. It must be maintained that for the Christian the Great Commission still stands. It has not been abrogated. Even if God so chose to save men—on the basis of Christ—without knowledge of Christ it would be inferior to one's knowing Jesus Christ in this life personally. But to not take the Great Commission seriously is to deny Christ.

A Functional Approach to the True Religion

If a Christian confronts a religious man in another tradition, par-

---

51 George D. Smith, *The Teaching of the Catholic Church* (New York: The Macmillan Co., 1960), p. 610.

ticularly in the Orient, in dialogue about the relative merits of the non-Christian faith, he is beset with problems of misunderstanding from the outset. The Oriental generally thinks differently from the Westerner. We define truth as logical consistency between propositions arising from experience or reasoning. In some Oriental cultures this is not the case. Some Buddhists, for example, meditate upon a one-handed clap which is a logical impossibility. In many cases the traditional beliefs are so ingrained with rituals, festivals, and the social system that inconsistency is not felt. Thus a "true" religion is not raised as an issue.

If one is to argue for Christianity in its truthfulness it must be done from the standpoint of function. That is to say, Christian faith will better meet the needs of humanity than Buddhism or Hinduism. Thus Christian faith would have greater value in its function in the person's life.

The first area of function is the realm of *motivation*. This area can be viewed as having four aspects. First, the brand of faith in the New Testament takes seriously the deliverance from bondage to fear. "Perfect love casts out fear" (1 John 4:18). It mounts a battle against ignorance, lust, and hate.

A second aspect of motivation is in relation to truth. Christian faith makes a sharp discrimination between truth and error, between idols and the reality for which they are substitutes.

A third factor is Christian faith's claim to bring the man of faith to a knowledge of the Creator, who has revealed himself. Along this line, knowledge of the Creator places the creation or nature in proper perspective. The fact that nature is not divine, that man has it for his sustenance and life, gives the groundwork for an adequate view of society. Thus Christian faith gives the best view of society and the self. The fact that man *is* demands a dignified explanation of his existence.

A fourth area in motivation relates to the possible hope for the present life as well as the meaningful personal existence of the life to come.

The second area of function is in *explanation*. Christian faith, it might be argued, gives a simple but highly consistent and meaningful explanation of important issues. Christian faith offers an explanation of the origin and cause of our universe with its uniform laws and processes. Christian faith explains in a more realistic way the facts of human misery in their various forms in terms of sin. Thus Christian faith takes seriously the fact of sin and the holiness of God in ethical dimensions. Along the same lines it gives a better explanation of the origin and destiny of man in terms of life and the meaning of death. Christian faith has a more meaningful eschatology than other faiths regarding the fulfilment of personality.

A similar approach is that of Donald Walhout. In describing the relationship between Christian faith and world religions, he speaks of Christianity as being the existential fulfilment of other religions. He sees this in the "fulfillment of man's basic need for reconciliation with God and his neighbor." [52] In light of this, the desire of a Buddhist to rid himself of desire finds its fulfilment in Christian faith in the consecration of human selfhood to God. The striving of the Yogi to achieve release from life is fulfilled in Christ, who makes life real, abundant, and divinely ordained. Where religion reaches out for the absolute principle of the universe, Christian faith identifies the unknown power as coming from the God who reveals himself.

However, where a religion is going in the opposite direction to "Christ and the practice of Christian love," [53] then Walhout holds that Christian faith stands in judgment over it. The opposite direction that a religious person may take is to go away from reconciliation to God. When men turn away from reconciliation, they turn from the means of a basic fulfilment in their lives.

Christian faith in regarding itself as the true and final revelation of God has no ground for boasting. Truth knows only responsibility and humility, but often suffers because it is the truth. If the claim of Christian faith is true, how can one know of the content of it? How may a seeker inform himself of God's revelatory act? How can one have the experience of faith? Is this knowledge that someone tells me? Is it internal in myself? Is it open for all to read and know? To this problem we now turn in the next chapter.

Those Who Have Never Heard

The so-called problem of the "heathen" or those who have never heard of the gospel of Jesus Christ, poses a real question in theology. Various proposed answers can be drawn from the history of religious thought.

Universalism has had a recurring appeal to many. Universalism is the belief that God will ultimately welcome all to heaven. Universalism

[52] *Interpreting Religion* (Englewood, N.J.: Prentice-Hall, 1963), p. 433.
[53] *Ibid.*, p. 434.

has assumed two general forms: rational and biblical. These are not always distinguished as such. Rational universalism tends to argue that it is unreasonable to suppose that a God of love and justice would condemn the greater part of mankind. It is often associated with the biblical concept of love and the argument that God's love will not be defeated. *Apocatastasis,* or universalism, is found in the works of Clement and Origen in the second and third centuries of the church.

The biblical form is found—not always without the rational association—in modern theologians.[54] The charge is made that Karl Barth has taught a biblical form of universalism. The primary line of argument is that the death of Christ is universal in its scope.

Barth starts from the doctrine of election in John Calvin. The fact that God elects man is the heart of the gospel. Its place in theology comes before one can consider the person and accomplishment of Jesus Christ. Using the term "predestination" with reference to God's electing man, Barth says: "Predestination means that from all eternity God has determined upon man's acquittal at His own cost. It means that God has ordained that in the place of the one acquitted He himself should be perishing and abandoned and rejected—the Lamb slain from the foundation of the world. . . . Predestination is the non-rejection of man. It is so because it is the rejection of the Son of God." [55]

Calvin had spoken of double election: the election of some to heaven and the election of others to hell. Barth rejects the so-called "horrible decree" to damnation. However, there is yet a double election and all of it takes place in Christ. Man is elected in Christ, and man's rejection because of his sin also takes place in Christ who becomes the rejected man. Thus election does not refer to a few chosen people but to Christ. Man is redeemed in Christ. "Belief in our rejection is the perverse belief in what God has not decreed." [56]

Outwardly Barth rejects the doctrine of universalism, but his view of the death of Christ seems to harmonize with the idea of *apocatastasis*.

At the opposite extreme of universalism can be located Calvinism

[54] Cf. John Macquarrie, *Principles of Christian Theology* (New York: Charles Scribner's Sons, 1966), p. 322.

[55] Karl Barth, *Church Dogmatics* (New York: Charles Scribner's Sons, 1957), II-2, 167.

[56] Gerrit C. Berkouwer, *The Triumph of Grace in the Theology of Karl Barth* (Grand Rapids: Wm. B. Eerdmans Publishing Co., 1956), p. 107.

in which all men are condemned in sin. Inasmuch as the sin of man is universal, both through his relation to the first man who sinned as well as sins of his own experience, judgment may universally fall upon all men. All of mankind could be condemned justly on this basis. However, God does have mercy upon the elect and delivers some through the death of the Son of God.

Besides the views associated with Wesley above, there is another middle-ground approach. Among some Roman Catholic theologians a distinction is made between the ideas of redemption and salvation. Redemption is what Christ did for all people. All men are redeemed. Salvation is related to the individual and what he does personally concerning his relation to God. The redemptive act brings man back to a state of decision like that of Adam who started man in sin. Man must then decide whether he will receive salvation. However, this solution is only a beginning one for the problem of those who have never heard of Jesus Christ. Salvation in the Roman sense is related generally to the reception of the sacraments in the Church. It would offer little hope to those who are yet in ignorance or those who lived in antiquity. One would have to argue beyond this like Aquinas does in the quotation above.

In conclusion, a few remarks are in order. The Christian has a consummate faith that God is just and merciful in his dealings with man. God seeks to do good to man. The reason that there exists something and not nothing is attributed to the motive of God's love. In viewing the problem of those who have never heard, the Christian sees deep profundity in Abraham's question to God in arguing for mercy toward the man Lot, "Shall not the Judge of all the earth do right?" (Gen. 18:25).

Any solution must not abrogate the implications of the Great Commission. Yet, it must be fairly remarked that if the Great Commission had been taken seriously by Christian people, the communication of the gospel to men and women would not have been impossible. However, the larger question of people before Christ's Commission remains. In this we return to Abraham's faith.

Last, while there are records in which men have been converted by unusual experiences in distant lands without the help of a missionary, these are unusual. A theology of evangelism and missions must be built upon what the individual Christian is commanded to do, and not what God does in his way.

III. How May I Know About God?

The first business of our religion is to provide us with an authority—an authority which shall be at once as intimate to active life as Mysticism is to the life contemplative, and more objective than the most Roman Church.
P. T. Forsyth, *The Principle of Authority*

Not the authoritarian state, not the infallible Church, not the inerrant Book, not the subjective preference of the individual, not the weight of social custom and tradition, but truth is the only sovereign, kingly authority known to man.
Bernard Ramm, *The Pattern of Authority*

Inspiration is, therefore, usually defined as a supernatural influence exerted on the sacred writers by the Spirit of God, by virtue of which their writings are given Divine trustworthiness.
B. B. Warfield, *The Inspiration and Authority of the Bible*

The sola Scriptura principle does not mean that, whenever there is a claim to revelation, the Christian must judge it by the criteria of revelation presented in Scripture itself. Man, we believe, apart from the Scriptural revelation, does not have a criteria to judge revelation. This is why Wesley desired to be a "man of ane book."
William Hordern,
The Case for a New Reformation Theology

There are two issues, among others, that may account for a good deal of the division in the mainstream of Christianity. The problem of authority is one, and the matter of church polity is the other. The problem of authority is another way of asking, "Who can tell me about God?" This question in one form or another is quite old and is reflected in the encounter of the religious people of Judaism and Jesus. "By what authority are you doing these things, and who gave you this authority?" (Matt. 21:23). One might apply this question to many areas in the religious life. Why does one believe God to be merciful? Why does one receive baptism? Why does one condemn adultery as evil? Why bear testimony of your faith in Christ? Why not some other belief, action, religious ceremony, and testimony? The answers given to these questions arise out of an appeal to some source for them.

Ideally speaking, an authority should be as stable as the polar star and should speak to every man in the same way.[1] But a brief survey of denominational structures shows that this is not the case. Before setting forth what seems the better solution, we must sketch the types of authority to which men have appealed.

Types of Authority

The Inner Light, or the Light Within

The term "Inner Light" can refer to anything from the light of the Logos (John 1:9), who is shining in all the world to prepare the hearts of men for the preaching of the gospel, to the direct immediate voice of the Holy Spirit. It can refer to: (1) personal apprehension as opposed to belief on the basis of authority; (2) perception of moral truth in which one discerns right from wrong; (3) the individual's duty in a particular matter—for instance, in choosing what is God's will for one's life; (4) the knowledge of God and of life in relation to him, which is experienced immediately.[2]

The divergent meanings attached to the term "inner light" make it difficult to criticize it in general. If one were to equate the Inner Light with the Holy Spirit, one might criticize the results arising out of the equation. For instance, some highly immoral things have been perpetrated on the claim that the Spirit has given the inner command to certain courses of action. More meaningful is the question, How do we know there is a Holy Spirit? Where do we learn this? Inasmuch as we learn of the Holy Spirit in the Scriptures, this pushes us back to another authority. There is authority for the Spirit in the Scriptures, but without the Scriptures, one might argue that all one

---

[1] Sören Kierkegaard, *On Authority and Revelation,* trans. Walter Lowrie (Princeton: Princeton University Press, 1955), pp. 60–61.

[2] Edward Grubb, *Authority and the Light Within* (Philadelphia: John C. Winston Co., 1908), pp. 64–68.

might speak about remains nothing but inward feelings without a corresponding Being who exists externally. The Society of Friends has emphasized the Inner Light the most. Yet it has recognized the problems associated with this type of authority and has been forced to make modifications in its emphasis on it. Two limitations came about: (1) closer orientation toward the Scriptures, and (2) the "sense of meaning" which arose out of a group agreeing on the "message of the Spirit." The last limitation was designed to thwart the possibility of fanatical individualism which occasionally arose in Quakerism.

If one is to equate the Inner Light with a type of intuitionism, another type of problem arises. Intuition means to see things as a whole, or synoptically. It has been called a shortcut to knowledge, as in the case of Archimedes who saw the solution to his problem "at once" without reaching it in a slow rational way.

However, if intuition is defined in this way it loses its authority, for it becomes internal rather than external. For some intuitions, people are put in hospitals; and other intuitions lack "public character"; that is, they cannot be reproduced in other people's lives. Intuition involves a certain amount of relativism, which is not a sufficient authority in religion.

While we criticize intuition as a religious authority, there is a sense in which it is very important. After one has surveyed the material in any realm, there comes a point in which one responds as though saying, "I see the truth of it." The truth of this can be seen against the background of a person who refuses to accept a well-reasoned, highly logical argument. In essence, he is saying, "I see your reasoning, but in spite of my inability to refute your argument, I 'see' that it is wrong." There comes the point in which the "eye of the soul" says yes or no to something confronting it.

As an authority, intuition is not as stable as the polar star. Intuition perceives; it does not produce the content of faith.

Conscience

Conscience as an authority in the religious life has been a popular guide. "Let your conscience be your guide" is an expression approved by many. What is the conscience? The word occurs some thirty-one times in the New Testament and means "joint knowledge" or "seeing with." Conscience as a concept receives one of its greatest expositions in the New Testament. In the New Testament it is that "faculty which reminds us, by stimulating feelings of guilt and shame, when we are doing wrong." [3] It seems quite obvious that this faculty needs educating and reeducating. Conscience is capable of being elevated, and the emphasis of Christian faith on living one's life in the fellowship of the church and the hearing of God's Word underlies the insufficient nature of conscience. Conscience must not be isolated from the Christian view of man in sin. Conscience can be repressed and perverted. Its sense of fairness can be warped by greed, its sense of purity can be tainted by lust, and its sense of holiness can be blackened by pride. It is, therefore, usually argued that conscience is quite relative and undependable. While recognizing some of the truth of this "it is significant . . : that no group custom enjoins lying, stealing, or murder indiscriminately, since such a law would lead to complete chaos within the group. There is thus a limit to the relativity of law in the conscience of man." [4] Another factor in the relativity argument is overlooked. Because diverse peoples do such diverse deeds and regard these actions as "right," it is concluded that the conscience is fully relative. However, this is to assume that if people know what is right, they will do it. Such an assumption overlooks the insights into human nature and man's basic selfishness.

A modern development concerning conscience is to regard it as a "faculty of reason by means of which we recognize, as rational beings, what conduct is befitting our true human nature and calling." [5] Joseph Butler (1692–1752) spoke of it as a "superior principle of reflection" which passes on all courses of action without being consulted or advised. James Martineau described it as the estimating power that chooses between two competing instincts. However, Martineau went further in evaluating conscience. Because man has something of the divine nature breathed into him and "our knowledge of God is regarded as his dwelling in us," Martineau sums up the strivings of human thought in the past, " 'the word of conscience is the voice of God.' " [6]

Not only must conscience come in for criticism as a single authority

---

[3] M. Halverson and A. A. Cohen (eds.), *Handbook of Christian Theology* (Cleveland: World Publishing Co., 1965), p. 61.

[4] Reinhold Niebuhr, *The Nature and Destiny of Man* (New York: Charles Scribner's Sons, 1941), I, 275.

[5] Halverson and Cohen, *op. cit.*, p. 61.

[6] *The Seat of Authority in Religion* (London: Longmans, Green and Co., 1890), p. 46.

in religion, but it is unable to answer the question: Can it give us information about God? Conscience may take the biblical standard of ethics and function in one's life, but it cannot take the initiative to secure a knowledge of God. It may respond to a knowledge of God, but this very fact points conscience to some other way of knowing. If we are to know God, we must seek this information elsewhere.

Conscience as an authority is not fully adequate. The criticisms of conscience parallel those of intuition above. Conscience does stand in need of education. If it is equated with the voice of God, then on what authority is this done? This raises again the relation to the Bible. Certainly no such equation is made there. Conscience cannot point to an objective standard to which all people may appeal. It is granted that a well-trained conscience is a vital part in the spiritual life, but the question arises: Where does it receive its training? The answer to this question points to something else. Conscience, moreover, may accuse or acquit, but what does it do when it stands in need of forgiveness? Conscience has an appropriate place in faith, but we cannot grant it first or even second.

Religious Experience

The term "religious experience" has been used in so many different ways with varying degrees of objective reference. It can mean the feeling of dependence, peace of conscience, contrition, the test of truth by its workability, the God-consciousness of Jesus, conscience, Christian consciousness, and intuition. It can also refer to the *testimonium spiritus sancti internum*, or the internal testimony of the Holy Spirit, of Calvin.[7]

Before we consider an example of religious experience as the authority in religion, we must not imply that religious experience is not important. Even where objective authorities such as the Bible are held, religious experience has been important. John Wesley, for example, preached for a "warm heart" long before Friedrich Schleiermacher was born. But Schleiermacher was one who tended to place religious experience in a preeminent place. The logic of Schleiermacher is the conclusion that one might write one's own Bible out of religious experience.

For a short exposition of the role of experience as the authority in

---

[7] Edwin E. Aubrey, "The Authority of Religious Experience," *The Journal of Religion*, XIII (October, 1933), pp. 433–49.

religion, we shall use Auguste Sabatier.[8] When the gospel of Jesus Christ is preached, "there is awakened in the heart of the seeker a religious consciousness identified with that of Jesus; it gives a consciousness of inward reconciliation with God and divine sonship." [9] Thus, this gospel, though proclaimed by the most imperfect preaching, brings about the repetition of the "religious and moral consciousness of Jesus." [10] The divine verities revealed in the consciousness of Jesus impose themselves by their own virtue on the seeker.[11] What is this consciousness of Christ or the divine verities? It is a threefold experience—"the experience of our deliverance from evil, of our filial union with God, and of our entrance into eternal life." [12] In this and in this alone is Christ's authority supreme. To the person who would protest that one could not have a subjective criterion, Sabatier would reply that one could have no other.

The influence of Schleiermacher via Sabatier and others has been great on modern religious liberalism. As meaningful as religious experience may be, certain questions make us aware that it, too, is secondary. From what source do we receive information about the Christ that is preached? Is not the religious experience the outgrowth of something else, namely, the declaration of a fact, a gospel, a doctrine concerning a person? How does one grow beyond this particular experience? Can there be any certainty in religious life when it is based purely on experience? Any reasonable answer to any of these questions seems to lead to something more objective as the cause of religious experience.

Reason

What can reason do in giving me knowledge of God? We boast of our reasonableness, but in actuality much of our reasonableness is based on a set of personal prejudices from which we start. If God is hidden, then reason in itself remains helpless. Reason may produce conclusions about God's existence drawn from various phenomena as evidenced in the first chapter. We have seen also something of the

---

[8] *Religions of Authority and the Religion of the Spirit,* trans. Louise S. Houghton (New York: McClure, Phillips, and Co., 1904).

[9] *Ibid.,* p. 274.

[10] *Ibid.,* p. 274.

[11] *Ibid.,* p. 288.

[12] *Ibid.,* p. 294.

gap between the reasonable conclusion and the actual experience of God.

Reason often suffers under the limitations placed on it. The eighteenth century, the so-called age of reason, accepted a religion within the bounds of human reason. It claimed the right of reason to question all areas of theological inquiry and developed a religion based on what reason could accept. Religion with these limitations amounted to little more than a belief in God, who deserves to be obeyed. This meant that man should live ethically, and God would bring about justice and equity in the future life. A modern religious movement that combines many of these features of reason as authority in religious matters is Unitarianism and certain types of liberalism.

Deism as a meaningful religious movement is dead. A religion based solely on reason is little better off than atheism. The god who is removed from the world of man is hardly worth worshiping. Certainly his distance from the affairs of man leaves us with scant knowledge of him. Granting that he exists, it would be impossible to declare whether God loves or hates man. More generally, reason exalts itself against the idea of God and makes man in his reason the measure of all things. Reason alone cannot get us to God, but God can come to our reason which is far more thrilling.

The Church

The church is vitally concerned with the question: How may I know God? The church professes to have an answer, but it is not an answer that she has found, but one that has been given, thereby becoming the reason for her existence. The church is not like an electronic instrument, making advances into the unknown and coming up with God. Instead, the church is receptive. God has come to it. If the church knows anything it depends on the self-revelation of God. The church professes that God has done this.

When the question of authority enters the discussion, Roman Catholic theory must receive special treatment, for it is the most extreme and highly developed view. The Roman Church claims authority in three areas: (1) interpretation of the Scriptures, (2) preservation and teaching of tradition, and (3) the infallibility of the pope.

The authority of the Church in interpretation of the Scriptures implies the claim of the Church to the sole right to interpret the Scriptures. But she also claims that the "most important part of the Bible (the New Testament) is born from the heart of the church." [13] Which came first, the church or the Bible? The Roman answer is the Church.[14]

The second area in the Roman claim is the preservation and teaching of tradition. The Council of Trent (1545–63), in sessions four through eight, declared tradition to be of equal status with canonical Scriptures. Tradition is the oral teaching of the early Church Fathers. "They did not write under the inspiration of the Holy Spirit, but their testimony is of great importance with regard to the general conceptions existing in the early Church." [15] But the guarantee of the Spirit in the teaching office of the church is said to be such that the church, in its continuing function as teacher, will not be led astray.

The third area in the claim relates to the infallibility of the pope. Papal infallibility is a narrow doctrine relating only to *de fide* statements, or matters of faith and morals. A *de fide* statement is made when the pontiff speaks *ex cathedra*, that is, from the chair of Peter.[16] "Infallibility is only assured when the Pope is speaking *ex cathedra* . . . when he is speaking officially as the head of the Church, and has the definite intention of making a statement which shall be accepted by the Church as infallible." [17]

Recent developments in Roman Catholicism raise the question in the Protestant mind whether the traditional stance of the Roman Church has been changed. Basically, the answer seems to be no. The

---

[13] *A Handbook of the Catholic Faith*, ed. John Greenwood (Garden City: Image Books, 1956), p. 143.

[14] The question as stated in popular advertising by the Knights of Columbus in popular magazines is somewhat misleading. It should be: Which was first, the church or the writing down of the Scriptures? Obviously, the church was established about twenty years before any extant Scripture was written down. But there is no possibility of the establishment of the church, any church, without the prior message which is contained in writing in the Scriptures. Whether it was written down or preached orally is beside the point. That it was eventually written down is important, but the Scripture message has the logical priority.

[15] *Handbook of the Catholic Faith*, p. 150.

[16] Should one reject *de fide* statements, he would be called a heretic. Protestants often unwittingly assume a wider range of application for infallibility than the doctrine actually supports. *De fide* statements are very limited.

[17] *Handbook of the Catholic Faith*, p. 130.

attitude of the Roman Church is more irenic in many areas, but little is changed in terms of the doctrine on the authority of the Church.

In Vatican II, the decree on ecumenism, it is admitted that the Church stands in need of "continual reformation," and it is declared that "deficiencies in conduct, in Church discipline, or even in the formulation of doctrine (which must be carefully distinguished from the deposit itself of faith) . . . should be appropriately rectified at the proper moment." [18] The real question basic to ecumenism concerns what has been deposited in the "deposit of faith."

Concerning the three areas as related above, Vatican II reaffirms the traditional opinions. Some of the new phrasing of statements may lead non-Romanists to disappointment.

The authority of the teaching Church is reaffirmed in the Dogmatic Constitution of the Church. It states that "God's people accept not the word of men but the very Word of God . . . (but) all this it does under the lead of a sacred teaching authority to which it loyally defers." [19]

The preservation and teaching of tradition receives a new emphasis in Vatican II. The Council of Trent in the sixteenth century had declared the Scriptures and tradition to be equally authoritative in light of the Reformation principle of the Scriptures only. Vatican II speaks of the "one deposit of the Word of God, which is committed to the Church" but which can be divided into two elements: "sacred tradition and sacred Scripture." [20] Revelation when written down becomes tradition. Vatican II implies that tradition has been handed down reliably through the centuries by the teachings of the bishops—unchanged, uncorrupted, and without error creeping in.

With reference to the matter of interpretation, the Dogmatic Constitution on Revelation says,

The task of authentically interpreting the Word of God, whether written or handed on, has been entrusted exclusively to the living teaching office of the Church, whose authority is exercised in the name of Jesus Christ. This teaching office is not above the Word of God, but serves it, teaching only what has been handed on, listening to it devoutly, guarding it scrupulously, and explaining it faithfully by divine commis-

---

[18] *Documents of Vatican II* (New York: Guild Press, 1966), p. 350.
[19] *Ibid.*, pp. 29–30.
[20] *Ibid.*, p. 117.

sion and with the help of the Holy Spirit; it draws from this one deposit of faith everything which it presents for belief as divinely revealed.[21]

The last element of our interest, papal infallibility, was reaffirmed. In the Dogmatic Constitution of the Church, Vatican II asserts, "All this teaching about the institution, the perpetuity, the force and reason for the sacred primacy of the Roman Pontiff and of his infallible teaching authority, this Sacred Synod again proposed to be firmly believed by all the faithful." [22] It also asserts that even when the pontiff is not speaking *ex cathedra,* but does speak in matters of faith and morals, the faithful are to submissive in mind and will.[23]

With the reaffirmation of these elements in Roman theory of religious authority, how are we to evaluate them?

The first question is: What authority is used to support this three-fold authority? The answer to this can be seen in the documents of Vatican II, where numerous references are made to the Scriptures. This looks good; however, two concerns are raised in appealing to the Scriptures to support papal theory.

First, the appeal to the Scriptures gives the illusion of biblical evidence. But no exegesis or interpretation of these Scripture passages is set forth. They are quoted on the assumption—*a priori*— that the passages "prove" the statements referred to in the doctrinal statements. The passages are known to prove the doctrinal statements because the teaching office of the Church declares it so. How do we know there is a teaching office of the Church? The appeal is made to the Scriptures which must be interpreted by the infallible teacher before it can be known. Obviously, one would not arrive at papal infallibility merely from reading the Scriptures without the teaching office of the Church. This circular type of support is fundamental to Roman theology.

The second concern is that the appeal to the Scriptures in the documents of Vatican II is generally meaningless. The teaching authority of the Church attempts to secure a foundation for itself in the Scriptures, but it requires the teaching authority to give certainty that this is what a given passage supports. The central issue becomes: Do the Scriptures without external inference support the infallible teaching role of the Church in its chief teacher, the pope? Most non-Romans would answer no!

Thus the question needs to be raised anew: What *did* Jesus promise his disciples? The fact that Christ promised to be with believers unto the ends of the earth does not guarantee infallibility any more than his presence in the believer guarantees that a Christian will not sin. The Church has erred as well as sinned. This is why there must be a continuing reformation in doctrine as well as practice. The infallibility of the pope is a presumptuous doctrine. An infallible council is said to have declared the pope infallible and immediately ceased being infallible itself. Infallibility is also suspect in light of certain pontiffs who were charged with teaching heresy.[24]

Another issue concerns the teaching authority of the Church in relation to the Holy Spirit. Roman theory connects the Holy Spirit to the Church, whereby the Church is taught directly concerning certain matters.[25]

On this matter, the Scriptures describe the role of the Spirit with reference to Christ and the Scriptures. Justification of a doctrine cannot be made on the grounds that the Church is led by the Spirit,[26] especially when the doctrine cannot be founded by fundamental exegesis of the Scriptures and appears contrary to its whole tenor.

With reference to tradition and the Church's role in preserving and interpreting it, the whole idea is connected with a developmental principle.

Rome does seem to acknowledge that development in doctrine is good. But it is a more fitting generalization to say that in religion, development goes in the direction of degeneration.

Degeneration in doctrine can be seen with reference to the traditional teachings about Mary. The New Testament speaks of Mary as a woman of faith, human in the full sense of the word with reference to sin, a real marriage, and death. With the development of analogies between Eve and Mary by certain Church Fathers and inferences made on Scripture passages having no connection at all to Mary, slowly an ideology about Mary has developed. Thus Vatican II could

---

[24] Cf. George Salmon, *The Infallibility of the Church* (London: John Murray, 1888).

[25] Cf. *Documents of Vatican II*, pp. 73, 76, 86.

[26] Cf. *Ibid.*, pp. 86–96, and the statements on Mary.

speak of her as "Queen of all" (p. 90), "Advocate, Auxiliatrix, Adjutrix, and Mediatrix" (p. 91).

The Council continues to say concerning the titles accorded to Mary, "These, however, are to be so understood that they neither take away from nor add anything to the dignity and efficacy of Christ the one Mediator" (pp. 91–92).

But how can this be? By all rules of language and logic it does take away. By the concept of development, Rome has slowly painted itself into a theological corner that it cannot get out of, without denying infallibility, nor defend by the Scriptures. At the same time it cannot defend its teaching authority without appealing to the Scriptures. But the Scriptures will not support it on any fair exegesis. The danger of development as a theological principle is that logically it is quite conceivable that Rome may "develop" in doctrine to preaching faith in Mary rather than faith in Christ, perhaps on some analogy that the mother is worthy of more honor than the Son.

This issue is emphasized by Berkouwer who wrote, "Whenever another source of knowledge is placed alongside Scripture as being of equal value, we observe that eventually Scripture becomes relegated to the background. . . . Since the Council of Trent tradition has advanced further and further into the foreground." [27]

In conclusion, our point is that there is a prior authority to the church as infallible teacher in matters of religion. It is this prior authority to which we now turn.

The Scriptures

The Scriptures have a relationship to the church which calls for clarification. The Scriptures give authority for the existence of the church. However, the church has no message except as it declares the content of the Scriptures.

The key to the question, how may I know God? is bound up with the Scriptures. The line of reasoning is this: If God is in any sense personal, which the Bible affirms, then it is impossible to genuinely know a person unless he reveals himself. One may know the physical description of another person—height, weight, color of hair, eyes, and other features—but until that person begins to speak forth from

---

[27] G. C. Berkouwer, *Recent Developments in Roman Catholic Thought* (Grand Rapids: Wm. B. Eerdmans Publishing Co., 1958), p. 18.

the depths of his being, real knowledge of the person is impossible. However, once the person begins to speak, we then perceive what kind of person that "hidden person" is.

Using this analogy, we may speak concerning the "hidden God." We have no visual features to begin with. If we are to know God he must speak to us. This is the only sure way of knowledge of him. One may question it as legitimate, but it is surely true that we will not learn of God unless he so wills. Christian faith affirms that God has revealed himself. The Old Testament is received as a story of preliminary self-revelation in a number of ways.

God's self-revealing took place in a decisive unique way in the Incarnation. The story of this and its meaning is recorded in the New Testament. This is why the New Testament assumes such a large role in the life of the church. Christian faith proclaims the appearance of God in human history in the person of Jesus Christ. In him we have a true knowledge of the nature of God. In him we have a knowledge that conscience, reason, or intuition could not give. Jesus Christ is the authority for religious experience, as well as the basis of the church. But all of these things are meaningless without the self-revelation of God in Christ.

Having introduced the Bible as the *record* of God's self-revelation, we must proceed to speak of the authority of the Bible. Almost all Christians accept the Bible in some sense. The degree to which it is accepted or modified by secondary authorities, such as the church, reason, and the Spirit, and the belief concerning the Bible make it a unique source.

There are, however, certain movements within and across denominational boundaries that accept the Bible in a unique sense. From the standpoint of the modern religious situation in Protestantism in general there are two opposing concepts regarding the Bible as the authority of religious life.

First, there is a view that the Bible is the infallible, inerrant, verbally inspired Word of God. The most definitive expression of this position in modern times has come from the old Princeton professors: Patton, Hodge, Warfield, and Machen. J. Gresham Machen (*d.* 1937) declared that the Bible is the only source of information about God that man can trust.[28] The unchanging is the Bible. Its unchange-

---

[28] *The Presbyterian Guardian,* October 7, 1935, p. 42.

ableness comes from being the Word of God. Machen repudiated the
use of relativistic terms such as the Bible *contains* the word of God.
"No we say, in the Christian fashion, that the Bible *is* the Word of
God." [29] Concerning its inerrancy, he wrote:

I hold that the Biblical writers, after having been prepared for their task
by the Providential ordering of their entire lives, received, in addition to
all that, a blessed and wonderful and supernatural guidance and impulsion by the Spirit of God, so that they were preserved from the errors
in other books and thus the resulting book, the Bible, is in all its parts the
very Word of God, completely true in what it says regarding matters of
fact and completely authoritative in its commands.[30]

This is not a mechanical theory of inspiration in which the penmen
wrote without involvement of personality.[31] The writers used sources,
questioned eyewitnesses, referred to documents, and labored in research.[32]

This theory is expressed about the *autograph* manuscripts only;
that is, those manuscripts coming *directly* from the writers, and not
the King James Version or any translation or any of the thousands of
extant manuscripts in the original languages.

What we believe is that the *writers* of the Biblical books, as distinguished
from scribes who later copied the books, were inspired. Only the autographs of the Biblical books, in other words, the books as they came from
the pen of the sacred writers, and not any one of the copies of those
autographs which we now possess, were produced with that supernatural
impulsion and guidance of the Holy Spirit which we call inspiration.[33]

The most crucial issue in the position of Machen and others comes
not in the question of the autograph manuscripts. The crucial question is: If God gave an inerrant, infallible, autograph manuscript,
why did he not preserve it from error in the matter of transmission?
Machen dodged this issue. He declared, "God has given us a marvel-
ously accurate, though not a supernaturally accurate, transmission,
from generation to generation, of what those inspired writers

---

[29] *Ibid.*
[30] J. Gresham Machen, *Christian Faith in the Modern World* (New York:
The Macmillan Co., 1937), pp. 36–37.
[31] J. Gresham Machen, *Christianity and Liberalism* (New York: The Macmillan Co., 1923), p. 74.
[32] *Ibid.*
[33] Machen, *Christian Faith in the Modern World*, pp. 38–39.

wrote." [34] If the autographs were important then, an adequate reason for their loss must be given. There seem to be no valid ones.

Second, there is the view that the Bible is the infallible guide to lead us to salvation in Christ Jesus. There is possibility of great latitude here. A more liberal view is that the *Bible that we have* does contain errors. "The Bible itself is by no means infallible. In it are to be found the erring words of men as well as the authoritative word of God. The contrary accounts of chronology, numbers of soldiers, and other details show that the writers are prone to mistakes." [35]

This position can be pushed to its most extreme point to make the Bible merely an account of the discovery of God by men. On the other hand, in neoorthodoxy,[36] the Bible *contains* the word of God. The emphasis is on revelation whereby the Bible is a record of the true Revelation, Christ the incarnate Word. The record is still a marred record because of the human element of writing down, transmission, and preservation. But it is the instrument of revelation.[37] The true Word or Logos is revealed in the written Word.

The great division seems to be between conservatives of all stripes over against neoorthodoxy and more liberal trends. What is the way out? First, it must be recognized that the division is not as great as it seems. The conservatives are arguing in support of a Bible that does not exist, and the neoorthodox are supporting the Bible that exists. The problem is often posed in an either/or framework. Either declare for inerrancy or settle for an unreliable Bible. This is not the issue at all.

The autograph manuscripts will probably never be discovered, and even if they should be turned up, they will only confirm what has been known all along—namely, the present manuscripts are *reliable*, *authentic*, and *certain*. The science of textual criticism has provided a remarkably trustworthy text as a result of working with

---

[34] *Ibid.*, p. 41.

[35] L. Harold DeWolf, *The Case for Theology in Liberal Perspective* (Philadelphia: Westminster Press, 1959), p. 47.

[36] The term "neoorthodoxy" is generally used to designate the theological vantage point of Karl Barth and Emil Brunner, along with those who accept their position. It is midway between liberalism and conservatism. It retains the seriousness of sin, the uniqueness of revelation in common with conservatism, while it is orientated toward a critical study of the Scriptures in common with liberalism.

[37] Karl Barth, *Church Dogmatics*, I-1, trans. G. T. Thomson (Edinburgh: T. & T. Clark, 1936), 125.

thousands of Hebrew and Greek manuscripts that are extant. The real issue is, therefore, to recognize the text that we have, and live with it.

In criticism of the Bible as a single authority, the following observations can be made. First, the authority of the Bible rests not in itself but in the person declared in it. Jesus Christ is the subject and authority behind the Bible. Second, the Bible is not simply a "paper pope." The Bible alone would be a dead book apart from the living Spirit of God who uses it as his instrument.

In spite of these observations the Bible has a central role in answering the question: How may I know God? It is central in a way that the previously discussed authorities are not. We shall return to this matter, in part, in presenting the next type of authority.

A Pattern of Authority

In the survey of various authorities that have been proposed as a guide for the religious life, we have seen some basic problems when each has been singled out to stand alone. In the final analysis, we have to turn to a pattern of authority [38] or a *discrimen*, a word "designating a configuration of criteria that are in some way organically related to one another as reciprocal coefficients." [39]

This category covers a variety of views and combinations. Bishop Charles Gore presented the following order: The church is the authority, but the Spirit and the Scriptures have their own roles to play. The church teaches, the Spirit converts, the Bible edifies. [40] In seeking to answer the question as to "the source, seat and organ of authority in the Church of Christ," Edward G. Selwyn spoke of its source as the Spirit of God. Its seat is in the common mind of the church; its organ of expression is in the Scriptures, creeds, dogmatic formulations, its liturgical forms and phrases—"whatever in short has nourished and borne fruit in the lives of the saints." [41]

Although the above combination of authorities gives an illustration of a pattern, it must be rejected for the simple reason that we do not

---

[38] Bernard Ramm, *The Pattern of Authority* (Grand Rapids: Wm. B. Eerdmans Publishing Co., 1957), p. 18.

[39] Robert Clyde Johnson, *Authority in Protestant Theology* (Philadelphia: Westminster Press, 1959), p. 15.

[40] In *Lux Mundi*, ed. Charles Gore (London: John Murray, 1890), p. 339.

[41] *Essays Critical and Catholic* (London: SPCK, 1926), p. xvi.

know that there should even be a church, Spirit, or even tradition without the use of the Bible to support these ideas.

If we are to have an adequate pattern of authority, or a *discrimen*, in which we do justice to order as well as the materials used, it must assume the following reciprocal relation: Christ-Bible-Spirit. Although we must discuss these separately in some chronological order, the reciprocal relationship must not be forgotten.

The authority of Christ-Bible-Spirit.—The primary fact of Christian faith is Christ. He is the authority for religious experience. He must be the beginning point, for only a person can be an authority. Religious authority cannot be either a doctrine, book, creed, or church, for the simple reason that these are nonpersonal as they stand in isolation. When they are examined more closely, each is reduced to something else—persons. What kind of persons stand behind each item? A doctrine has been drawn up by theologians; the Bible was recorded by men who heard God speak, or observed historical events; a creed grows out of theological conflict between persons of different thought; and the teaching authority of the church functions through persons. If all of these persons are honest in themselves, they will confess that their ostensible purpose was to bear witness to the living Christ.

If the role of Christ is diminished, it is questionable whether any authority is worth defending. For it is not just any person that we are speaking of, but Christ who is said to be the Son of God, the Saviour of the world. Thus he is a "communing person." [42] Our final authority "is our new Creator, the choosing, saving God Himself in action." [43] Religious authority is intimately connected to commitment, for it is in obedience that regeneration takes place.

If we are to speak of Jesus Christ as authority, how do we know about him? How much would we know of him without the Bible? The Bible preserves for us the untarnished picture of Jesus, the Christ. If this is so, is not the Bible the prior authority? No, because the Bible has no purpose or authority apart from Jesus Christ. Consequently, the Bible must be defined in reciprocal terms to Christ.

The Bible supports the picture of Christ and the authority of the

---

[42] Peter Taylor Forsyth, *The Principle of Authority* (London: Independent Press, 1913), p. 63.
[43] *Ibid.*, p. 53.

person of Christ supports the Bible. Without the Bible, our knowledge of Christ might be that of an emaciated figure or a stern judge as dictated in medieval times. The Bible is the recorded message that always stands in judgment over the perverted pictures of Christ that do arise. But behind the Bible stands the authority of Christ, and the two must not be isolated from each other. This is evident in the words of Jesus concerning the Holy Spirit, or the Comforter who comes from him and who witnesses of him in the Scriptures.

The Bible becomes the unchanging medium through which the authority of Christ is expressed. The Bible serves as the medium of his confrontation to men. It is the written Word through which the incarnate Word speaks. Thus, the Bible is not an obstacle, moving the revelation one step away from us, but a means "ordained by the Revealer between the Revelation and us." [44]

The third coauthority then is the Spirit. Without the testimony of the Spirit to the message of the living Christ in the Bible, we are helpless in establishing a sense of religious certainty. John Calvin spoke of this problem in his *Institutes*. The Scriptures are dependent upon the testimony of the Spirit, who is given by Christ the prior authority. Calvin wrote:

If, then, we would consult most effectually for our consciences, and save them from being driven about in a whirl of uncertainty, from wavering, and even stumbling at the smallest obstacle, our conviction of the truth of Scripture must be derived from a higher source than human conjectures, judgments, or reasons; namely, the secret testimony of the Spirit. . . . The testimony of the Spirit is superior to reason. For as God alone can properly bear witness to his own words, so these words will not obtain full credit in the hearts of men, until they are sealed by the inward testimony of the spirit.[45]

Thus, in the same breath that we talk of the authority of the Bible we must also speak of the authority of the Spirit, for they cannot be separated either. The Spirit is linked with the Word, and we know of his action because of what is written in the Word. Fanaticism with reference to the Spirit does not become a danger when the words of Scripture concerning the Spirit are heeded.

---

[44] *Ibid.*, p. 134.
[45] *Institutes of the Christian Religion*, trans. Henry Beveridge (Grand Rapids: Wm. B. Eerdmans Publishing Co., 1957), I, 71–72.

The relation between the Spirit and the Scriptures was expressed in the Second London Confession, written in 1677. It is worth noting:

The Holy Scripture is the only sufficient, certain, and infallible rule of all saving Knowledge, Faith, and Obedience. . . . All which [referring to the canonical books of the Bible] are given by the inspiration of God, to be the rule of Faith and Life. . . . The Authority of the Holy Scripture for which it ought to be believed dependeth not upon the testimony of any man, or Church; but wholly upon God . . . the Author thereof; . . . our full perswasion, and assurance of the infallible truth, and divine authority thereof, is from the inward work of the Holy Spirit, bearing witness by and with the Word in our Hearts. . . . Nevertheless we acknowledge the inward illumination of the Spirit of God, to be necessary for the saving understanding of such things as are revealed in the Word.[46]

Without the Spirit's working in a reciprocal relationship to the Scriptures, man would not ordinarily conclude that the Bible is God's word to him. With the power of God's Spirit in convicting the sinful heart of man, man sees himself in the pages of the Scriptures and comes to Christ who died for him.

The authority of the church.—The church has authority only as it preaches the gospel of Christ. Its authority is derived from his Commission, but he does not give up his governing authority over the believer. Like the believer, the church as a whole must stand under the judgment of the Head and his authority role for the church. We believe "in the Church because of Christ and not in Christ because of the Church." [47]

What is the role of the church then as an authority? The history of the church is not to be cast out as though only meaningful thought has come about in the twentieth century. The great Christian men of the past have contributed much good in the way of interpretation of the Scriptures and pastoral insight into its meaning for human life. We can profit by instructing ourselves with their help as long as all thought in the religious sphere is subjected to the mind of Christ Jesus as reflected in the Scriptures.

Great minds in the history of Christian faith have contributed to the formation of creedal statements. These formulations have been

---

[46] William L. Lumpkin, *Baptist Confessions of Faith* (Philadelphia: Judson Press, 1959), pp. 249–50.

[47] Forsyth, *op. cit.,* p. 316.

useful as long as they were true to the real constitution of the church, the Scriptures. The church today has the delegated authority to teach and preach the gospel of Christ. Yet its message must not be founded upon anything but the Scriptures, which speak of Christ as witnessed to by the Spirit of God. In all things the church is subordinate to this threefold reciprocal authority.

Reason, conscience, and experience.—These three have their place and role but it is a humble one. Reason stands unable to find meaningful knowledge of God until it is enlightened by him. Once God has spoken concerning himself and once he enlightens man's heart, man the sinner can assimilate such knowledge. The conscience remains in a secondary position to the Scriptures. Conscience cannot inform man of God, but conscience can be informed of God and thereby become enlightened and helpful in living. The conscience can only condemn, it cannot forgive; it cannot provide in itself material for an ethic, and it certainly cannot redeem.[48] When conscience is taught by Christ through his Word, it may become quite sensitive to God's Spirit. But even then it is only a secondary authority for religious guidance.

Experience is also important in its proper place. The authority is not in the experience, but the *experienced;* that is, religious experience is the outgrowth of meeting Jesus Christ. Experience is thus the product of the gospel's declaration and response. Consequently, experience must always refer back to its norm and origin. In religious experience, the Spirit of God encounters man in the present age on the basis of the historic gospel which declares what Christ has done for man.[49] Arising out of this encounter is the experience that we know and are known by God. To be known by God is to experience redemptive hope.

The conclusion is that we need a structure of authorities with Christ as the prior authority for all. If the Bible alone is set forth as the sole authority, one may tend toward bibliolatry. If the Spirit alone is the authority, one tends toward mysticism or fanticism. If the church alone is the authority, it tends to authoritarianism. If reason is the sole authority, one tends toward humanism or deism. These tendencies are offset when "Christ is the authority who speaks

---

48 *Ibid.,* p. 404.
49 *Ibid.,* p. 122.

through the Bible and makes its authority meaningful and alive. His Spirit conforms to the image of his written Word which becomes the life and authority of the church." [50]

Definitions

Because the Bible plays an important role in the pattern of authority there are certain concepts that need definition concerning it. It is common to speak of the Bible in terms of inspiration, as containing a revelation, and the reader's needing illumination. What does this mean?

1. *Inspiration.*—Almost all Christians speak of the Bible as inspired. The difference is over the extent of inspiration. Very early in the history of the church there was a tendency to speak of *verbal inspiration.* Perhaps the first writer to express such a viewpoint was Clement of Alexandria. A hundred years after Clement, Gregory Nazianzus wrote that "every slightest line and stroke of Scripture is due to the minute care of the Spirit and that even the slenderest nuance of the writers is not in vain or displayed to us in vain." [51] The term verbal inspiration has endured in the history of Christian thought, although with different meanings in different contexts. The old Princeton school accepted the definition of Francis L. Patton who wrote that "The books of the Bible . . . were composed by men who acted under the influence of the Holy Ghost to such an extent that they were preserved from every error of fact, of doctrine, of judgement; and these so influenced in their choice of language that the words they used were the words of God. This is the doctrine which is known as that of PLENARY VERBAL INSPIRATION." [52]

Among some conservative writers there is a confusion of terms. Some have equated plenary verbal inspiration with another theory called "dictation." The dictation theory implies that the Scriptures were dictated by God to the writers in much the same fashion as an executive dictates a letter to his secretary. If the Scriptures were dictated it would rule out any meaning for passages like Luke 1:1–4,

---

[50] Dallas M. Roark, "Authority in Protestantism: 1890–1930," *The Journal of Religious Thought,* XXII (1965–66), 22.

[51] Barth, *Church Dogmatics,* I-2, 517.

[52] *The Inspiration of the Scripture* (Philadelphia: Presbyterian Board of Publication, 1869), p. 92. (The capitalization is Patton's.)

in which the writer declares his dependence upon other sources. It is thus a mistake to identify these two theories together as some do.[53]

A second type of inspiration is that defined by Karl Barth. Barth tries to make use of the term verbal inspiration. "If God speaks to man, He really speaks the language of this concrete human word of man. That is the right and necessary truth in the concept of verbal inspiration." [54] Barth proceeds to say that although God has spoken to man in man's terms and although human words are not the final, ultimate symbol concerning the truth of God, yet these human forms of expression have the value of a "commission" in his service and they, for all practical purposes, speak with authority to us. We have no other vehicle but human words.

2. *Revelation.*—The word "revelation" is really a very narrow term. Sometimes the entire Bible is said to be a revelation from God. This is incorrect. Much of the Bible stands under the term "inspiration" with a lesser amount of it under the term "revelation." Much of the history of the Old Testament, as well as that of the New Testament, is the result of research. Inspiration merely means that the writers were directed by the Spirit of God in order to provide a sufficiently reliable account. Revelation strictly refers to an unveiling to man of something he could not know by ordinary investigation. For instance, the story of creation, the virgin birth of Jesus, the deity of Christ, foretelling of prophecy, and the coming of Christ: all of these could not be known without a direct declaration from God. Jesus Christ himself is *the* revelation of the nature of God to man. "The real content of revelation in the Bible is not 'something' but *God* Himself. Revelation is the self-manifestation of God. . . . Revelation everywhere includes within itself a negative presupposition: without it man is always in some way or other in a kind of darkness or bondage." [55]

3. *Illumination.*—The term "illumination" refers to the work of

---

[53] J. Clyde Turner in *These Things We Believe* (Nashville: Convention Press, 1956) equates verbal inspiration with dictation under a heading of mechanical inspiration. He wrote, "Some believe in plenary verbal inspiration, that is, that every word of the Bible was dictated by the Holy Spirit, either directly or indirectly" (p. 3). It is possible to see such an equation in the history of the church, but it is not the sophisticated form of the term "plenary verbal inspiration" in modern use.

[54] *Church Dogmatics,* I-2, 532.

[55] Brunner, *Revelation and Reason,* p. 25.

God's Spirit in teaching the individual concerning Christ, usually in
relationship to the Scriptures. It does not imply a new revelation of
any sort. It is comparable to a personal grasping of God's revelation.
Illumination may be regarded as the existential moment in which
one perceives that God's work is concerned with oneself. Augustus H.
Strong gave the following examples to help distinguish these terms
from one another.

(1) Inspiration without revelation, as in Luke or Acts, Luke 1:1-3;
(2) Inspiration including revelation, as in the Apocalypse, Rev. 1:1,11;
(3) Inspiration without illumination, as in the prophets, I Peter 1:11;
(4) Inspiration including illumination, as in the case of Paul, I Cor. 2:12;
(5) Revelation without inspiration, as in God's words from Sinai, Ex.
    20:1,22;
(6) Illumination without inspiration, as in modern preachers, Eph.
    2:20.[56]

Conclusion

One of the implications of the problem of authority, or the question of how may I know about God, is what I am going to do about
it. It is inconceivable from the standpoint of the New Testament to
think of a Christian apart from a relationship to the fellowship of the
church. The issue is no less pressing in modern times, but it is more
complicated.

In bewilderment, many view the denominations with a shake of
the head without any proper assessment of the real truth in the matter. Inasmuch as there are differences, many conclude they cannot
all be true churches. But the matter is not like deciding between
Buddhism and Islam. The issue is not an either/or situation. Within
denominations there is far more that is held in common than that
which divides. This is not to conclude either that there is not an issue
of truth involved.

A quick checkup on creedal statements in many denominations
reveals that there is greater unity in Protestantism than there is division. The name "Christian" is bigger than any one denomination. It
is quite possible to be at one with many other denominations in es-
sentials and have charity at the point of nonessentials. But many
people expect the church to agree absolutely on everything, whereas

[56] *Systematic Theology* (Philadelphia: Judson Press, 1907), p. 197.

this is not expected of anybody in any subject area or any organization elsewhere.

Where does one begin in a discussion of differences? The answer revolves around the issue of authority.

At the foundation of every corporation there is a charter of incorporation. The charter lays down the guidelines for the development of the corporation. Without pushing the analogy too far in the direction of organizational spirit, something similar is the case in Christian faith. At the foundation of Christian faith is Christ, speaking through the Bible. Therefore any judgment concerning a denomination or church must be made from the standpoint of *adherence* to the charter, or the Bible. Thus we have the problem of *approximation* to the biblical standard. The closer the church is to the New Testament, the closer it is to being near the true pattern of the charter.

In light of the preceding statement, two comments are needed. Approximation as a principle does not involve minutiae such as whether one calls his Bible school a Sunday school; or whether musical instruments are rejected in the worship service; or whether one does or does not wear lipstick. It does involve important matters such as personal commitment to Christ as Saviour, meaningful but not magical ordinances, carrying on the work of the Great Commission in teaching and discipling all nations, and the growth of a fellowship of committed men and women.

The other comment relates to the gap between what is acknowledged as the biblical truth and the captivity to tradition that has grown up through many generations. As increased materials become available, showing the New Testament message in its simplicity and purity, the man of Christian faith must be ready to acknowledge its meaning for his religious life. Because tradition stands under the judgment of Christ in the Scriptures, we must be prepared to dump it over where necessary. The man of faith feels in his heart the common conviction with the apostles, "We must obey God rather than men" (Acts 5:29). This truth has application to the churches as well as in the realm of personal obedience.

IV. Who Is God?

This absolute and unique "I," beside whom there can be none else: this "I" who alone summons us to "hear" Him, and this "Thou" to whom alone we are to turn for succour absolutely —this is the meaning of "Lord," just as in a remarkable passage in Hosea we read: "It is thou!" It is from this point that dogmatic reflection must start, from this absolute Lord, not from a neutral definition of the Godhead.

Emil Brunner, *The Christian Doctrine of God*

We cannot get behind God—behind God in His revelation—to try to ask and determine from outside what He is. We can only learn and then attempt to repeat what He Himself alone can tell us and has told us—who He is.

Karl Barth, *Church Dogmatics*

When Christian faith speaks of God as a "person," it maintains both the activity of God as an expression of his will and the personal and spiritual nature of the Christian relationship between God and men. The term "person," which naturally is a figure of speech, stands guard against the transformation of the conception of God into an abstract idea, and against its being understood as a force of nature.

Gustaf Aulén, *The Faith of the Christian Church*

What can the thinking man say about God? This question has become more crucial since man has continued in his conquest of our world and the space around it. Can man no longer speak to God "up there," as Bishop John A. T. Robinson contends? [1] What can we say about the idea of God that is meaningful? On what basis can we say it? These questions have elicited different answers from different perspectives.

---

[1] *Honest to God* (Philadelphia: Westminster Press, 1963), pp. 10–28.

Rational method.—Through the influence of Neoplatonic philosophy, theologians speak of the attributes by the method of *vias,* or ways. The first way was *via negationis,* or the way of negation. This involves speaking of God without the imperfections in man. God is without sin, without limitations, without death, and other qualities. This has little in common with the Christian view of God who reveals positive knowledge of himself. The second way was *via eminentiae,* or the way of eminence. One attributes to God in the form of perfection all the good attributes of his creatures. If man has limited knowledge, God has infinite knowledge. If man is powerful, God is omnipotent. The third way was *via causalitatis,* or way of causality. This predicates of God the necessary attributes to explain the world of nature and intelligence.

At best these are human attempts to speak of God. If God is hidden, or *Deus absconditus,* then these statements reveal to us little more than human opinion. It is not possible for human nature as it is to come to a realistic view of God. The sinfulness of man distorts his picture of what God is like. Karl Barth declares concerning the *vias* or ways: "God is the One who is free even in His being for us, in which He is certainly not to be apprehended only by means of negative concepts. Again, so far as the *via eminentiae* is concerned, it is not true that as our concepts try to surpass earthly realities in the form of superlatives they necessarily move towards the love of God turned to the world and manifested in the world." [2]

We must turn elsewhere for our knowledge of God.

Logical positivism.—Logical positivism, with its emphasis on the use of language and the principle of verificational analysis,[3] declares that nothing meaningful can be said about God, because verification of the transcendent Being cannot be made in the same sense that other facts can be verified. Metaphysics, or the discussion of a transcendent reality, is to be eliminated.

---

[2] *Church Dogmatics,* II-1 (Edinburgh: T. & T. Clark, 1957), 347.

[3] A. J. Ayers says concerning the verification principle, "The criterion which we use to test the genuineness of apparent statements of fact is the criterion of verifiability. We say that a sentence is factually significant to any given person, if, and only if, he knows how to verify the proposition which it purports to express—that is, if he knows what observations would lead him, under certain conditions, to accept the proposition as being true, or reject it as being false."—Alfred Jules Ayers, *Language, Truth, and Logic* (New York: Dover Publications, n.d.), p. 35.

Serious objections can be raised concerning whether language is limited in the fashion that these philosophers contend. Some of the men in this movement have modified their position concerning the nature of language. Although we are not attempting to discuss the objections systematically, we would note the diverse viewpoints of Ludwig Wittgenstein and John Hick. Wittgenstein modified his earlier views to say that there are many "language games" in which many different types of nonverification statements can be made that are meaningful, and prayer is included in the list.[4] John Hick defends the idea of eschatological verification of the existence of God. At the end of life one can prove or disprove the existence of God.[5]

The student of theology can learn much from the use of language, but as a Christian he cannot assent to the central motif that it is meaningless to talk about God.[6]

Religio-genetic.—Karl Barth uses this phrase to describe the approach of Schleiermacher, and it can be applied to Ludwig Feuerbach. Schleiermacher "tried to interpret the attributes of God as an objectification of the individual aspects of the religious self-consciousness." [7] From his consciousness man concludes that God is eternal, omnipresent, omnipotent, and omniscient. When he reacts against his conscience, he feels that God is holy and just. When he resolves his state of disharmony, he conceives that God is love and wise. Feuerbach, in a similar vein, believed that God is a projection of man's best thoughts.[8] It is true that men make gods after their own image. But even then men have been warned of the dangers of idol worship. Christian faith rejects such a beginning point and speaks of the revelation of God. To this we now turn.

Biblical revelation.—It remains an axiom that if we are to know about God in any meaningful way our knowledge must come from him. Self-revelation can be our only hope of a valid knowledge of God. The Christian faith maintains that God has revealed himself in

---

[4] Cf. Frederick Ferré, *Language, Logic, and God* (New York: Harper & Row, 1961), p. 59.

[5] *Op. cit.,* pp. 253–74.

[6] Note: See Tillich's comment, "If the logical positivists cared to look at their hidden ontological assumptions as inquisitively as they look at the 'public' ontologies of the classical philosophers, they would no longer be able to reject the question of being-itself."—Paul Tillich, *Systematic Theology* (Chicago: The University of Chicago Press, 1957), I, 231.

[7] Karl Barth, *Church Dogmatics,* II-1, 338.

[8] Cf. Ludwig Feuerbach, *op. cit.,* pp. 17 ff.

many different ways. Its primary emphases are on the revelation through men appointed as prophets, or spokesmen for God, and the finality of self-revelation in the Incarnation. The appearance of Jesus Christ in human history marks the turning point in the groping of man for a certain knowledge of God. The Incarnation means that God has descended, and when man knows Jesus Christ he knows God the Father also (John 14). The record of the appearance of Jesus Christ and its meaning for salvation is contained in the New Testament.

It would be foolish to presume that knowledge of God is the only important item considered in the Incarnation. If God does exist for the sake of knowledge, it would be good to know him. But the important fact is that the Incarnation did not take place to give a certain true knowledge of God, but it took place for the redemption of man. Knowledge of God without redemption would be of little value. On the other hand, one could not know redemption without some knowledge of God.

Incomplete knowledge.—The Christian faith has never maintained that it knows everything about God. The Bible is designed for the purpose of salvation (John 20:31). But it is necessary to maintain that our knowledge, as far as it goes, is true knowledge. One can make the statement that all assertions about God are symbolic, but this must not be understood to mean that the symbols are not meaningful. Paul Tillich declares that the only nonsymbolic thing one can say about God is that he is "being-itself." [9] Is not this symbolic in the final analysis? Words never fully convey the whole story, but words are all that we have for communication. We must use them carefully, for there comes the limitation in which they will not carry any more freight. We have to use them as far as they will go.

One example will help point up our problem. Some theologians are down on the phrase "personal God." It carries with it the ideal of individuality. But here we are in a dilemma. If we do not say "God is personal," we do not use the highest form of existence that we know apart from God. If we do use it, we run the risk of making God conform to an image of man's personality. In this matter we must use the best and highest term we have and realize that it does not express all that can be expressed about God.

---

[9] *Op. cit.,* p. 238.

Definition.—To give a comprehensive definition of God is quite impossible. Theologians have attempted to give short definitions for practical use. Augustus Strong, a Baptist, wrote, "God is the infinite Spirit in whom all things have their source, support, and end." [10] The Westminster Confession, which Charles Hodge regarded as probably the best ever written by man, says, "God is a Spirit, infinite, eternal, and unchangeable, in his being, wisdom, power, holiness, justice, goodness, and truth." The New Hampshire Confession of Faith, a Baptist work, declares:

We believe that there is one, and only one, living and true God, an infinite, intelligent Spirit, whose name is Jehovah, the Maker and Supreme Ruler of heaven and earth; inexpressibly glorious in holiness, and worthy of all possible honor, confidence, and love; that in the unity of the Godhead there are three persons, the Father, the Son, and the Holy Ghost; equal in every divine perfection, and executing distinct but harmonious offices in the great work of redemption.

Each statement of the Confession is anchored in biblical assertions.

A modern attempt to define God in propositional form does not fare as well as more historical assertions. Paul Tillich's definition offers extreme latitude: "God . . . is the name for that which concerns man ultimately." [11] This definition could fit primitive animism as well as apply to the sophisticated philosophical theology of Paul Tillich. It will fit any form of man-made idol. It cannot be an adequate definition for the living God. Even if God is not the ultimate concern of men, he is still the Lord and Judge of the world.

The Bible does not give a systematic definition of God. One has to appeal to various assertions of the Scriptures. It is from the data of the Scriptures that we are able to say that God is Spirit, or that he is holy.

The attributes.—Theologians have used various arrangements to deal with the various attributes, or characteristics, of God. They have spoken of natural and moral attributes—the natural relating to his existence and the moral to his truthfulness and goodness. Others have spoken of intransitive and transitive attributes. The intransitive relate to the being of God and the transitive relate to his effects. Per-

---

[10] *Systematic Theology* (Philadelphia: Judson Press, 1907), p. 248.
[11] *Systematic Theology*, I, 211.

haps the most common are incommunicable and communicable. The incommunicable relates to his being, while the latter speaks of attributes for which there is a likeness in the human spirit. We prefer not to follow an arbitrary division such as this. We shall begin with self-revelation of God and deal with the various ways in which God has revealed himself.

The Self-Revelation of God

The Name of God

A beginning point of self-disclosure is by means of one's name. There are many nouns and adjectives ascribed to the Being who is also called God. But God is not his name. However, the God of Abraham, Isaac, and Jacob is known by a name. His name is usually written in English as Yahweh (a transliteration) or Jehovah (a poor transliteration). More than 6,700 times God is called Yahweh in the Old Testament. This is in contrast to the term *Elohim* (God) which appears only 2,500 times. There are other names used to designate God such as *El Shaddai,* the Almighty God, *Adonai* or Lord, and others. The significant name is Yahweh. This is his personal name. Just as I introduce myself by my name, so God has given us his name—Yahweh. Emil Brunner maintains that the name should not be translated, as is done in Exodus 3:14, "I AM That I AM." This detracts from the more significant fact that God has revealed himself by name. Brunner also states that such a translation tends to make God an object of philosophical definition rather than the self-revelation to Israel. [12]

The revelation of Yahweh emphasizes that God is no longer hidden but chooses to disclose himself to man. He is not content to remain in self-sufficient isolation. He moves toward man to make him his own. The culmination of his revelation by name is the final revelation of possible relationship in Jesus Christ whereby we can call God "our Father." Jesus came to reveal the Father (Matt. 11:27), and it is by the Spirit that man cries out in faith, "Abba!" or "Father" (Rom. 8:15–16).

The fact that God reveals himself by name should warn us against such vague appellations as "The First Cause," "The Moral Law,"

---

[12] *Christian Doctrine of God,* p. 120.

"The World Soul," "The Unmoved Mover," and other similar terms. When one is content to speak in vague generalities about God's self-revelation, one does little in honoring God.

The self-revelation of God by his name is to be placed above what one might learn from looking at the creation. Having existed from eternity without need of a creation, God did not have to create. The fact that there is something as opposed to nothing points up his "outgoing" nature. In connection with this we might raise the question of the possible knowledge of God through nature. Modern theology has been divided on this issue, especially theologians Karl Barth and Emil Brunner.

Barth has maintained in the past that there is no knowledge of God apart from the historical revelation. Brunner maintains that there is revelation in the creation, which is to be distinguished from a so-called "natural theology." The matter of a natural theology deals with the issue of whether man has an innate knowledge of God. The Scriptures seem to indicate that revelation in creation is a possibility, because from this type of knowledge man is charged with guilt for his idolatry. The book of Romans concludes that man is without excuse, because he continues to corrupt the revelation of God within the creation (Rom 1:19–20). If one maintains the careful distinction between "natural theology" and "revelation in nature," then the biblical answer is that there is some knowledge of God.[13]

The value of "revelation in nature" is in terms of man's responsibility. Regardless of how much one stresses it, it is not a redemptive knowledge that comes to man. He still needs the good news of redemption, regardless of his astute deductions from the creation.

God as Person

It is extremely important to note God's self-revelation with regard to the concept of person or personal. Some reject the word "person" and use instead the term "personal," declaring, "The symbol 'personal God' is absolutely fundamental because an existential relation is a person-to-person relation. Man cannot be ultimately concerned about anything that is less than personal."[14] The word "person" is not

---

13 "But even apart from explicit Biblical evidence, the Christian Idea of the Creator should itself force us to admit the reality of a revelation in Creation; for what sort of Creator would not imprint the mark of His Spirit upon His Creation?"—*Ibid.*, p. 133.

14 Tillich, *op. cit.*, I, 244.

fully adequate to describe him, but we could not be satisfied with an impersonal "it," or "thing." Certainly the term "person" is a better concept than an impersonal one.[15] The word "person" or "personal" embodies ideas that are important when one speaks of God. We must speak of God as self-determinative, self-conscious, and active. All of this is in the term "personal." [16]

It is necessary to speak in person-to-person relationships with God and man as prerequisites for religious experience. This explains why man has had the tendency to attribute souls to the inanimate objects that he worships. Man is not satisfied with that which is less than himself.

The idea of person is necessary to speak of other phases of God's self-revelation. It is difficult to think of God's loving without the requisite idea of person. If God is impersonal, an "it" or "thing," how can he understand right from wrong? And what is more important, how can he command me to do that which is right? Without the idea of person one might ask if God knows as much as man does in the moral sphere, for man does know something of right and wrong.

There are, to be sure, objections to the term "person," but it is the best one we have. It fits the biblical descriptions, for in the Old Testament God speaks of himself in the personal pronoun "I."

God as Holy

"A doctrine of God which does not include the category of holiness is not only unholy but also untrue." [17] To say that God is holy means that he transcends all that is human and earthly; defined in an ethical sense, this means that he is pure, without sin, and righteous. "To be holy is the distinguishing mark peculiar to God alone: it is that which sets the Being of God apart from all other forms of being." [18] In an ethical sense, holiness emphasizes the necessity of the atonement for man provided by God. Without an atonement, a covering, man cannot enter the holy presence of God without being annihilated.

Aulén states that the holiness of God is significant in four ways: (1) "It asserts the purely religious character of the idea of God." This is placed in opposition to religion's being a matter of morality

---

[15] Brunner, *Christian Doctrine of God,* pp. 139–140.

[16] Buswell, Jr., *op. cit.,* p. 36.

[17] Tillich, *op. cit.,* I, 215.

[18] Brunner, *Christian Doctrine of God,* p. 158.

and ethics. (2) It emphasizes "the majesty of God" in opposition to transforming Christianity into a panacea for attainment of human happiness and enjoyment. God's holiness is unconditional in his confronting men. (3) It emphasizes God's "unfathomableness" in opposition to rationalistic religion, which accepts only what reason can comprehend. (4) "It repudiates all attempts to identify the divine and the human in contrast to mysticism." [19]

The revelation of God in his holiness is often pitted against his self-revelation in love. If one is to speak correctly the two can never be separated. One must speak of holy love. Holiness means that God is true to himself and his will in expressing his love. Love that is without self-respect is not true love. With regard to redemption, both love and holiness are expressed. To say that God loves means that he seeks man's good. To say that he is holy in his love means that he deals with man's sin in harmony with his own nature. He does not take a light view of sin.

God alone is holy. It is possible that certain objects may be revered and respected as holy. One may attach certain dread and awe to objects, but in the Bible the term is primarily used with reference to the nature of God in his self-revelation: he is holy.[20] One might note Barth and Brunner's criticism of Otto.[21] "God's holiness is not a quality in and of itself; it is that quality which qualifies all other qualities as divine. His power is holy power; his love is holy love." [22]

Holiness and wrath—related to the concept of God's holiness is the idea of wrath. God in holy love draws men to himself. In love he seeks to deal with their sin. When love is rejected, judgment follows. "In the presence of divine love, there are, fundamentally, only two possibilities—either it subdues man, or it does not. In the former case the judgment of God restores and saves; in the latter case it rejects and separates." [23] Even in wrath and judgment the love of God is involved. Judgment comes in the form of separation from God, because love will not overrule the independent action of the human will. It can "will" to reject God's acceptance.

[19] Op. cit., p. 120.

[20] Cf. Rudolf Otto, The Idea of the Holy (New York: Oxford University Press), 1958.

[21] See Brunner, Christian Doctrine of God, pp. 157–58; and Barth, Church Dogmatics, II-1, 360.

[22] Tillich, op. cit., I, 272.

[23] Aulén, op. cit., p. 172.

The judgment of God has been called the "strange work" of God [24] because it is outside of his declared intention to save men. This takes place where the Son is "not known, not loved, not trusted, not recognized." [25] One cannot turn the assertion around and say that love is God, as the Christian Scientists do.

God Is Love

The simple assertion that God is love (1 John 4:8) is overwhelmingly profound. This means that everything that one can say about God involves a statement relative to his love. If one asked the reason for God's love, there is "only one right answer: because it is His nature to love." [26] The New Testament employs a special word with reference to God's love. It uses the verb *agapao,* meaning to love in the sense of goodwill and benevolence. It is a love not based on the personal worth of the object, but it is a love that creates worth. Man in sin is loved in spite of his unloveliness. The verb *agapao* is to be distinguished from another word used, which is *phileo*—the type of love prompted by respect and admiration as among men. This is not the sense in which the Gospel of John declares that "God so loved." It is, therefore, *agape* that is the superior love of God. *Agapao* creates a response where there is no equality in love. It is an uncaused love.

One can see, therefore, that it is *agape* (the noun from *agapao*) that stands behind the significance of the atonement. This is the love that is outgoing and self-giving, even though the recipient is not worthy of it. The New Testament speaks of this love in contrasts: "While we were yet sinners Christ died for us. . . . While we were enemies we were reconciled to God by the death of his Son" (Rom. 5:8–10). One cannot understand the message of the New Testament, the gospel, without reckoning with this unique love.

The love of God has significance for human relations. Only God can command us to love our neighbors. The Categorical Imperative of Kant can at best invoke men to respect each other, but there is a difference between respect and outgoing love. The love of man for his neighbor becomes a reality only when man becomes a new creature in the love of God. It becomes a mockery to command love toward men without a relation to the one who is Love. Barth has

---

[24] Brunner, *Christian Doctrine of God,* p. 230.
[25] *Ibid.*
[26] Aulén, *op. cit.,* p. 133.

stated that the definition of a person can only have meaning as one
loves God and is loved by God in return. Without being associated
with the love that is divine, man never really knows what it means
to be a true person.

God as Lord

When Moses was given the Ten Commandments (Ex. 20), they
had as authority behind them this significant statement: "I am the
Lord your God." God has revealed himself as Lord. As the Lord
who creates, he lays down the foundation of life in moral terms.
As Lord, he can legislate what is right and wrong. In the final analysis
the escape from relativities in ethical systems lies in coming to the
one who is authoritative and nonrelative. The lordship of God means
that he stands above human history and judges men in their actions.
As Lord, he directs history to its planned consummation. But supremely as Lord he enters the affairs of mankind to redeem a hopeless
man-centered situation. Out of the continuing self-degradation of
man, he brings meaning and salvation to those who acknowledge his
lordship.

The lordship of God is a necessary concept for us to grasp the
surety of his promises. The guarantee of the covenant promise of
forgiveness in the death of Christ would be meaningless apart from
him who is able to perform his promises.

Last, it is by the Spirit that we call him Lord, says the apostle
Paul. In submission to his reign over our lives we acknowledge his
right, his redemption, and his righteousness.

God as Grace

Grace is the silent presupposition of the existence of all men. With
the creation of the world, the grace of God has been continuously
expressed, either silently or openly. With all the emphasis in the
Old Testament on the Torah or law, behind the concept of God's
law there is grace. To see how obvious this is, one has only to ask
the question: why has judgment not fallen for my sins before now?

Sheer rebellion against the law should bring immediate punishment.
God has not chosen the role of policeman of the universe, to bring sharp
punishment immediately. One must realize that in God's power and
knowledge no sin goes unnoticed. Instead, he has chosen to express
his grace to the end that man might repent of his bent toward self-

destruction. Grace, as revealed by the God of all grace (1 Peter
5:10), comes from the Greek word *charis* and means "kindness
which bestows upon one what he has not deserved." [27] Berkhof defines it as "the unmerited goodness or love of God to those who have
forfeited it, and are by nature under a sentence of condemnation." [28]
To say that God is gracious, therefore, is to speak of something that
belongs to the very nature and essence of the being of God.[29]

Grace has many relations in the New Testament. It is the basis
of God's gifts to man in Jesus Christ (Eph. 1:6; 2:8–9). Grace is
the motive of redemption (2 Cor. 8:9). By grace through faith the
believer is justified (Rom. 3:24). In the knowledge of his grace we
wait for the consummation of our salvation and the appearing of our
Lord Jesus Christ (Titus 2:11–13).

Within the realm of theology there are two conflicting definitions
of grace. In the above definition grace is understood as a benevolent
disposition on God's part that governs all his actions toward man.
The opposite viewpoint is that defined by Roman Catholic theologians: Grace is defined as a supernatural gift, a divine substance
that is imparted from God through the sacraments to man. "Grace is
a positive reality superadded to the soul." [30] Sanctifying grace is a
"real quality infused into the soul and making it Godlike—a quality
which is of permanent character, to be destroyed only by sin." [31]

One can see the implications of this type of definition. We will
point out only two.

First, the loss of grace is possible through mortal or deadly sin.
By certain sins one loses his place in the body of Christ and, like a
dead cell, is passed out of the body. Roman theologians proceed
to speak of actual grace—still a substance—that is necessary for
the avoidance of sin. But one can enter spiritual death even after
he is redeemed.

The second area relates to baptism. Children who die unbaptized
have not received the supernatural substance in baptism and therefore are denied the beatific vision and salvation. B. V. Miller stated,

27 Joseph Henry Thayer, *Greek-English Lexicon* (New York: American
Book Co., 1889), p. 666.
28 L. Berkhof, *Systematic Theology* (Grand Rapids: Wm B. Eerdmans Publishing Co., 1953), p. 71.
29 Barth, *Church Dogmatics,* II-1, 356.
30 George D. Smith, *The Teachings of the Catholic Church,* p. 552.
31 *Ibid.,* p. 588.

concerning the unbaptized child, "There is no measure or proportion between the natural happiness that will be their lot in limbo, and the inconceivable felicity of heaven, of which man's carelessness may so easily deprive them. Moreover, it must be clearly understood that the child dying without baptism is definitely lost." [32]

This is a most natural logical deduction with regard to baptism in the concept of grace as a spiritual substance. It would be an impossible conclusion for the biblically oriented writer who begins with grace as the basic attitude of God. One cannot alter this attitude of God who wills that all men be saved. Grace is manifest even in judgment, for God gives to man his own way of separation. One can never be in doubt as to whether he is in the grace of God. This is evident from the definition. Falling from grace on the biblical ground is a contradiction in terms. It is not to be equated with the question of whether one can be lost after conversion.

God as Free

God alone has freedom. Even though God grants certain freedom to man, he does this in his (God's) freedom. We cannot speak of freedom merely in the area of negations or absence of limitations. "Freedom in its positive and proper qualities means to be grounded in one's own being, to be determined and moved by oneself. This is the freedom of the divine life and love. In this positive freedom of His, God is also unlimited, unrestricted and unconditioned from without. He is the free Creator, the free Reconciler, the free Redeemer." [33]

The Bible speaks of the freedom of God. In his creation God expressed his freedom. There was no outside pressure on him to bring the world and man into existence.

The freedom of God in reconciliation means that he was under no compulsion to save man. His freedom is a presupposition of the whole story of salvation history. God's entry into history, at first through individuals in the Old Testament and then finally in the person of his Son, expresses the fact of God's freedom. To conclude that God is locked out of his created world is to confess that he is not free. Freedom means that he is above the world as it runs its

---

[32] Quoted in *ibid.*, p. 358.
[33] Barth, *Church Dogmatics*, II-1, 301.

course according to his laws and in the world transcending the law as he so wills, working in the form of a miracle.

A further word about God's freedom and man's freedom must be made. It is within the context of the freedom of God that he freely creates man with limited freedom. There are certain freedoms that man does not have. He cannot by himself, unaided, violate the law of gravity. He cannot continually turn back death or reverse the life cycle. He cannot turn back the calendar of time. But man does have a measure of freedom, particularly with different choices in life. All of this is within the context of God's willing that man should have this freedom.

Freedom is the supposition of prayer. God has willed in his freedom that man call upon him. "God is and wills to be known as the One who will and does listen to the prayers of faith." [34] Without the freedom of God, one could not suppose the possibility of God's answering prayer. We cannot limit the results of prayer to a cliché such as, "Prayer makes me adjust to the adverse circumstances." It might do that, but prayer goes beyond that to the direct response of God's acting within human history. "We need not hesitate to say that 'on the basis of the freedom of God Himself God is conditioned by the prayer of faith.' " [35]

The freedom of God stands in opposition to the idea of determinism. The Bible is opposed to a deterministic view. The great difference lies in the fact that Yahweh is personal. What he does will in freedom is done so in love. Determinism implies a strict machine-like universe, where even God is bound to a pattern of movement that is impersonal.

God as One

The Bible declares that God is one. Affirmed by Christians, misunderstood by others, both Testaments declare that there is one God (1 Tim. 2:5; Deut. 6:4). This statement negates polytheism, dualism, and henotheism. It means positively that the doctrine of the Trinity is monotheistic in its expression. Theologians have sometimes used the word "simple" with reference to the unity of God to express the indivisibility of God. Wherever he acts, he acts completely and wholly as God. He cannot be divided.

---

[34] Barth, *Church Dogmatics,* II-1, 510.
[35] *Ibid.*

The concept of oneness can be misleading. All monisms are not monotheistic. Pantheism is a unitary expression, but it is not the picture of Yahweh in the Bible. One can make a monism out of nature, reason, spirit, fate, duty, and others, but this is not the biblical doctrine of the unity of God. To say that God is one is to declare that there is none like him. This sentence makes shipwreck of all other religious ideologies. "Beside God there are only His creatures or false gods, and besides faith in Him there are religions only as religions of superstition, error, and finally irreligion." [36]

A final word of warning on the oneness of God. In trying to understand God's self-revelation, many attempt to divide up the persons of God. In the Incarnation, which is attributed to the Son, it is no less the redemptive work of the Father and Spirit. Various works of God are attributed to one person or another of the Godhead, but it is the one Lord who is active in all.

God as Righteous

The expression "righteousness of God" is capable of radical misunderstanding. With reference to God it can be used in two diverse senses. First, God is righteous in the sense of being holy. God is without sin. It was this sense that drove Martin Luther to question, before his conversion, whether God was really loving. This sets forth righteousness as a *standard*. God alone is righteous. In the period of Luther's discovery of a different concept of God, the popular mind was set on thinking of God as the righteous judge. Therefore, it was difficult to conceive of Christ as sympathetic and compassionate.[37] The idea of God's right actions goes back deep into the Old Testament. We meet with it early in the book of Genesis in which Abraham, in questioning God concerning Lot in Sodom, asked the question, "Shall not the Judge of all the earth do right?" (Gen. 18:25). The other extreme of the expression is in the passages on judgment in the New Testament in which God will judge righteously. The wicked shall not escape from his deeds and impenitence (John 17:25; 2 Tim. 4:8; 1 John 2:29; 3:7; Rev. 16:5).

Second, God is righteous in *redemption*. At this point the word

---

[36] Barth, *Church Dogmatics*, II-1, 444.

[37] The emphasis on the stern role of Christ the judge helped the growth of intermediaries between Christ and man. The compassionate role of Mary, the mother of Jesus, fits into this pattern of thinking.

"righteous" does not convey the meaning of the Scriptures. Righteousness used in this second sense is a gift of God (Matt. 6:33) which is accorded the believer by his faith in Christ (Rom. 4:5; 5:17,21). One would have the meaning if one spoke of this as "righteousness *from* God," as Nygren does.[38] The mighty act of salvation is God's intervention in man's sinful life to give his righteousness, whereby man is accepted by God because of Christ's death.

Thus, because this meaning of God's righteousness is disclosed, one is able to declare that God helps, saves, and forgives sin.[39] When Paul states the theme of his epistle to the Romans, he says that in the gospel (1:16) "the righteousness of God is revealed through faith for faith" (v. 17). "Through the atonement on the Cross of Christ God realizes in sinful man, and in sinful humanity, His Holy and Merciful plan for humanity as a whole. This is the righteousness of God in Jesus Christ." [40]

The fuller impact of this can be seen in the question and answer of the Heidelberg Catechism.

How art thou just before God? Only by faith in Jesus Christ, that although my conscience accuses me, telling me that I have grievously sinned against all commandments of God and have never kept a single one of them, but have always been inclined to evil, yet God, without any merit on my part, of pure grace has granted and imputed to me the complete satisfaction, righteousness and holiness of Christ, as though I had never committed any sin and had myself performed all the obedience which Christ has rendered for me, if only I will accept these benefits with a believing heart.[41]

The recovery of this Pauline doctrine in Romans was one of the great features of the Reformation. This is one of the great Scripture truths that warm the heart of sinful man. It promises hope where man could have no hope otherwise.

God as Knowledge and Wisdom

The knowledge of God is incomprehensible to human understanding. The Bible describes his knowledge in inclusive terms. God knows

---

[38] Anders Nygren, *Commentary on Romans* (Philadelphia: Fortress, 1949), p. 147.
[39] Cf. Brunner, *Christian Doctrine of God*, p. 275.
[40] *Ibid.*, p. 276.
[41] Barth, *Church Dogmatics*, II-2, 404.

the past, the present, and the future. There is nothing hidden from him. He knows intimately the world in which we live, for he is its Creator. But his knowledge of the world is not expressed as the main element in the Bible. The more important knowledge relates to the needs of man in redemption. We are to rejoice in God's knowledge of us, for when the Bible speaks of God's knowing us it implies his redemption of us, or entering into fellowship with us.

God knows our needs before we pray (Matt. 6:8), he knows us by name (Rev. 21:27), and knows the future day of the coming of the Lord (Mark 13:32). To know the past and possibly the present would not be too difficult to comprehend, but to speak of the future knowledge that God has we are bereft of understanding. Yet this is the biblical description that God has given of himself. What is more mystifying is the assertion that God knows past possible actions if certain other possibilities had been available (cf. 1 Sam. 23:11 ff.).

The omniscience, or all-knowledge, of God must not be imposed upon the free will of man to imply a lack of freedom. Sometimes people reason that since God knows all the actions of people beforehand, these actions must come to pass, since he foreknew. This is to put the cart before the horse. The foreknowledge of God has nothing to do with bringing certain actions to pass. God can know what a free creature can and will do. His knowledge is not the cause of subsequent actions.

Buswell treats prayer briefly in the area of the foreknowledge of God. Because God knows of our prayers beforehand, he has thus "built the answer to our prayers into the very structure of the universe. He knows that we will pray and that we will pray in a spontaneous manner, as a child cries to his father. God has put the universe together on a principle of personal relationships in which He answers prayer, and we can, in a measure, understand his loving provision only on the basis of His omniscience." [42] One must not conclude from such a statement that one is predestined to pray. Instead, God simply knows beforehand that we will pray.

One other implication of God's knowledge is that God's knowledge is intimately related to his redemptive purposes. When the Bible speaks of God's "knowing" men, it generally means that he loves men. We must remember that God does not know something

---

[42] *Op. cit.*, p. 61.

because it is, but it is something because God knows it: "Everything does not exist in itself but in God, in His knowledge of its possibility and its actuality." [43]

Associated with the area of the knowledge of God is the wisdom of God. Barth speaks of the wisdom of God as "the inner truth and clarity with which the divine life in its self-fulfilment and its works justifies and confirms itself and in which it is the source and sum and criterion of all that is clear and true." [44] Berkhof is more to the point. He speaks of the wisdom of God as a perfection, "whereby He applies His knowledge to the attainment of His ends in a way which glorifies Him most." [45] There can be little comparison between human and divine wisdom. Human wisdom relates to the living of life in a manner compatible with the Creator's purpose. Divine wisdom is related to his actions in sustaining his world, in spite of its sin and rebellion, to bring meaning where there was none, and purpose out of a runaway creature. Man is not to glory in human wisdom but in the wisdom of God, who seeks out man to redeem him (Jer. 9:23–24). One can hardly understand the patience of God in his dealing with men apart from the standpoint of God's wisdom. His patience implies his wisdom in dealing with his creatures.

God as Almighty (Omnipotent)

There is considerable room for misunderstanding in this heading because the terms used may not carry the meaning intended. Many theologians do not speak of the omnipotence of God because the term is equated with absolute power, *potestas absoluta*. Omnipotence often means that God can do everything. Consequently, absurd questions can be raised, such as, "Can God make a rock he cannot lift?" or "Can he make the past not to have existed?" The Bible does not speak of the power of God in this manner. Certain things stand out in answering this.

First, we must retain a close reading of what the Bible does say about God's power. Although the Bible does not speak of the word "omnipotence," the word may be used if the philosophical baggage is dropped from its meaning. The Bible speaks of God's power in a unique way.

---

43 Barth, *Church Dogmatics,* II-1, 559.
44 *Ibid.,* 426.
45 Berkhof, *op. cit.,* p. 69.

Second, God's power is not understood as blind force. If we separate God's power from his love, we are speaking of a god that does not exist, and who if he did exist would be a despot indifferent to the created world. "We cannot speak of a living God except insofar as his sovereignty is understood as identical with the sovereignty of divine love." [46]

Third, God's power is always associated with his self-revelation as holy and righteous in all that he does.[47] His power is not identified with omni-causality in which everything comes to pass in a fatalistic way. He is not a slave to his power.

Fourth, omnipotence conveyed the idea of a ruling power over everything, but the Bible speaks of God's limiting himself in power. God has created man who has power to stand over against God and oppose him. The creature has relative independence.

Finally, the power of God is related to his will. There is no difference "between what God *wills* and what He can *do*." [48] "Whatever contradicts His being is impossible for Him" [49] and reduces itself to absurdity. His will is that he be Lord of history, and his power is manifested in its expression and limitation according to his wisdom and knowledge to bring to pass his redemptive plan for mankind. God has power to achieve his will, and apart from his power there is none other.

God as Omnipresent

To say that God is omnipresent is to declare that "there is no place in the world where God is not." [50] Wherever God is he is there in "his whole Being." [51] This last phrase is important to guard against diffusing God throughout the universe, a little here and a little there. God is where his power manifests itself. There is no place where his power is not manifest, not even is hell without his sustaining force. Omnipresence "is the sovereignty on the basis of which everything that exists cannot exist without Him, but only with Him, possessing its own presence only on the presupposition of His presence." [52]

---

[46] Aulén, *op. cit.*, p. 146.
[47] Barth, *Church Dogmatics*, II-1, 544.
[48] Brunner, *Christian Doctrine of God*, p. 253.
[49] Barth, *Church Dogmatics*, II-1, 535.
[50] Brunner, *Christian Doctrine of God*, p. 257.
[51] Berkhof, *op. cit.*, p. 60.
[52] Barth, *Church Dogmatics*, II-1, 461.

Having declared God's nearness, one must admit that in man's relationship to God there is a distinct "farness" from him. At times God comes "closer" than at other times. His "closer" relationship to man took place in the Incarnation of the Son of God. When Jesus is designated as Emmanuel, we witness the joining of God's Son in manhood. The Christian doctrine of the indwelling of the Spirit speaks of God's presence within the heart and destiny of man that separates the believer from the unbeliever. The latter is sustained by God's power but is "far" from him. Sin blinds the heart to God's power, and the alienated creature builds the universe around himself, shutting out God. But he must have God's power even to do this.

While affirming the omnipresence of God, we must not identify the creation with God. The omnipresence of God does not depend upon the universe, although we visualize God's presence in spatial terms. Omnipresence points up the dependence of the universe on God for its continuing existence. Perseverance is simply the continuous creativity of God in which he holds the created things together. Tillich declared, "God is essentially creative, and therefore he is creative in every moment of temporal existence, giving the power of being to everything that has being out of the creative ground of the divine life." [53]

The Christian faith abhors two things equally well: one is pantheism, in which the creation is identified with God; and the other is deism, in which the world is set in motion and God does not interfere with it. The doctrine of God's omnipresence in sustaining the world affirms elements of both of these. It affirms with deism that God is not identified with the creation, and it affirms with pantheism that its existence is dependent upon the power of God upholding it.[54]

Theologians usually speak of these two truths under the headings of transcendence and immanence. God is above the world and yet in it. Both ideas are necessary to express the biblical picture. The two can be illustrated by a rabbi's parable on the beautiful rose in relation to the sun. The rose grows up and puts forth a beautiful blossom because the sun is transcendent, sending forth its rays. At the same time, the rose blossom affirms the immanence of the sun as it takes the rays to itself and puts it forth in beautiful red, yellow, or pink. The sun is both there and here.

---

[53] *Op. cit.*, I, 262.
[54] Against the deistic view, Aulén quotes Sorley: "Surely a God who does not interfere will hardly be missed" (Aulén, *op. cit.*, p. 157).

God as Glory

The biblical words for glory in the Bible are *kabod* in the Old Testament and *doxa* in the New. "*Kabod* is light, both as source and radiance." [55] Just by being himself, God is glorious, as light by itself is full of radiance and brilliance. *Doxa* speaks of honor which God has himself. The glory of God is, therefore, God's dignity and right in maintaining himself against his creation and its corruptions. God's glory is "the self-revealing sum of all divine perfections. It is the fulness of God's deity, the emerging, self-expressing and self-manifesting reality of all that God is." [56] One cannot speak of God without declaring him to be the Lord of glory.[57]

God not only has glory in himself, but desires that man glorify him. If man is to glorify God, he must hear the word of God to turn from his sin and trust in God. To glorify God is to be obedient to his will. The believer glorifies God in obedience. The believer receives the glory of God in Christ (John 17:22). The believer shall behold the glory of Christ in the presence of God when he returns (John 17:24). The climax of creaturely glorification comes in his ultimate transformation in Christlikeness (1 John 3:2).

God's Eternity

A usual type of definition of eternity is that it is God's infinity in relation to time. That is to say, God has been from infinite time backward to infinite time forward. Although this may be a popular type of definition, it is incorrect. There was a time at which time did not exist. This was in eternity. Yet we must not say that eternity is timelessness. God is from eternity to eternity. He is the eternal being. Eternity can be described as pretemporal, supertemporal, and posttemporal. God always existed prior to creation. He is pretemporal: that is, before time began. The term "supertemporal" is used because it expresses the idea that God is above time while it is going on. After time has ceased, God in his eternity is posttemporal. To all of this God "is simultaneous, i.e., beginning and middle as well as end, without separation, distance or contradiction." [58]

---

55 Barth, *Church Dogmatics*, II-1, 642.
56 *Ibid.*, 643.
57 1 Cor. 2:8; Psalm 139:11–12; John 15, 17.
58 Barth, *Church Dogmatics*, II-1, 608. (Cf. Barth, *Church Dogmatics*, II-1, 622–29).

Time, on the other hand, is a creation of God. It involves the before and after relationships of human existence.[59] While God yet remains eternal he has relationships in time. God fills time and indwells it but remains eternal also. In the discussion of the doctrine of the Trinity, a term is used that can be helpful here. *Perichoresis* refers to the interrelationships of the persons of the Trinity, mutually indwelling and yet remaining distinct within one another. The relationship between God in eternality and time is similar. God remains eternal but fills time.

God is acutely aware of time. The Incarnation took place in time. The Christian faith cannot conceive of God as mere timelessness. A. E. Taylor makes the blunt comment, "If God does not know the difference between yesterday and tomorrow, He does not know as much as I do." [60]

The relationship of time and eternity is one that is difficult to solve, but the biblical assertions of the eternity of God and his appearance in time must be affirmed.

Problems in the Doctrine of God

Spatial Terminology

In the upheaval of much modern theology, considerable criticism has been directed toward traditional methods of speaking about God. Bishop John A. T. Robinson and others have rejected terminology which implies spatial relation.[61] They argue that "up" or "down" for heaven and hell has no meaning to modern minds in the space age. Instead of God up, down, or out there, Robinson makes the transition to the "Ground of our Being." [62] Just how much this symbolism improves on the older symbolism only time will tell.

The real problem relates to whether one should jettison the time-honored terminology of the Bible. The return of Christ is described in spatial terms—just as he ascended, so he will return. If we are to speak of God in heaven "up there," it is generally recognized that it is not an abode visible to the naked eye. If it should turn out that God is yet "out there," it is also true that Christian faith has always

---

59 Buswell, *op. cit.*, p. 47.

60 *Ibid.*, p. 46.

61 *Honest to God,* p. 17.

62 *Ibid.*, p. 47.

maintained that God is "down here." The symbolism of God "up there," emphasized his otherness to man and the creation. The symbolism of God "down here" has always meant his nearness in the Incarnation and the working of his Spirit to bring men to himself.

The problems associated with space travel point up the problem of symbolism. When an astronaut is outside of the earth's pull, there is no up nor down. If a meaningful term is substituted, it could well be such a term as "home." Up or down may not mean much when one is between here and the moon or another planet, but the effort to return "home" would be quite meaningful.

The comparison may be fruitful for talk in theology. To be in sin is to be away from home—away from fellowship with God—regardless of where one is. To be reconciled is to return to him, to home.

The Problem of Evil

Nicholas Berdyaev, the Russian existentialist, wrote: "The rationalistic mind of modern man thinks the chief hindrance to belief in God, the chief argument for atheism, is the existence of evil, and the sorrow and suffering it causes in the world. It is difficult to reconcile the existence of God, the all-good and almighty Providence, with the existence of evil, so strong and powerful in our world. This has become the classical and only serious argument." [63]

Speaking in a similar manner, Harold Titus calls the problem of evil the "atheistic fact." [64]

There are several categories of so-called evils. Some speak of natural evils, such as floods, earthquakes, tornadoes, and other elemental phenomena which destroy life and property. Others speak of social evils involving poverty, war, and hunger.

A discussion of the problem of evil calls for distinguishing between evils that man causes to other men and evils that invade man's life seemingly uncaused by other men.

The evils that man causes to other men are more readily understood than the second type. Man is one of the greatest enemies of man. To explain this requires the concept of man's freedom. Berdyaev wrote, "Evil is inexplicable without freedom. Evil is the child of freedom." [65] Freedom of man is a necessary supposition to respon-

---

[63] *Op. cit.*, p. 187.
[64] *Op. cit.*, p. 429.
[65] *Op. cit.*, p. 188.

sibility. Unless man is free to be disobedient, he cannot be held responsible for his action. A determined creature is not a moral creature. On the other hand, man is not absolutely free. He cannot stop his dying, defy the law of gravity, or go for long without certain physical needs. Freedom, however, is particularly meaningful for moral issues. This freedom to rebel against God, against one another, and against society collectively may help us understand some of the evils of the world. On this, C. S. Lewis has written: "When souls become wicked, they will certainly use this possibility to hurt one another; and this, perhaps, accounts for four-fifths of the suffering of men. It is men, not God, who have produced racks, whips, prisons, slavery, guns, bayonets, and bombs; it is by human avarice or human stupidity, not by the churlishness of nature, that we have poverty and overwork." [66]

Without the ingredient of freedom, one could not have a basis for understanding human history. The question may arise concerning the delay of God's judgment on human actions. Is God helpless, unable, indifferent? The answer rests in what kind of God we conceive the deity to be. If we stress sheer justice, we may think of him as a superpoliceman who will not tolerate evil, and by his knowledge of transgressions will proceed to eliminate the offender. Thus justice would be conceived from a stimulus-response view. When evil—the stimulus—appears, justice or the response of God would be swift and immediate. If such a concept were actual, then who would be left living? We would all perish.

If we conclude for God's mercy—which the Bible surely does—we must be prepared to see the design of redemptive possibilities. God seeks the sinner to come to repentance. He is patient with us even in our freedom and sin.

The second type of evil is more difficult to cope with. What is to be made of tornadoes, earthquakes, and disease? Is freedom any help here? Can it be that *all* of creation is involved in some form of rebellion? Or to put it another way, is there an intruder in the world of man and his environment who has brought disharmony to the creation?

This appears to be the answer of C. S. Lewis in dealing with the matter of disease and pain. He points out that disease is associated

---

[66] *The Problem of Pain* (New York: The Macmillan Co., 1962), p. 89.

with Satan (Luke 13:16; 1 Cor. 5:5). This is quite significant, for evil is thereby associated with intelligence, shrewdness, and negative purpose. Because there is a tendency on the part of evildoers to involve and corrupt others, one might proceed to relate this fact to the creation. Satan has not only brought man to disharmony with God, but has sown disharmony in man's world.

Can we relate disease to disharmony and tyranny, as is reflected in man's experience? If one may view a disease as caused by an organism out of harmony with its normal habitat, we may then speak of its tyrannizing another organism. Some illustrations may be used to speak of this. Cancer, for example, seems to be a type of life corruption in which cells feed on other cells. Leukemia involves the attack of one type blood cell life on another. Many diseases seem to follow this pattern—life intruding upon other types of life and attempting to lead a parasitic existence—to tyrannize. How would this differ from the balance of nature? It differs in that the balance of nature is related to the world below man, whereas man, being a moral creature, transcends the balance. From the point of faith, the Scriptures declare that man is the lord of the creation, and its creatures, other than man, are for his use. Thus animal life is not to lord it over man.

This type of analysis is interesting, since new diseases appear when old ones seem conquered. Evil is not static but grows in sophistication. If we may speak of disease as disharmony caused by an outsider—an intruder invading and influencing the world below man—it would be a parallel to man's experience when in freedom he was tempted to rebellion, whereby he was tyrannized by the same intruder.

How far should this analogy be pushed? The extent will be limited by the analogy itself. Man is not as bad in rebellion as he could be. His life is not as evil and chaotic as possible. By the same analogy our world is not as chaotic as possible, nor is it as diseased and corrupt. The chaos that exists is balanced out by orderliness somewhat parallel to the story of man's fractured existence. Chaos and order exist side by side in man as it can be perceived in the world beneath man.

Another question arises in regard to what has been said. Can we relate this freedom being used by an intelligence that is able to tyrannize man's habitat through it and by means of it to revelation?

Some form of explanation along these lines is implied in the Scriptures (Rom. 8:20–23). The influence of evil and its disharmony did not stop with man but permeated the whole creation and still has a hold on it. The man of faith looks forward to his and the creation's release from its tyranny when he enjoys the liberty of God.

A side issue to the problem of evil concerns suffering. Suffering is a by-product of the intrusion of sin into the world. Suffering cannot be regarded as God's means for perfecting character before the advent of man's original departure into sin. However, in spite of the tyranny of sin and the enslavement attendant to it, God is able to thwart sin and achieve victory in men's lives.

As life *now* exists we may say that suffering is the occasion of personality and spiritual development. Paul gives such a viewpoint in Romans: "We rejoice in our sufferings, knowing that suffering produces endurance, and endurance produces character, and character produces hope, and hope does not disappoint us, because God's love has been poured into our hearts through the Holy Spirit which has been given to us" (5:3–5). It may be questioned, given our present sinful world, whether such character development can come in any other way than through suffering. But this is not to affirm that evil is necessary to produce good. Better is to say that God helps man to achieve good in spite of evil. God is not thwarted from expressing his love in making something of the man of faith, although that man previously exercised his faith to corrupt his relation with God.

A useful analogy to illustrate these ideas is presented by C. S. Lewis concerning man's relation to a dog. Man has attempted to tame a dog so that he may love it and that the dog may serve him. He is not motivated by the love of the dog or from a desire to serve the dog. In the process of expression of his love to the dog, the dog's ultimate interests are preserved. The dog is chosen rather than some other creature because it has possibilities for a better life with the man than if left to its own natural habits. The man seeks to make the dog more lovable than it was before. With this in mind the man does certain things to remove the offense to his love.

The dog has a smell and habits that offend the sensitivities of the master. Thus, the man takes the dog and washes it with soap and water, he housebreaks it, "teaches it not to steal, and is so enabled to love it completely." [67] From the dog's point of view, if he were a theologian, all of this would make him doubt the goodness of his master, "but the full-grown and fully-trained dog, larger, healthier, and longer-lived than the wild dog, and admitted, as it were by Grace, to a whole world of affections, loyalties, interests, and comforts entirely beyond its animal destiny, would have no such doubts." [68]

All of this is to say that God pays man an "intolerable compliment" by giving him a love that demands the transformation of his person. The transformation is painful.

[67] *Ibid.*, p. 43.
[68] *Ibid.*, p. 44.

V. The Trinity

*O Lord, one God, God the Trinity, whatsoever I have said in
these Books that comes of thy prompting, may thy people
acknowledge it: for what I have said that comes only of myself,
I ask of thee and of thy people pardon.*

Augustine, *The Trinity*

*To know Christ is to know His benefits, not as the Schoolmen
teach, to know His natures and the modes of His incarnation.
. . . There is no reason why we should spend much labour over
these supreme topics of God, His Unity and Trinity, the
mysteries of creation and the modes of the Incarnation. I ask
you, what the scholastic theologians have achieved in so many
ages by occupying themselves with these questions alone?*

Philipp Melanchthon, *Loci Theologici*

The doctrine of the Trinity is a key article of the Christian faith,
even though it is one of the most difficult to comprehend. The word
"trinity," however, is not used in the Bible. Tertullian (*ca.* A.D. 160–
240) was the first to use the Latin word *trinitas*.

In a discussion of the doctrine of the Trinity, there are certain
preliminary things that need to be clarified.

First, we must admit the concept of mystery. This must not be the
admission of the Trinitarian only. Even the Unitarian must acknowledge that he professes only a skimpy knowledge of the essential being
of God. But mystery does not negate inquiry or revelation. We admit
with Augustine that "enquiry concerning the incomprehensible is
justified, and the enquirer has found something, if he has succeeded
in finding out how far what he sought passes comprehension." [1] If the
Trinity is a mystery, it is yet important, for it explains other mysteries. The doctrines of the Incarnation and indwelling of the Spirit

---

[1] A. Augustine, *The Trinity*, trans. John Burnaby ("The Library of Christian
Classics," [Philadelphia: Westminster Press, 1955]), VIII, 129.

would have little significance without a knowledge of the Trinity. Rather than being a burden to the intellect, the Trinitarian concept of God "illuminates, enriches, and elevates all our thought of God." [2]

Second, we must, in a discussion of the Trinity, continue to remind ourselves that man is created in the image of God, and not God in the image of man. Man is thus only a faint image. Therefore, when dealing with the data of the biblical revelation we must remember that God is not the peculiarity, but man is. Man has a tendency to view God as suprapersonal, that is, to compare God with man by using man as the standard of being. In reality man is infrapersonal, that is, God is the standard of comparison in relation to man, and man is the peculiar creature. If we wish to do justice to the person of God as far as we can understand him, we must not denounce God because of the simple, single personality of man. God cannot be reckoned a monstrosity because he is different from man.

Third, the doctrine of the Trinity is the expressed result of formulating the biblical information concerning the relation of the Father to the Son and the Spirit. If one asks, "How are the three persons related to one another?" the answer one receives is some doctrine of the Trinity. The doctrine is not idle philosophy and metaphysics to which we may be indifferent.

In the early centuries of the church, when the issue of the Trinity was debated, the issue centered around the nature of Christ. Was he of the same nature as God, or was he of a like nature? In other words, was he God, or was he a great and majestic, but created, being? The difference was summed up by two very similar words. Was Christ *homoiousion,* that is, of a like nature to God, or was he *homoousion,* that is, of the same nature? The difference in the two words cannot be exaggerated even though a single letter, the *iota* or "i," makes the difference. Carlyle and Gibbon have epigrammed that the fate of the world hung on a single letter. In reality the difference is that significant. It is a question of tremendous importance.

Positively put, the Trinity means that God is incarnate in Jesus Christ. God has come himself to redeem man; he has not sent a second-rate envoy. Love gives personal attention to important matters.

---

[2] B. B. Warfield, *Biblical Foundations* (Grand Rapids: Wm B. Eerdmans Publishing Co., 1958), p. 84.

Long ago, Anselm attempted to answer the question of why a lesser being than God could not have redeemed man. He reasoned that man would of necessity be the servant of whoever redeemed him. Thus anything less than God would involve man in idolatry. Although this is reasonable, it is preferable to answer the question from the standpoint of love's personal involvement.

Fourth, we must distinguish between the facts of the Trinity and the doctrine of the Trinity. The traditional formulation of the Trinity is a product of debate upon the meaning of the scriptural statements. The church must reflect upon the scriptural statements, but this does not elevate the doctrine to the level of the Scriptures. Indeed, we must not accept an ancient doctrine merely because it is ancient but because it is true. The formulation that has been traditionally accepted as orthodox from the Nicene Council on must stand or fall on the basis of the Scriptures.

With these observations in mind, we will turn to study the data of the Trinity in the Scriptures.

Biblical Evidence for the Trinity

Although older theologians were accustomed to speak of the Trinity anticipated in the plural name for God (*Elohim*), the Trisagion of Isaiah 6, the Suffering Servant passages in Isaiah, and the personification of wisdom in the Old Testament, we are bound to base the doctrine on the New Testament. Gregory of Nazianzus (A.D. 329–89) posited that the Old Testament revelation established in the people of God the foundational fact of the unity of the Godhead. Thus the Trinity is not a *certain* fact of revelation until the Incarnation takes place.

One passing observation about the Shema, or the monotheistic statement of Deuteronomy is of interest. When the pious Jew recited, "Here, O Israel: The Lord our God is one Lord" (6:4), he used a word in that confession that can be understood in a latent Trinitarian sense. The phrase "our God is *one*" can be understood in the sense of unity, or community. The word "one" involves more than numerical meaning. It designates oneness—in accord, togetherness in the same place, or unity of mind. Centuries after the writing of Deuteronomy, the Dead Sea community designated itself as "the community" or the "oneness" with the same meaning of the word in the confession of Deuteronomy 6:4. As interesting as this may be, we must still confine ourselves to understanding it as latent anticipation of the New Testament.

The New Testament gives to us a unique set of data concerning the Father, Son, and Holy Spirit. There have been some, however, who have felt that the doctrine of the Trinity was imposed on, or imported to the New Testament. Adolph Harnack, for instance, deprecated the doctrine of the Trinity as the "Hellenizing of Christianity." Others have sought the source of the doctrine in Babylonian or Hindu ideology in which there are triads of gods. Such similarities are superficial. The Jews of the New Testament were rigidly monotheistic and held such polytheism in contempt.

The data of the doctrine of the Trinity did not evolve over centuries but is a fixed possession of the New Testament from the very beginning. The doctrine expresses the experience of the first eyewitnesses. The disciples had worshiped God the Father as Jews; in the man Jesus they came to know one who was the Son of God and to whom they accorded the title "Lord." Their experience on the day of Pentecost was the fulfilment of the promise of the Son before his ascension and that of the Father through the prophets.[3]

The data for the doctrine of the Trinity are of two types. First, there are statements that relate the three names together. The Great Commission (Matt. 28:18–20) is an example of this. The Father, Son, and Spirit are mentioned together in the annunciation account in Luke 1:35. The Holy Spirit is the power of the Most High, and the fruit of Mary's womb was to be the Son of God. In the baptismal scene of the Gospels (Luke 3:21–22; Matt. 3:16–17; Mark 1:10–11; John 1:32–33), the Spirit descended on the Son with the pronouncement of the Father's good pleasure in him. The Fourth Gospel sets forth the promise of the Son concerning the indwelling Comforter sent from the Father (John 15:26). There are other statements [4] in which a composite witness to the Father, Son, and Spirit are mentioned, but our attention must now be given to the second type of evidence.

The second type of evidence is that which speaks solely of the

---

[3] Compare Charles W. Lowry, *The Trinity and Christian Devotion* (New York: Harper & Bros., 1946), p. 67; and John Mackintosh Shaw, *Christian Doctrine* (London: Lutterworth Press, 1953), pp. 90–91; and Warfield, *op. cit.*, p. 89.

[4] Cf. 1 Cor. 12:4–6; Rom. 8:9; 2 Cor. 13:14; Eph. 4:4–6; 1 Peter 1:2; Jude 20–21.

Deity of the Son or the Spirit without reference to the other two. For example, in John 1:1 reference is made to the divine nature of the Word, the Son, without mention of the Spirit. Thus evidence for the deity of Christ is evidence for the Trinity. The same principle holds true for the statements concerning the Spirit.

In considering this type of evidence it must be remembered that the first Christians were converted Jews with a strict monotheistic background. They had no bent toward polytheism, and it was not easy to ascribe deity to a human being. In addressing Jesus as Lord, they recognized in him the attribute of divinity. The simple statement that "Christ is Lord" (Rom. 10:9) points up the early belief in the Trinity. In Christ the fulness of deity dwells bodily (Col. 2:9). The doubting heart of Thomas confessed Jesus as "Lord and God" (John 20:28), a confession that would be blasphemy concerning any other person. In the book of Titus, word is given concerning our hope and the appearing of the "great God and our Saviour Jesus Christ" (2:13). The early confession of Peter was that Jesus is the Son of God (Matt. 16:16). In John's Gospel Jesus was accused of blasphemy (10:36) for making himself equal with God. In chapter 8, Jesus made an equation that the Pharisees could not overlook. He said, "Before Abraham was, I am" (v. 58). He equated himself with the name of God in the Old Testament, "I am" (Ex. 3:14).

Before concluding reference to the Son, we can note that the attributes or qualities that are generally designated to the Father are also attributed to the Son: holiness (2 Cor. 5:21), omnipotence (Matt. 28:18), eternity (John 1:1; 17:5), life (John 1:4), immutability (Heb. 1:11–12), omniscience (Matt. 9:4), omnipresence (Matt. 28:20), creation (John 1:3), judgment of all men (Matt. 25:31–46), prayer and worship (John 14:14).

The New Testament word on the Holy Spirit is not as prolific as that on the Son. The divine nature of the Holy Spirit is set forth in the Scriptures in a personal way. The Holy Spirit is not an impersonal "it" but a personal "he." In the apostolic rebuke of Peter to Ananias, the lie was told not to men but to God the Holy Spirit (Acts 5:3–4). Philip was directed by the Holy Spirit to the eunuch (Acts 8:29). The Holy Spirit directed the early church in its missionary activity (Acts 10:19–20; 13:2). The Spirit is the promise of the Son proceeding from the Father (John 14:16–17). The Spirit helps the believer in prayer (Rom. 8:26), and we are warned against grieving the Holy Spirit of God (Eph. 4:30). Furthermore, the Spirit gives gifts for the service of God (1 Cor. 12), he regenerates (Titus 3:5; John 3:5), teaches (John 16:13), and sanctifies the believer (1 Peter 1:2). To conclude our thoughts about the Spirit, the so-called unpardonable sin emphasizes that the Spirit is holy and that sin cannot be committed against a more august person.

In discussing the biblical statements relating to the Trinity, there are certain principles that will help clear up some of the difficulties.

First, the principle of subordination in action. The principle of subordination in *action* must be clearly and carefully distinguished from subordination of *nature*. One form of false doctrine in the early church made the Son a subordinated creature in nature. The New Testament does not warrant such an assumption. There is, however, a subordination in action. This means that in order of activity and mode of action the Father is first, the Son is second, and the Spirit is third. B. B. Warfield has declared, "Whatever the Father does, he does through the Son, by the Spirit." [5]

Second, Augustine, following Athanasius, declared that texts implying subordination of the Son to the Father must refer to the Son as incarnate in the form of a servant and not in the form of God. The Son is inferior to the Father in his human nature only (cf. John 14:28 and 10:30).

Third, the New Testament is primarily concerned with the work and action of the persons of the Trinity and not with their metaphysical relationship. Consequently a detailed doctrine is not elaborated in the Bible.

Fourth, we must not divide the Triune God into three Gods as though the Son alone has the work of redemption apart from the Father and the Spirit. The love of God the Father gives the motive for redemption; God the Son is the Redeemer; and God the Spirit inhabits the believer in application of redemption. Thus certain actions are attributed to one or another of the persons but that action involves no less than the entire being of God.

To conclude our remarks on the scriptural data and the Trinity, we must observe that the doctrine of the Trinity sums up a great deal of the gospel. Concerning God the Father, it embodies his

---

[5] *Op. cit.,* p. 110; compare Rom. 2:16; 3:22; 5:1; Eph. 1:5; 1 Thess. 5:18–19; Titus 3:5.

promise of a "Christ to us." Of the Son, it is a word of "Christ for us." Of the Holy Spirit, it is a word of "Christ in us."

The Dogma of the Trinity

The distinction has been made between the *facts* and the *doctrine* or dogma of the Trinity. The doctrine involves the real problem of relating the facts. Does not a father imply a son and a son a father? From where and how does the Spirit proceed? The answers to these questions give us a doctrine or dogma.

Many were the problems and controversies in working out the doctrine of the Trinity. One of the great problems centered around language. The same terms were often used in totally different relations. After much debate, the doctrine was expressed in these orthodox terms:

"The Catholic Faith is this: that we worship one God in Trinity and Trinity in Unity, neither confounding the Persons nor dividing the Substance; for there is one Person of the Father, another of the Son, and another of the Holy Ghost. But the Godhead of the Father, of the Son, and of the Holy Ghost is all one; the glory equal, the majesty coeternal. For like as we are compelled by the Christian verity to acknowledge every Person by Himself to be God and Lord, so we are forbidden by the Catholic Religion to say, There are Three Gods or three Lords." [6]

The creed is misleading for our generation in terms of language. The word "person" does not have the same meaning for us that it had for the writers of the creed. Its use in the creed indicated "a permanent, individual mode or manner of Divine existence." [7] The meaning of the Latin *persona* (English person) was "mask," as used by an actor to portray different characters on the stage. On the other hand, the early Greek Christians used the word "hypostasis," which meant subsistence or substance, or referred to "something which has substantial existence in its own right and not as a mere quality or adjective of something else." [8] The Greek fathers spoke of "three persons in one substance."

---

[6] The Athanasian Creed. It is one of the later creeds but one of the fullest in expression. Its date and origin are uncertain.

[7] Lowry, *op. cit.*, pp. 80–81.

[8] Shaw, *op. cit.*, p. 95.

It becomes apparent that terminology was a real problem in the early church. It is not less a problem for the modern mind. If we do not speak of the Trinity in terms of "person" with the idea of self-consciousness, we run the danger of destroying the clear-cut personal distinctions spoken about in the biblical references to God, Christ, and the Spirit. If we speak of God in terms of person, with all its contemporary implications, then the Trinitarian concept seems to border on the side of tritheism. But if we do not use the term "person," we use less than our highest term and run the danger of speaking of God in impersonal terms, and if we do we stand to lose what is unique to the Christian concept of God.

Some theologians discarded the phrase "three distinct persons." John of Damascus described the Father, Son, and Holy Spirit as "being immanent in one another though there is no confusion or mixture." [9] Basil declared, "Everything that the Father is, is seen in the Son, and everything that the Son is belongs to the Father. The Son in his entirety abides in the Father, and in return possesses the Father in Himself. Thus, the hypostasis subsistence of the Son is, so to speak, the form and presentation by which the Father is known, and the Father's hypostasis (subsistence) is recognized in the form of the Son." [10]

Emil Brunner remarks that a problem arises when we place the Son alongside the Father rather than to see the Son in the Father and the Father in the Son.[11] The Son is not *separate from* the Father, but *distinct in* the Father. Likewise, the Spirit is through the Son and not alongside the Son. This accords with the phraseology of John's Gospel, "Believe me that I am in the Father and the Father in me" (14:11; cf. 14:20; 17:21).

Whatever objection one may have about the creedal statements of the doctrine of the Trinity, the doctrine itself must be seen against the attempt to guard against certain serious heresies. The formulators of the creedal statement were intent on rejecting the ideas: that God is too far removed to be concerned for man, that the creation is evil and only spirit is good, that man's redemption took place by a creature less than God.

---

[9] R. S. Franks, *The Doctrine of the Trinity* (London: Gerald Duckworth & Co., 1953), p. 120.

[10] J. N. D. Kelly, *Early Christian Doctrines* (New York: Harper & Bros., 1958), p. 264.

[11] *Christian Doctrine of God*, pp. 229–30.

Augustine presents his plea concerning the Trinity: "As for our present enquiry, let us believe that Father, Son, and Holy Spirit are one God, maker and ruler of the whole creation: that Father is not Son, nor Holy Spirit, Father or Son; but a Trinity of mutually related Persons, and a unity of equal essence." [12]

Analogies of the Trinity

The doctrine of the Trinity presents such a deep mystery to the mind that it gropes for some analogy to increase its understanding. We shall catalog a number of analogies but not without the principle that analogies at best are quite inadequate.

Physical.—*Water* has a trinity of three forms: liquid, vapor, and solid. In a drink of wine, water, and honey each element permeates the whole. An *egg* has the yolk, white, and shell. A *rope* has three strands, but they are woven together to form a unity. A *triangle* has three sides to show that the Father is not the Son or the Spirit, and vice versa, but one triangle. *Relationships* involve one man who is at the same time father, husband, and son. *Humanity* gives a picture of three persons: Peter, Paul, and John, but a single humanity. A *tree* has its root (Father), stem (Son), and fruit (Holy Spirit). The early Church Fathers used the *sun*, the ray and the point of the ray. *Sonship* offers an analogy suggesting the Trinity. If God has a Son, his Son would have the same nature as he. God was always a Father; otherwise, he would be changeable and evolving. The Son is of an eternal nature as the Father. He was one with the Father from eternity. This analogy does not refer to the Spirit but does point up the relationship to the Father by the Son.

Psychological.—The most profound psychological analogies come from Augustine who completed his work *De Trinitate* in A.D. 417. If man is made in the image of God, said Augustine, then the best analogies should be found in man. There is, first, the analogy of love. If God is love, then a lover must have a beloved. The spirit of love unites the two together. Thus we have God the Father as lover, God the Son as beloved, and God the Spirit as the spirit of Love. The analogy of Augustine is incomplete after the first two steps. Later writers attempted to improve on the analogy by explaining how the third person is a necessity. Perfect love is without jealousy and requires a third with whom to share love.

---

[12] *Op. cit.,* p. 58.

In the trinity of mind, knowledge, and love, Augustine began with the mind, proceeded to its knowledge of itself as mind, and then the mind's love of itself. Of these he wrote, "These three are one, and if perfect they are equal." [13]

A third analogy set forth by Augustine is the trinity of memory, understanding, and will in the single life of a person.

The value of the last two analogies lies in their presenting three functions from a single essence. They also set forth a coexistent or coinherent factor. However, the analogies are weak in that they are *in* one person while God *is* three-personal.

In attempting to set forth helpful analogies on the Trinity and the problem centering around the word "person," we sympathize with the statement of Augustine that we say three persons, not to express the Trinity, but in order not to keep silent.

The Trinity and Other Doctrines

The doctrine of the Trinity does have an important bearing on other doctrines. Consider first the doctrine of revelation. Where do we obtain our knowledge of God? The Bible declares that Christ is the final and most complete expression of God's revelation to us (Heb. 1). In the final analysis God only can reveal God. In the fourth century Athanasius rightly argued that if Jesus was not the true Son of God and God incarnate, then he could not communicate a "true knowledge of God, since He can neither see nor know His own Father accurately."

Without the revelation of Jesus Christ, we are thrown back upon our own resources for obtaining a knowledge of God. In all honesty we must confess that a god that can be discovered by human effort is hardly worth discovering. If my idea of God is really mine, then I could attach little significance to it at all. If Jesus Christ is not God incarnate, I must confess that I know nothing of God and am thrown back upon a theology based on nature and the nebulous God of reason.

When the Trinity is rejected, the alternatives are generally Unitarianism or some form of vague pantheism. Unitarianism rejects the incarnate self-revelation of God in Jesus Christ. While Jesus may have been a man of significant religious insight, he cannot be regarded as the God-man in the traditional sense of the term. Thus the Unitarian only knows of God by reason and not by revelation.

---

[13] *Ibid.*, p. 60.

Pantheism obscures the distinctions between God and man, and in some senses all men are manifestations of the divine. This fusion of the divine and the human wipes out the unique significance of Jesus Christ. His cross and its meaning become transformed into a principle that is an example for all people. Self-sacrifice becomes the principle for men to live by and therein lies their salvation—not in Christ's death! At the same time the pantheist's god is not yet made, because the world, being a part of God, is always changing and progressing. Pantheism tends to break up into polytheism where, in its more refined form, the beautiful in nature, genius in man, and truth in the mind become objects of worship. Thus facts of the Trinity are intimately related to a thoroughgoing doctrine of revelation.

The doctrine is important also for its relation to salvation. Among other things implied is that God, the Creator, is also Redeemer. God was in Christ reconciling the world to himself. If Jesus Christ was not incarnate deity, then our salvation rests upon a creature little higher than ourselves. Redemption would not rest in the nature of God. There is no room for Christian joy over the firm foundation of redemption if salvation does not rest in God alone.

The concept of the Trinity is important for the believer's orientation toward an understanding of God. If we disparage the facts relating to God's self-disclosure we are disparaging God himself. One should not show a kind of callousness to God's love wherein he seeks to reveal to man his inner nature and essence. He was not under obligation to reveal himself, but the fact that he did sets forth the truth that the lover seeks to communicate to the beloved. Calvary is not the only expression of his love: the revelation of himself as Father, Son, and Spirit is another expression of love. To be indifferent to it is a kind of insensitiveness that is difficult to conceive in men who profess to love God. God has spoken, and if we would know his love we must seek to understand his nature.

The implication for this doctrine can be carried further in its relation to almost any Christian doctrine. Without the implications of the Trinity, the church becomes transformed into a lecture club or mutual aid society without a definite *kergyma* for declaration. The Christian hope, the return of Christ, is watered down to a kingdom of man, and the range of doctrine beginning with justification by faith, regeneration, sanctification, the indwelling of the Spirit, and Christian life receive a totally different but humanistic treatment.

VI. Jesus, the Christ

It is very important, therefore, to note that in Scripture the confession of the deity of Christ is not at all regarded as a threat to, or as competitive with, monotheism.

G. C. Berkouwer, *The Person of Christ*

The equation "very God and very man" must always be regarded as an equalizing of the unequal. As we have made it plain earlier, the incarnation of the Logos is not a change from His own nature or His own mode of being as the divine Word into the nature and mode of being of a creature, nor yet the rise of a third thing between God and man.

Barth, *Church Dogmatics*

Jesus speaks with divine authority and now we have to make our choice: Either he speaks the truth or he does not. If he does not, we have again two possibilities: He utters falsehood either consciously or not. Should it be deliberate falsehood, he is the greatest deceiver known to history; should it be unconscious falsehood, he is the most pathetic victim of religious megalomania known to history. Given these possibilities we prefer to believe that Jesus Christ spoke the truth and had the right to speak with divine authority simply because He was God.

H. de Vos, in Berkouwer, *The Person of Christ*

The Son of God, the second person of the Trinity, being very and eternal God, of one substance, and equal with the Father, did, when the fullness of time was come, take upon Himself man's nature, with all the essential properties and common infirmities thereof, yet without sin: being conceived by the power of the Holy Ghost, in the womb of the Virgin Mary, of her substance. So that the two whole, perfect, and distinct natures, the Godhead and the manhood, were inseparably joined together in one person, without conversion, composi-

tion, or confusion. Which person is very God and very man,
yet one Christ, the only Mediator between God and man.
                                        Westminster Confession of Faith

When certain unknown Jewish men were encountered by the person named Jesus, there had to be a commanding power in his personality in order to explain why they left their normal vocations and followed him. Little by little these men came to understand him until one of them had the spiritual perception to declare, "You are the Christ, the Son of the living God" (Matt. 16:18). In the weeks and months of the life of Jesus, they came to marvel, doubt, despair, and finally to perceive in his resurrection that a very unusual person stood before them.

After Pentecost, they began to declare to the world a message centered around the events of the crucifixion, burial, and resurrection of Jesus. As the message was proclaimed beyond the boundaries of Jewish culture, both at home and abroad, clearer definition of who Christ was had to come to pass. As believers began to describe the person of Jesus, who was called the Christ, they grappled with the problem of his unique nature. Many views had to be condemned, until finally a statement came forth in A.D. 451 at the Council of Chalcedon which has come to be the traditional orthodox statement of the doctrine concerning the person of Christ. The history of Christological controversies, however, did not really end with Chalcedon. Some of the heresies that were condemned in the past have continually cropped up in one form or another. Arianism is revived in Jehovah's Witnesses, and liberalism is refined Ebionism.

Any age has the ever-present danger of consciously or unconsciously reviving a heresy. The only safeguards lie in a thorough understanding of the Scriptures with a knowledge of the history of doctrine as a guideline.

The treatment of the complex person of Christ must always necessitate two approaches, that of the biblical material and then the doctrinal deductions in the history of thought.

The Biblical Data

The problem of Christology begins with the statement, "The Word became flesh" (John 1:14). This statement combines a transcendent being with a physical being. How are they related to each other? That is the problem of Christology. The writer very obviously intended to relate the two separate natures to each other. Karl Barth suggests, "If we paraphrase the statement 'the Word became flesh' by 'the Word assumed flesh,' we guard against the misinterpretation . . . that in the incarnation the Word ceases to be entirely Himself and equal to Himself, i.e., in the full sense of the Word of God. God cannot cease to be God." [1] Thus we must speak of a true Incarnation, or "becoming man," of the Logos, and "it can be said that 'He became flesh, not that He has been changed into flesh, but that He has taken living flesh on our behalf and has become man.' " [2]

When we turn to the other New Testament data concerning the life of Jesus, we see that some actions are clearly those of a super-human power, while others can be only attributed to a truly human power.

Divine Characteristics [3]

Self-consciousness.[4]—From his early age, Jesus is described as being on unusually unique terms with God (Luke 2:49). He claimed a unique equality with God (John 10:30). Jesus maintained that men who knew him knew God the Father (John 14:9), and believing in him was equal to believing him that sent him (John 12:44–45). His self-consciousness pointed up that he alone reveals the Father and that there is no true knowledge of the Father without the Son (Matt. 11:27). This seems to be the evident implication, for it was precisely for blasphemy that the people were about to stone him (John 10:32–33; 19:7). The Gospel of John gives the boldest description of things taking place, which could be accomplished only by one greater than human. Jesus promised the prepared heavenly dwelling

---

[1] *Church Dogmatics* I-2, 160.

[2] Kelly, *op. cit.,* p. 285.

[3] Cf. Kelly, *op. cit.,* p. 138, where he declares, "The New Testament writers generally regarded Christ as pre-existent; they tended to attribute to Him a twofold order of being, 'according to the flesh' i.e., as man, and 'according to the spirit,' i.e. as God. So deeply was this formula embedded in their thinking that F. Loofs justly labelled it 'the foundation of all later Christological development.' "

[4] We are indebted to Loraine Boettner for his cataloging of the Scripture references in the description of Jesus' life. See his *Studies in Theology* (Grand Rapids: Wm. B. Eerdmans Publishing Co., 1953), pp. 140–268.

where his followers shall be with him (John 14:1–6). He promised that the prayers of the faithful shall be heard (John 14:14), and upon his departure the "other Counselor" would be given.

During his trial he was asked whether he was the Messiah. His reply was, "I am; and you will see the Son of man sitting at the right hand of Power, and coming with the clouds of heaven" (Mark 14:62). For this he was charged with blasphemy and condemned to death. In the Great Commission he laid claim to "all power" and charged that his name, along with the Father and the Holy Spirit, be the name of benediction for baptism. Without doubt it is difficult to tear these statements out of the Scriptures. We cannot penetrate beyond these statements, as Bultmann seeks to do,[5] to distinguish words Jesus uttered from words supposedly attributed to him without imposing a presupposition that never existed in the New Testament writers' mind.

The apostolic recognition.—By apostolic awareness we want to imply two references.

First, we note recognition of him by those who knew him most intimately. Peter has to be listed first. He uttered the words of recognition of Jesus' messianic office (Matt. 16:16). An important confession is that of Thomas who doubted at first about the resurrection but came to confess, "My Lord and my God!" (John 20:28). Paul is the latest apostle to speak forth. He is emphatic in declaring, "He is the Son of God" (Act 9:20), "the image of the invisible God" (Col. 1:15), incarnate God in all its fulness (2:9), and the form of God made in servitude (Phil. 2:7).

There are others in the lifetime of the apostles who made similar confessions but who were not enrolled in the apostolic band. John the Baptist declares Jesus to be the Lamb of God, the baptizer with the Holy Spirit, and the Son of God (John 1:29–34). Stephen describes his heavenly vision in terms of Jesus' sitting at the right hand of God (Acts 7:56).

Second, apostolic recognition must be noted in reference to the combined testimony of the New Testament books. There seems to be no New Testament book without references, either in statement or in title, to the uniqueness of Jesus. Many books contain the introduction

[5] Rudolph Bultmann, *Form Criticism* (New York: Harper & Bros., 1962), pp. 71–74.

with reference to Jesus who is the Christ, or the anointed one of God. Furthermore, "throughout the New Testament Christ is called 'Lord,' not merely in the sense in which men are invested with authority or dignity or ownership, but in the sense of Absolute and Supreme Sovereign, Preserver, Protector." [6]

The titles ascribed to Jesus are of value in estimating his person. One can multiply the number of titles but the more significant ones speak of Jesus as Lord (Phil. 2:11), "Lord of lords" (1 Tim. 6:15), "the Lord of glory" (1 Cor. 2:8), "the mediator" (Heb. 12:24), and "God . . . blessed for ever" (Rom. 9:5).[7] In addition, the New Testament connects the name "God" with Jesus nearly a dozen times.[8]

Miracles.—The older and often conservative theologians appeal to miracles with reference to the deity of Christ. We can admit all that is claimed by these writers except perhaps the conclusions. The miracles of Jesus do have an important place in his life. We cannot admit a priori with Hume and Renan that miracles are impossible. Miracle, moreover, should not be defined as an unknown law which may be discovered in due time. A miracle has real significance only in terms of a personal act of God in contradiction to his power in upholding the universe. From the latter point all things could be considered miraculous. This does not seem to be the intention of

[6] Boettner, *op. cit.*, p. 149.

[7] Boettner has an extended list. Jesus is called "King of Israel," John 1:49; "The Saviour," II Peter 1:11; "Master," Mt. 23:10; Jude 4; "Son of God," John 1:34, 20:31; "Son of Man," Mt. 17:9; "Jesus," Mt. 1:21; "Christ," Mt. 16:16; "Saviour," John 4:42; Acts 5:31; "Messiah," John 1:41; 4:25–26; "The Lamb of God," John 1:29; "The Word," John 1:1; "The Only Begotten Son," John 3:16; "Redeemer," Gal. 3:13; . . . "The Image of God" II Cor. 4:4; "The Effulgence of His Glory," Heb. 1:3; "The Very Image of His Substance," Heb. 1:3; "Great High Priest," Heb. 4:14; "The Author of our Salvation," Heb. 2:10; "The Author and Perfecter of our Faith," Heb. 12:2; "The Head of the Church," Eph. 5:23; . . . "The Power of God, and the Wisdom of God" I Cor. 1:24; "The Bread of Life" John 6:35; "The Living Bread," John 6:51; "The True Vine," John 15:1; "The Door," John 10:7; "The Holy and Righteous One," Acts 3:14; "The Prince of Life," Acts 3:15; . . . "The Lord God," Rev. 1:8; "My Lord and my God," John 20:28. These titles assume more significance when it is understood that they come from a strictly zealous monotheistic background. *Op. cit.*, pp. 151–52.

[8] "John 1:18 (Aleph B. C. text); 20:28; I John 5:20; Heb. 1:8; II Pet. 1:1; Acts 20:28; Rom. 9:5; 2 Thess. 1:12; Titus 2:13, and perhaps Acts 18:26; I Tim. 3:16."—*Ibid.*, p. 151.

the writers of the New Testament. J. Gresham Machen defined a miracle as "any deviation from, or transcendence of, the order of nature due to the interposition of a supernatural cause." [9] The emphasis is on the direct act.

In a discussion of miracles it is important to stress that they are not isolated events separated from the person of Jesus and the claim to divine power. It is not as though a mere human were performing them. It is quite natural to be suspicious concerning the claims on the part of anyone, but this is no mere man. Man he is, but more than man. Many are suspicious of the miracles of the New Testament and classify them with miracle stories in other religious cultures. The circumstances in each case are different. Generally the miracle stories of the world religions can be shown to have arisen centuries after the founder of a particular world religion. In the case of Jesus, this is not so. Within the apostolic generation, his miraculous birth is claimed, miracles were performed, and references to him as divine take place. There was really no question concerning the role of miracles in the lifetime of Jesus; instead, it was always a question of the source of his power.

It would be easier in a scientific age to dispense with the idea of miracles, and we agree with Machen that the New Testament would be easier to believe without them. But it would not be worth believing.[10]

It is difficult to conclude, however, that miracles prove the divinity of Jesus. If miracles prove the truthfulness of a claim, then the door is open for all forms of claims. Miracles would then prove the claims of the Christian Scientists, Pentecostals, and Roman Catholics: for all claim miracles of one sort or another.

In reality all that miracles provide is the claim to be heard (Deut. 13:1-3; 2 Thess. 2:9). The message is the determining factor of truth. The Bible does speak of false signs as well as false messages. Jesus has to be judged on the basis of what he said and above all for what he did. His miracles are the frosting on the cake.

An impartial reading of the New Testament must drive one to conclude that its writers knew of Jesus as divine in a unique sense of

---

[9] *Christianity and Liberalism,* p. 103.
[10] *Ibid.*

the word. This is only one feature of his makeup. We turn now to
the other feature.

Human Characteristics

Virgin birth.—The New Testament is likewise emphatic about the
human nature of Christ as well as the divine. The words of John
that the Word was *made flesh* emphasize his likeness to man. There
is also another point of departure and that is the virgin birth. Two
books, Matthew and Luke, relate the story of Jesus' birth. It is implied
in other passages.[11] The virgin birth lays stress on the real humanity
of Jesus. He had true flesh and blood. This was an important declaration against Greek culture and philosophy which could not admit that God could have real contact with flesh which was believed to
be evil. One can see the Johannine dispute with this mode of thinking
in his warning: "By this you know the Spirit of God: every spirit
which confesses that Jesus Christ has come in the flesh is of God"
(1 John 4:2); and conversely, everyone who "does not confess Jesus
is not of God" (v. 3). So crucial was the conflict in the early centuries
that the phrase "born of the Virgin Mary" was incorporated into the
Apostles' Creed. Its primary intent was to contend for the true
humanity of Jesus.[12] Jesus was a true man like other men, but he was
also more than man.

With the modern tendency to doubt[13] the virgin birth, the question
is sometimes raised concerning whether it must be accepted. Emil
Brunner, along with others, regards it as a peripheral matter.[14] However, the question of doctrine is never the question of how little can I
accept. The intent is a full exposition of biblical truth. Concerning
the virgin birth, Barth warns, "The Church knew well what it was
doing when it posted this doctrine on guard, as it were, at the door
of the mystery of Christmas. It can never be in favour of anyone

---

[11] J. Gresham Machen, *The Virgin Birth of Christ* (New York: Harper &
Bros., 1930).

[12] William Hordern, *A Layman's Guide to Protestant Theology* (New York:
The Macmillan Co., 1957), pp. 19–20.

[13] A recent news release on a survey by a team of University of California
sociologists showed that only 57 percent of Protestants believed in the virgin
birth, while 81 percent of Roman Catholics did.

[14] *Christian Doctrine of Creation and Redemption,* trans. Olive Wyon (Philadelphia: Westminster Press, 1952), p. 354. Brunner declares concerning the
virgin birth, "Thus we must assume, either, that the Apostles were unaware
of this view, or, that they considered it unimportant, or even mistaken."

thinking he can hurry past this guard. It will remind him that he is walking along a private road at his own cost and risk." [15]

It is both unfair and wrong to attempt to equate the story of the virgin birth of Jesus with similar stories that have appeared in other religions. The story of Jesus appears from the beginning, whereas the others are due to the influence of centuries of time intervening. Likewise, there is no similarity and connection between the gospel story and the myths of ancient religions. By and large, these myths are connected with fertility of the soil, and they explain the cyclical wheel of death and life. They are repeated every year, whereas the birth and resurrection of Jesus are once-for-all-time events. Christ's birth is in the realm of history, whereas the myths know nothing of historical events. Concerning the so-called parallels, Barth says: "In the case of these alleged parallels the similarity can never be more than verbal, because the divine agents in the miraculous births spoken of in this connexion are definitely not God in the full and strict sense of the word, but at best gods, that is, hypostatisations of the feeling of man for nature or his reflection of history, hypostatisations behind which man is everywhere only too visible as the proper lord of the world and as the creator of its deities." [16]

Physical and emotional responses.—With the virgin birth as the starting point, the Scriptures speak of other features of Jesus' human life. The first word was growth in physical strength and wisdom (Luke 2:40). In his ministry he grew tired and fatigued (John 4:6), his physical body needed sleep (Matt. 8:24), sustenance (Matt. 4:2; 21:18), and water to quench his thirst (John 19:28). In the realm of emotion, Jesus expressed joy (John 15:11) and sorrow (Matt. 26:37). His life was characterized by compassion (Matt. 9:36) and love (Mark 10:21). In addition, he expressed righteous indignation toward those who withheld faith in himself (Mark 3:5).[17]

His humanity received special emphasis toward the latter part of his ministry. The events prior to his trial cannot be understood with-

---

[15] *Church Dogmatics,* I-2, 181. Cf. his statement in *Dogmatics in Outline,* p. 100. "One thing may be definitely said, that every time people want to fly from this miracle, a theology is at work, which has ceased to understand and honor the mystery as well, and has rather essayed to conjure away the mystery of the unity of God and man in Jesus Christ, the mystery of God's free grace."

[16] *Church Dogmatics,* I-2, 197.

[17] Boettner, *op. cit.,* pp. 183–84.

out a full concept of his humanity. In the garden, he offered up prayer to his Father for strength in the critical hour. He perspired as only one does under great physical strain (Luke 22:43–44). His death was a real death. There was no stage-playing involved. His body was prepared for burial, and had not the sabbath occurred, stopping burial preparation on the one hand, and the resurrection, making it unnecessary on the other hand, Jesus' body would have received the full Jewish burial preparations.

The sinlessness of Jesus.—Jesus, the Christ is declared to be sinless. He asks the question, "Which of you convicts me of sin?" (John 8:46). Many other New Testament references speak of Jesus' sinlessness.[18] The question involved in whether Jesus was sinless or not is an outgrowth of the profound conviction that he was human first of all, and then divine. The book of Hebrews speaks of the common life of Jesus, living among the sinful but without sin. However, the fact of his sinlessness sets him apart from mankind. This, coupled with the fact that Jesus came to expose sin, is the reason that "the world" hates him (John 15:18–22).

There are two questions that must be dealt with in connection with the human nature of Jesus, as well as in connection with his sinlessness. The first question relates to his baptism by John the Baptist. Baptism is connected with the confession of sin (Matt. 3:6). The implication for Jesus was a confession similar to that of the people who received John's baptism. Was not Jesus confessing the same guilt that belonged to the multitude? The passages related to Jesus' baptism do not imply this. First, John declared that he himself should be baptized by Jesus. He is aware of a unique person in Jesus. Jesus countered with the words that he should be baptized "to fulfil all righteousness" (Matt. 3:15). The act of submission to baptism fulfils his personal role of humiliation under law. "Christ submits to an ordinance of God and is in this respect no exception. He belongs to this people and has come to do the will of the Father. Hence he wishes to receive baptism, too, and this does not mean that he himself has succumbed to the power of sin and therefore needs the baptism of repentance. But he is bound to this people and thus bound he will bear its guilt." [19]

Second, the Gospel of John declares that Jesus' baptism was heaven's

---

[18] 1 John 3:5; 1 Peter 2:21–22; Heb. 4:15.

[19] G. C. Berkouwer, *The Person of Christ,* trans. John Vriend (Grand Rapids: Wm. B. Eerdmans Publishing Co., 1954), p. 245.

way of declaring who the Messiah was (John 1:33–34). Third, without attempting to impose a text on another text, Jesus' baptism could be viewed in light of Peter's definition of baptism as a testimony of a clear conscience before God (1 Peter 3:21). Baptism portrayed for Jesus, without the necessity of repentance, what it portrayed for the other people with repentance.[20] Baptism, for Jesus, declared his sinlessness before God.

The next question in light of the sinlessness of Jesus is whether there was a possibility of his sinning. The question is sometimes framed in this manner: Was Christ only able not to sin (*potuit non peccare*) but did avoid sinning, or was he not able to sin (*non potuit peccare*)? If the latter answer is true, that Christ was not able to sin, in what sense can one speak of a true temptation?

Theologians have spoken of a *communicatio idiomatum* or a communication of properties, which means that the properties of both natures of Christ are ascribed to each other. Therefore, the human nature would be under the realm of enabling grace in which it could not sin. The danger, however, is that of making the issue into a theological syllogism. As a rule, the sinlessness of Christ is affirmed on the basis of his not being able to sin. But the temptation is then placed in a different context from ethical wrong. J. O. Buswell declared that "Jesus is a Person with a character, and being Himself, it would be *morally* impossible (not physically impossible) that He would sin." [21] He used the illustration approvingly of a man who *could* beat his wife but who would not. Berkouwer contends:

One must hold, with the church, that those are wrong who are content to say that Christ was able not to sin. But one must be on his guard against an abstract mode of reasoning about the confession of Christ's sinlessness and against playing down the reality of the temptation. . . . The moment the Scripture introduces the temptation in the wilderness it mentions

---

[20] Baptism portrayed a clear conscience and this seemed to be the testimony of Josephus in the first centuries. He wrote, "Who [John] was a good man, and commanded the Jews to exercise virtue, both as to righteousness towards one another and piety towards God, and so to come to baptism; for that the washing [with water] would be acceptable to him, if they made use of it, not in order to the putting away of some sins, but for the purification of the body; supposing still that the soul was thoroughly purified beforehand by righteousness."—*Antiquities of the Jews*, book 18, chapter 5, section 2, quoted in Dana and Mantey, *A Manual Grammar of the Greek New Testament* (New York: The Macmillan Co., 1951), p. 104.

[21] *A Systematic Theology of the Christian Religion*, II, 61.

Christ's being filled with the Holy Spirit. In his life there is a mysterious incapacity for sin stemming from his love and mercy. Scripture refers to the sinlessness of Christ as his permanent *deed*. . . . The purpose of the temptation in the wilderness is not that Christ should commit some *ethical* aberration but that he should be persuaded from entering upon the road to suffering.[22]

Berkouwer, therefore, limits the real temptation to the role of Jesus' sufferings and the great temptation is that he should depart from it. However, "He could not elude his suffering because he did not want to elude it." [23]

The truth of the life of Jesus could be stated in terms of an analogy in which gold is tried, but it is part of its nature that it always stands the test.

One other word about the sinlessness of Jesus is in order. The Scriptures speak of his being made sin who knew no sin, "so that in him we might become the righteousness of God" (2 Cor. 5:21). The intent is not that Christ became sinful but that he entered into the judgment and life of man who was in sin. His outward situation was that of a sinful man.

The Unity of His Person

For the sake of description, we have been referring to Jesus as having human and divine characteristics, but this division is never referred to in the Scriptures. When Jesus speaks it is always with the unity of his person. He says, "I say to you." [24] He never declares that I speak this with reference to my divine nature, or with reference to my human nature. When he speaks, it is Jesus the Christ who is Lord that is speaking. Frankly stated, there is *no* evidence for anything but unipersonality in Jesus.

The Doctrines Concerning Christ

Orthodoxy

There have been many doctrines propounded concerning the person of Christ. For four hundred years, the church struggled with the question. After much controversy, the statement of the Council of

---

[22] Berkouwer, *The Person of Christ,* p. 261.
[23] *Ibid.*
[24] Matt. 5:18,20,22,26,28,32,34,39,44. Many more could be given.

Chalcedon in A.D. 451 was regarded as the orthodox position. This is the position held in common by both Roman Catholic and Protestant traditions. Although Baptists have never been a creedal people, they have generally accepted the general truths set forth there. It is beneficial for the student to see the results of the years of theological labor and struggle. We quote it:

Following, therefore, the holy Fathers, we confess and all teach with one accord one and the same Son, our Lord Jesus Christ, at once perfect (complete) in Godhead and perfect (complete) in manhood, truly God and truly man, and, further, of a reasonable soul and body; of one essence with the Father as regards his Godhead, and at the same time of one essence with us as regards his manhood, in all respects like us, apart from sin; as regards his Godhead begotten of the Father before the ages, but yet as regards his manhood—on account of us and our salvation—begotten in the last days of Mary the Virgin, bearer of God; one and the same Christ, Son, Lord, Only-begotten, proclaimed in two natures, without confusion, without change, without division, without separation; the difference of the natures being in no way destroyed on account of the union, but rather the peculiar property of each nature being preserved and concurring in one person and one hypostasis—not as though parted or divided into two persons, but one and the same Son and Only-begotten God the Logos, Lord, Jesus Christ, even as the prophets from of old and the Lord Jesus Christ taught us concerning him, and the Creed of the Fathers has handed down to us.[25]

There are certain terms which need explanation. First, the Son is declared to be perfect or complete in regard to his manhood. He is truly man of a reasonable soul and body. The idea of human nature, however, has changed over the centuries. We must not assume that the Son of God adopted a human person and inhabited that body. Buswell seeks to define nature as "a complex of attributes, and is not to be confused with a substantive entity." [26] Pursuing this line of thought, Buswell declares: "We can without equivocation, accept the implication and declare that Jesus had a human spirit. I mean this, . . . not in the sense that He had two spirits, but in the sense that His eternal *ego,* His personality, took to itself in the incarnation all the essential attributes of a human spirit. *He had a human spirit in the sense that His spirit became human.*" [27]

[25] J. F. Bethune-Baker, *An Introduction to the Early History of Christian Doctrine* (London: Methuen & Co., 1903), p. 287.
[26] *A Systematic Theology of the Christian Religion,* II, 52.
[27] *Ibid.,* 53.

Following the same line of thought that "a 'will' is not a substantive entity, but a behavior complex," Buswell then speaks of two wills of Christ as defined by the Council of Constantinople in A.D. 680. He writes, "Our Lord Jesus Christ . . . took to Himself a human volitional behavior pattern when He took to Himself all the essential attributes of human nature." [28]

Boettner speaks of the union of the Son of God with an "impersonal generic human nature. This human nature had no personality apart from the Divine nature, but came to consciousness and found its personality only in union with the Divine." [29] Boettner then likens this to the relation between the human body and spirit. Without true personal life, the body is devoid of reason and sensation, yet it is the physical nature of man. Speaking from the standpoint of John 1:14, Barth contends that " 'flesh' does not imply a man, but human essence and existence, human kind and nature, humanity, *humanitas*, that which makes a man man as opposed to God, angel, or animal." [30]

The second phrase for our consideration is "bearer of God." Generally the phrase is rendered "Mother of God," which grates on the nerves of Protestants. Unfortunately the English translation does not carry the intent of the Greek word *theotokos*. The Greek word "fixes attention rather on the Godhead of him who was born. To deny that she [Mary] was Theotokos was really to deny that he who was born of her was God as well as man." [31] The term really has no suggestion that Mary gave birth to the divine nature of God.

Is Chalcedon a dead issue? Hardly! There are those in the heritage of theological liberalism who regard it as a form of dogma which should never have been brought into existence.[32] Those who are enamored by rationalism, certain forms of pantheism, and cultism have yet to make terms with Chalcedon. On the other hand, there are those who accept it in essence but deny the necessity of going beyond the biblical data on the subject. Jesus Christ is the God-man. There-

[28] *Ibid.*, p. 54.
[29] *Op. cit.*, p. 199.
[30] Barth, *Church Dogmatics,* I-2, 149.
[31] Bethune-Baker, *op. cit.*, p. 262.
[32] DeWolf, *op. cit.*, p. 73. "As an ontological theory the Chalcedonian Creed, with its ancient metaphysical categories, is quite impossible for most of us. Yet, as an expression of our apprehension of God through the man Jesus, it speaks for our faith, as for theirs in the fifth century."

fore, Brunner concludes, Chalcedon is bound to the past and the biblical word is sufficient.[33]

The importance of Chalcedon is that it defined the doctrine concerning the person of Christ for the primary purpose of safeguarding against heresy. It does not explain how the Incarnation took place. It does explain where the lines can be drawn and heresy denounced. We do not turn to Chalcedon because of traditionalism, but we look at it for the purpose of linking ourselves with a formal statement which attempted to safeguard the biblical message that Jesus Christ is the Word made flesh.

Unaccepted Views Concerning Jesus Christ

In the attempt to come to a comprehensive statement on the person of Jesus Christ, many views were set forth. Obviously not all of them could be right, and several were condemned as heterodox, or erroneous. We need to view these attempts from the right perspective. It is easy to write off the ancients who came to be regarded as heretics without thinking of their motive and purpose. In some cases they were sincere men who were striving to find and formulate answers to the greatest problem of their time: namely, who is Jesus Christ? As it happened, they came up with the wrong or inadequate answers. Others, however, were attempting to impose paganism on Christian thought and thus the motive was false.

The value of the following brief sketch of the unaccepted views of Christ rests in seeing that old heresies arise in new disguise in almost every period.

Ebionism.—The Ebionites were Jewish followers of Jesus who solved the problem of the divine nature of Christ by denying it altogether. There seems to be a difference of opinion among them over his virgin birth, but some conceived of him as a human on whom the Spirit of the Lord came. After the enduement with the Spirit, Jesus assumed his prophetic office and "through his piety became the Son of God." [34] This type of Jewish influence can be seen, in part, in the Judaizers

---

[33] *The Christian Doctrine of Creation and Redemption,* p. 362.

[34] Reinhold Seeberg, *Text-Book of the History of Doctrines,* trans. Charles E. Hay (Grand Rapids: Baker Book House, 1956), p. 88. Cf. H. A. Wolfson, *The Philosophy of the Church Fathers* (Cambridge: Harvard University Press, 1956), p. 587.

who nearly succeeded in getting the church to observe the Jewish law. Only by ignoring the New Testament can one conclude for this view.

In modern times, the attitude of the Ebionites can be paralleled in the thinking of some religious liberals. Liberalism has little use for dogmas of the past. It attempted to throw off the dogmatic formulations concerning the person of Christ and return to what was presumed to be the simple religion of Jesus. The distinction, the *religion about* Jesus versus the *religion of* Jesus, was accepted by liberalism.[35] The "recovered" view of Jesus as held by some liberals was essentially parallel to the Ebionites.

Adoptionism.—Adoptionism has a relationship to the Ebionites. The adoptionists believed that Jesus was like any ordinary person, but at one point in his life was adopted as the Son of God. The point at which he became the Son of God, or "adopted," was at birth or at his baptism.[36] Paul of Samosata, the most important representative of adoptionism, declared that "the Logos came and dwelt in Jesus, who was a man." [37] Adoptionism denied the Incarnation in the true sense of the word. A real union of the Logos with man as expressed in John 1:14 is rejected.

Adoptionism has been a real temptation to the church. However, it does a real disservice to the meaning of the New Testament. It is evident that "adoptionism has isolated the Scripture witness to Christ as truly man from the total context of Scripture." [38] Berkouwer concludes that "in order to find Adoptionism in the New Testament, one must make a radical selection in Scripture—a selection which obscures the mystery of the person and work of Christ." [39]

Docetism.—This is a view associated with the Greek word meaning "to appear." Docetism was influenced by that strain of Greek thought which regarded spirit as good and matter and flesh as evil. Thus it was impossible for them to conceive of God's really coming into contact with human flesh. What seemed to be the Incarnation was really only an appearance. Jesus was not a real human being but one

[35] Cf. Harry E. Fosdick, *The Hope of the World* (New York: Harpers, 1933), pp. 103–4. Also Fosdick's *The Modern Use of the Bible* (New York: Macmillan & Co., 1924), pp. 181–86; 102.
[36] Seeberg, *op. cit.*, pp. 104–105.
[37] *Ibid.*, p. 164.
[38] Berkouwer, *The Person of Christ*, p. 176.
[39] *Ibid.*

"who only appeared in human form." [40] Basilides, one of the advocates, declared "that Christ came in phantasm, was without substance of flesh, did not suffer at the hands of the Jews, but instead of him, Simon was crucified; hence we are not to believe in him who was crucified." [41]

Docetism has to reject the events recorded in the Gospels because of its philosophical ideas taken over from Greek thought. However, the New Testament takes a strong stand against anyone denying the humanity of Christ. The letter entitled First John says, "Every spirit which confesses that Jesus Christ has come in the flesh is of God." [42] In fact, the Gospels, as well as other epistles, draw a picture of the genuine humanity of Christ. [43]

A modern modified type of Docetism is Christian Science. It denies the reality of the Incarnation. It presupposes that matter is evil and that God could not become a corporal man subject to death. [44]

Apollinarianism.—Apollinaris (b. A.D. 310), bishop of Laodicea, in Syria, reasoned that it was impossible to combine the divine and human natures of Jesus, the Christ. Accepting the trichotomous nature of man as being body, soul, and spirit, he argued that the human nature of Jesus was composed of body and soul but the divine Logos took the place of the spirit. On this basis the human nature of Jesus would not be complete.

Apollinarianism was rejected by the Council of Constantinople in 381. As a doctrine it was really a form of Docetism by suggesting that Jesus was not a real or complete man. It would be questionable whether he should be called a man at all, and the whole gospel story is based on a divine deception of a person who seemed to be man but was not. Apollinarianism raised questions concerning the completeness of redemption. If Jesus were without a human spirit, a real part of man's nature, then it was concluded that something in man's redemption would be overlooked.

Great emphasis was attached to the necessity of Christ's being like man in all respects, except for sin, in order for him to be the

---

[40] Wolfson, *op. cit.*, p. 588.
[41] Quoted in Seeberg, *op. cit.*, p. 96.
[42] 1 John 4:2,3; Cf. 1 John 5:5,9; 2:18–19.
[43] Luke 24:36–43; John 20:17,27; Heb. 2:17.
[44] Cf. Mary Baker Eddy, *Science and Health* (Boston: 1934), pp. 314, 322–32.

Redeemer of man. A being less than man could not enter wholly into man's plight. Gregory of Nazianzus summed up this thought concerning the incompleteness of the Incarnation with reference to the matter of redemption in saying " 'What has not been assumed cannot be restored; it is what is united with God that is saved.' " [45]

Nestorianism.—Nestorius, bishop of Constantinople, was charged with having taught that the two natures of Christ merely existed in conjunction with each other without a clear union. Nestorianism implied that there were two natures and two persons rather than two natures and one person. Nestorianism was first condemned at the Council of Ephesus in A.D. 431 and later at the Fifth Ecumenical Council meeting at Constantinople in A.D. 553.

Whether Nestorius himself was really heterodox is debated,[46] but at least Nestorianism, as historians have come to understand it, would have involved a simple moral unity between the two natures. The Incarnation would be a simple relationship between the human and the divine rather than the Word's becoming flesh.

Eutychianism.—Eutyches was a monk of Constantinople who attempted to defend the unity of Christ's person. He may have been rash to the point that his statements imply more than he wanted to say. Eutychianism has come historically to mean a view that when the divine and human natures came together a fusion took place that made Jesus Christ a *third* entity, or nature. Eutyches declared, " 'I confess that our Lord was of two natures before the union, but after the union I confess one nature.' " [47]

With the union of the two natures into one the humanity of the incarnate Word is no longer *homoousion,* i.e., of like substance with man, but is absorbed into the divine nature. Whatever the personal position of Eutyches might have been, the ideas associated with his name were rightly condemned.

In conclusion to this brief survey of the more prominent heresies, we believe that they were rightly rejected by church councils. Although there may have been many political, ecclesiastical, and tactical

---

[45] Kelly, *op. cit.,* p. 296.

[46] With the discovery of the *Bazaar of Heracleides* in the early part of this century, J. F. Bethune-Baker and F. Loofs have attempted to defend Nestorius of the charge of heresy. It is certainly true that Nestorius was a victim of ecclesiastical politics, but whether he can be completely exonerated is a continuing question.

[47] Seeberg, *op. cit.,* p. 267.

implications in their rejections, the consensus of opinion is that these ideas were wrong. Summed up, Ebionism and Docetism rejected the reality of the two natures. Arianism and Apollinarianism could not accept the integrity of the natures. Nestorianism, Adoptionism, and Eutychianism denied their proper union.[48]

There are no elaborated theories concerning the mechanics of the Incarnation in the Bible, but it is emphatic that with relation to God the incarnate Word is one with him by nature; and with relation to man, he is true man by nature also.

There are certain ideas associated with modern times that require a few comments.

Modern Views Concerning the Christ

After the period of the early heresies, there were few new developments in the doctrine concerning the person of Christ. The Middle Ages saw some outbreaks of old ideas, but little else. The two views discussed below are associated with different periods. The first idea is associated with Luther, though it has roots back in the period of the Church Fathers. The other idea is often associated with a serious type of biblically oriented liberalism.

Communicatio idiomatum.—The term refers to the communication of properties, or communication of attributes. In the Incarnation the properties of the divine nature are communicated to the human nature and vice versa. However, the doctrine is generally slanted toward the attributing of the divine attributes to the human nature.[49] The Lutheran view of the bodily presence of Christ in the Lord's Supper is contingent upon this doctrine. Christ's body is omnipresent because the incarnate Son is omnipresent. Therefore, the literal body is present in the elements.[50]

There are some serious questions connected with this doctrine. Not only does it lack a scriptural foundation but it "implies a fusion of the divine and the human natures in Christ." [51]

Kenosis.—The kenosis doctrine concerning the person of Christ came forth from the motivation of doing justice to the unity of Christ's consciousness.[52] There is also an attempt to account for the growth

---

48 Strong, *op. cit.*, p. 672.
49 Berkhof, *op. cit.*, p. 325.
50 Berkouwer, *The Person of Christ*, p. 272.
51 Berkhof, *op. cit.*, p. 326.
52 Berkouwer, *The Person of Christ*, p. 30.

and development in the life of Jesus. Building on Philippians 2:6–8, in which Christ "emptied himself," it was declared that the attributes of deity were laid aside. Thus the humanity of Jesus was emphasized along with the growth of his divine self-consciousness and calling.

It is questionable whether the Scriptures will allow such an interpretation of these passages. Should it succeed exegetically, it "is no longer evident that it is truly God who comes to us in Christ. A genuine union is then out of the picture." [53] Berkouwer further concludes, "At the end of the road, when the reconstruction of Christology was undertaken, arose the danger of the complete humanization of Christ." [54]

Conclusions and Implications

As we reflect upon the biblical view of Christology, we must conclude with the Scriptures that Jesus, the Christ, was more than mere man. He is *vere Deus* and *vere homo*. This has been the teaching of the Christian faith since the time of the apostles. With the rise of liberalism in the late nineteenth and early twentieth centuries, a distinction was drawn between the religion *of* Jesus and the religion *about* Jesus—said to be the work of the corrupter, Paul. This much is implied by this distinction: Christianity is built upon a falsehood, or a mistake.

At the same time, we must remark that the gospel declaring the incarnate Word has had more power in transforming lives than the gospel of human virtue and achievement, which is supposedly the true gospel. Athanasius was correct to say that only God can save the fallen race. " 'We ourselves were the motive of His Incarnation; it was for our salvation that He loved man to the point of being born and of appearing in a human body.' " [55]

Where there is an attempt on the part of modern man to write off the divine-human nature of the person of Christ, there is a return to some form of ancient heresy or rationalism. The doctrine assumes such an importance that the words of Scripture need to be reiterated: "Whoever confesses that Jesus is the Son of God, God abides in him, and he in God" (1 John 4:15). But whoever confesses otherwise, let him beware.

---

[53] *Ibid.*
[54] *Ibid.*, p. 31.
[55] Kelly, *op. cit.*, p. 284.

VII. The Holy Spirit

*My own complaint against most writers on the Holy Spirit is
that they know too much.*
          Quoted by Ramm, *The Witness of the Spirit*

*The Holy Spirit in the New Testament sense is the presence of
God which bears witness to, and makes effectual, the historical
Christ as a living personal presence. The operation of the Holy
Spirit is necessary for the Word about Christ to become the
Word of Christ for us, and for the Word of Christ to become
the Word of God.*
    Brunner, *The Christian Doctrine of the Church, Faith,
    and the Consummation*

*Only if they were not God could a definition be given at this
point, such a definition as would be more than a description of
the fact that God Himself is to the fore in His revelation. But
what is to the fore in God's revelation is the Father, the Son,
and the Spirit. A first-class definition of these three could thus
only be given if the Father, the Son and the Spirit are not God.*
                     Barth, *Church Dogmatics*

To write about the *person* of Christ is one thing but to speak of the
Spirit of God is another. Many of the things spoken in regard to the
Holy Spirit are only an extension of what the Bible declares about
the person of Christ. In fact, the Bible does not give an extensive
treatment of the Holy Spirit. Brunner declares that the scope of the
New Testament utterances is not such that we can "summarize them
in a 'Doctrine of the Holy Spirit.'" [1]

In comparing the doctrines of Christ and the Holy Spirit in the
history of Christian doctrine, one can say that the church went far

---

[1] Brunner, *The Christian Doctrine of the Church, Faith, and the Consummation,* trans. David Cairns and T. H. L. Parker (Philadelphia: Westminster Press, 1962), p. 9.

beyond the New Testament data in defining the doctrine of Christ. On the other hand, the judgment has been made that the church "fell considerably short of the New Testament in defining the doctrine of the Holy Spirit." [2] Both facts being true, namely, the limitation of scriptural utterance and absence of creedal definition, there is little to draw on. Perhaps we are in a better position to say what the person and work of the Spirit are not than we are to say what they are.

However, what the Bible records about the person of the Holy Spirit is tremendously important. The data is not such that we can dismiss it lightly. A whole movement within the ranks of Christianity, the so-called Third Force, has emphasized the role of the Holy Spirit in several unique ways. The "Third Force" refers to segments of churches, sects, and fellowships which can be termed "Pentecostal" in one sense of the word or other. However one judges this movement with reference to its relationship to other Christian groups, its doctrine of the Spirit must be evaluated from the standpoint of the Scriptures and what the Scriptures regard as the Spirit's proper work.

The Biblical Data

In discussing the doctrine of the Holy Spirit one has to begin with the foundation material, i.e., the Scriptures. Without this we would only be able to conclude with the remnant disciples of John the Baptist at Ephesus that we have not even heard that there is a Holy Spirit. The significance of this statement is based on the Jewish belief that since the time of the prophets—who had ceased with Malachi—the Holy Spirit had been withdrawn from Israel.[3] Now the gospel as preached by Paul spoke of the outpouring again of the Holy Spirit.

The data on the Spirit's being is such that there is sufficient warranty to speak of the Holy Spirit as a person. He is not viewed in the New Testament, as is sometimes expressed in the Old Testament, in the form of a divine force or power. In the New Testament he speaks (Acts 8:29), commissions (Acts 13:4), forbids (16:6–7), intercedes (Rom. 8:26), guides (John 16:13), teaches (John 15:26), and indwells the believer (John 14:17). The common attributes of will

---

[2] George S. Hendry, *The Holy Spirit in Christian Theology* (Philadelphia: Westminster Press, 1956), p. 37.

[3] George Foot Moore, *Judaism* (Cambridge: Harvard University Press, 1954), I, 421.

(1 Cor. 12:11), knowledge (1 Cor. 2:10–11), and love (Rom. 15:30) are his. His very name is Holy Spirit, and wrong can be committed against him (Acts 5:3; Heb. 10:29).

If one raises objections one must do so on rational rather than scriptural grounds, for in the Scriptures he is called Spirit of God (1 Cor. 2:11). His presence is ubiquitous (Psalm 139:7), whereby he indwells the hearts of all believers (John 14:17). The interchange of the different titles speaks of the same person of the Holy Spirit who dwells in the believer (1 Cor. 6:19), who is the temple of God (1 Cor. 3:16), and this is equivalent to "Christ in you" (Col. 1:27).

Beginning with these biblical equations we can go on to discuss certain ideas.

Inasmuch as the Spirit came at Pentecost in a unique way, are we to conclude that prior to Pentecost the Spirit was absent or did not exist? If one answered affirmatively, then there is no answer to such references in the Old Testament in which the Spirit of the Lord moved upon the waters in creation (Gen. 1), or in the history of Israel whereby God directed its development through prophetic leadership—leadership in whom the Spirit of God rested. The obvious conclusion is that the Spirit of the Lord was, is, and shall forever be, because he is of the same nature as God.

In light of the statement that the Spirit of God has continuity with the nature of God and is at one with him, one can look to certain manifestations of the Spirit in a unique way and see these manifestations in light of his eternalness. In light of this the baptism of Jesus has a relationship to the diverse manifestations of the Spirit. The significance of his baptism, in which the Spirit descended upon him, is that indication is given whereby Jesus is marked off as the "permanent bearer of the Spirit." [4] In this context the closeness of the Trinitarian relationship is declared as well as the distinctiveness of the persons. The Spirit and the Son are not separated, but also they cannot be identified; that is, they cannot be confused.[5]

Similarly, viewing the unique manifestation of the Spirit at Pentecost, several basic ideas come forth. First, the Spirit came according to promise and therefore his ministry is to be viewed in relation to the words of Christ. Second, the Spirit does not supersede the presence of

---

[4] Hendry, *op. cit.*, p. 19.
[5] Barth, *Church Dogmatics,* I-1, 542.

Christ. The faith of the church must always be Christ-centered, not Spirit-centered. Third, the Spirit witnesses to the fact of redemption which has the central place in the proclamation of the church. Fourth, the Spirit universalizes the work of redemption. By this is meant that the time barrier of centuries is broken, and the Spirit makes it possible for the atonement to have meaning and power for the twentieth century, or contemporary witnesses in any era. Without this continuity of the Spirit the later generations would know of Christ only in a historical sense of knowing a fact. But because of the resurrection and the universalizing activity of the Spirit, the modern generation, as well as intervening ones, can know a Person.

Another idea related here is that worship is Trinitarian in nature. The Christian worships the Father through the Son in the Spirit. Jesus spoke of true worship as being spiritual in nature, for God is Spirit (John 4:24). The baptismal formula implies the same concept. This relationship is not detailed to any large degree in the Scriptures and what God has not given we cannot in certainty know. The traditional doctrine of the relationships within the nature of God is summed up by Barth: "By being the Father in Himself from eternity God brings Himself forth from eternity as the Son. By being the Son from eternity, He comes forth from eternity from Himself as Father. In this eternal bringing forth of Himself and coming forth from Himself, He posits Himself a third time as the Holy Spirit; i.e., as the love which unifies Him in Himself." [6]

In this we have to confess a mystery.

The Work and Activity of the Spirit

In the New Testament we are given more information on the work of the Spirit than on his person.

Redemptive Activity

The Spirit's work in the individual begins in the area of redemption. Redemption implies a need of knowing one's helplessness. Jesus spoke of the Spirit's work in terms of the conviction of sin (John 16:8–9). Without this sense of self-understanding, man the sinner does not know from what heights he has fallen. Awareness of his own sin makes regeneration become a possibility. Jesus described this as a new birth (John 3:5). The apostle spoke of it as a new creation

[6] *Church Dogmatics*, I-1, 552–53.

that takes place within the life of man (2 Cor. 5:17). This is also described in terms of the washing of regeneration and renewing of the Holy Spirit (Titus 3:5). When redemption is an accomplished fact the Spirit does not depart from the believer but indwells him (Eph. 1:13). Again, Jesus promised the spirit who would dwell *with* us and *in* us (John 16:17).

At this point, one may speak of the continuing redemptive activity of the Spirit in transforming the believer into the image of Christ. This has been commonly called sanctification. In the continuing growth in Christian understanding and grace, the believer is to bear the fruits of the Spirit, listed as "love, joy, peace, longsuffering, kindness, goodness, faithfulness, meekness, temperance" (Gal. 5:22). Sanctification could also be described as seeking to have the mind of Christ (Phil. 2:1–4). The ultimate transformation to the likeness of Christ will come at his Parousia (1 John 3:2). The future transformation means that perfection is unattainable this side of death. Where perfection in Christian living is professed, the seriousness of sin is usually watered down.

Gifts of the Spirit

A gift of the Spirit is a qualification granted to the believer to enable him to accomplish his Christian calling. There are a number of gifts listed in several parts of the New Testament. Paul tells the Corinthians of the gifts of wisdom, knowledge, faith, healing, working of miracles, prophecy, discerning of spirits, *glossalalia* or tongues, interpretation of tongues, apostleship, teaching, the gift of helping, and administration (1 Cor. 12:8–10,28). To other churches he speaks of the gift of liberality (Rom. 12:8), the gift of evangelism (Eph. 4:11), and the gift of the ministry (Eph. 4:11).

These are gifts related to Christian living in all of its diversity. One may go beyond the gifts of the Spirit to say that personal ability of any order is a gift of God. Personal talents are not achieved. We cannot boast in our native talent, for we did not produce it ourselves. There is therefore no ground for boasting in the possession of any gift of life.

One implication of the gifts not always recognized is that God does not call a man to a church vocation for which he has not been equipped. But each has his own gift (1 Cor. 12:6–7), and each is under obligation to serve the body of Christ in accord with his gift.

Because of the diversity of the gifts of the Spirit, it is presumptuous to exalt one gift over the other or assume that all believers should have the same gift (1 Cor. 12:29–30).

There is an order within the various gifts of the Spirit. Paul names apostles first, prophets second, and teachers third (1 Cor. 12:28). In comparing preaching with the gift of tongues, the latter is placed in a secondary role with the admonition to seek the higher gifts.

Before turning to a discussion of two particular gifts of the Spirit, it should be laid down as a principle that possession of any gift is not a guarantee of spiritual depth. The church at Corinth possessed all the gifts; but its members were described by Paul as babes, unable to assimilate solid spiritual food (1 Cor. 3:1–3).

The gift of healing and the gift of tongues are gifts that perplex some modern Christians.

The gift of healing is a gift presumed to be exercised by such diverse groups as Pentecostals and Episcopalians. It is clearly mentioned in the New Testament as a gift (1 Cor. 12:9), and James encourages his readers to exercise the prayer of faith for the sick (5:14).

A distinction must be made between divine healing and faith healing. The passages in the New Testament speak with reference to divine healing. God can and does heal, but this is not contingent upon our faith but upon his mercy and will. Faith healing, on the other hand, stresses the necessity of faith on the part of the sick and implies that if they are not healed it is due to a lack of faith on their part. It tacitly implies that one has the right to be healed. It seems evident that the gift of healing is not a guarantee for healing all people. In Ephesus, Paul was used by God to heal many people, but later on he could do nothing for Trophimus (2 Tim. 4:20) or Timothy, to whom he sent a message that he should secure some medicine for his stomach's sake (1 Tim. 5:23).

Where healing is regarded as every Christian's right, there are certain nonbiblical conclusions at work. *First*, there is no promise in the Scriptures that every person has the right to be healed. If there were, this could go on theoretically until the person would never die. *Second*, when some men suffer, they achieve a personality of greatness that perhaps would not have been possible without a measure of suffering. This is not to justify suffering as a means of achieving good but to recognize a fact of life. Physical infirmity and spiritual growth are related in the history of great names within the church. Pascal never knew a healthy day in his life, and Luther was always haunted by a sense of despair. The same holds true for others. *Third*, we must remember that Paul had the gift of healing but was unable to secure deliverance from his "thorn in the flesh," for it was in God's wisdom a means of expressing his power in Paul's life.

Faith healing has been overrun by fraudulent practices. Several years ago a study was made of the healing movement by a Southern Presbyterian. He secured permission to observe in the meetings of many different "healers," and his findings are as follows: First, "All healers make use of a certain psychological phenomenon which is called 'the ready-made frame of desire.' " [7] That is, crowds come expecting to be healed. Second, they operate on the well-known fact that about 80 percent of the ills that trouble Americans are psychosomatic. This means that the healers look for those who have inorganic diseases. Third, the healers generally screen the applicants. People suffering from organic diseases like cancer, polio, and tuberculosis are screened out of the lines. Fourth, healing "techniques" are applied. The near blind are turned to face the floodlight which brings any shadow into sharp relief and the sight is said to be "coming." For the deaf a large pocket watch is pressed against the "temporal bone." Depending on the fact that few people are stone deaf, the "ticking will penetrate the auditory nerve by means of vibration through the bone." [8] Other techniques are used for specific cases.

The important question is: are the healings genuine? Stegall and Harwood conclude that they are devoid of a real relationship to apostolic miracles. [9] Any changes that take place for the better can be explained on two bases—suggestion or deliberate fraud. [10]

We conclude that divine healing, but not faith healing, is the key to understanding the idea in the New Testament. The account in James (5:13–16) speaks of church order in which the elders, not a healer, are called to pray. There are no offerings taken, no books or records sold, and no personal prestige is to be gained. The prayer of faith on the part of the elders is emphasized, not the faith of the sick. In the

---

[7] Carroll Stegall and Carl C. Harwood, *The Modern Tongues and Healing Movement* (Denver: Western Bible Institute, n.d.), pp. 7–8.

[8] *Ibid.*, p. 10.

[9] *Ibid.*, p. 27.

[10] *Ibid.*, p. 28.

New Testament only five people who were healed are said to have faith. In the case of the other twenty-four, there is no reference to faith. In addition, it is difficult to require faith on the part of Lazarus who is dead. But there is a legitimate role for the church to play in praying for the sick. This is a ministry given by Jesus (Matt. 25: 31–36), and it has not terminated.

The gift of tongues, or glossolalia, was first exercised on the day of Pentecost. There are only two significant accounts of the phenomenon, Acts 2 and 1 Corinthians 12–14. A comparison of these two accounts is necessary.

The gift of tongues at Pentecost was used to address men, to communicate ideas, to preach the gospel concerning Christ, that people who spoke in various dialects might understand. The question has been raised whether it was a miracle of speaking or hearing, but apart from this it does not have the problems associated with 1 Corinthians.

Glossolalia was used at Corinth to address God and was understood only by use of an interpreter. Moreover, glossolalia involved individuals alone, and minimized preaching and its importance (cf. 1 Cor. 14:2–5,13–14,19,27–28).

There are two basic views on the Corinthian experience: one is that the "tongues" were languages, and the other is that they were ecstatic utterances. The latter idea has received the greater support. There are some serious questions in receiving the last opinion, although it is the most popular. First, it is a big jump from languages in Acts to ecstatic utterances in Corinth. Second, glossolalia was a sign for unbelievers (1 Cor. 14:21) and this refers to an Old Testament passage: "By men of strange tongues and by the lips of foreigners will I speak to this people." It seems more probable that the stranger would be impressed by languages than by ecstatic utterances. If the Corinthian phenomenon were ecstatic utterances some scholars would equate it with similar phenomena in mystery, heathen, and primitive religions. It is certain, however, that the Corinthian experience was understood by Paul to be a gift of God.

Whatever was the nature of the tongues, Paul gave definite direction concerning their use. They were not to be used in public worship without someone who could interpret (1 Cor. 14:28), and even then no more than two or three were to speak. In contrast to present phenomenon, speakers-in-tongues in Corinth were able to control themselves. One must be cautious in equating contemporary glossolalia with the New Testament experience.

What is the value of the gift? Any answer to this question must include the initiatory nature of the day of Pentecost. Pentecost is the beginning of a great spiritual fact, the age of the Spirit. When the foundation had been established the framework was no longer needed.

Glossolalia arrested the attention of Jerusalem, but once it focused its attention on the disciples something else became all the more important—the preaching of the apostles. The sign was incomplete in itself and needed preaching to complete it. In other words, the gift of tongues is not the capstone of the Christian faith. Paul's estimate of the secondary place of glossolalia is emphatic: (1) note the comparison between five words of understanding and ten thousand words in a "tongue:" (2) note the prominence of prophesying, which can be translated as preaching; and (3) note what edifies or builds up the church (14:22–23; 15:3,5,24,29).

One question needing an answer is whether glossolalia is a present-day gift of the Spirit. Some argue Yes on the basis that God is always the same. In periods of revival it is said that strange things happen. Others argue No on the basis that the tongues were like miracles and served as a temporary aid to the church in getting started.

Whatever the answer to the question above, we are suspicious of any movement that is productive of division when the Scriptures place the gift in a secondary position. (See appendix.)

We must keep in mind that the church at Corinth was the *only church* seemingly to have the gift beyond Pentecost. This should enjoin caution. Second, present-day advocates *often imply* that everybody has the right to speak in tongues. Even if it is a gift today, there is not a word of support for this implication. Third, there seems to be little practical use of glossolalia. If missionaries did not have to study the foreign language of his mission area, a practical use of the gift could be found, but this is not the case. Fourth, the danger in the present-day movement is that it becomes the badge of spirituality leading to spiritual pride. The advocates of speaking in tongues work to involve other Christians in this experience to the neglect of the proper role of the proclamation of the gospel.

New Testament Terms

There are certain terms that lend themselves to misunderstanding among Christians. Without a precise understanding of certain terms relating to the Spirit, confusion and anxiety often result.

The baptism of the Spirit.—This term, occurring in Mark 1:8 and John 1:33, can be defined as the activity of the Spirit in which estranged man by his faith in Christ is placed (immersed or baptized) into the life-giving relationship in Christ. This happens when one believes. Regeneration and the baptism of the Spirit are simultaneous. One receives the Spirit when he believes (Eph. 1:13). There is no text commanding believers to seek the Spirit's baptism. Why seek that which one already has? The baptism of the Spirit is something that all believers have by virtue of their believing and trusting in Christ. The certainty of the Spirit in one's life does not depend upon feeling but upon the promise of God. The promise is that the man who trusts in Christ as Saviour is the recipient of the Spirit.

The filling of the Spirit.—The fulness of the Spirit is comparable to growth in sanctification or in purity of life. The ultimate picture of the believer is Christlikeness. Being filled with the Spirit does not imply that one has more of the Spirit (quantitatively), but that the Spirit has more of the believer in his divine control. On this basis there are ebbs and flows of knowing the presence of the Spirit. One is more usable at times than at others. The fulness of the Spirit can be lost (decrease in influence) and regained over and over, whereas one does not lose the baptism of the Spirit, or one's place in Christ. It is evident, on many different occasions in Acts, that the disciples prayed and were filled with the Spirit. At a later time they were again filled. The Spirit in this sense is not a substance that is used up, but relates to one's dedication to the kingdom of God which is more intense at certain times than at other times. The apostles were not men who *stayed* filled with the Spirit to the highest degree. It seems evident that "the fulness of the Spirit" was connected with their present commission of service. When a new point of service came they were filled with God's grace, ready for the confrontation. It is doubtful whether man could stand a continuous emotional stress involving a continual fulness.

It is important to maintain the distinction involved in this term with relation to assurance of salvation. The ebb of the Spirit's influence does not involve a loss of redemption. Falling from grace is a contradiction in terms if grace is understood in the New Testament sense of mercy or benevolent favor. Faith knows the promise of God that his Spirit is with us to the end.

The indwelling Spirit.—The fact that the Spirit of God indwells the inner life of the believer is important. The Spirit of God links the contemporary life of the believer to the redemptive acts of Christ's death. The living Spirit makes Christian faith alive and keeps it from being a paper religion bound to a lifeless book. Where this concept is lost, various forms of barren religion give birth to a substitute in the form of mysticism. Mysticism arises where moralism or barren dogma has fallen on deaf ears.

An understanding of the role of the Spirit of God can offset these dangers. The promise of Jesus concerning the Spirit is that the Comforter would take his place and abide with us and *in* us (John 14: 16–17). To the Romans, Paul wrote of the Spirit of God dwelling within (8:9–11). Other passages speak of the same.[11] The role of the Spirit's presence is that the believer is assured of the validity of his faith in Christ. His presence is the guarantee that one shall be resurrected as Christ was. As the believer abides in Christ, he is led to pray with the Spirit who intercedes for him (Rom. 8:26). It is by the Spirit that we are taught the meaning of the Scriptures for our lives (1 John 2:27). It is the Spirit who lifts our heavy hearts to hope for things better when our circumstances do not warrant such (Rom. 15:13). The Spirit directs, when we are willing, in applying the concepts of the New Testament to our world situation (Rom. 8:14; Gal. 5:18). Without the presence of God's Spirit, contact with the taproot of Christianity has been severed. The presence of the Spirit in the life of the believer removes Christian faith from the realm of human striving and places it alone in the category of grace and life.

This emphasis in Christianity is to be distinguished from classical mysticism. Classical mysticism attempts a unification of the believer with God or the World Soul through steps of purgation, contemplation, and, finally, the experience of oneness in ecstasy. Even Christian mysticism as seen in the Middle Ages is different from the New Testament theology on the presence of the Spirit within the believer. Christian mysticism parallels classical mysticism in purification and contemplation but differs in imitating Christ. Imitating Christ refers

[11] Cf. 1 Cor. 3:16–17; 6:19; 2 Tim. 1:14; 1 John 2:27; 3:9; 4:4,12–13,15; James 4:5.

to the use of ascetic exercises in seeking spiritual illumination. Christ is viewed more as an example than as a mediator. In the New Testament, in contrast, "it is clear that we have not to do with an immediacy without a Mediator." [12]

The experience of unification differs also. In classical and medieval mysticism it can involve a vision of the essence of God, or it can mean that the will of the person is dissolved into the Eternal. The goal is absorption of the person into the divine, as a drop of individual spray returns to a unity with the ocean.

Christian mysticism is opposed to the foregoing. At no time in Christian mysticism is the personality to be lost and in no sense does the Spirit become identical with ourselves.[13] The doctrine of the indwelling Spirit loses its meaning apart from the mediatorship of Christ. Mysticism of the classical type tends to reject the historical importance of Christ. It is impossible to gain a closer relationship to God than that which is found in the Spirit of Christ's presence within man. In finding Christ one finds God. Apart from Christ, one never finds God.

On the guidance of the Spirit in the life of the believer, it might be laid down as a principle that the Spirit does not command believers to do that which is contrary to the Scriptures. The Bible sets forth guidelines concerning the work of the Spirit, and one needs to expect harmony between the Spirit's activity and the Scriptures. People who defend their actions on the basis of deep-felt conviction when that action is contrary to the Scriptures must come to question their long deep-felt feelings. It may be that feeling and imagination have gotten the upper hand. One's immediate sense of what the Spirit of God declares, apart from the Scriptures, may be the result of egotistical desire for personal advancement.

One problem relating to personal conviction involves people desiring to enter the ministry. Occasionally one sees men who profess a call to the ministry. In preparation their academic work is poor, their ability to speak is halting, and their facility for getting along with people is low. The possibilities of a church's retaining such a person as pastor are very low. The solution to this problem lies in differen-

---

[12] Brunner, *Christian Doctrine of the Church, Faith, and Consummation*, p. 17.
[13] Cf. Karl Barth, *Church Dogmatics*, trans. G. Bromiley (Edinburgh: T. & T. Clark, 1958), IV-2, 519.

tiating between a call to the ministry and the sincere desire to serve God in a dedicated way. Undue emphasis has been placed on the ministry as the most dedicated of callings. God "calls" to a diversity of vocations. If God has not given native ability for a specific calling—and this includes the ministry—one may question whether God is directing toward this area of service.

The Church and the Spirit

The Scriptures speak of the believer as being baptized in one Spirit into one body. Without the Spirit one cannot enter into the body of Christ. Without implying any idea of election, one may say that it is the Lord who incorporates the believer into the church (Acts 2:47). In this manner, the Spirit is free and is not bound to sacraments.

The story of the church is the epic of how the Spirit of God has acted in history and spoken through it. The church is by no means the successor to Christ. The church is the instrument of the Spirit of Christ who is directing its destiny. "The Spirit is the true vicar of Christ, Christ's *alter ego*, and was known as such in the Church by the fact that he was encountered in the same role of Lord (*Kyrios*) as Christ himself had been." [14] In its outward appearance, the church seems always beset by human troubles. In its inward structure as the body of Christ it has the heartbeat of the Saviour and stands with ultimate perfection. Because of its humanness, the church has not been infallible. There is no doubt about the infallibility of God's Spirit but the humanness of the believer has not always been open to the directing of God's Spirit.[15] The history of church councils will bear out the fact that not every man was delivered from erroneous thinking. One shudders to think about, and hesitates to affirm, the fact that orthodox doctrine is simply the result of which idea got the most votes.

In Roman Catholicism there is a separation of the Spirit from the Scriptures and the Spirit is regarded as the life or soul of the church. Thus it can be maintained that the church continues to be taught by the Spirit without any necessary dependence on the Scriptures. This

---

[14] Hendry, *op. cit.*, p. 65.

[15] Cf. *A Handbook of the Catholic Faith*, p. 124. "The mission of the Holy Spirit is so to guide the leaders of the Church that they do not fall into error, and with them the whole Church of Christ."

amounts to nothing more than a return to the "inner light" as the authority of the church, a concept that Rome is generally careful to disassociate itself from. The biblical image of the work of the Spirit is his association with the Scriptures, the words of Christ, and it is through this media that he speaks. It is true that the Spirit indwells the body of Christ, but the church is taught by the Spirit through the Scriptures, not independent of them.

The modern church needs to know the fellowship of God's Spirit through Christ. The restlessness of the modern church can be explained in part by its refusal to acknowledge the mediating role of God, the Holy Spirit.

Conclusion

The doctrine of the Spirit, like the doctrine of the Trinity, deals with a vital but often neglected part of the Christian faith. Remove this basic element and Christian faith is shorn of its power. Reject the role of the Spirit, and Christian faith becomes an ethical standard which no man can achieve. The indwelling of the Spirit, however, means that man can be transformed, renewed, regenerated. It removes the story of Jesus from being a story about a man of the past and makes the fruit of the life of Christ a present reality for man's redemptive needs.

VIII. The Atonement: The New Covenant

To banish the Atonement from the creative centre of Christianity is in the long run so to attenuate Christ as to dismiss Him from Christianity, and condemn Him to be outgrown.
Forsyth, *The Cruciality of the Cross*

If we study the history of religion with the question, "What does forgiveness mean here and how is it obtained?" we find that the law which governs this question is the following: that the more a religion rises from a sacrificial system into "more spiritual" regions, the easier forgiveness becomes, or as a rule the very idea of it disappears altogether behind mystical ideas or those of a philosophy of identity. If this does not happen then a rigid moralism, impressive enough in its way, is developed (Zarathustra, the Stoics), in which the thought of righteousness leaves no room for forgiveness at all. Thus either we find forgiveness connected with a (more or less primitive) sacrificial cult, or we find religion without sacrifice and without forgiveness.

Brunner, *The Mediator*

An enlightened Judaism can preach a gospel of forgiveness, but our Christian religion has primarily to do with the terms of forgiveness; not with God's readiness to forgive, but with His way of redemption; not with his willingness but with His will; and with His will not merely as His aim, but as His deed; not as intended, but as achieved. The feeble gospel preaches "God is ready to forgive"; the mighty gospel preaches "God has redeemed."

Forsyth, *Cruciality*

The atonement is a central fact of the Christian faith. It is true that "he who understands the cross aright—this is the opinion of the Reformers—understands the Bible, he understands Jesus Christ." [1] However, there are conflicting opinions concerning the significance of the cross. The doctrine of the atonement, unlike some other doctrines settled in council formulations, has never been settled, nor has it been in controversy, as have issues like the person of Christ. There has not been one theory of the atonement that has prevailed universally over other theories. There are only theories: some have prevailed and waned only to receive new emphasis at a later time. All theologians within the Christian tradition agree that Christ died for our sins, as Paul states. Just how he died for and how he redeems man becomes the central problem of the atonement.

Perhaps the easiest way to approach the theories of the atonement is chronological.

Classical Theory

One of the theories held in the early period of the church was the classical or ransom theory. Simply stated, the ransom theory is based on the notion that Christ's death constituted a ransom paid to Satan, in order to cancel the just claims which he had on man. Origen is usually given credit for this theory. "He is the first Christian theologian to teach clearly that the death of Christ is a ransom paid to the devil in exchange for the souls of men, forfeited by sin; that the devil over-reached himself in the transaction owing to the perfect purity of the soul of Christ which it was torture for him to try and retain; while Christ, both for Himself and for all who will follow Him, triumphed over the devil and death." [2]

Although there were other theories existing, the classical view won many influential men to its support. Not all expressed it with sophistication. Gregory of Nyssa used grotesque language in advocating the theory. He wrote: "The Deity was hidden under the veil of our nature that so, as with ravenous fish, the hook of the Deity might be gulped down along with the bait of flesh; and thus, life being introduced into the house of death, and light shining in darkness, that which is diametrically opposed to life and light might

---

[1] Emil Brunner, *The Mediator,* trans. Olive Wyon (Philadelphia: Westminster Press, 1947), p. 435.

[2] J. K. Mozley, *The Doctrine of the Atonement* (London: Gerald Duckworth & Co., 1953), p. 102.

vanish; for it is not in the nature of darkness to remain when light is present, or of death to exist when life is active." [3]

Gregory did recognize that his theory involved deception, but he sought to justify it. He concluded that "the enemy effected his deception for the ruin of our nature but God by His device not only conferred benefit on the lost, but on him, too, who had brought the ruin." [4]

The classical theory generally held sway in some form or other until the time of Anselm and Abelard. It was in Anselm, however, that a new theory came into being that would win out over its opponents. However, in modern times the classical theory has been revived and transformed somewhat by Gustaf Aulén. Aulén seeks to show that this theory underlies the theology of Luther in the Reformation and is the only adequate view for the understanding of the Scriptures. Says Aulén concerning Luther:

His frequent use of the idea of the deception of the devil is closely connected with an important element in his theory, the thought of the Hidden God (*Deus absconditus*). Luther returns to this theme in a number of places, and the term varies somewhat in meaning. But one side of his meaning is that the Revealed God (*Deus revelatus*) meets us in the world as a Hidden God; God was present, hidden, in the despised man Christ, in his lowliness, and in his self-devotion to suffering and to death. This is the idea that underlies the image of the devil's deception. In Him the mightiest of all powers was present hidden: but the "enemies" did not understand this fact when they assailed Him. Hence the language about the devil's deception is the expression of a very deep thought of Luther.[5]

The classical theory died out for many reasons. Of primary importance is the appearance of Anselm's succinct work on the atonement, *Cur Deus Homo?*, which took the doctrine seriously. A second factor in the demise of the classical theory was its incompleteness. While the term is used in the Scriptures, there are many other terms that deal with the meaning of the death of Christ, and these are basically ignored in the classical theory. Last, the theory did not commend itself to wide acceptance because of its crudeness, its implied

[3] Sydney Cave, *The Doctrine of the Work of Christ* (Nashville: Cokesbury Press, 1938), p. 127.
[4] *Ibid.*
[5] *Christus Victor* (New York: The Macmillan Co., 1958), p. 110.

duplicity, its tacit admission that perhaps the devil had some right-
ful hold on man. Better things were ahead for the doctrine of the
atonement. To these we now turn.

Anselm and the Concept of Honor

The theory of Anselm has had a number of labels, such as the
"commercial theory," "the satisfaction theory," "the Latin theory."
Anselm's work, *Cur Deus Homo?—Why God Became Man*—appeared in the twelfth century. Anselm placed great emphasis on the
absolute necessity of the atonement. The need for the atonement,
according to Anselm, is the nature of God. Man's sin was in not
giving to God the honor due him by his very nature. Dishonoring
God is sin. Withholding honor to God puts man in debt to him.
Because God is infinite, his honor takes on infinite proportions, and
sin against God becomes infinite in consequence.

Anselm wrote: "This is the debt which man and angel owe to God,
and no one who pays this debt commits sin . . . and this is the sole
and complete debt of honor which we owe to God. . . . He who
does not render this honor which is due to God, robs God of his
own and dishonors him; and this is sin." [6]

Since it was "right" for man to repay God the honor he took
from him in the act of disobedience, God, as the righteous judge of
the universe, *must* demand satisfaction. Otherwise, he would be
acting contrary to his nature. Thus, according to Anselm, since the
offense was against an infinite being, the satisfaction must be infinite.
But it is impossible for man who is finite to make infinite satisfaction.
Anselm concluded: "For God will not do it, because he has no debt
to pay; and man will not do it, because he cannot. Therefore, in
order that the God-man may perform this, it is necessary that the
same being should be perfect God and perfect man, in order to make
this atonement." [7]

In mercy God sent Christ, who being both sinless and infinite
could make an infinite satisfaction through his suffering and death on
man's behalf. Since Christ was not under obligation to die, because
of his sinlessness, he did more than was required of him, thus ac-
quiring extra merit or favor in God's sight. Not needing merit, it is
given to man whereby man's sins are remitted.

---

[6] *Cur Deus Homo?* (LaSalle, Ill.: Open Court Publishing Co., 1958), p. 202.
[7] *Ibid.*, p. 246.

A summary of Anselm's thought does not do justice to the simplicity and the masterful handling of a theological discourse. In review of Anselm's work, the following reservations must be offered. The theory seems to be dominated by Anselm's contemporary feudal life, where the relation of the king and subject was overdrawn. This influence is seen in Anselm as well as the customs of Germanic law and the penitential system that had grown up in Western theology.[8]

More serious is the motivation of the theory. The atonement must have as its basis God's holy love, not his honor, for the New Testament does not begin with anything else than God's love. Another problem relates to the concepts of satisfaction and merit. If Christ made full satisfaction for the past sins of man, what happens when new trespasses come? When Anselm speaks then of the "merit" he goes beyond the requirement of his theory of satisfaction. Anselm's theory of merit is alien to the New Testament idea of atonement.

Other questions may be raised which are serious. For example, why must God insist on full satisfaction of his honor when Jesus commanded his disciples to forgive seventy times seven? It may be rightfully argued in rebuttal to this question that we should forgive because we are sinners, whereas God is not under the same condition. But the question still persists, especially when we think of God in terms of love rather than honor.

A contemporary of Anselm, Peter Abelard (1079-1142), raised critical questions about Anselm's theory as well as set forth his own view. In criticism, Abelard asks how God could be pleased with the death of his Son "when God ought to have been the more angered against man, inasmuch as men acted more criminally by crucifying his Son than they ever did by transgressing his first command in paradise through the tasting of a single apple." [9] Abelard proceeds to ask, "If that sin of Adam was so great that it could be expiated only by the death of Christ, what expiation will avail for that act of murder committed against Christ, and for the many great crimes committed against him or his followers? How did the death of his innocent Son so please God the Father that through it he should be reconciled to us?" [10]

---

8 Cf. Mozley, *op. cit.*, p. 128.

9 *A Scholastic Miscellany: Anselm to Ockham,* ed. E. R. Fairweather ("The Library of Christian Classics," [Philadelphia: Westminster Press, 1956]), X, 282.

10 *Ibid.*, pp. 282–83.

To top off his criticism, Abelard said: "Indeed, how cruel and wicked it seems that anyone should demand the blood of an innocent person as the price for anything, or that it should in any way please him that an innocent man should be slain—still less that God should consider the death of his Son so agreeable that by it he should be reconciled to the whole world!" [11]

These are serious questions that Abelard raised. While they pose serious questions to Anselm's theory, they can be answered adequately in another theological context. Having dealt with his criticisms, let us turn to the theory of Abelard.

Peter Abelard and Example Theory

We have seen that Abelard rejected the views held by those before him as well as those of his contemporary. Abelard began with the fact of God's love and grace. In his commentary on Romans, he wrote: "Through this unique act of grace manifested to us—in that his Son has taken upon himself our nature and preserved therein teaching us by word and example even unto death—he has more fully bound us to himself by love; with the result that our hearts should be enkindled by such a gift of divine grace, and true charity should not now shrink from enduring anything for him." [12]

Abelard continued his exposition of this theme in declaring that Christ's appearance now wins man his freedom from slavery and man now acts "out of love rather than fear." Abelard believed that the separation between man and God was solely in man. God was desirous for men to return to him, and Christ simply reveals this continuing love on God's part. Abelard points to Abraham and Cornelius as examples of men who had faith and were accepted by God apart from baptism. God's love is expressed in its fullest by the words of Jesus: "Greater love has no man than this, that a man lay down his life for his friends" (John 15:13). What is the meaning of Christ's death for man? Abelard answered:

In two ways He is said to have died for our faults; first, because ours were the faults on account of which He died and we committed the sin of which He bore the punishment; secondly, that by dying He might take our sins, that is, the punishment of sins, introducing us into Paradise at the price of His own death, and by the exhibition of such grace, because

[11] *Ibid.*
[12] *Ibid.*, p. 283.

as He says, "no one has greater love" (John 15:13), might draw our minds away from the will to sin and incline them to the fullest love of Himself.[13]

The simplicity of Abelard's theory is disarming. God wishes to forgive. Nothing stands in the way of man's receiving that forgiveness other than man himself. No atonement is necessary. God's love has been expressed in Christ and not attained by Christ's death. Christ has come to give man the assurance that God yet cares.

How does Abelard fare in the hands of his critics? Bernard of Clairvaux assailed Abelard, contending that Christ is nothing more than a teacher in Abelard's theory. He drew a parallel between Adam and Christ and argued that the example of Adam made one a sinner. He further charged that Abelard was teaching a salvation by devotion, not by regeneration. All examples of humility and devotion are useless apart from the act of redemption. For Bernard the real issue was instruction *or* restoration. Actually Bernard insisted on both, but he rejected an example theory for the meaning of Christ's death.

Other critics have hit upon its one-sidedness with reference to the biblical data. It appears naïve concerning the nature of man and his corruption in sin. If Abelard's theory were true, there would be no atonement in the true meaning of the word; all that remains is what has always been true—God's love to man. In this case, Abelard's question of Anselm returns home. Could God be pleased even in this death?

John Calvin and the Penal Theory

John Calvin regarded the obedience of Christ as the proper beginning point in the discussion of the atonement. He was obedient even unto death (Phil. 2:8). Without obedience, his life and death would have been meaningless. Because Jesus Christ was the Son of God and without sin, he came obediently to redeem man. How does he redeem in his death? Calvin said, "Our acquittal is in this—that the guilt which made us liable to punishment was transferred to the head of the Son of God" (cf. Isa. 53:12).[14] Calvin proceeded to draw a parallel between the death of Christ and the sacrifices in the Old Testament. Jesus Christ became the "propitiatory victim for

---

[13] Cave, *op. cit.*, p. 159.
[14] *Institutes of the Christian Religion*, I, 439.

sin . . . on which the guilt and penalty being in a manner laid, ceases to be imputed to us." [15] In this is found the "penal" idea; namely, that Christ took the penalty due to man.

Bearing the penalty of sin is not the whole story. Calvin stressed the role of the resurrection of Christ which is the completion of salvation. It is "not by his death, but by his resurrection, that we are said to be begotten again to a living hope." [16] Because the resurrection is a reality, the risen Christ has promised the Comforter to abide in the believer, enabling the "faithful followers not only to live well but also to die happily." [17]

Calvin dealt with one of the problems often associated with the idea of expiation or propitiation. Propitiation often implies a sacrifice to secure the favor of God. Calvin described the death of Christ as a propitiatory death. How is this related to God's mercy? Calvin declared that "such modes of expression are accommodated to our capacity, that we may the better understand how miserable and calamitous our condition is without Christ." [18] The love of God is the motivation for the atonement, but God cannot love sin—he must deal with it. This is the wrath of God spoken about in the Bible. Calvin wrote: "Therefore, in order that all ground of offense may be removed, and he may completely reconcile us to himself, he, by means of the expiation set forth in the death of Christ, abolishes all the evil that is in us, so that we, formerly impure and unclean, now appear in his sight just and holy." [19]

The theory of Calvin has had widespread influence. It has been accepted far beyond the boundaries of the Reformed churches. Even those opposed to Reformed theology in many ways accept the penal theory of the death of Christ.

How does Calvin pass with the critics? The central criticism remains that of Abelard in his criticism of Anselm—the problem of substitution. God seems just in requiring that sin be punished, but justice seems neglected when an innocent person is punished to make atonement for the sinner. It may be granted that substitution is possible in certain areas such as debt payment, serving one's country, and so on. But the question is raised, can there be substitution for

15 *Ibid.*
16 *Ibid.*, 446.
17 *Ibid.*, 448.
18 *Ibid.*, 435.
19 *Ibid.*, 436.

the penalty imposed because of sin? Supporters of the view say that Jesus Christ is different at this point: He can be what no one could be—our substitute for sin's penalty.

A secondary criticism is that much support for the theory is based on the Old Testament sacrificial system rather than on the words of Jesus concerning his own view of his death. A thorough-going view of the atonement must begin with the New Testament and assimilate Old Testament data only as the New Testament warrants it.

Another problem, in common with almost all the other views, is the Trinitarian "illusion." The statements of the New Testament speak of God's sending his Son to save man, creating the illusion of an innocent third party. While the Incarnation and redemptive act are attributed to the Son, the illusion must be offset by the frank statement that "God was in Christ reconciling the world to himself" (2 Cor. 5:19). It is God who loves, God who comes, God who takes our sin to himself, God who forgives. There is no act of injustice, although the "illusion of discourse" seems to imply it.

In conclusion, we need to ask whether the concept of penalty is adequate in explaining the death of Christ. It has been time-honored in the history of Protestant thought since the Reformation. Is there a better, more comprehensive method of dealing with the meaning of Christ's life and death? We hope to set forth such a proposal in the latter part of this chapter.

Socinus and the "No Atonement" Theory

Faustus Socinus (1539–1604) was an Italian emigré who settled in Poland. Socinus was a rationalist in theology along with a strong appeal to the Scriptures. In the Racovian Catechism, which was drawn up in 1605, the viewpoint of Socinus was set forth. Its reference to the atonement is significant in its criticism of other views rather than for any profundity in the development of a positive view.

In opposition to the other views of the atonement, Socinus protested that if God had forgiven in the old covenant without satisfaction, how much more would he forgive in the covenant of grace. He asked: "Why should God have willed to kill His innocent Son by a cruel and execrable death, when there was no need of satisfaction? In this way, both the generosity of the Son perishes, and, instead of a most benign and munificent God, with supreme impiety and unspeakable sacrilege, we concoct for ourselves a God who is base and sordid." [20]

Socinus regarded it to be "false, erroneous, and exceedingly pernicious" [21] to believe that Christ died to pay the debt of man's sins. He charged that satisfaction and forgiveness are opposites. If satisfaction is made for wrong, then one cannot speak of forgiveness. Socinus concluded that God forgives men freely; thus satisfaction is rejected.

What is the meaning of Christ's life and death? Jesus Christ, a being blessed by God, is the Teacher of men. He has appeared to show men the way of faith and obedience. Faith is the way "by which we both embrace with our soul the promises of Christ, and henceforth seek, to the best of our ability, to keep His precepts." [22] Actual obedience on the part of the follower is stressed. Faith and obedience make redemption a matter of human achievement, but it is coupled with forgiveness when man has failed. Jesus Christ is transformed from the "way-maker" into a "way-show-er."

In an evaluation of Socinus, one might say that he failed to rise above his basic criticisms of others but with the additional involvements of taking the good news out of the gospel. Socinus stringently criticized the problem of an innocent death in other theories, but he offered no better explanation of Christ's innocent death than to say that he demonstrated his love for man by dying the most ignominious death. Just how his death is an expression of God's love is not said. Even if it could be shown to be an expression of Christ's love, it would still make God a tyrant—a thing Socinus wanted to avoid.

With the exception of its regard for Jesus Christ, Socinianism is a return to the level of Judaism. The gospel that God has done something unique in Jesus Christ is lost. The questions that Socinus raised were meaningful, but his answers were more reactionary than constructive. If we are to understand the New Testament, we must go beyond Socinus.

Thus far we have endeavored to set forth the "types" of atonement that have had significant influence in the development of doctrine.

---

[20] Cave, *op. cit.*, pp. 201–2.

[21] Robert L. Ferm, *Readings in the History of Christian Thought* (New York: Holt, Rinehart & Winston, 1964), p. 248.

[22] Adolph Harnack, *History of Dogma,* trans. Neil Buchanan (New York: Russell & Russell, 1958), VII, 159.

Many variations have been made. It is true also that the terms used to describe the theories are not consistent from author to author. It is still an open question as to whether the atonement has been adequately treated in the history of Christian thought. We now turn to an attempt to do better justice to the data of the New Testament.

Canon Mozley has wisely said that if the atonement is to mean anything to the individual, one must "do justice to three things—to the meaning of the Bible, to the meaning of the moral consciousness, and to the meaning of Christian religious experience." [23] Not all interpretations of the cross will fit Mozley's canons of adequacy. In fact, it seems that the prevailing views of the atonement have been influenced by the culture of the times over against the first canon, the meaning of the Bible. The classic view of the atonement seems unduly influenced at the point of deception.

The Anselmic view is structured on the lines of an outdated feudal system. Abelard ignores certain emphases in the Bible, even though he adheres to the Bible for certain of his ideas. The penal theory of Calvin and others seems to be molded by legal ideas that go beyond the legal implications of the New Testament. The starting point of each theory is inadequate in itself. The concepts of satisfaction, example, penalty, and so on are only part of the complete picture. They are, at best, branches on the tree, and the trunk is a wholly different thing.

The life and death of Jesus Christ require an adequate explanation insofar as one is capable of making it. Although we may acknowledge that the death of Christ involves mystery beyond full comprehension, we are yet compelled to go as far as we can in understanding it.

Presupposition of the Atonement

The only adequate presupposition for the life and death of Christ is holy love. The atonement is not a matter of love only; it is holy love. Love alone can be misconstrued, and God becomes a doting old grandfather who will overlook and forgive anything without requiring a new creation on the part of the believer. In this case, God wants his creature's love at the price of overlooking his sin. Holy love does not overlook the seriousness of sin, as Anselm was so concerned

---

[23] *Op. cit.*, p. 204.

to emphasize. Holy love thus requires moral regeneration. Holy love is that which purifies and purges from the believer that which is contrary to the nature of God.

These concepts are expressed in John 3:16. The motive of the Incarnation—hence atonement—is love. To be merely loving, God could have declared that sin is forgiven. But to be holy in his love, God dealt with the sinfulness of man, thus getting to the root of the problem—the transformation of the self. Forsyth declared, "Even a loving God is really God, not because He loves, but because He has the power to subdue all things to the holiness of His love . . . even sin itself to His love in redeeming grace." [24]

Holy love is necessarily set against other presuppositions. The atonement cannot be viewed as a "deflection of God's anger." [25] There is no warranty for suggesting that God be divided up whereby a wrathful Father is opposed to a loving Son. Parallel to this is the idea that the atonement secures God's grace for sinful man. If there is any one truth evident it is that the atonement is a *result* of God's grace. It is falsely assumed that the sacrificial system of the Old Testament began with the idea of appeasing an angry God. Instead, the theory behind the system is that God *instituted* it so that man could have an entrée into his presence.

One of the difficulties of the appeasement idea or propitiation concept is explaining how another can be substituted in punishment. Even if it be argued that in human law or feudal law someone can substitute for another, there is yet the corollary question of explaining why I must yet die if Christ died for me. Why does not his death erase the possibility of my death? If death be spoken of in terms of spiritual alienation rather than the physical event, then why must physical substitution be insisted upon for the sinner?

If satisfaction is the key presupposition, as it was with Anselm, then the problem comes as stated by Mozley. "If . . . God's honor is the consideration, it is not obvious why repentance should not be accepted as a satisfaction to that honor." [26] If the God-man makes the full satisfaction, then there is no room for forgiveness on the part of God the Father. It seems to boil down to the fact that there is

---

[24] P. T. Forsyth, *The Cruciality of the Cross* (New York: Hodder & Stoughton, 1910), p. 60.

[25] Mozley, *op. cit.*, p. 184.

[26] *Ibid.*, p. 130.

no forgiveness; instead, man is given a reward because of the Son who justly earned all that is given.

On the other hand, the biblical data of the atonement seems to set forth something more far-reaching than merely an example, as in Abelard. There is so much more in the New Testament that relates to the idea of sacrifice than moral example. The New Testament is given over to recounting the death of Christ in such a way that it seems to be central to the entire twenty-seven books. Although the mind of modern man rebels against the idea of atonement, it is the essential story. "The essence of the Gospel consists in this, that here is a real event, a sign of the real gulf between God and man and a sign of the real movement of God, an event which shows up both the seriousness of our position and the unspeakable wonder of the Divine Love." [27] The atonement is a serious judgment against such low concepts concerning God that "God will forgive, that is his business." [28]

Methodology

The assumption seems to be made by many writers that it is impossible to build a coherent view of the atonement from one presupposition. Some writers oppose the atonement ideas as understood in the Pauline epistles to that of the Gospels and Hebrews. Others analyze the various phraseologies in the New Testament without an attempt at synthesis. The theories developed around a single motif have often been inadequate to the diversity of scriptural data.

A procedure of study for many has been that as set forth by Leon Morris in his book *The Apostolic Preaching of the Cross*. Morris treats the Hebrew terminology in the Old Testament, then the Septuagint equivalents, rabbinical concepts, and then finally the usage in the New Testament.[29]

A proper method of study must begin with the New Testament. It is true that the New Testament is a continuum of the Old Testament, but with a difference. This difference involves the freedom of interpretation of Old Testament passages by New Testament writers. Two examples will illustrate this fact.

In the case of messianic expectations, we see the difference be-

---

27 Brunner, *The Mediator*, p. 487.
28 Cave, *op. cit.*, p. 301. (The words of Heine.)
29 (Grand Rapids: Wm. B. Eerdmans Publishing Co., 1955).

tween the fulfilment and the prophetic hope. The hope was largely political and when the Messiah was crucified, even the disciples lamented, "We had hoped that he was the one to redeem Israel" (Luke 24:21). He did redeem Israel in an unexpected and different way from the Old Testament hopes. The other example is that drawn from Jeremiah. In this work we are told that a difference shall prevail. Jeremiah declares that the new covenant will be "not like the covenant which I made with their fathers" (31:31 ff.). We are to expect, therefore, both continuity and discontinuity between the two Testaments. We must not interpret the New Testament by the Old or any other non-Christian document. Rather, we must let the New Testament speak first and let its judgment fall where it will on Old Testament concepts of sacrifice and atonement.

The Central Motif

Is there a single motif that is adequate to explain the diverse terminology concerning the meaning of the death of Christ? We propose that *the life and death of Jesus must be seen in terms of the fulfilment and establishment of the new covenant.* This concept is adopted because it is the most extensive word of Jesus concerning his own understanding of his death. The fulfilled new covenant is expressed most poignantly in the Last Supper.

The Lord's Supper is the institution enjoined upon the church whereby it remembers the content and significance of his death. It seems safe to say that his death can be understood from the perspective of his institution concerning the meaning of both the supper and his death. The account of the Last Supper and its declared meaning is given in all three Synoptics, in 1 Corinthians, and is implied in John's Gospel. In each case, Jesus declared concerning the cup, "This is my blood of the covenant" (Mark 14:24; Matt. 26:28; Luke 22:20; 1 Cor. 11:25). In the Synoptics this is connected with the fact that remission of sin is involved in the pouring out of the blood of the covenant. Inasmuch as the account has due emphasis in relation to his death, it must not be ignored.

The primacy of the covenant about to be established has its beginning in the words of Jesus. It is confirmed in other areas of the New Testament. "Christ has obtained a ministry which is as much more excellent than the old as the covenant he mediates is better, since it is enacted on better promises" (Heb. 8:6–7). We are also told that Jesus is the "surety of a better covenant" (Heb. 7:22). The death of Jesus was, therefore, a death involving the establishment of the new covenant. Not only was the covenant prophesied by both Jeremiah and Ezekiel, but the terms are interpreted to us in the New Testament.

The particular role of Jesus' death is important. He poured out his life to ratify the covenant which was foretold. The "cutting" or making of a covenant in the Old Testament was made with the death of an animal (Jer. 34:18). In this the blood of the covenant was an important feature. In this regard, the Passover ritual is perhaps important. In the original Passover, there is no mention of atonement. For this reason, it is significant that Jesus died during a Passover week rather than the Day of Atonement. The Passover display of the blood on the door lintel could well refer to the renewal of the covenant. When the blood was displayed, the covenant was brought to mind, and the angel of death passed over (Ex. 12:13).

In the same manner that the Old Testament covenant was established and renewed from time to time, so the new covenant was established by a more sure promise. Instead of the death of an animal, the death of God's Son is the means for its establishment. It is in this precise form that the new covenant is better than the old.

Luther, in explaining the meaning of the Lord's Supper, places these words as though Jesus spoke them:

Behold, O sinful and condemned man, out of the pure and unmerited love with which I love you, and by the will of the Father of mercies . . . , apart from any merit or desire of yours, I promise you in these words the forgiveness of all your sins and life everlasting. And that you may be absolutely certain of this irrevocable promise of mine, I shall give my body and pour out my blood, confirming this promise by my very death, and leaving you my body and blood as a sign and memorial of this same promise.[30]

The new covenant idea can incorporate the meaning of the various terminologies in the New Testament under its heading. The passages speaking of *blood* can be understood as the establishment of the covenant. The passages relating to *justification* present the believer's

---

[30] Martin Luther, "The Babylonian Captivity of the Church," *The Three Treatises* (Philadelphia: Muhlenberg Press, 1960), p. 158.

standing in the covenant. The passages speaking in terms of *redemption* set forth the power of the new covenant by the Spirit. The passages speaking of *reconciliation* declare the meaning of the new covenant to alienated mankind.

First, consider the place of the *blood,* the establishment of the covenant. Traditionally, the blood of Christ has had an important place in the idea of atoning for sin. First John speaks of "the blood of Jesus his Son" cleansing us from all sin (1:7). The question has been raised concerning how the blood cleanses. There is no rational reason why the blood of animals or that of the human body of Christ should cleanse. Some have declared that the blood atones "simply because it is God's appointment or ordinance." [31]

There is more significance and meaning in the word "blood" if it is seen as ratifying or establishing the covenant of God. The terms of 1 John 1:7 are written in a covenantal relationship. Each statement begins with an "if." We have the same thought expressed in a different context in Hebrews 10:29. The blood is the blood of the covenant and is declared to be the means whereby we are sanctified or set apart unto God in a covenantal relationship. The blood of the covenant thereby speaks of forgiveness of sin, which is cleansing itself.

In considering the other passages of the New Testament, it is not difficult to see them in the light of ratifying the covenant.

Apart from the Last Supper accounts in the Synoptics, which it must be recalled is our starting point of the new covenant, the first significant mention of the blood of Christ is in John 6. The only realistic understanding of the passage is in reference to the Lord's Supper. At no time was there any hint of cannibalism in the life of Jesus (vv. 52–53). By the same token, verse 63 tells us that the words are *spirit.* They were meant to be understood as an analogy. To what are they analogous? Again, an answer is the Last Supper, where he spoke of the covenant of his death and life. By receiving the elements, that is, flesh and blood, we are accepting the covenant that God made with us.

In Romans 3:25 if *hilasterion* (in KJV, propitiation) be understood as mercy seat, or the place where God shows mercy, then the blood is really the blood of the covenant whereby we know we

[31] Mozley, *op. cit.,* p. 12. (Mozley sums up the point of view of Davidson and his work on the atonement.)

have obtained mercy. If not, the question remains, how does blood expiate the guilt of the sinful?

In Romans 5:9, we are justified by his blood. It should be observed that there is a close relation between justification by faith and the concept of blood as related to the new covenant. Justification means that one is accepted in the presence of God. We are accepted through Christ by faith, and that even when we are not sinless. The cleansing of the blood of Christ holds the same analogy. The blood of Christ does not perfect us but rather speaks of the new covenant whereby God accepts us in repentance and faith and thereby gives us his Spirit that continues to work in us and sanctify us. The new covenant only points to our ultimate transformation, just as justification points to our ultimate sanctification.

In Ephesians 1:7, we are told of redemption through his blood. But it is within a context of the Son and our blessings through him before the foundation of the world. God chose us from eternity (v. 4), but the fact is only revealed in time through his blood, which is the covenant of our redemption and the guarantee of the forgiveness of sin (1:7). The basis for the redemption and the covenant is also given—"the riches of his grace."

The seeming intent of Ephesians 2:13 is to contrast the Gentiles without a covenantal relationship to God with the fact that the blood of Christ now makes them members of the covenantal community.

In Colossians the blood of Christ can be associated with a covenantal relationship also (1:20–23). We are reconciled by the blood of the cross, "provided [we] continue in the faith, . . . not shifting from the hope of the gospel which [we] heard." This suggests a covenant which God has made and man affirms it by faith or rejects it by unacceptance.

In 1 Peter 1:2 a similar situation prevails. Obedience and sprinkling of blood are connected just in the same way a covenant is issued. The sacrifice of Christ was destined before the foundation of the world (1 Peter 1:19–24). In this context, confidence in God is expressed because Christ was raised from the dead. The purifying of our souls is that related to obedience to the truth. In this case the truth would be the acceptance of the covenant based on Christ's death.

In Revelation 1:5, the question is again to be asked, "How are we washed from our sins in his blood?" (KJV). The Revised Standard

Version translates the amended text as "freed," which agrees with a covenant of forgiveness as we have set it forth.

The blood of Christ receives the longest treatment in Hebrews (chapters 9, 10, and 13). Christ is the mediator of the new covenant (9:15), which is established by his blood (9:14). The new covenant was only possible because of Christ's death, just as the first covenant was not ratified without blood. As under the law everything was set apart, regarded as holy before God, with blood, so the shedding of the blood of Christ is the means by which the believer is set apart, regarded as accepted in God's presence, and thereby receives the forgiveness of sin. In Hebrews 10:14–18 the final offering of Christ is again associated with the establishment of the covenant. In Hebrews 13:20 the blood is emphatically connected with the covenant. The writer declares, "The God of Peace who brought again from the dead our Lord Jesus, the great shepherd of the sheep, by the blood of the eternal covenant."

Thus, we have observed the more significant passages on the blood of Christ and have seen that they can be understood from the standpoint of referring to a ratification of the covenant.

Second, *justification*: the believer's standing in the covenant. In relation to any idea of the atonement in the New Testament, one must consider the usage of the word "justification." The most pertinent passages are in Romans. Abraham is said to have been justified by believing (4:3). By asking certain questions concerning his justification, one must conclude that Abraham was justified when he was the passive recipient of the covenant of God (Gen. 15:6 ff.). Abraham was not made perfect, or sinless, but was reckoned as such because of obedience in the covenantal relationship of faith.

In Romans 4:5, we are told that God justifies the ungodly. Abraham is the father of the faithful (v. 16), and we are reckoned as righteous also (v. 24). The same analogy, under which Abraham was accepted because of the covenant, holds for us also.

The fact that we are given acceptance before God while we are yet ungodly demands explanation. God offers the new covenant and we accept it by faith. (Throughout our lives we are always involved in sin of one degree or another.) The evidence and surety of the covenant and its guarantee to us are the death and resurrection of Christ. Had it been merely the death of Christ alone, we could not have any assurance and hope. The resurrection distinguished the death of Christ from being merely the death of a good man. It sets forth the seal of the covenant's validity as well as the fact that he is the Son of God.

Third, *redemption*: the power of the new covenant by the Spirit. A great emphasis is often placed on the Old Testament and papyri usage, but we will not impose either these or etymological usages on the New Testament use. Thayer defines *Apolutrosis* in the New Testament as "deliverance effected through the death of Christ from the retributive wrath of a holy God and the merited penalty of sin." [32] This is the very thing expressed in the new covenant. In it God has promised to put away our sins and grant forgiveness. What is this but the removal of the wrath of God? Such is the declaration to us in the death of Christ.

In some instances the idea of redemption is linked with the concept of blood, thus making possible a tighter link in this theory. Such is the connection in some manuscripts for Ephesians 1:7 and Colossians 1:14. In Hebrews 9:15, redemption is linked with the establishment of the new covenant. In Hebrews 9:12, an eternal redemption is said to be the result, because he entered the holy place taking his own blood.

A related term of redemption is *ekagorazo*, which occurs twice in relation to redemption proper. "Christ redeemed us from the curse of the law, having become a curse for us" (Gal. 3:13). We are not told how we are redeemed from the curse of the law but there is a basis for understanding that we are no longer under its control because we are under a new covenant, the old having passed away. In Galatians (4:4–5) we are told that Christ redeemed us from the law. We receive "adoption as sons" because we are "children of Abraham" (3:29), and thereby heirs of the covenant of faith (3:24–25).

Another passage relating to redemption certainly lends itself to a covenantal understanding. Titus 2:13–14 speaks of the great "God and Savior Jesus Christ, who gave himself for us to redeem us from all iniquity and to purify for himself a people of his own who are zealous for good deeds."

What does "redeem" mean? The word *lutroo* means to loose or redeem, liberate by payment or ranson. We are redeemed only at the present in a forensic sense, and we are purified only in an

---

[32] *Op. cit.,* p. 65.

ultimate sense. In the atonement of the new covenant we are liberated from our iniquities at the price of the Son of God who makes the covenant with his life. We are purified as God's Spirit continues to work in our heart.

A similar word, *lutron,* occurs twice in the four Gospels. Jesus said that the Son of man came to "give his life as a ransom for many" (Matt. 20:28, Mark 10:45). We are not told how this ransom price is to be received. We could argue that it is to be interpreted from the standpoint of the covenant and the tremendous price involved in the death of Jesus, which established the new covenant.

Another similar word is *antilutron,* which occurs in 1 Timothy 2:5-6, concerning "the man Christ Jesus, who gave himself as a ransom for all, the testimony to which was borne at the proper time" (RSV). The word *antilutron* is translated ransom, or as Thayer defines it, "What is given in exchange for another as the price of his redemption." It does not seem adequate to isolate the word *antilutron* from what follows in the context. If we consider the passage from the standpoint of the new covenant, the passage makes good sense. Christ is the one mediator, and also the mediator of the new covenant. The testimony of the new covenant, as well as the guarantee, comes at the point of his death and resurrection.

Yet to be considered are two related words, *hilasmos* and *hilasterion.* The first occurs in 1 John 2:2 and 4:10; the second in Romans 3:25. There is debate about the translation of *hilasterion,* whether it should be translated "propitiation" or "mercy seat." [33] The more significant debate concerns whether either word should be translated expiation or propitiation. One of the key issues is whether or not God should be accorded wrath. The argument centers around the atonement. In line with our explanation of the atonement, the argument is misplaced. The real question of wrath does not come at the atonement but at the *judgment.* The new covenant is established and sets forth God's love for man. If the new covenant is rejected, then the wrath of God appears. If the Son of God is spurned and the blood of the covenant is profaned, then appears the wrath of God (Heb. 10:29).

The basic meaning behind expiation or propitiation is that atonement has been made in some way or the other. Greek lexicons do not

---

[33] Morris, *op. cit.,* pp. 125 ff.

help in making a distinction between expiation and propitiation, for Arndt and Gingrich define *hilasmos* as "expiation, propitiation." [34]

The point of the passage is that of dealing with our sins. Christ is the atonement and the atoner. Our sins are put away from us. Is this not what the new covenant means? God has remembered our sins no more. They are forgiven upon entry into the new covenant. The same meaning holds true for 1 John 4:10. God has forgiven our sins; this is shown by the death of Christ as a sign of the new covenant.

Fourth, *reconciliation*: the meaning of the new covenant. Morris declares, "The chief difficulty to be solved in the New Testament use of reconcile, reconciliation, etc., is whether, in the process of reconciliation, God can be said to be reconciled to man, or whether the process is one in which man only is reconciled." [35]

There is no problem in seeing that man has alienated himself from God. Sin has produced a chasm that must be bridged for man. In laying down a new covenant the way is opened for man. This is an obvious truth of Ephesians 2:16: "reconcile us both to God;" Colossians 1:21–22: "you . . . he has now reconciled;" and 2 Corinthians 5:19: "God was in Christ reconciling the world to himself."

There is, however, no reference to the fact that God is reconciled. Yet, such is implied in some sense of the word. God has not and does not tolerate the sin of man. He has reconciled himself in some sense by virtue of his willingness to put away the sin of man. Our view does not take a light view of sin: instead it is so serious that only God can put away sin and receive man. In this case we have the same analogy of the new covenant to the old covenant. God made a covenant with Abraham before the law of sacrifice was instituted. Abraham was accepted because of his faith in God's covenant. With the making of a covenant there was shedding of blood of animals (Gen. 15:8–18) for its establishment. We do *not* read that Abraham won God's favor through sacrifice. Abraham was accepted, forgiven, and received in God's presence, and the covenant was the sign to Abraham that all of this was true.

In the new covenant we have the same story. God made a covenant in the person of his Son; man is to be received, his sins forgiven on

---

[34] William F. Arndt and F. Wilbur Gingrich, *A Greek-English Lexicon of the New Testament* (Chicago: University of Chicago Press, 1957), p. 376.
[35] Morris, *op. cit.*, p. 192.

the basis of the covenant which is established by the shedding of blood. We who were alienated, who were enemies, children of sin, are promised forgiveness, newness of life through the regeneration of God's Spirit, who is the promise of the covenant—all on the condition of receiving the new covenant.

Implications of the New Covenant

Having dealt with the new covenant in relationship to the various terminologies, it is now germane to turn to the treatment of the new covenant in relation to other aspects of the role of Christ.

First, the death of Christ as the establishment of the new covenant fulfils the eternal purpose of God.

Relating to the promise of God from eternity.—The matter of redemption is something that took place from eternity. We were chosen in him before the foundation of the world (Eph. 1:4); and the life and death of Christ is the manifestation in time and space of the grace of God to us. The introduction to Titus speaks of the eternal life that God promised "ages ago" (1:2). The ability to lay down his life and receive it again comes only from the transcendent Father (John 10:17–18). But he came for the purpose of laying down his life. The words, "It is finished!" (John 19:30), indicate a consummation of purpose. Paul spoke of himself as a preacher of the mystery that is revealed only now in Christ (Eph. 3:3–6). In due time "God sent forth his Son, born of a woman" (Gal. 4:4). God did not spare his own Son but delivered him up for us (Rom. 8:32). Jesus described his life in terms of being sent to suffer many things (Luke 17:25). The Son came to seek and to save the lost (Luke 19:10). This was his purpose before the Incarnation. From his youth he was aware of being about his Father's business (Luke 2:49). Part of his work was to destroy the works of the devil (1 John 3:8). This he does by the gift of the Spirit who renews and directs our lives and gives us grace to overcome.

In his classic passage in Philippians, Paul speaks of the fact that Christ humbled himself, forsaking the glory of heaven to bring redemption to earth (2:6–11). In the Son dwells all the fulness of deity who came to reconcile all things to himself (Col. 1:15–20).

These and many other sources could be used to show that the life and death of Christ was a work of God, planned from eternity. In viewing the death of Christ from the standpoint of establishing the new covenant, we do justice to the exactness of God's treatment with his people in all dispensations: law and grace.

Relating to the first and second man.—The biblical point of view toward sin is that something quite radical took place in Adam. Paul speaks of all dying in Adam, and all being made alive in Christ (1 Cor. 15:21–22). Although a covenant is not described in the first chapters of Genesis, the same elements are there.

The permissiveness concerning Adam's behavior, as expressed in Genesis 2:16, may be contrasted to the "you shall not eat" in Genesis 2:17. These two verses imply terms of obedience and rebellion. If we may presume a reference to covenant relations, we may also conclude that the covenant relation was broken by sin. Covenants that were made later were broken. The people of God occasionally reaffirmed their covenant relationship but then turned aside into sin. It was because of the failure of the previous covenants that a new one was prophesied. The old covenant was helpless in making men righteous. The law of the Spirit of life in Christ Jesus has set the believer free from the old covenant (Rom. 8:2–4).

In establishing a new covenant, Jesus did it in a unique fashion. As the second Adam, he was without sin (Heb. 2:17; 4:15), and thereby able to help the weak. Through Christ and the fruit of his covenant, there is a restoration of relationship and personality. Through Christ's Spirit, man is "renewed in knowledge" (Col. 3:10) and "true righteousness and holiness" (Eph. 4:24), all of this being the result of the indwelling of the Spirit through the new covenant relationship. He worked in a fashion that was not evident under the old covenant.[36] The apostolic preaching proclaimed that "forgiveness of sins is proclaimed to you, and by him every one that believes is freed from everything from which you could not be freed by the law of Moses" (Acts 13:27–39).

Relating to the covenant with Abraham.—The covenant with Abraham was prophetic of the new covenant in which all the nations would be blessed. Paul wrote to the Gentile Christians, "Now we, brethren, like Isaac, are children of promise" (Gal. 4:28). Abraham believed God, and he was accepted by God because of it. Salvation

---

[36] Under the old covenant, the Spirit was bestowed for a special ministry, often temporarily, and then withdrawn; in the new covenant the Spirit is given to man with whom he will remain forever. The role of the Spirit in the Old Testament is surely a limited one. See Rene Pache, *The Person and Work of the Holy Spirit* (Chicago: Moody Press, 1954), pp. 30–35.

has not changed in essence. In the new covenant, salvation is, like Abraham's, by faith. The guarantee is now sure because of Christ's death and resurrection, but the means of acceptance is still the same. This is the understanding of Hebrews when the author writes, "The Holy Spirit also bears witness to us; for after saying, 'This is the covenant that I will make with them after those days, says the Lord: I will put my laws on their hearts, and write them on their minds,' then he adds, 'I will remember their sins and their misdeeds no more.' Where there is forgiveness of these, there is no longer any offering for sin" (Heb. 10:15–18). The true sons of Abraham are those who have faith (Rom. 4:13–17). The intent of Jesus was to fulfil, not destroy (Matt. 5:17). As such, the promised covenant finds its fulfilment in him and in him alone.

Relating to Christian privilege.—The Scriptures describe the Christian's privileges in terms of the elements promised in the coming covenant, or the established covenant in Christ. We are with Paul "ministers of a new covenant" (2 Cor. 3:6), and are given "the Spirit as a guarantee" (5:5), which is the promise of the prophets concerning the coming covenant; God indwells the believer, likewise a promise of the Father (2 Cor. 6:16) in setting forth the new covenant. Victory over sin, Satan, and death are only possible through the benefits of the covenant—the Spirit of God.

Second, the new covenant fulfils cosmic significance. It was the merit of the classical view of the atonement to set forth the victory of Christ over the powers of evil and darkness. After the atonement, the world was no longer in the hands of darkness and Satan but under the rule of Christ. The emphasis was placed on deliverance from the power of evil.

Crude terminology centering around deception was often used to express how the flesh of Christ hid the fishhook of his divinity. The new covenant gives fuller meaning to the cosmic significance of the death of Christ than the classical view. After the new covenant was established, deliverance from sin is made possible through the Spirit who indwells the believer. The believer did not have this in the Old Testament. In potentiality, the New Testament believer is victorious over all the temptations and harassments of Satan. Although the disciple yet faces the temptations of life, and sometimes succumbs to them, he has the power of the Spirit of God within him to overcome life and death. The same power that raised Christ will raise us up also (1 Cor. 6:14). With the new covenant "the ruler of this world" is cast out (John 12:30–33). The witness of Hebrews is that through death, the establishment of the covenant, Christ destroys him who has the power of death, and delivers all those who through fear of death were "subject to lifelong bondage" (Heb. 2:14–16).

All of these benefits of victory, we repeat, are a result of the promise connected with the new covenant. The Spirit promised in the new covenant relationship enables the victory.

Third, the new covenant concept does not have some of the problems and questions that other views possessed.

A common objection and problem of the so-called objective views of the atonement is in reference to the implications of Christ's death. If we are redeemed by Christ's death, why do Christians yet die? Certainly if Christ's death is redemptive, one can justly argue that total redemption has not been achieved. At best it only relates to a way of escape from spiritual death. Why is man's physical nature yet subject to death? There is no answer to this issue in the traditional views of the atonement.

The new covenant is not beset by this question, for the death of Christ is the guarantee of the Christian's victory *through* death. The covenant is related specifically to the forgiveness of sins and the indwelling of God's Spirit. These are the guarantee of the covenant rather than physical deliverance.

An objection raised against the satisfaction theory of the atonement is, how could sin be forgiven before the cross? Certainly the death of Christ assumes great importance. If there is salvation in no other name than that of Jesus, how could there be forgiveness even by Jesus before his death? For our view there is no problem. God forgave before the cross as well as after the cross. Forgiveness was based upon repentance and faith in God. It still is! The proclamation of the kingdom was in no way different in essence from that of the prophets. The proclamation is repent, and forgiveness shall follow (Luke 24:47). The new covenant of promise has greater implications for the repentant since the time of Christ. He has a greater surety (Heb. 7:22) in the new covenant because God, in the person of the Son, has given a better guarantee of his mercy than the Old Testament saints knew.

An overlooked area in the traditional theories is to explain how the old covenant was fulfilled and the new started. Generally, little attention is paid to the establishment of it. It is assumed. But the fact that the New Testament (new covenant) is so named is important. Hebrews has much to say about the inadequacy of the old and the establishment of the new covenant with the death of Christ.

Another serious question concerning some of the theories, such as Anselm, Calvin, as well as the classical, is, Why cannot God simply forgive as man is commanded to do? This poses no problem for the view of the new covenant. In it one sees the fact that God declares his forgiveness. Christ suffered for our sins because man could not and would not accept the fact that God forgives. Who can forgive sin but God? Nothing stands in the way of forgiveness except unbelief on man's part. Socinus raised the right questions but gave the wrong answers. He wondered why God could not forgive without satisfaction. In his view the death of Christ was unnecessary.

The new covenant speaks of God's forgiveness without satisfaction or honor being restored. God has not suffered in honor. In his forgiving attitude toward man he has not suffered nor increased his personal glory. The Son's death is not meaningless, as in Socinian thought, but the means whereby God establishes the new covenant with man. His was a meaningful death.

The difficulty with the Socinian theory is that the atonement amounts to nothing, and salvation is by achievement of a high moral code given by Christ. For him religion meant "correct thinking and correct behavior." [37] But in the new covenant, salvation is by sheer grace. We are granted forgiveness. The covenant with the benefit of the Spirit is all of grace in Christ.

The question of Abelard is a real serious question for the penal and satisfaction theories. He asked, "How can the death of the innocent Son so have pleased God the Father that through it He is reconciled to us who have so sinned that on this account the innocent Lord was killed?" [38] Abelard's question is based on the "Trinitarian illusion" mentioned above. The question is not of significance to the new covenant view because it is God in the Son who has already reconciled himself to man and shows this in establishing a new covenant.

We would now return to the standard of Mozley, in summing up, in that the atonement must do justice to the meaning of the Bible, moral consciousness, and the meaning of Christian religious experi-

---

[37] Cave, *op. cit.*, pp. 203–4.
[38] *Ibid.*, pp. 159–60.

ence. It is apparent that the new covenant can carry the freight of the total terminology of the New Testament. The new covenant does establish the doctrine in line with the moral consciousness of the New Testament, and it is true to the doctrine of Christian religious experience, for it speaks of the Spirit of God bearing witness within our hearts that it is so.

IX. The Nature of Man

Without the presuppositions of the Christian faith the individual is either nothing or becomes everything. In the Christian faith man's insignificance as a creature, involved in the process of nature and time, is lifted into significance by the mercy and power of God in which his life is sustained. But his significance as a free spirit is understood as subordinate to the freedom of God.

Reinhold Niebuhr, *The Nature and Destiny of Man*

It is beyond doubt that there is nothing which more shocks our reason than to say that the sin of the first man has rendered guilty those, who, being so removed from this source, seem incapable of participation in it. This transmission does not only seem to us impossible, it seems also very unjust. . . . Certainly nothing offends us more rudely than this doctrine; and yet, without this mystery, the most incomprehensible of all, we are incomprehensible to ourselves.

Pascal, *Pensées*

The principle of "Creative Evolution," that is, the appearance of new forms of life which cannot be explained in causal terms, and the significance of nonmechanical factors are today admitted by scientists of high standing. That theory of Evolution which believes that everything can be explained in causal terms, exists today less in the brains of scientists than in those of theological apologists—as that which they oppose—and in the minds of popular materialistic philosophers—as that which they absolutely believe.

Brunner,
The Christian Doctrine of Creation and Redemption

The fact that man can transcend himself in infinite regression and cannot find the end of life except in God is the mark of his creativity and uniqueness; closely related to this capacity

*is his inclination to transmute his partial and finite self and
his partial and finite values into the infinite good. Therein lies
his sin.*

Niebuhr, *Nature and Destiny*

*The final sin of man, said Luther truly, is his unwillingness
to concede that he is a sinner.*

Niebuhr, *Nature and Destiny*

The doctrine of man, generally coming under the rubric of anthropology, is important for a number of reasons. First, it is a subject that can be discussed at great length with the unconfessing world.
The unbelieving man is yet man. Second, what man believes about
man will determine much of the movement of history. One only has
to look at three men.

Friedrich Nietzsche is the man that one must know to understand
the drive for power, as seen in the Third Reich of Germany or the
fascism of the Italian Mussolini. Karl Marx has placed his imprint
upon the minds of millions. It is his view of "man" that is important.
It is not primarily the emphasis on economics that sets Marx apart
but "the ideas of human dignity and of justice, that of the identity of
the idea of man and the ideal of society, and lastly the understanding
of the historical nature of human existence." [1] The other man, Sig-
mund Freud, gives us a view of man as understood from the sex
instinct, and his nature as man must be interpreted from this standpoint. It is evident that a "man's view of himself determines his
life." [2]

There is thus a difference between anthropologies. This is evident
in the following ways. There is the scientific discipline of anthropology which attempts to uncover the facts of man's historical existence.
Man has a history that is worth knowing. Mankind has lived in a
world that can be observed. His scientifically observed life must not
be regarded as useless. What man is physically and chemically often
affects what he is creatively.

Philosophical anthropology is very much interested in the subject

---

[1] Emil Brunner, *Man in Revolt* (Philadelphia: Westminster Press, 1947),
p. 37.
[2] *Ibid.*, p. 33.

of man. What is man? What is life? What is his body? Does he have a soul? Such questions are of interest to philosophy. There is a considerable identity of interest between philosophical anthropology and theological anthropology. The latter is unique in that it seeks a special understanding of man in revelation. It turns to the Scriptures for a measure of the knowledge that it accepts. Theological anthropology cannot agree with the words of Alexander Pope that "the proper study of mankind is man." If this were all that we had to go on, our task would be rather disappointing. In spite of the gross misconceptions attributed to it, the biblical picture of man ultimately is the most realistic and most optimistic one available.

There are two ways of approaching the biblical Christian doctrine of man. First, one can gather all the statements concerning man in the Bible and put them in order. This is the method most commonly used. But there is a problem in understanding man from this standpoint. If sinful man is not what he once was, how can we understand what he ought to be now? Where is the pattern for understanding him? Even though it is possible to build an anthropology on compiled texts, it falls short of a connecting link between the present and the past. "We are not in any position to infer from any residual lineaments in the Biblical picture of sinful man the true essence of man as God created him." [3]

Another approach is to begin with *the man,* Jesus who is the real man. "The nature of the man Jesus alone is the key to the problem of human nature. This man is man." [4] In this case, anthropology depends on Christology. In looking at Jesus we see ourselves. "In Him are the peace and clarity which are not in ourselves. In Him is the human nature created by God without the self-contradiction which afflicts us and without the self-deception by which we seek to escape from our shame. In Him is human nature without human sin." [5]

There is merit in this method. We know little about the first man, but this man shines forth in the light of history. Perhaps the phrase speaking of Christ as the "second Adam" gives a commentary here. "The same Christ who is accepted by faith as the revelation of the

---

[3] Barth, *Church Dogmatics,* III-2, 30.
[4] *Ibid.,* p. 43.
[5] *Ibid.,* p. 48.

character of God is also regarded as the revelation of the true character of man." [6] In knowing Christ we know what we should be.

We now turn to the special items in the doctrine of man.

The Creation of Man

The appearance of man on the face of the earth is a fact we accept. The questions of *how* man arrived and *when* are not so easily solved. Theologians in the past have accepted the Genesis account without question. With the rise of modern science, new problems arose. Frequently theologians begin with the scientific data on man's past and attempt to squeeze the biblical account into their scientific explanations. What is needed, however, is for both disciplines—science and religion—to receive sincere treatment at the hands of the other.

Genesis 1–3.—History or Myth?

A decisive issue in the doctrine of man relates to the early chapters of Genesis. How are they to be understood? Are they historical? Are they myths in the deep sense of that word, conveying profound theological truths concerning man? There are three ways at least that one may regard these chapters.

Traditional.—The traditional view of the early chapters of Genesis is that they describe God's creative activity compressed into six twenty-four-hour days. Man is created on the sixth day and is very young in age. The idea of creation taking place at 4004 B.C. has been influential since the time of Archbishop Ussher. When various sciences came to assert that man is much older, it was easy to see how the two disciplines conflicted. Something had to go. Some Christians gave up the historical view of the early chapters in Genesis, others gave up science and compartmentalized their faith, while still others sought some different approach. Many proposals were set forth, of which too few had any merit, such as the gap theory of the old Scofield Bible. We shall discuss the top two contenders current in theological circles.

Creation revealed in six days.—The six days mentioned in Genesis are six twenty-four-hour days in which at one point in man's history God told the story of creation to man. The story is quite old. On

---

6 Niebuhr, *op. cit.*, I, 146.

each day in which the story was told it may have been written down on a stone tablet similar to the manner in which the Babylonians wrote their version of the story. Inasmuch as the first Hebrews came from a Babylonian culture, one would expect a similarity in literary styles. The six days, in which God said to man the story of the past, are not related to the age of the earth or the age of man. The fact of Genesis is the fact of man's life, beginning with God as Creator. One may find broad parallels between the development from simplicity to complexity in the account of Genesis and the geological table, but Genesis gives no indication of the age factor at all.

The merits of this view are: (1) It is not cluttered with any chronology; (2) it may find a general concordism with the facts of science; (3) it retains the integrity of the concept of a "day" as it is understood in the Hebrew sense of an evening and a morning; and (4) it fits into our understanding of the culture of the ancient past.[7]

Genesis is a myth.—Unfortunately, the word "myth" means to many people something fictitious. There are many meanings of the term. Theologians use it to speak of a literary type, or vehicle, which conveys profound theological truths. As such it conveys the deepest truths about man's nature and existence.

If the story of Genesis is accepted as myth, it then becomes the story of *everyman*. It has been the story of man since his existence. It is yet the story of man to come. Man is confronted with the issues of right and wrong, and has to choose between them. The story points up to the fact of man's continued choice for sin against God. Paul Tillich says, "The story of Genesis, chapters 1–3, if taken as a myth, can guide our description of the transition from essential to existential being. It is the profoundest and richest expression of man's awareness of his existential estrangement and provides the scheme in which the transition from essence to existence can be treated." [8] The account in Genesis becomes the story of mankind every day of its life rather than an event that happened once long ago to one man.

There is value in regarding the account from the mythological

---

[7] See Bernard Ramm, *The Christian View of Science and the Scripture;* Wiseman, *Creation Revealed in Six Days;* Russell Mixter, *Evolution and Christian Thought,* and *Modern Science and Christian Faith.*

[8] Paul Tillich, *Systematic Theology* (Chicago: The University of Chicago Press, 1963), II, 31.

point of view. It escapes the problem of traditional theology, which will be considered later, in which the descendants of Adam seem to be held guilty for something they did not do. Yet it does not have an adequate answer to the question concerning why each person comes to the point of personal rebellion. We will come to that later.

Adam—Name or Noun?

This question is closely related to the section above. Two points of view are in contention here. First, Adam is not the name of an individual historical man but refers to Man. It is argued that the word for Adam is really not a proper noun at all, but a general term for man, like mankind. The same applies to the "woman" until she is given a proper name in Genesis 3:20. Thus it is concluded that the references in Genesis refer not to a particular man but give the story of every man.[9] Tillich speaks of these early chapters as myth and interprets them as a state of "dreaming innocence." The account refers not to a single man but to a state of potentiality which was before time and place, but yet to be.

The second point of view holds that Adam was a historical man. It is true that the Revised Standard Version of the Bible translates the word used in the King James for Adam as "man." It never speaks of Adam until Genesis 3:17 and continues to do so thereafter with the exception of 3:20 and 5:2. The name Adam is used in the Gospels only once (Luke 3:38). In the Epistles it has a doctrinal framework, comparing the first transgression of "Adam" with the obedience of Christ, the second Adam.[10]

The types of objection to Adam as a historical man are: (1) grammatical usage in the early chapter; (2) the problem of equating Adam with ancient primitive man as science "knows" him; and (3) the built-in problem of guilt, associated with the traditional doctrine of sin in which mankind is judged for Adam's sin. These objections are not insurmountable but must be resolved to restore this position to its importance.

There is perhaps a third alternative which could be introduced, but

---

[9] Brunner declares that the simple story of man's coming into being points up a fourfold truth: "Body and mind belong equally to the nature of man, neither is to be deduced from the other, the spirit is 'from above' and the body 'from below'—and, this is the most important, they are both destined for each other, and in a definite way adapted to one another."—*Man in Revolt*, p. 374.

[10] Cf. Rom. 5:14; 1 Cor. 15:22,45; 1 Tim. 2:13–14; Jude 14.

which is not widely held. The solution could lie in maintaining both. Adam could well refer to the first historical man, for, after all, mankind had to begin somewhere. The story of Adam could well be understood from the existential point of view in which each man sees himself deciding between "truth or falsehood." Why not have your cake and eat it too?

Man Versus the Animals

Delaying for the time the question of man's origin, we need to ask concerning the difference between man and the animals. One can parallel various physical similarities between man and other higher animals. Man's larger brain, his upright stature, and his thumb-opposing first finger are significant differing physical characteristics. "Man is the only animal which can make itself its own object." [11] Man can "look" at himself as well as have a consciousness of the world as apart from himself. This reflects the rational nature of man. It is possible to speak of animals reasoning within limits, but man alone has "the power of abstraction and generalization." [12] Animals do not produce books on philosophy and theology.

Unique to man are the realms of religion and morality. Although man continues to turn toward idolatry and corruption of religion, he is the only worshiping creature. Man alone stands in responsibility in moral issues. Only man is a murderer. Brunner speaks of the human nature being expressed in desiring something "mental for its own sake, something beautiful for the sake of its beauty, something good for the sake of goodness, something true on account of its truth, something holy for the sake of its holiness. No animal reveres its dead. Where there is reverence for the dead, there already human nature is present." [13]

James Orr stressed the rational religious and moral faculties of man as well as his capacity for speech and his progressive creative ability in the "arts, institutions, and sciences." [14]

However similar man is to the creatures below him, he is quite distinct from them. We agree with Brunner that the humanness of

[11] Niebuhr, *op. cit.*, I, 55.

[12] James Orr, *God's Image in Man* (Grand Rapids: Wm. B. Eerdmans Publishing Co., 1948), p. 62.

[13] *Christian Doctrine of Creation and Redemption*, p. 81.

[14] *Op. cit.*, p. 65.

man is something "which cannot possibly be derived from the animal kingdom." [15] The appearance of mind requires "mind" to explain it.

Man's Age

The length of man's walk on the earth calls for a revolution in traditional thinking. Unfortunately, Archbishop Ussher's chronology has been imposed upon the Scriptures and seems often to be accepted as part of the Bible. The once familiar date of 4004 B.C. for the creation of man was a result of adding the genealogies in the Old Testament. This no longer can be accepted. Even the very conservative B. B. Warfield wrote that "the question of the antiquity of man has of itself no theological significance." [16] The Bible does not give a date for the beginning of man. The genealogies themselves serve to give only the *line* of descent, not the length of time for the descent. Warfield further declared, concerning the genealogies:

Their symmetrical arrangement in groups of ten is indicative of their compression; and for all we know instead of 20 generations and some 2,000 years measuring the interval between creation and the birth of Abraham, two hundred generations and something like 20,000 or even 2,000 generations and something like 200,000 years may have intervened. In a word, the Scriptural data leaves us wholly without guidance in estimating the time which elapsed between the creation of the world and the deluge, and between the deluge and the call of Abraham. So far as the Scripture assertions are concerned, we may suppose any length of time to have intervened between these events which may otherwise appear reasonable.[17]

If one is going to accept the biblical accounts with reference to Adam as being historical, then he will have to adjust his thinking about the past. We cannot think of Adam as wearing a blue serge suit and having all the conveniences of modern man. Rather the word "primitive" must be used to describe his existence. If Adam was an existent person, the first man, his primitive state must antedate that of other such men such as the Neanderthal man. Until some technological advances were made—remember that the first man had much to learn—man would have resorted to primitive dwellings,

---

[15] *Christian Doctrine of Creation and Redemption*, p. 80.
[16] *Biblical and Theological Studies*, ed. Samuel G. Craig (Philadelphia: Presbyterian & Reformed Co., 1952), p. 238.
[17] *Ibid.*, p. 247.

created crude instruments, and established some means of survival. Even though some reject Adam as being a historical first man, man the first had to begin somewhere. Whenever he did begin he must have been primitive in the true sense of the word. Nevertheless, he was yet man.

We have seen that others reject any possible identification of a historical Adam with primitive man. Brunner does so maintaining that there is no visible chronological continuity of these creatures with the history of Israel. Accepting the story of Adam in Genesis as the story of Everyman, Brunner is not concerned with the age of man or any creature.

Various figures have been proposed for the age of man's life on earth. The oldest would reach back about five hundred thousand years. This may seem a little high. But the Neanderthals seem to have had some religious life about one hundred thousand years ago. It may be safely said that the further the figure is projected into the past, the less certainty there is. On the other hand, we may say that man is no recent being. One need remember that man was in America as early as 10,000 B.C. Agriculture seems to have originated as early as 8000 B.C.

Evolution and Creation

Any doctrine of man in the area of theology should consider the subject of evolution. To do so is to invite misunderstanding, misinterpretation, and, if one were to attack the doctrine of evolution undoubtedly he would be labeled an obscurantist, to be compared to a vestigial remain from anti-evolutionary days. The prestige of modern science is so great that for anyone to look askance upon one of its tenets is to ask for trouble.[18] However, criticism there must be; but it must not be motivated solely from religious motives. The telling criticisms, if any, must come from the scientific community, or defects in logic.

Perhaps a beginning point in the dialogue should center around definitions. Evolution as a term is defective. Its ambiguity is nowhere more evident than among biologists themselves. Evolution has come to mean two diverse things—evolution as a fact and evolution as a faith.

Evolution as a fact.—This is a theory about change within the

---

[18] Cf. Anthony Standen, *Science Is a Sacred Cow* (New York: E. P. Dutton Co., 1958).

species. Individuals in a species are quite related, although varying slightly from one another. This aspect of the concept of evolution includes the mixing of two species which would give rise to a third, such as the mixing of the golden-winged warbler and the blue-winged warbler producing the hybrid, Lawrence's warbler. This type of evolution is a proven fact. It has been observed and verified.

In this sense, evolution poses no problems for theology. But because of the ambiguity around the term "evolution," some other popular term should be adopted by biologists to be used consistently and universally. Perhaps a term like "development" as opposed to "evolution" might be suggestive. The controversy in evolution comes in the second meaning associated in the term.

Evolution as a faith.—Development in biology may be opposed to evolution. The first is based on fact, the second requires a leap of faith. A sketch of this faith is summed up by Theodosius Dobzhansky: "Evolution is a continuous process, composed, though, of small discontinuous mutation steps. From the continuity of evolution it follows, of course, that forms intermediate between the now-living organisms must have existed in the past. Provided that man and the simplest virus are really descended from common ancestors, then, if all organisms which lived in the past were fossilized and recovered, we would see an unbroken chain of organisms intermediate between man and the virus." [19]

What is there to say about this faith-sketch? Evolutionists frequently make faith statements in a dogmatic form on the one hand but admit there is no evidence for the statement on the other. Note the following statement:

"The evidence shows conclusively that man arose from forebears who were not men, although we have only the most fragmentary information concerning the stages through which the process has passed." [20]

The evidence mainly appealed to for support of this conviction is the fossil remains. But of this, Dobzhansky declares that "the fossil record of primates is unfortunately meager." [21] Concerning man there are no intermediate fossil remains and there is no evidence, according to Dobzhansky, of more than a "single human or human-like spe-

---

[19] *Evolution, Genetics and Man* (New York: John Wiley & Sons, 1966), p. 285.
[20] *Ibid.*, p. 319.
[21] *Ibid.*, p. 325.

cies." [22] But while this is admitted on the one hand, the statement of the evolutionist's faith is that the evidence is said to be conclusive.

In a more candid mood one should simply admit: "I do not have any proof for my belief that man has evolved from an apelike creature, but I *believe*—and many share this conviction—that this is what happened. I cannot prove it but by applying the fact of the *developmental theory* of evolution to the appearances of fossil life I believe that life evolved this way. I infer from the known fact to the unknown and I construct my theory on this faith."

This is not the general candor of the evolutionist. He does not divide his fact and faith so nicely. Hence the ambiguity in the issue.

Evolution as a faith has been criticized in the following ways.

1. Concerning the origin of life. The origin of life is faced with the dictum of Pasteur that presently "life arises only from pre-existing life." [23] Is it possible that Pasteur's "law" did not apply in the origin of life? It is a tacit conclusion of a philosophy of science that laws do not change with age. A law of nature might be proved to be wrong in due time, but a true law does not become invalid solely on the basis of time change. If Pasteur's law is true, it becomes an issue for the origin of life as presently conceived by evolutionists.

The two proposals that are usually set forth have not succeeded in convincing evolutionists in general. The first is that "spontaneous formation of complex proteins and nucleoproteins" gave rise to the early forms of life. But in spite of declaring that this is "a most improbable event," [24] Dobzhansky takes the leap of faith that with aeons of time the highly improbable will occur, and did occur, and with this faith assumption, life starts its long evolution. The second proposal is that viruses are the link between the living and the non-living, but this is also problematical, for the nature of a virus is parasitic and "no free living viruses are known." [25]

---

[22] *Ibid.*, p. 333.

[23] *Ibid.*, p. 17.

[24] *Ibid.*, p. 19.

[25] *Ibid.*, p. 14. If success crowns the continuing attempts to synthesize life, philosophers will be posed with renewing the old question: what is the nature of matter? It may be that matter is no longer "just matter," but as it is reduced down to sub-atomic particles it may be much more "mental" than material. The idealist may find more support for his thesis that life is ultimately mind. If the scientist takes "so-called matter" to produce life which grows and reproduces with some direction, the old question will be raised: from what sources did it receive its pattern of growth? Is it possible that every particle of our universe is more "alive" in a way we have never thought possible or dreamed of? Will we have to discard the opposites of mind and matter?

At this point, the honesty of many biologists is that they must admit a complex lack of evidence concerning the origin of the first forms of life, but their faith in the theory enables them to conceive of life arising in a way that their evidence prohibits at this period. Some express their faith comprehensively, as Simpson, in affirming that "although many details remain to be worked out, it is already evident that all the objective phenomena of the history of life can be explained by purely materialistic factors." [26]

2. *The next problem relates to the appearance of life in the fossil record.* It is the general conclusion of biological evolutionists that all the major phyla appeared in the Cambrian Age, about five hundred million years ago, in a period that lasted about eighty million years. The appearance is sudden. The fossils do not record forms suggesting the forms of life before the Cambrian Age, nor do they give us transitional forms. Furthermore, Simpson notes as a fact that the phyla *fail* to "appear in the order which would be expected as 'natural' on the basis of increasing complexity." [27]

By applying the known to the unknown, the fact of the present to the unknown of the past, the evolutionist can assume that life evolved before the Cambrian forms appeared. But he has no evidence and should admit that his faith enters his theory. The evolutionists and the creationists meet at this point. Both can affirm nothing more than that life appears in the Cambrian. The first confesses his faith in life evolving previous to the Cambrian forms, while the second may confess that the sudden appearance of life may mean that God created life in what we designate the Cambrian Age. The man of science decries "miracle," [28] but at present his faith that life arose from non-life necessitates a miracle in the same sense that the man of religion does. Both should be aware of what they are doing. Both are making faith statements.

3. *The problem of mechanism.* Assume for argument's sake that life has evolved from a few simple cells. There is yet difficulty in explaining how it has come about. Faith enters the picture for the evolutionists again. Two proposals stand against each other with difficulties in each. The majority of biological evolutionists agree that new species "originate through the selection and fixation of small mu-

---

[26] George Gaylord Simpson, *The Meaning of Evolution* (New Haven: Yale University Press, 1949), p. 343.

[27] *Ibid.*, p. 31.

[28] Cf. *ibid.*, p. 16.

tations." [29] Dobzhansky voices the objection to this in declaring that "mutations do not produce new species. The mutants of Drosophila are still flies which belong to the same species of Drosophila to which their ancestors belonged." [30] The second opinion—defended by Goldschmidt, is that development of new species has come about by great mutations. This poses the possibility of a reptile egg hatching a bird. Contrary to this possibility is the general opinion of most evolutionists that "the development of the living world rarely if ever involved major changes produced by single mutational steps." [31] What causes mutations and how to bring them about is yet an unsolved issue.[32] The solution may come or it may not; but, so far, no satisfactory theory is acceptable. The faith of the evolutionist is that it will be solved.

4. The problem of classical evidence. Certain types of evidence are said to support evolution as a faith: (1) the argument from recapitulation, or embryology; (2) the evidence of the fossils; (3) distribution of animals; and (4) comparative anatomy and vestigial remains.

While the arguments have been used to support evolution as a faith, they may be understood in a way that does not support evolutionary faith. For example, the tonsils and appendix were once thought to be useless, but more recent evidence indicates that they still have use in the human body for producing antibodies.

It is not our purpose here to review these classical arguments with alternate explanations, for this has been done elsewhere. It is only necessary to note the alternative possibility to indicate that the classical evidence does not necessarily support the faith of the evolutionists.[33]

5. The problem of reductionism. Evolution as a faith labors under the charge of reductionism. Reductionism—attempting to reduce all of reality to one mode of thinking—has always been a problem with man in his search for understanding. Evolution as a faith attempts to

---

[29] Thomas S. Hall and Florence Moog, Life Science (New York: John Wiley & Sons, 1955), p. 441.
[30] Evolution, Genetics and Man, p. 83.
[31] Ibid., p. 84.
[32] Ibid., p. 86.
[33] Cf. Robert E. D. Clark, Darwin: Before and After (Grand Rapids: International Publications, 1958), pp. 168–87; and Modern Science and Christian Faith (Wheaton: Scripture Press, 1948), pp. 58–98.

reduce man's history of life to a single explanation. The attempt is worthy, but life is too complex and complicated. Against this attempt stands the fact that intermediary forms have not been found. But a popular text used in many colleges declares the faith of the authors that "it is now more reasonable to believe that the intermediate forms have not been found than that they never existed." [34]

Moreover, the reductionist tendency appears contrary to the evidence that certain forms have not changed for up to four hundred million years. The little marine brachiopod Lingula is one such example.[35] It may be assumed that it developed or evolved to its present form from something else. But without evidence to the contrary it may equally be validly assumed that it did not. It depends upon what your theory demands. The evidence of a prior, different form is lacking in the fossil record. Other examples appear in the fossil record which have not changed for similarly long periods of time, and both Dobzhansky and Simpson make several references to them.[36]

The issue in reductionism is: how far may I carry my theory? Can I impose what is factual concerning development of species to the evolution of phyla or across phyla? The faith of evolution says you may, but the evidence for this is yet missing.

6. Phyla and the "kinds" of Genesis. The earliest evidence of life involves the major phyla. As long as the evolutionist does not insist on his faith centering on a single cell beginning point, there may be more in common between evolution and the religious document in Genesis than at first appears. The Bible records that God created "kinds," a term without an exact biological synonym, but which may hold some counterpart to the broad term like phyla. This points up part of the misunderstanding between the creationists and the evolutionists. The creationists readily admit development within the phyla from the simple to the complex but reject the faith-proposition of some evolutionists that life has evolved across phyla. The issue here is the same as in the problem of reductionism: how far may I apply my particular theory on species to the general story of phyla?

In light of the above problems, various comments may be made. The faith aspect must be recognized in the second facet of evolution-

---

[34] Hall and Moog, *op. cit.,* p. 442.
[35] Dobzhansky, *op. cit.,* p. 296.
[36] Cf. *ibid.*

ary theory. In light of this the evolutionist should not look down his
nose at other people who reject or hesitate to affirm his theory because of the lack of evidence. He should have equal respect for those
who have faith that it did not happen the way he outlines, but who
may have faith that the appearance of life is related to God, who
initiates it and directs it.

There are decisive ethical implications for the larger theory of
evolution, and evolutionists apparently seem to smart under the
charges, for many of them devote some few pages to developing an
evolutionary ethic.

Evolution with its associated tendency toward materialism has a
direct bearing on ethics, for what a man thinks concerning metaphysics—the nature of life, man, the universe, and God—is directly
connected with how he *lives* life. It is significant that Adolf Hitler
was highly captivated with evolutionary teachings, and the German
Youth Movement was indoctrinated with these views. Nazi Germany,
in part, is the consequence of it. The Soviet Union likewise officially
sponsors materialistic evolutionary views. Karl Marx read Darwin
in 1860 and wanted to dedicate his *Das Kapital* to Darwin who de-
clined the honor. Mussolini likewise was influenced by evolutionary
theory. It is true that other factors influenced the lives and events of
these men, but it remains a truism that a man lives the way he thinks.

A well-known philosopher has recently raised again the issues in
evolution. Mortimer J. Adler, director of the Institute for Philosophical Research in Chicago, assesses the problem as follows: Evolution supposes that man is a creature among other creatures. If he is
different, it is a superficial difference, not a radical difference. Without the radical difference between man and the brutes "those who
now oppose injurious discrimination on the moral ground that all
human beings, being equal in their humanity, should be treated
equally in all those respects that concern their common humanity,
would have no solid basis in fact to support their normative principle.
A social and political idea that has operated with revolutionary force
in human history could be validly dismissed as a hollow illusion that
should become defunct." [37]

Adler proceeds to say that various scales may be erected for evaluating humans, and on this basis he asks, "Why, then, should not

[37] Mortimer J. Adler, *The Difference of Man and the Difference It Makes*
(New York: Holt, Rinehart & Winston, 1967), p. 263.

groups of superior men be able to justify their enslavement, exploitation, or even genocide of inferior human groups, on factual and moral grounds akin to those that we now rely on to justify our treatment of the animals that we harness as beasts of burden, that we butcher for food and clothing, or that we destroy as disease-bearing pests or as dangerous predators?" [38]

Evolution as it is presently held does not allow for radical discontinuity—that is, for an immaterial element such as spirit or soul—between man and the beast and therefore it cannot allow for a radical difference between them. This means then that ethics as it has commonly been conceived is a *logical* impossibility as the inferences are drawn concerning man's evolutionary arrival. The fact that evolutionists attempt to develop some form of ethics for man is inconsistent with evolutionary philosophy. Ethics becomes transformed in the process from being related to what is right and wrong in relation to God to a system of behavior that is functional for the preserving of life and harmony in society.

The alternative to this position is the reaffirmation of the ingredients of traditional theism in which man is a unique person, a special creation, a being who will share life with God in eternity, and who has free will and moral responsibility. Here alone is the real meaning for ethics, for treatment of man as equal, for personhood, and teleology. Here too is the basis for meaningful civilization.

The final statement should refer all of this back to the story of man's origin, our main concern in this section. What can we say? The only meaningful thing is that man appeared on the face of the earth at one point in geologic history. There is no evidence concerning the "how" of his arrival. How did he arrive there? The faith of the Christian urges him to say with the Scriptures—God created. No fossil evidence can give us the fingerprints of God. The faith of the evolutionists urges him to say that man has evolved from some prior form. But he too is without the print of the intermediate form. Both must be aware of what they are doing.

The Image of God

The Bible declares that man was made in the image and likeness of God (Gen. 1:26-27; 5:1; 9:6). What does it mean to be in God's

---

[38] *Ibid.*, p. 264.

image? [39] First, it does not mean a physical image. There are those, Mormons, for example, who speak of God as having a physical form. To contemplate God in physical form does violence to the Bible as well as to misunderstand the use of anthropomorphic expressions. Statements like the arms, eyes, and ears of God are anthropomorphic; that is, to speak of God in human terms for the sake of communication. The Bible also speaks of the wings of God, God as a rock, but nobody wishes to literalize these as they do the others, for that would be going too far. Jesus spoke of God as Spirit (John 4:24), and Spirit alone is able to do the works of God. Spirit alone as a term is able to convey the highest meaning for the being of God. To conceive of God as having a physical body is to reject the words of Jesus.

Second, the image of God has been defined in terms of qualities or substances. Berkhof sums up the image of God in man as consisting of the

... soul or spirit of man, that is, in the qualities of simplicity, spirituality, invisibility, and immortality. (b) In the psychical powers or faculties of man as a rational and moral being, namely, the intellect and the will with their functions. (c) In the intellectual and moral integrity of man's nature, revealing itself in true knowledge, righteousness, and holiness (Eph. 4:24; Col. 3:10). (d) In the body, not as a material substance, but as the fit organ of the soul, sharing its immortality; and as the instrument through which man can exercise dominion over the lower creation. (e) In man's dominion over the earth.[40]

Third, the Roman Catholic theology has generally drawn a distinction between image and likeness. Roman Catholic writers have generally followed Irenaeus who made this distinction in the second century. The first man was created with two types of life, the natural life which corresponds to the image idea, and the supernatural life which is the likeness of God. The supernatural life is composed of sanctifying grace, with hope, charity, and the moral virtues of justice, prudence, temperance, and fortitude.[41] When man sinned, he lost the supernatural life or the likeness while retaining the natural

---

[39] "The Biblical doctrine that man was made in the image of God and after His likeness is naturally given no precise psychological elaboration in the Bible itself. Nor does Biblical psychology ever achieve the careful distinctions of Greek thought."—Niebuhr, op. cit., p. 151.

[40] Berkhof, op. cit., p. 207.

[41] F. J. Sheed, Theology and Sanity (New York: Sheed & Ward, 1953), p. 157.

life or the image. The natural image of God involves freedom, spirituality, and immortality of the soul.

In evaluating the Roman view, the first question centers around the legitimacy of making a distinction between likeness and image. The distinction rests upon unsound grammatical use because the Hebrew language is quite repetitive in nature, and repetition only gives fulness of thought rather than differences in the qualitative makeup of man. A second objection involves what sin did to the nature of man. Barth is correct in saying that man "cannot achieve any essential alteration of the human nature which he has been given." [42] Again, he declared, "Sin is not creative." [43]

The effects of sin point up a basic difference between Thomist and Reformed thought. The Roman theologian would say that man is *deprived*; that is, his supernatural life has been taken away. The Reformers asserted that man is *depraved*; that is, man's actions are permeated by sin. The Thomist position implies that man is not complete now in nature but is corrupted by sin.

Fourth, the *imago dei* (image of God) is not a substance but a relationship. This concept begins with Kant's dictum that a person is a responsible being. One cannot look at man as an isolated individual complete in himself. Instead, he is an individual-in-community and has his meaning in responsibility to the Thou. Thus man is still in the image of God; even when he is godless, he is still responsible. Sin does not diminish his responsibility; on the contrary, the greater the sin the greater his responsibility. Thus the "freedom of man is never freedom to repudiate his responsibility before God. It is never freedom to sin." [44]

This view has certain advantages. First, all men are created equal in the image of God—they are all responsible creatures. Inequality in talents increases the need for personal responsibility in the community of God. Second, man cannot change his nature in sin. He may deny it, rebel against his Creator, but he is still man-in-responsibility. Third, it does not have one of the problems that the traditional viewpoint has. The Reformers spoke of a relic of the image of God which was quite defaced. When a pessimistic view is pushed to its extreme it is difficult to explain some of the virtuous acts of man.

---

[42] *Church Dogmatics*, III-2, 227.
[43] *Ibid.*, p. 206.
[44] *Ibid.*, p. 197.

Without concluding that man is always virtuous, this view recognizes that man "bears witness to his original relation with God;" [45] man is still responsible. Fourth, the individual as responsible necessarily incorporates elements of the other views such as rationality and spirituality, for only persons have accountability to God.

The Nature of Man

Reinhold Niebuhr makes the statement that "all modern views of human nature are adaptations, transformations, and varying compounds of primarily two distinctive views of man: (a) the view of classical antiquity, that is of the Graeco-Roman world, and (b) the Biblical view." [46] The Christian faith has always had the difficulty of letting the classical view dominate itself. Niebuhr also states:

The Christian view of man is sharply distinguished from all alternative views by the manner in which it ". . . emphasizes the height of self-transcendence in man's spiritual stature in its doctrine of the 'image of God;' [. . . by its insistence] on 'man's weakness, dependence and finiteness' [and its affirmation that] 'the evil in man is a consequence of his inevitable though not necessary unwillingness to acknowledge his dependence, to accept his finiteness and to admit his insecurity, an unwillingness which involves him in the vicious circle of accentuating the insecurity from which he seeks escape.' " [47]

Classical Greek

Much of the thought of the early Christian thinkers, as well as medieval Catholicism, was influenced by Plato and Aristotle. There are two emphases that come from Greek thought which determined the direction early Christian thought would take. First, the rational nature of man was given the most prominent place. Reason was the creative principle and as such was "identical with God." [48] Second, a dualism was maintained between the body and mind or reason. The mind or spiritual principle was good in contrast to the body which was evil.[49] The body was considered the prison house of the soul and consequently inferior. One can see the influence of this type

---

[45] Brunner, *Man in Revolt*, p. 105.

[46] *Op. cit.*, p. 5.

[47] *Ibid.*, p. 150.

[48] *Ibid.*, p. 7.

[49] There are two strains in Greek thought in contradiction to each other. One stresses the idea that the body, being material, is evil. The other emphasis stressed body culture. The Olympic games stem from this heritage.

of thinking in early monastic practices of fleeing the world and subjecting the body to austere practices.

We cannot emphasize too strongly that the Bible records nothing of this type of dualism. To that we now turn.

Biblical View of Man

In the Bible man is spoken of as a living soul. Traditionally, man's nature was spoken of as being composed of body and soul. It is biblically more correct to speak of him, however, as a living soul. The biblical emphasis is on the unity of man in his existence. One sees this in Barth when he declares, "I am not only my soul; I am my soul only as I am also my body. I am not only my body; I am my body only as I am also my soul. Hence it is certainly not only my body but also my soul which has awareness, and it is certainly not only my soul but also my body which thinks." [50]

Because of the unity of man it is not correct to divide up functions of being into substances. One cannot attribute thinking to the soul, but the one man thinks. One cannot say simply that the body suffers and the soul cannot suffer, but that the one man suffers. Our descriptions of our existence are often more unified than our thinking. We say rightfully "I think," not just my mind thinks; "I am hungry," not just my body is hungry. These and other statements are the utterance of the one subject I, who at the same moment is soul and body.[51]

Another question of importance is the relation between soul and spirit. Spirit and soul are never separated in the New Testament. When they are distinguished, "spirit is the principle of the soul." [52] To speak in other words, man, being a besouled body, *has* spirit, "but we cannot simply say that he *is* spirit." [53] Only as man has spirit can we speak of his becoming a soul. This distinguishes man from the beast. When the sustaining power of God's Spirit is withdrawn from man's bodily life, death comes, and the body returns to the dust of the earth while the person of the body enters the judgment of his Creator.

---

[50] *Church Dogmatics*, III-2, 400. One cannot come to the conclusion that there is no thinking without the body, for "the soul is man's self-consciousness taking place in the body." (*Ibid.*, 401).

[51] *Ibid.*, 394.

[52] Niebuhr, *op. cit.*, p. 151.

[53] Barth, *Church Dogmatics*, III-2, 354.

It has been customary for some to speak of the immortality of the soul separated from the body. Note carefully that this term technically means that after death the soul lives on endlessly and the body is dead endlessly. Of course, this is the Greek concept of human existence and not the biblical idea. Immortality of the soul implies an indestructible substance created by God and it has no end. This is also Greek thought and not biblical anthropology. The soul, according to biblical thought, can be conceived as immortal only as long as God gives it its existence. It has no existence on its own right or power. Soul is continually dependent upon Spirit for life. The Christian speaks of the everlasting life because of sustained existence by the power of God. It is incorrect to speak of eternal life for man, for eternal life belongs only to God. Man's life has a beginning; God's being does not.

The difference in attitude toward life and death can be viewed in comparing the accounts of the death of Socrates and Jesus. For Socrates, death was a release to be experienced without fear and agony. Jesus displayed the Hebraic view of death in which death is a real threat to personal existence.

Dichotomy or trichotomy.—A question debated from the early centuries of the Christian church is whether man is of two parts (body and soul—dichotomy), or three distinct parts (body, soul, and spirit—trichotomy). The dichotomist appeals to scriptural passages such as Genesis 2:7; Job 32:8; 33:4; Matthew 10:28; 1 Corinthians 5:3, and others. The trichotomist appeals to these passages also but seeks to clinch his argument particularly from 1 Thessalonians 5:23 and Hebrews 4:12. The first passage speaks of "spirit and soul and body." The second passage speaks of the living Word of God, "piercing to the division of soul and spirit." With regard to these it is obvious that completeness and depth of soul are the intended ideas. Nobody argues for man's nature being divided into four parts or five. Yet, Jesus spoke of loving the Lord God with "all your heart, and with all your soul, and with all your mind, and with all your strength" (Mark 12:30). One may ask, why should one argue for a trichotomy on the basis of 1 Thessalonians and Hebrews and not argue for a quadripartite or more?

The argument over the two points of view has gone on since the early church. Perhaps it may be said that the dichotomists have been the more influential. However, if one emphasizes that man is not divided in his existence, but is a unitary being, then the question of dichotomy or trichotomy is not a very significant one.

Origin of the soul.—If man is a living soul, how does each new-born babe obtain his spiritual nature? This question has been spoken of traditionally as the origin of the soul. Generally three answers have been offered: preexistence of the soul, traducianism, and creationism.

1. Preexistence of the soul. This viewpoint has had little support in the history of Christian thought and is dependent on Greek philosophical thought for its origin. One Christian exponent of it was Origen, who declared that God had created in the beginning a fixed number of rational essences. These souls, or rational essences, were all endowed with free will and were by their very nature supposed to imitate God. It was dependent upon them to follow him or fall away by neglecting him. The rational essences became involved in the rebellion of the devil or other demons, and so God made the world as the place for their punishment. Thus each soul was imprisoned in a body as its punishment.[54] Therefore, each new human offspring is a product of punishment in which God places within the human body a soul. Its imprisonment remains until death when the soul is released. In one sense, man is similar to being a "fallen angel."

One of the main reasons that this view has had so little support in the history of Christian thought is that it is not dependent upon biblical statements for its evidence.

2. Traducianism. The word comes from "traduce," meaning to transfer, cross over. Theologically it means that the soul is inherited, along with the body, from the parents. Traducianism was held also in the second century. Tertullian formulated it and, under his and later writers' influence, it came to be widely held.

Traducianism means that the souls of men are contained in Adam in some sense, because each soul has been derived ultimately from the original breath of God breathed into Adam. There is much more to be said for this viewpoint than the one above. First, the Bible says nothing about a continuing inbreathing of the breath of life into each new human being. Propagation seems to be by physical means alone. Second, the passages used to argue against the position (Eccl. 12:7; Isa. 42:5; Zech. 12:1; Heb. 12:9; Num. 16:22) do not necessarily

---

54 Kelly, *op. cit.*, pp. 180–81.

mean any more than the fact that God is Creator of man's soul in an ultimate sense.

Objections are raised on the basis that it is a type of materialism. Traducianism seems to make the soul a piece of material that is transmitted from generation to generation. However, this seems to be based on a misunderstanding of the words regarding man's spiritual nature. His spiritual essence is not flesh, but it *is* something. It seems there are certain qualities of personality that can be transmitted from generation to generation, such as a family of musicians and musical ability, and this need not be conceived in physical terms.

3. Creationism. Creationism is the idea that each new soul is a direct creation of God. Each new soul is ethically and morally pure. It then comes into contact with the body that is sinful or fallen. Berkhof says, "It may simply mean that the soul, though called into being by a creative act of God, yet is pre-formed in the physical life of the foetus, that is, in the life of the parents, and thus acquires its life, not above and outside of, but under and in, that complex of sin by which humanity as a whole is burdened." [55]

Creationism, like the other viewpoints, was held early in the history of the church. It was held by such men as Ambrose, Jerome, and Pelagius.

The objections to creationism are mainly two. First, the strongest objection is that it involves God as the author of evil, at least indirectly, for God places a pure soul within a body that will ultimately corrupt it. The second great objection is that it makes the parents responsible for the body of the child but omits the impartation of the soul so that it is an independent element apart from the parents.

The issue of creationism versus traducianism is one that is difficult to solve. Even the great Augustine, who was very much concerned about this problem, could come to no solution. J. O. Buswell, in his *Systematic Theology*, concludes, "I would conclude with Augustine therefore, that on biblical grounds we cannot firmly establish either the traducian or the creationist view of the origin of the human soul." [56]

One problem in the whole discussion has been the either/or terms of the question. It is possible that *both* of these are aspects of the

---

[55] Berkhof, *op. cit.*, p. 199.
[56] I, 252.

real truth. We agree with Brunner in his statement about the synthesis of the problem:

I, this human being, am evidently both a product of my ancestors and a new creation of God. We must assign the continuity to the preservation, the new element to the creation of God, whereby the question may remain open whether or not as a whole and apart from man each individual as such, in spite of all continuity and explicability of its elements from its antecedents, is something new. This must in any case indubitably be claimed for the human person. Every human being is a new creation of God; every one is an original, and none is a product of a series, although in its cultural manifestation the originality may be very slight. Each human being is not only an individual but a person, and therefore directly related to God as its Creator.[57]

The Beginning of Sin

In any discussion of the biblical story of the beginning of sin, one must face the prior question of "from where did sin come?" The Bible does not offer a philosophical answer to the origin of sin. Certain presuppositions are found there however. God is holy and cannot be regarded as originating sin. God is not such that he can be tempted to sin. Beyond this, there are only hints recorded in the Bible concerning the origin of sin. The Gospel of John records the words of Jesus in saying that the devil is a murderer from the beginning (8:44). The first letter of John speaks of the devil as sinning from the beginning (3:8). First Timothy 3:6 alludes to the sin of the devil as being that of pride. Jude 6 declares that the angels kept not their own principality but left their proper habitation.

If the sin of the angels was a sin with regard to turning away from God in process of questioning his goodness, this does find its parallel in the temptation story in Genesis 3. What had been successful in the angelic realm turned out to be quite successful in the human realm. The account of the serpent in Genesis 3 is important. Niebuhr avers that the Christian has not been wrong "in identifying the serpent with, or regarding it as an instrument or symbol of, the devil. To believe that there is a devil is to believe that there is a principle or force of evil antecedent to any evil human action. Before man fell the devil fell. The devil is, in fact, a fallen angel. His sin and fall consist in his effort to transcend his proper

---

[57] *Christian Doctrine of Creation and Redemption*, p. 35.

state and to become like God. This definition of the devil's fall is implied in Isaiah's condemnation of Babylon." [58]

There are several lessons in the Genesis story. First, even the devil himself was created good, and evil comes from his transgression against God. In this sense, evil involves the turning from the Good, the Creator, to the self. Second, the appearance of the devil within the Garden of Eden story shows that man's rebellion is not a matter of caprice or evil perversity on his part. The circumstances were not rigged so that man was forced to sin. Third, man himself is not the inventor of evil. There is a basic difference between man's sin and the sin of the devil. The devil is the inventor of sin and the first one involved in it. His sin is "pure defiance, pure arrogance, purely intellectual and spiritual sin. Human sin always contains an element of frailty, of the nonspiritual, or the sense element." [59] Fourth, the sinful creature—either angelic or human—tends to corrupt those surrounding it. The guilty party becomes an evangel of evil.

The conclusion, then, that we must reach in beginning the story of man's departure from obedience to God is that man was created good. Sin is an intruder from the outside, and man begins his walk into sin by turning from obedience to God.

The Nature of the First Sin

The first sin of man was not a sexual one. In *Letters from the Earth,* Mark Twain caricatures the story of Genesis and speaks of Adam and Eve's discovery of sex.[60] Not only does Twain not understand the psychology of sex, but he also does great injustice to the biblical picture of sex. He speaks of it as something that is forbidden and evil. This is a perversion of the biblical concept of God making man and woman for each other.

In a more serious vein, theologians have attempted to characterize the first sin under some single word, as rebellion, pride, unbelief, but this is an attempt to simplify matters. It is perhaps true that all of these things are involved in the first sin of mankind. The first sin of man must also have some relationship to that which is recorded about man later in his history. The New Testament speaks of certain features of sin, and in this case, it is pride that is the beginning of

---

[58] *Nature and Destiny,* p. 180.

[59] Brunner, *Christian Doctrine of Creation and Redemption,* p. 108.

[60] *Letters from the Earth,* ed. Bernard Devoto (New York: Harper & Row, 1962).

consequent sins. Niebuhr declares that "pride is more basic than sensuality and that the latter is, in some way, derived from the former." [61] Pascal defines sin in these terms, "This I is hateful. . . . In one word it has two qualities: It is essentially unjust in that it makes self the center of everything and it is troublesome to others in that it seeks to make them subservient; for each I is the enemy and would be tyrant of all others." [62] Pride issues in the self-wilfulness of man in which he exalts himself in the place of God. The ultimate end is self-glorification. Further, pride issues in the attempt to gain freedom from God.

Reinhold Niebuhr, in his classic work *The Nature and Destiny of Man*, speaks of the sin of man in terms of pride. Unfortunately, the word "pride" has come to mean for us a conceited or swelled-head attitude. But pride in the sense that Niebuhr uses it is related to self-centeredness. It refers to overconcern with one's self. Speaking then in terms of pride, pride is treated under three different categories by Niebuhr, although they are never quite distinct: pride of power, pride of knowledge, and pride of virtue.[63]

The *pride of power* is dealt with on two different levels. "The first form of the pride of power is particularly characteristic of individuals and groups whose position in society is, or seems to be, secure." [64] However, one can never find this sort of security, for doom may be impending around the corner. The second form of the pride of power is more obviously "prompted by the sense of insecurity. It is the sin of those, who knowing themselves to be insecure, seek sufficient power to guarantee their security, inevitably of course at the expense of other life." [65] This type of power issues in forms of greed, insecurity, fear of obscurity, and in other ways.[66]

The second form of pride is the *intellectual pride* of man. "In-

---

[61] *Op. cit.*, p. 186.

[62] *Ibid.*, p. 187.

[63] *Ibid.*, p. 188.

[64] *Ibid.*, p. 189.

[65] *Ibid.*, p. 190.

[66] Cf. Paul Tillich: "*Hubris* is not one form of sin besides others. It is sin in its total form, namely, the other side of unbelief or man's turning away from the divine center to which he belongs. It is turning toward one's self as the center of one's self and one's world. This turning toward one's self is not an act done by a special part of man, such as his spirit. Man's whole life, including his sensual life, is spiritual. And it is in the totality of his personal being that man makes himself the center of his world. This is his *hubris*; this is what has been called 'spiritual sin.' Its main symptom is that man does not acknowledge his finitude."—*Systematic Theology*, II, 50–51.

tellectual pride is thus the pride of reason which forgets that it is involved in a temporal process and imagines itself in complete transcendence over history." [67] The ultimate consequence is that one who is guilty of intellectual pride is unaware or is ignorant of his own ignorance. It is the sin of making one's self think that he has become the final thinker.

The third type is *moral pride*. "Moral pride is revealed in all 'self-righteous' judgments in which the other is condemned because he fails to conform to the high arbitrary standards of the self. Since the self judges itself by its own standards, it finds itself good. It judges others by its own standards and finds them evil when their standards fail to conform to its own. This is the secret of the relationship between cruelty and self-righteousness." [68]

Niebuhr concludes that "the sin of moral pride, when it has conceived, brings forth spiritual pride. The ultimate sin is the religious sin of making the self-deification apply in the moral pride explicitly." [69]

Results of Original Sin and the Problem of Guilt

Even when the Bible is not received as the revelation of God, it can be freely admitted that there is something radically wrong with man. Man's inhumanity to man makes the thoughtful observer wonder what can adequately explain all of these problems. Why is it that man takes to selfishness and sin naturally? Any answer given to this question will probably bring into the discussion the phrase "original sin."

Original sin is used to describe what Adam did in corrupting himself as well as the human race.[70] The latter implication, i.e., what we

---

[67] Niebuhr, *op. cit.*, p. 195.

[68] *Ibid.*, p. 199.

[69] *Ibid.*, p. 200.

[70] William Hordern, in *The Case for a New Reformation Theology*, says that the term "original sin," despite its misuses, "must be retained. It points up the fact that all man's sins stem from his original sin, the sin that is logically first" (p. 130). Further, he says, "It is also original in the sense that it describes a situation that we inherit. . . . Sin is something that has somehow got its hold upon the human race as a whole." However, Hordern goes on to say that the doctrine of original sin has brought much confusion and embarrassment to the Christian faith. He declares that one cannot "reconcile the imputation of Adam's guilt to his descendants. We do not need help from Adam to make us guilty. Our own sin is quite sufficient for that" (p. 131).

inherit by being sons of Adam, is vitally important to any doctrine of man-in-sin, for it involves the issue of guilt. Another term, the "fall of man," describes man's departure from God into sin and rebellion. The two ideas are summed up in the *Westminster Shorter Catechism*: "The sinfulness of that estate whereunto man fell, consists in the guilt of Adam's first sin, the want (lack) of original righteousness, and the corruption of his whole nature, which is commonly called original sin; together with all actual transgressions which proceed from it." [71]

This definition can be accepted, but the real issue comes in adding the answer of Question 16, which speaks of the covenant being made with Adam. Then it says, because of Adam's transgressions, "All mankind descending from him by ordinary generation sinned in him and fell with him in his first transgression." This is the aspect of the doctrine of man that offends modern consciousness. This view is still defended by men of the Reformed tradition who are conservative in their theology. Brunner, however, remarks that although the theory of original sin has been held from the time of Augustine, it is "completely foreign to the thought of the Bible." [72] He adds that the Bible does say that in Adam all have sinned, but it does not tell us how all of this took place.[73]

We have two basic questions closely related to each other: What are the effects of Adam's sin upon his descendants? Where does guilt enter the life of the individual? Before any proposals are offered, it must be noted that the source of disagreement centers around the passages of Paul in Romans 5:12 and 1 Corinthians 15:22.[74] How are we to interpret these passages? In what sense do all die in Adam? If all die in Adam, am I guilty in Adam? Or to put it another way, can there be vicarious guilt? Can I be blamed for something I did not do?

In the following exposition we shall state the proposed answers and attempt to relate the two basic questions.

---

[71] *Westminster Shorter Catechism*, Question 18.
[72] *The Christian Doctrine of Creation and Redemption*, p. 103.
[73] *Man in Revolt*, p. 142.
[74] "Therefore as sin came into the world through one man and death through sin, and so death spread to all men because all men sinned" (Rom. 5:12). "As in Adam all die, so also in Christ shall all be made alive" (1 Cor. 15:22).

The Augustino-Calvinistic View

From the time of Irenaeus there have been those who regarded Adam as the source of all the sinfulness of mankind. Through Adam's sin men have become enslaved to the devil.[75] In this instance the passage in Romans is understood as saying that death has come upon all men because they all sinned in the one man Adam. Augustine, as did Calvin later, spoke of the fall or sin of Adam as producing a human race of perdition. Man is so shot through with sin that the Reformers spoke of his being totally depraved. Even the virtues of the heathen were regarded as splendid vices; that is, his outward acts of charity were corrupted through ulterior motives. Nothing good was to be found in man and his only good was to find salvation in Christ. From the Calvinistic perspective one may say that man is shot through with sin from the top of his head to the sole of his feet.

However, such a statement concerning the moral position of man can be misleading. The idea does not mean that man is as bad as he can be, nor does it exclude the idea that man does have individual acts that can be said to be praiseworthy. It means "first, that sinners have no natural affection for God; secondly, that they cannot remedy this defect by resident moral powers. They can only vent pride and selfishness on new and more refined levels." [76]

The position sounds quite severe. It means that man by birth becomes a sinner. How is this so?

Adam is regarded as standing in a twofold relationship to the human race. He is first the natural head of the human race, the father of all living. We are all sons of Adam by birth; from him we have our physical body. This itself does not imply any involvement of his offspring with the problem of sin and guilt except to ask ultimately how can righteousness be the offspring of the unrighteous? The second aspect is that of Adam's covenant relationship. Because Adam was the *representative* of all his descendants, his act of will, therefore, was also their act of will. The Reformed theologian Berkhof wrote,

Because he was the federal representative of his race, his disobedience affected all his descendants. In his righteous judgment, God imputes the

[75] Kelly, *op. cit.*, p. 171.
[76] Edward John Carnell, *The Case for Orthodox Theology* (Philadelphia: The Westminster Press, 1959), p. 72.

guilt of the first sin committed by the head of the covenant to all those who are federally related to him, and as a result, they are born in a depraved and sinful condition as well, and this inherited corruption also involves guilt. This explains why only the first sin of Adam, and not his following sins nor the sins of other forefathers, is imputed to us, and also safeguards the sinlessness of Jesus, for He was not a human person and therefore not in the covenant of works." [77]

Man is therefore born with the defects of Adam along with being guilty because of his sin. The great objection is that it runs contrary to man's sense of fairness. How can he be blamed for something that happened before he was born? Equally as serious is the question: Can there be guilt without personal involvement and responsibility? It does not solve any of these questions to reply that "you were there in Adam." I was in my father in the same sense but I do not inherit his goodness any more than I am responsible for his sins. If there is anything evident in the book of Romans, it is personal responsibility for one's own sins—not somebody else's.

Neo-Pelagian View

Close to the end of the fourth century a British monk named Pelagius came to Rome. He taught that there is no relationship between Adam's sin and the corruption of the race, nor is there any guilt involved. Man is born innocent and free, like Adam before his rebellion against God. Man has the ability also to live a sinless life if he so desires. He even believed that some men before the birth of Jesus had lived without sinning. The assumption is made that man is capable of fulfilling the commands of God. They are not impossible of performance, because God as Creator would command only what we are capable of doing.

The views of Pelagius are adopted by modern Christian existentialists. Some modern theologians reject any connection between Adam and the sin of any other man. Basically, each man is born in a state of innocence and, like Adam, faces daily the matter of deciding his relationship to God. This has much in common with Pelagius

---

[77] *Op. cit.*, pp. 242–43. Buswell in his *Systematic Theology of the Christian Religion* follows much the same line of thinking, basing his viewpoint on the *Westminster Shorter Catechism* in which "the Covenant being made with Adam not only for himself but for his posterity, all mankind descending from him by ordinary generation, sinned in him, and fell with him in his first transgression" (I, 312).

but it departs in affirming that all men in fact have sinned and men do not live in perfection. The passage in Romans is to be understood in the sense that all men die because all men sinned in their own right and not particularly because Adam sinned. Niebuhr asserts that even Augustine, who rejected Pelagianism and spoke of inherited corruption, inserted a qualification on the passage in Romans 3:23 so that it read, "For all have sinned—whether in Adam or in themselves—and come short of the glory of God." [78]

In describing such a position, Brunner states that no connection exists between the first sin and the sin of the tiny child. When then does the first sin take place? Brunner rejects the possibility of any reconstruction of the matter. If forced to make some decision he declared: "It is the moment when the little child first becomes conscious of himself as an 'I,' and when he actually expresses it, the very moment which Fichte extolled as the birth of man." [79] Although born innocent, the only recollection we have is that we have always been sinners. Such is also the history of man in general— history is seen to be filled with sin.

What does this view do then with the early chapters of Genesis? The Genesis account is understood as the story of *every man*. It is a true fact that all men come to place themselves in opposition to God. All men refuse their creatureliness and place their own word above the word that God has concerning them.

The problem in this position is to explain why every man always does this. Brunner's solution is as follows:

Our solidarity in sin also refers to past generation. It refers to our individual past as well as to that of humanity. We are not aware of any moment in our existence when we were not sinners. So far as our consciousness is concerned, the state of "being a sinner" began with our first sin. But this first sin cannot be reconstructed by us in psychological fashion; it is lost in the mists of infancy or childhood. So far as our recollection as persons is concerned, we are aware of ourselves as sinners. The same is true of humanity as a whole. So far as it can be perceived in history, it is seen to be sinful. [80]

Why is it then that men do turn aside into sin? Two answers may be advanced among others. Paul Tillich, a modern existential

[78] *Op. cit.,* p. 261.
[79] *Christian Doctrine of Creation and Redemption,* p. 100.
[80] *Ibid.*

theologian, speaks of the creation of man as synonymous with the fall. It seems to be the nature of the created to make the transition "from essence to existence. He creates the newborn child; but, if created, it falls into the state of existential estrangement." [81] However, one may well ask if this does not imply that the creative work of God is really bad. This is especially true concerning the first man. The second answer would be that sin is a corporate thing, and humanity has been involved in sin for so long that the innocent child quickly learns to express his own will against the wills of those around him.

Although this view is strong in establishing the fact of personal responsibility and of making guilt a consequence of personal sin, it is weak in explaining the universal phenomena of why men depart into sin. The objection raised against the Reformed view (How can I be blamed for something I wasn't there to do?) is revised to read, "How can I be blamed for something when I was too young to know better?" In summary, Neo-Pelagianism denies a relation between Adam's sin and his descendants and between Adam's guilt and personal guilt.

The Thomistic View

First suggested by Athanasius, eventually accepted by Thomas Aquinas, the Roman Catholic theory stands between Augustinianism and Pelagianism. The Roman Catholic view depicts Adam as having two types of life. He had the natural life to which was added as a gift the supernatural life. The supernatural life includes the theo-logical virtues of faith, charity, and a desire to be with God. When man disobeyed God, he lost the supernatural life. In consequence, man is simply deprived of something that he once had. After Adam's sin, he still has his natural life but now it is tainted with the tendency toward sin, but yet having the ability of the will to do otherwise. "Original sin is thus described negatively. It is the privation of some-thing which does not belong to man essentially and, therefore, cannot be regarded as a corruption of his essential nature." [82] With regard to guilt, a child is born neutral, or innocent. In this there is similarity to Pelagianism, but with a difference. The un-baptized child, who dies in infancy, because of moral neutrality, is

81 Tillich, *Systematic Theology*, II, 44.

82 Niebuhr, *op. cit.*, p. 248.

neither condemned to hell nor admitted to heaven. Neutrality is not innocence, for the child is denied the beatific vision of God. Baptism becomes the key for full restoration to God's fellowship.

Romanism is not fully consistent in its view of sin and man. It attempts to explain why children take to sin as they do—being born with a tendency to sin—but this is very little improvement over Calvinism. The unbaptized infant who dies is theologically no better off in Romanism than in Calvinism. The fact of rejection from God's presence without baptism logically means that concupiscence, or the inherited tendency to sin, is condemnatory for men. It is a distinction without significance! In essence, the unbaptized child bears the result of somebody's guilt—a fact similar to the Reformed position.

The View of Some Baptists and Others

Some Baptists have spoken of Adam's sin resulting in a tendency of his descendants to sin. The question of Job about the impossibility of a clean thing coming from an unclean one is pertinent. How can the innocent come from the sinful? How is it that my child manifests selfishness in ways that he has never observed in anyone else? The question, Is man a sinner because he sins or does he sin because he is a sinner? has been posed in an either/or fashion. For this position, both sides are true. Man takes to sin readily because he is man, he *appears* to be born with a bent toward selfishness. At a very early age a child moves from making legitimate demands for his physical needs to demanding constant attention, entertainment, and care. If the perceptive parent is not aware, the child will build a small universe around himself. Selfishness continues to grow with age unless it is disciplined—and it does require discipline.

The second part of the question—is man a sinner because he sins?—is also true. Here is where guilt really enters. There cannot be guilt without personal involvement in sin. To be clear in the matter, we must say that there is no guilt involved in the things that a child does in his early "unresponsible years." Yet, during this time, as a son of Adam he manifests the usual sins of adulthood: selfishness, self-centeredness, anger, and so on. It is only when the child comes to an age in which he realizes that these actions are wrong and that he is a responsible being for his actions that guilt may enter.

Is there biblical precedent for such a position? We are really dealing with what is called "the age of accountability." Although this

is not grounded in the Scriptures as a definite term, one may see the idea in the Jewish practice of Bar Mitzvah ceremonies in which a boy of thirteen assumes the obligations of the religious law of God. In this sense can be understood the words of Paul when he wrote, "I was once alive apart from the law, but when the commandment came, sin revived and I died" (Rom. 7:9). In a similar sense can one understand John 1:9: "The true light that enlightens every man was coming into the world." This is saying that all men at one point in their lives are enlightened so that they are regarded as responsible for their own decisions. Much must be made of personal decision about sin and about God.

The advantages of this position are obvious. It has affinity to those positions that affirm man's helplessness in working out his own salvation. It affirms the *sola gratia* (by grace alone) platform of the Reformation. It emphasizes, in contrast to the Reformed position, the aspect of freedom and responsibility. It is concerned with present personal guilt rather than with the guilt of someone who lived in the past. It attempts to account for the universal turn toward sin but not at the expense of freedom. It limits guilt to what one is personally involved in. It grants that children do not merely learn to be sinful, they manifest their heart's departure into sin. At the same time it is not freighted with implications of guilt for which there is no ground of responsibility at an early age.

In conclusion to this section, it is worth noting that a great deal of attention can be focused on how man has gotten himself into this mess. The following chart may help focus attention on the different views we have dealt with in this section.

MAN

Relation of Adam to His Descendants

Calvinism: Human nature is depraved in Adam; man does evil in attempting even to do good.

Thomism: Human nature is deprived with a tendency to sin which can be overcome.

Pelagian: All men are born innocent with no relation to Adam's sin. Sin is learned, but can be avoided.

Baptist: Man has a bent toward sin, may do outwardly good deeds occasionally, but is helpless in helping himself.

Relation of Adam to His Descendants Concerning Guilt

CHILD

Calvinism:	guilty in Adam	faith in Christ redeems
Thomism:	neutral (?)	baptism restores
Pelagian:	no guilt in Adam	faith for those who sin
Baptist:	no guilt until	personal faith in Christ
	responsibility	is necessary.

It is evident that we all find ourselves in sin. We are also aware that we are responsible for our actions personally. All of the concern about "how I got this way" may cause us to overlook "how I can get out of it." The central affirmation of the gospel of Jesus Christ is that man has a way out, an exit from the guilt of personal sin—and there can be no sin that is not personal. God has provided an escape. The mature man sees it as his only hope.

Excursus
Problems in the Doctrine of Man

The man of faith does have certain problems with the doctrine of man. The *problem of guilt* inherited, as implied in the Reformed doctrine, has been highly criticized by modern theologians. Brunner is particularly critical of it. He says, "The 'stumbling block' of the ecclesiastical doctrine, however, consists in this, that we are made responsible for sin which someone has committed." [83] He continues to insist that sin and responsibility stand together, or the idea of guilt is meaningless. He points up the fact that in the Bible, wherever one speaks of sin it is with reference to responsibility.[84] He argues that men can inherit much from their past, but "sin, godlessness, alienation from God, can never be inherited." [85] He objects to the Reformed doctrine in that it seems to make sin something that is communicated as a biological inheritance. He likewise points out that the Reformer's attempt to emphasize the helplessness of man in sin went to the point of having a "crude form of determinism." [86] The very meaning of the image of God, according to Brunner, is that man

---

[83] Brunner, *Man in Revolt*, p. 143.
[84] Brunner, *Christian Doctrine of Creation and Redemption*, p. 104.
[85] *Ibid.*, p. 105.
[86] Brunner, *Man in Revolt*, p. 146.

is always in a position of responsibility, whether in sin or out of sin.

On the other hand, it is quite difficult for the modern mind to appreciate the concepts involved in the Reformed position. Individualism is a concept that we have lived with, but corporateness is the word connected with the Reformed doctrine. It speaks of humanity as a mass and with a representative. The Reformers never deemphasized personal responsibility. Calvin would not acknowledge vicarious sin. Yet both concepts—inability to not sin, and responsibility—are held in common. At last, for Calvin, the two must be resolved in mystery in which God in his justice has a greater understanding of justice than man does.

The problem of freedom.—"The essence of man is his freedom." [87] Sin is meaningless without the possibility of its coming into being from freedom. Freedom "is his creaturely mode. It is adapted and therefore proper" to man.[88] The matter of freedom is important. It is interesting to contrast the first three centuries and the sixteenth with regard to freedom. It was developed against the Stoic doctrine of fate, and one can see it expressed in Justin, Origen, the Cappadocian Fathers, as well as Chrysostom.[89] In the sixteenth century the emphasis is on the bondage of man in sin and his inability.

What is the freedom we must speak of? First, there is not such a thing as absolute freedom. P. T. Forsyth said that if there were absolute freedom, it would be the worst kind of tyranny. The freedom of man is the freedom of being in dependence on God. "Man is only free when he is united with God." [90] Freedom is not such that one can turn away from his responsibility before God. "It is never freedom to sin." [91] The fact that man does sin brings about an enslavement. The freedom of man is that which Jesus spoke about in Matthew 16. In retaining our independence, we lose it. In denying ourselves, we gain freedom. To exert our freedom in sinning, we enslave ourselves and destroy our freedom. Modern man's problem is that he seeks freedom apart from responsibility. He has yet to learn that "in the Divine Love to have oneself and to lose oneself is the same thing." [92]

---

[87] Niebuhr, *op. cit.,* p. 17.
[88] Barth, *Church Dogmatics,* III-2, 194.
[89] Kelly, *op. cit.,* pp. 166 and 349.
[90] Brunner, *Man in Revolt,* p. 129.
[91] Barth, *Church Dogmatics,* III-2, 197.
[92] Brunner, *Man in Revolt,* p. 231.

The mentally retarded.—One question that theology has no scriptural basis for dealing with is the unfortunate position of the severely mentally retarded. Questions can be raised from many angles. Are these truly human? Responsible? Guilty? It seems to me that the question has to be dealt with on the basis of the relationship between body and soul. It is impossible on a chemical basis to answer whether they have a soul or not. However, if one can presume that the body and soul are a unity, then one can proceed to speak of the inability of the body-brain to carry the functions of the soul as it exerts to express itself. The soul is thwarted in expressing itself because of the incapacity of the body complex. One need never be tormented by anxiety over the issue of salvation. God has given us no basis for deciding differently. So one can only commit this to his mercy, which is the beginning point of the gospel in the first place.

X. The Christian View of Sin

Man may think that he can and should be gracious to himself, but this is impossible. He thinks and acts as his own helper, but believing that he is his own best friend he is all the time his own worst enemy.

Barth, *Church Dogmatics*

At the same time that sinfulness in human life is always defined as volitional, it also appears to faith in the form of a demonic spiritual power which commands and subjugates the human will. The solidary interrelationship of sin concretizes itself in inscrutable and obscure powers, a mysterious complex which cannot be accurately delimited and defined, and which slips away and becomes shadowy as soon as one tries to grasp and comprehend it.

Aulén, *The Faith of the Christian Church*

Since . . . the concept of sin always has reference to man as a whole, and furthermore, since God's judgment on sin is always an unconditional and radical rejection, in the presence of God it is meaningless to differentiate between serious sins which entail serious guilt and lesser sins which cause lesser guilt. The consciousness of guilt and the awareness of our own unworthiness do not become weaker because a sin, according to human estimation, is less serious. In this connection there is in reality no place for a graduation of sins as greater or lesser.

Aulén, *The Faith*

A theologian should be able to write meaningfully on the subject of sin, for this is the common experience of all mankind, whether it is acknowledged or not. The doctrine of sin is surrounded with two extremes. Sin can be regarded as insignificant in light of God's great love. Thereby one can wipe out all meaning for the basic facts of the gospel; i.e., the atonement in Jesus Christ. On the other hand, man can be regarded as being so vitiated with sin that he does nothing that is noble or good by human standards. We hope to avoid both positions.

Christian faith, by the nature of its message, places great emphasis on the doctrine of sin. The gospel is a message declaring how God has "put away" sin. The gospel is God's answer to man's rebellion.

Why Is Sin Sin?

On what basis can one speak of certain things as sin? There have been many diverse ideas promoted. Sin has been defined as: (1) a violation of community custom, which ultimately may be right or wrong; (2) an illusion, in which case it does not exist; (3) ignorance, in which case education would be able to eradicate it; (4) the manifestation of the beast-nature of man, in which case he should not be blamed for it as it is a part of his nature; (5) nonexistent, in which case one should not worry about it; and (6) a violation of conscience, which cannot be separated from its upbringing and thus is unreliable.

There is no basis for talking about sin, however, "except in a religious sense. The significance of the knowledge of sin can be known only as divine revelation illuminates the fact of sin." [1] In this regard when one talks about ethical standards there are ultimately only two great ethical systems that oppose the Christian viewpoint. There is, first, the naturalistic view which starts with the fact of existence and seeks to explain morality on the basis of natural facts. "Right" is a summary of the conclusions of experience. Thus the right is that which has proved useful to mankind in his community experience. Naturalism in its approach to living cannot ask the question of what one *ought* to do. "Morality—as generally understood—only begins where the natural instinct breaks down, that is, where one 'ought' to do what one does not want to do. The choice before the naturalistic moralist is either to deny the existence of such a 'sense of ought' or to give up his Naturalism." [2] Fortunately, many naturalists are not wholly consistent in this matter, for while they deny God, they hold a humanist outlook in ethics.

---

[1] Aulén, *op. cit.*, p. 259.
[2] Emil Brunner, *The Divine Imperative* (Philadelphia: Westminster Press, 1947), p. 37.

The opposing system is some form of idealism involving duty for duty's sake. "An act is not good if I do it because I like doing it, but only if I do it because I ought to do it, because I 'may' not do otherwise." [3] This ethic involves three concepts: The right may be known to reason and is not acquired from revelation; the right as known by reason must be binding on everyone without exception and this involves the idea of universal validity; and it must be able to tell everyone what one must do in particular cases.[4]

There are two major criticisms of the last view, which is ascribed to Immanuel Kant. First, it seems to equate the reasonable thing to do, or duty, with the law of nature which does not tell one what he ought to do. Second, there is concealed a principle which is contrary to the established standard of reason, and that is the standard of happiness: "Act in such a way that if everyone were to act as you do, a happy human society would result." [5]

Opposing these two great systems in one form or another is the Christian ethic based upon the biblical assertions. "What God does and wills is good; all that opposes the will of God is bad. The Good has its basis and its existence solely in the will of God." [6] The holiness of God is the basis for the good. "The Good is that which God does; the goodness of man can be no other than letting himself be placed within the activity of God." [7]

The Christian ethic is universal in its positive features. The commandment of love has an unconditional character which applies absolutely to all, in all circumstances, and in every kind of situation; "it is universal also through the worldwide breadth of the divine will, which wills nothing less than this: His Kingdom." [8] On the negative side, one can only declare something to be sin which violates the nature of God. Because it violates the nature of God it also violates the structural makeup of man and God's design for him. Thus man cannot rightly speak of sin without the fact of God's self-revelation. It is meaningless to speak of sin without reference to God's commands.

Viewing sin as related to God and man as God's creature, one

---

[3] *Ibid.*, p. 38.
[4] *Ibid.*, p. 39.
[5] *Ibid.*, p. 580.
[6] *Ibid.*, p. 53.
[7] *Ibid.*, p. 55.
[8] *Ibid.*, p. 59.

might say that sin is wrong because it is essentially self-deceptive and God desires nothing but the truth for man. In many cases sin—in its initial stages—has the halo of innocence. In others, a particular deed can be isolated from its effects and gives the impression of harmlessness. Second, and related to the deceptive aspect, is the fact that sin is self-destroying. The commands of God are related to life and sin violates what makes for life. Perhaps one other comment concerning the evil of sin is that man in sin becomes self-centered. When man shuts God out of his life and becomes a god unto himself, he cuts himself off from the best that life has. Self-centeredness cuts off fellowship with God, with man, and the world at large.

The Nature of Sin

Christian faith has always looked to at least two types of materials in the Bible concerning the nature of sin. It has analyzed the story of Adam in the book of Genesis, and it has made a synthesis of the statements on sin with regard to man in general. We shall attempt to deal with the nature of sin along these lines.

Sin had to begin somewhere.—The biblical record undoubtedly is to be understood from the standpoint of Adam's sin as the first. We have already discussed in chapter 9 the authenticity of the account. We also discussed in that chapter the matter of Adam's descendants and the problem of guilt associated with it. The reader is urged to review the material there.

The beginning of sin vitally affects the question of the nature of sin. The nature of Adam's sin centers in the words of unbelief or disobedience due to pride or egocentricity. One word does not adequately express all that was involved. It would perhaps be better expressed if one coined a hyphenated word such as "unbelieving-disobedience" or "disobeying-in-unbelief." The goodness of God was called into question in the Genesis story. The man Adam did not believe that God's warnings were true, and this led him to disobey. Disobedience cannot be understood apart from unbelief. The story is sometimes recounted to picture man as standing with two choices, either to obey or disobey. The man Adam was never given such a middle position in choice. From the beginning, the commandment of obedience was placed upon him. Sin for him was going against the command of obedience. Unbelieving-disobedience was a fact of experience for him as well as for all mankind.

The nature of "unbelieving-disobedience" is such that the self becomes the distorting factor of human life. To live in "believing-obedience" is to live under the dominion, the governorship of the Lord God. With unbelieving-disobedience, the self assumes the dominion and asserts its governorship and tyranny against the Lord God. Sin involves the swap of one rulership for another. However, in the case of man, it is not one tyranny for another, but the exchange of beneficent lordship for the anarchy of human freedom in which every person is a tyrant. The rule of the ego in a world of aspiring egos is the consequence of sin. Aulén states that "sin as unbelief and sin as egocentricity are one and the same thing seen from different points of view. Egocentricity is opposition to the divine will, and therefore 'unbelief.' Whenever this power rules, the fellowship with God is destroyed." [9]

The nature of sin is such that in manifesting its egocentricity as unbelieving-disobedience it corrupts all that it touches. How could it be otherwise? This is one of the emphases of the doctrine of original sin. Can this not be seen in the original account? The children of Adam and Eve are corrupted by their parents. Cain expresses the same unbelieving-disobedience as Adam and Eve. We are not advocating a mere example theory of the transmission of sin, but one can see the reason for this theory to rise. Even if one granted that children were born innocent, the egocentric nature of the parents would soon corrupt them. There is a solidarity of the race in sin that almost defies explanation.

The sin of Adam was not an insignificant act. Sin is not simply an isolated thing that has no connection with the present or the past, nor is it without implication for the personality of man. The nature of un-believing-disobedience is such that once a transgression is committed one can never return to the state of "un-sin" or innocence. Sin can be forgiven, but it has its devastating consequences. Sin has a cumulative effect. As sins pile up, it becomes easier for sin to assert itself. Sin can be compared to corrosion on a battery cable. The more corrosion, the weaker the battery power. The more sin corrupts the human personality, the less power to overcome it.

The relationship of unbelieving-disobedience to sensuality can be seen as the manifestation of the egocentric nature of man. The pleasure of the moment is not weighed against the future time in

---

[9] Aulén, *op. cit.*, pp. 264–65.

which indulgent egocentricity destroys itself and comes to judgment
before God. Sin is not to be defined merely in terms of the sensual
nature of man. Sensuality is only a manifestation of unbelieving-
disobedience. Sensuality is "the result of egocentricity, a 'seeking
one's own.' " [10]

Moreover, sin cannot be blithely defined as a form of intellectual
heresy. It is true that there is a correlation between what one thinks
and what one does, but sin is not simply the failure to believe this or
that doctrine. There is no virtue in trying to believe as little as
possible; on the other hand, the sin of man first relates to his lack of
trust and commitment.

The first sin of the race is important for the explanation of the
fact of sin as well as understanding the history of mankind. It is,
however, not the most significant fact in light of the subsequent story
of man. What is more consequential is the other side of the story of
man's personal sin.

Sin is personal.—We do not mean by this heading that Adam's
sin was not a personal act, but that our own sins relate to our
responsibility and not to Adam. We cannot write off our sins by
blaming others, as Reuben attempted to do with his evil involvement
in getting rid of his brother Joseph (Gen. 42:21–22).

Sin involves the whole person. Sin is not imposed on man, nor is
it accidental or commited without man's wilful involvement. Sin
corrupts the entire man. Man's perspective on ultimate things is
warped. He stands helpless in a world that is his making. He is not at
home in this world and his sin has alienated him from God's world.
He is like a man swimming upstream against violent currents. This
is one of the implications of the term "total depravity." It does not
mean that man is as mean as he could be, nor does it mean that one
must overlook certain "noble" deeds of heroism. It does mean that
sinful man cannot swim against the stream and remedy his sinful condition by his own moral strength.[11]

Sin is not separate acts which have no relationship to one another.
Sometimes writers make the distinction between the terms "sin" and
"sins." The word "sins" refers to the many separate acts or deeds
that are the result of sin. The basis for this distinction comes from
Romans 6, in which Paul speaks of sin as a tyranny or dominion

10 *Ibid.,* p. 265.
11 Carnell, *The Case for Orthodox Theology,* p. 72.

over man. This governorship of sin rules man until he is delivered from it by his "death in Christ," and sin thereby has no more rule over a "dead" person. In the same chapter, one is commanded to fight against sins. Such a distinction is quite necessary in seeing the relationship between individual acts and the reason we do them. Man has submitted himself to the slavery of sin and is its bondsman. He does its bidding in terms of his egocentricity, and it is not until he is delivered from the rulership of sin that he is on the way to the recovery of his whole self. It is the heart that must be changed, as Jesus said, for here, in the enslaved kingdom of the heart, is where sin comes from: unbelieving-disobedience manifests itself in desires contrary to the good of the person's structural design.

Personal sin implies responsibility. Luther posed the two alternatives: "Either man is responsible for nothing, or else he is responsible for his life as a whole." [12] Man is responsible for getting himself enslaved to sin and is responsible for his own delivery through commitment to Christ, who is the Deliverer. "Man is what he does. And he does what he is." [13] Man reels from one sin to another and he does it consciously: hence responsibly.

The New Testament Catalog of Sins

Any attempt to categorize the numerous listings of specific sins would be artificial and forced. Sometimes distinctions are made between sins against God and sins against the neighbor. "There is no sin against the neighbor which is not sin against God. The sin against the neighbor becomes sin just because it is sin against God." [14] In dealing with the subject of sins, the New Testament is quite prolific in its lists of sins. The sins are somewhat specific but do deal in general principles. It is not presumed that an entire cataloging of sins is found in the New Testament. There is value in looking at the list, however.[15]

Abusiveness, adultery, anger (two words), arrogance, a base mind, being bereft of truth, bitterness, boastfulness, carousing, clamor, conceit (or conceitedness), covetousness, a craving for controversy, cowardliness,

---

[12] Aulén, *op. cit.*, p. 283. (As Aulén phrased it.)
[13] Barth, *Church Dogmatics*, IV-1, 492.
[14] Aulén, *op. cit.*, p. 261.
[15] For an alphabetical listing, see Frederick C. Grant, *An Introduction to New Testament Thought* (Nashville: Abingdon Press, 1950), pp. 176–77.

debauchery, deceit, depravity of mind, disobedience, including disobedience to parents, disorder, dissension (two words), doglike behavior,
drunkenness (two words), enmity, envy, error, evil, evil eye (jealousy?
or bearing a grudge?), evil thoughts, extortion, faithlessness, (two
words), falsehood, false witness, fierceness, filthiness, foolishness or
folly (three words), fornication (also rendered immorality in RSV), foul
talk, gossip, greed (also rendered covetousness), mutual hatred, being
hated by men, hating God, hating good, haughtiness, heartlessness, homo-
sexuality (two words; and also sodomy, as below), idolatry (two words),
immorality, improper conduct, inhumanity, implacableness, impurity,
ingratitude, injustice, insolence, invention of evil, lying, malice, malignity,
man-slaying murder, murder of father or mother, party spirit, passion
(three words), evil desire, slavery to passion and pleasures, perjury, love
of pleasure, pollution, pride, profaneness, profligacy, wild profligacy (another word), quarrelsomeness, recklessness, reveling, reviling, robbery,
ruthlessness, selfishness, silly talk, sin, slander (three words), sodomy,
sorcery, strife (also rendered quarrelsomeness), base suspicion, theft,
treachery, ungodliness, unholiness, unrighteousness, wickedness (also
rendered evil or injustice), worship of demons, wrangling, wrath—a
total of 115 terms, not counting duplications.[16]

The variety in the above list, as well as its rather full coverage of
sins, is significant of the ethical life of the Christian.

There are some observations that should be drawn at this time.
First, the listing deals with individual sins. One will look in vain for
a community or national ethic in the New Testament. There is nothing
said in this list about the sin of war, for instance. Other national sins
are not condemned. Certainly one can extend from the personal to
the greater sin of the nation, but it must be remembered that the
passages deal with individuals primarily. When one is tempted to extend the list to apply to national policy, it may be questioned on the
grounds that the ethics of religion may be imposed on those who do
not share the Christian faith. Christian ethics presupposes a
"spiritual" background, that is, the experience of conversion, and
without this as a prerequisite, it would be unfair to suggest that other
people abide by its moral code.

Second, there is no distinction between the various categories of
sins. The list includes all types: physical, mental, and spiritual. The
condemnation placed on physical or sensual sins by our present

---

[16] These are drawn from the following passages: Mark 7:21–22; 2 Cor.
12:20; Gal. 5:19–21; Eph. 4:31; 5:3–5; Col. 3:5,8; Matt. 15:19; Luke 18:11;
Rom. 1:28–31; 13:13; 1 Cor. 5:9–11; 6:9–10; 1 Tim. 1:9–10; 6:4–5; 2 Tim.
3:2–4; Titus 3:3; 1 Peter 4:3; Rev. 9:21; 21:8; 22:15.

"religious" culture is out of all proportion to the other sins. It is ironic that we often condemn sins of the body that "burn out" due to the aging of the body, but do not condemn as severely the sins of the mind or spirit that intensify with advancing years. For instance, there is greater possibility in a grouchy person's becoming more grouchy. The cynic becomes more cynical. The man who is set against God becomes convinced more firmly in his opposition. All of this is not to overlook the possibility of repentance and the renewing of personality but to emphasize that the many distinctions between sins are artificial and wrong.

The Unpardonable Sin

The New Testament has a few references to a particular sin that is removed from the usual category of sins. It has commonly been called the "unpardonable sin" or "blasphemy against the Holy Spirit." There is no general agreement concerning the nature of the unpardonable sin.

One might approach the matter as Halford E. Luccock does. He proposes, in due reverence, a list of sayings that he would call, "Things I Wish Jesus Had Never Said." One he lists is Matthew 12:22–37. He concedes a sentiment for the idea that the words in the passage were uttered in great indignation and that perhaps at some other time Jesus would not have uttered them.[17] Such a comment with regard to ordinary men would be quite true; but, molded by purpose and knowledge of doing the Father's will, it seems difficult to write off such a reaction on the part of Jesus. For whether or not there is uttered here a statement out of anger, there is a basic truth—which Luccock also admits—which remains: Sin can become so deeply rooted within the personality that no change is ever desired. To this we will return.

Various attempts have been made to explain the nature of the unpardonable sin. They are not always mutually exclusive. First, it is sometimes defined as opposition to conversion. Often the passage from Genesis 6:3 is quoted to show that there is a time in which God will stop dealing with the human heart. But the words, "My spirit shall not abide in man for ever," refer only to the 120 years that Noah had to build the ark. After the 120 years, the flood would

---

[17] *The Interpreter's Bible* (New York: Abingdon-Cokesbury Press, 1951), VII, 692–93.

come. The passage has nothing to do with the unpardonable sin. So opposition to conversion is not the unpardonable sin. Many people have opposed conversion for long years and later became Christians. This viewpoint can become true at death. If one opposes conversion until he dies he is involved in unpardoned sin, but there was always a possibility that he could have been converted anywhere along the way.[18]

Second, the unpardonable is sometimes defined as the hardening of the heart and mind to the truth of the gospel. This has only a shade of difference in meaning from the above. The turning of the heart from truth to falsehood paves the way for more serious acts of rebellion. Aulén states, "When Christian faith speaks of a state of 'hardness of heart,' it understands thereby a definite rejection of the divine and gracious will characterized by the suspension of the consciousness of guilt." [19] Thus, one cannot continue to be stubborn in resistance to the gospel of Christ without its taking its toll in one's life. However, we do not feel that this is the unpardonable sin.

Third, the real truth of Matthew 12:22–37 and Mark 3:19–30 is that the unpardonable sin is a very definite thing. Jesus spoke concerning this after the Pharisees *attributed to an evil source that which was clearly the work of the Holy Spirit.* They attributed his exorcism of demons to the power of Satan. A good deed does not come forth from a foul creature. Only by the Spirit's power does it come about (John 3:19–21). "The unforgivable sin is the utter rebellion against God that denies him as the doer of his own acts." [20] To boil it down in three words, it is "calling good evil."

Why is it unforgivable? The basic reason is psychological, not theological. "It was evidence of a moral obtuseness and perverseness so deep-rooted that there was no hope of its ever being changed. Calling good evil ranges all the way from ascribing good actions to evil motives, to the supreme example cited in the . . . words of Milton's Satan, "Evil, be thou my good." [21] Sin can become so enslaving in its more sophisticated forms, in sensuality, pleasure,

---

18 Lange's commentary speaks of the sin as follows: "It is open and full opposition to conversion, and hence to forgiveness."—*Commentary on Matthew*, p. 224.

19 Aulén, *op. cit.*, p. 286.

20 *Oxford Annotated Bible*, eds. Herbert G. May and Bruce M. Metzger (New York: Oxford University Press, 1962), p. 1186.

21 *Interpreter's Bible*, VII, 693.

prestige, ambition, power, and popularity, that the person does not want to turn from it. A complete reversal of values takes place. Evil becomes the good. Good becomes the undesirable. However, all along there is nothing from God's standpoint that would prohibit forgiveness. The problem lies with the freedom of personality to remain enslaved in its reversal of values.

There are two other features that must be discussed in connection with the unpardonable sin. First, is it possible that believing people can commit this act? The general answer is no, because conscience and concern are still alert in them. Indeed one might well ask the question whether it is possible for anyone to commit this particular sin. One could question it on the basis of the details of the chapter. We do not have the presence of Jesus with us in body today, and we do not have his acts of healing. However, we *can* come to a complete reversal of values by attributing good things to evil sources. I simply raise the question without answering it.

The other feature is the distinction between sins against the Spirit and *the sin* against the Spirit. All that we ever do in sin is against the Spirit. We are admonished not to grieve the Holy Spirit (Eph. 4:30). But there is only one act which can be called the unpardonable sin.

The Unpardoned Sins

The unpardoned sins are those that are unconfessed when one dies. What is the implication for the man who lives a reasonably good Christian life but may be guilty of some sins which he has never confessed or turned from?

There are essentially two views to this matter within Christianity. First, the Roman Catholic position is to say that mortal sins, even in a "good" Roman Catholic Christian would be condemning and the man would, by his sinful act, bring the judgment of hell upon himself. If there were merely venial sins in his life, these would be taken care of in the state of purgatory. Unpardoned sins must be dealt with one way or the other.

The second answer comes from the Reformation viewpoint and is more closely anchored in the New Testament. The idea of justification or righteousness from God (Rom. 1:16–18; 3:20–24) means that a man is accepted by his faith in Christ. It does not imply that he is perfected once and for all in this life. The Christian life has its ups and downs. The man is still redeemed even when guilty of occasional acts of sin. However, his occasional transgressions do violence to his fellowship-relationship to God, but not to his redemption-relationship. It is impossible to be confessed up with regard to sins at all times. If one were going to try it, it might be possible to remember one's overt acts of sin, but what about the commanded actions of the New Testament—the so-called sins of omission? The sins of omission are also as damning as the sins of commission.

If one is going to grade sins, as the Roman Catholics do, one is always going to stand in jeopardy of casting himself into hell. On the other hand, the grace of God is his gracious receiving of trusting men and women in spite of their shortcomings. We are not trying to minimize sin at this point; on the other hand, it is so serious that we must affirm that God saves us in spite of ourselves, or we would not be saved at all. If we must remain perfect, then where is the need of grace?

There is another aspect to unpardoned sins. One can continue to live apart from God and the gospel of his Son. One comes to death and terminates life without committing his life to Jesus Christ. One dies unpardoned. This is to be distinguished from the unpardonable sin. The unpardoned sins become now unpardonable.

Distinction of Sins

Within the diversity of Christian faith there are different viewpoints concerning the types of sins. On the one extreme is the Roman Catholic view which regards sin within two categories. First, there are mortal sins. A mortal sin is "an act so grievously subversive of the moral order as to destroy the friendship existing between the soul and God, and to frustrate the end of the moral law, which is the due subordination of all created good to God, the infinite and sovereign good." [22] "The loss of grace being the immediate effect of moral sin necessarily involves eternal separation from God, should the sinner die unrepentant." [23]

It should be kept in mind that the Roman Catholic idea of grace is akin to a spiritual substance imparted to the soul like food is taken into the body by mouth. When mortal sin is committed, the food supply (grace) to the soul is cut off. Without the food supply the soul will perish. To regain the supply, the soul must repent and be

---

[22] George D. Smith, *The Teaching of the Catholic Church,* p. 927.
[23] *Ibid.,* p. 931.

absolved by receiving the sacrament of the Church which turns on the flow of grace again. (We do not want to be crude in this illustration, but it is necessary to distinguish paramount differences in the concepts of grace. It must be noted that in Protestantism in general, grace is not conceived as a substance, but as the benevolent attitude of God. This distinction has tremendous importance for the different views of sin and grace.)

Examples of mortal sin are "to injure either oneself or one's neighbor so that normal human duties become impossible to perform (i.e. suicide; total neglect of one's own spiritual welfare; theft or murder)." [24] To the age-old question that concerns many people, can a person be saved and lost? the Catholic answer is an emphatic yes!

Second, there are venial sins which "do not involve the loss of grace, and whose effects can be repaired by the supernatural principle of grace and charity which still remain in the soul." [25] The analogy of the word "stain" on the soul possibly suggests what is meant by this type of sin. Venial sins are not condemning sins. Of course, one will have to suffer for them. But even if purgatory be the goal of most Roman Catholics, they can be assured, regardless of how long they remain in a state of purifying suffering, that they will eventually reach the goal of heaven. Venial sins are committed by everyone and "not even the holiest person can avoid them altogether." [26] One cannot stack up venial sins to equal a mortal sin. It is also true that under given circumstances, the act committed might be either venial or mortal. If man commits an act which is really mortal but he thinks that it is venial, then it is venial. The same holds true for the person who believes that the sin he is committing is mortal even though it may be only venial in nature. This briefly is the Roman Catholic view regarding the differences in sins.

On the other side is the Protestant view which makes no distinction between the various sins. This view begins with the proposition of James: "Whoever keeps the whole law but fails in one point has become guilty of all of it." (2:10). In addition, the various New Testament listings of sins mingle them together. Jesus spoke in the same breath of evil thought and murder, of adultery and slander, of fornication and theft. Paul's listings in Romans commingle gossipers

24 A Handbook of the Catholic Faith, p. 391.
25 George D. Smith, The Teaching of the Catholic Church, p. 947.
26 Ibid., p. 949.

with murders and disobedience to parents in the same sentence with "haters of God." In Romans 13:13, he speaks of drunkenness in the context of jealousy and quarreling. In most of the other passages in the New Testament the same pattern holds true.

One of the reasons for the tendency to distinguish between sins, as the Roman Catholics do and others also, is because sins are different. However, the real important difference is in the *consequences* rather than in the matter of guilt. Adultery, for instance, has great consequence for it involves not just one person but a whole network of personality involvements. The presence of children involves a serious consequence as well as the possible breakup of two homes. However, Jesus spoke of the seriousness of lustful thinking in contrast to adultery. "Every one who looks at a woman lustfully has already committed adultery with her in his heart" (Matt. 5:28). Certainly lustful thinking does not have the involvements of the multi-personality which the actual act has, but it is still termed adultery by Jesus and is as serious as the committed act. There is also a difference between murder and the thought of murder, but each is liable to judgment.

Thus there are greater consequences in the committed act as opposed to the contemplated thought. But each is equally the same serious sin against God. Each is equally condemning.

The same holds true for the fact of falsehood, cheating, jealousy, gossip, and the many other sins listed in the New Testament. Yahweh is the God of truth with regard to witness, slander, or injustice. He has laid down certain claims with regard to himself and the rights of others. The Ten Commandments set forth his right of priority of all things, the reverence due his name, his day on earth, and his rule over man. Man also has certain rights: life—commit no murder; family—commit no adultery; property—commit no theft; reputation—commit no slander; and security—do not envy.

When distinctions are drawn between sins (and not the consequences) there is at work a theology which will eventually make many sins into virtuous acts. Such a tendency in theology will water down the concept of the holiness of God and end with the ability of man to atone for many of his petty sins. Such a distinction brings on the demise of grace and the exaltation of man's goodness. All of which is contrary to the New Testament.

The Consequences of Sin

The New Testament very easily sums up the consequences of sin: "The wages of sin is death" (Rom. 6:23). Many reasons have been marshaled to explain why sin has to be punished. Some have suggested that punishment vindicates divine righteousness; others have maintained that punishment brings reform to sinners; still others speak of punishment as a deterrent from further sinning. Great objections can be raised against all of these.

The real answer to the punishment of sin comes in relation to the creative design of man and the holiness of God.

With regard to the creative design of man, God has made man in such a way that the laws of nature and the laws concerning good and evil are for his own good. As long as man obeys the structure of order he can find happiness. In this sense, one can look at the law prohibiting adultery. The design of the Creator was for a man and woman to live together faithfully in love to one another. Where adultery enters, the picture of whole family structure is at stake. There is a breakup of loyalty. One cannot love two in marriage because two loyalties are contrary to the structure of monogamy. As man violates his vows of loyalty and trust he has violated the design of the Creator and thus alienates himself from him. Where the marriage vow is violated there are certain psychological results that automatically enter. One's mental life becomes subject to distressing disturbances which "rob him of joy, disqualify him for his daily task, and sometimes entirely destroys his mental equilibrium. His very soul becomes a battlefield of conflicting thoughts, passions, and desires. The will refuses to follow the judgment of the intellect, and the passions run riot without the control of an intelligent will. The true harmony of life is destroyed, and makes way for the curse of the divine life. Man is in a state of dissolution, which often carries with it the most poignant sufferings." [27]

This has a very real connection with the other factor: God's holiness. Not only does man violate the structural makeup of his nature, but he also violates the nature of the Designer. God is holy. The nature of God is such that the evil, unholy, wicked nature of man cannot enter *unprotected* into his presence without annihilation. With-

---

[27] Berkhof, *op. cit.*, p. 259.

out the continuing power and presence of God in his life, man the finite creature, has no other alternative than to die in violating the design of his existence.

One must bear in mind that salvation is simply the deliverance from the ultimate consequence of all of this. Physical death is not terminated, but pardon is granted to man and entry is made possible into the presence of God by his protection: the death of Christ in covenant.

The consequences of sin are fourfold:

Present miseries.—Some sins bear with them the seeds of consequences bringing misery, suffering, and sorrow to man. Certain sins bring harm to the body when sin is committed. The breakdown of physical life is only part of the misery. Unconfessed sin may haunt one's mental and spiritual well-being for years. Some sins may have no direct connection with the body but may eventually affect it when worry, guilt, and self-indictment disturb the soul of man. But it must be acknowledged that in some cases it *appears* that men prosper while sinning and the "righteous" seem to have only sorrow. Psalm 73 speaks of this experience. Although sin has possibilities for present life, judgment on sin is not completed until God's final judgment.

Spiritual death.—"Sin separates man from God, and that means death, for it is only in communion with the living God that man can truly live." [28] Alienation from God becomes final and eternal if conversion does not take place before death. One can speak of this as eternal death.

Physical death.—This is to be defined as the cessation of life as we know it in the physical realm. The body functions cease and the spiritual faculties of man no longer possess a channel of expression. There is a breakdown of all the component parts of human life. The body decays and the spirit is deprived of its earthly abode. That which made up the body again becomes earth and the form of man is lost until the resurrection brings the form into new being. The spirit departs the body to abide in its destined place. The spirits of the redeemed enjoy the presence of the Lord, while the spirits of the unredeemed begin to experience partial judgment which will not be complete until God's judgment takes place after the resurrection of all men. Then the spirits of the dead will be reunited with their raised

---

[28] Berkhof, *op. cit.,* p. 259. See Matt. 8:22; Luke 15:32; John 5:24; 8:51; Rom. 8:13.

and changed bodies to enter the future existence as a complete person.

This fact is somewhat borne out by man's physical life. The new-born baby is a dying creature. The body is continually replacing itself with new cells while the elimination of dead cells continues throughout life. Physical death becomes a reality when the body can no longer keep ahead of the need for repair and re-creation.

Death everlasting.—At this point death does not mean a termination of being and existence. Death everlasting means that the individual has decreed for his own existence an existence apart from the presence of God. This takes place forever. Just as in mortal life the rebelling person was sustained in his rebellion by God's power, so now in death everlasting his state of existence is sustained by God's power. Luther's comment that hell is God's hell remains true. The Bible says nothing of a termination point, presumably because the tendency of sin is to further the separation from God. The self-centered world of the sinful becomes all the more self-centered, and the shriveling up of the person keeps pace with the direction of sin.

A fuller treatment of this matter will be reserved for the doctrine concerning last things.

XI. The Christian Life

There is nothing so happy as a Christian who has never met a theologian.

Attributed to Vance Havner

If we will not bear the yoke of Jesus we have to bear the yoke which we ourselves have chosen, and it is a hundred times more heavy.

Barth, *Church Dogmatics*

Anyone who does truly good works has blessedness already in his faith, and therefore cannot find himself wanting first to rely upon his works.

Friedrich Schleiermacher, *The Christian Faith*

It seems to be adequate . . . to call it the experience of the New Being and to distinguish several elements in it which . . . can be described as the experience of the New Being as creating (regeneration), the experience of the New Being as paradox (justification), and the experience of the New Being as process (sanctification).

Paul Tillich, *Systematic Theology*

"All this I did for thee; What wilt thou do for me?" The New Testament does not speak in this way. It knows nothing of a Jesus who lived and died for the forgiveness of our sins, to free us as it were retrospectively, but who now waits as though with tied arms for us to act in accordance with the freedom achieved for us.

Barth, *Church Dogmatics*

What does it mean to be a Christian? How does one become a disciple of Christ? What does being a Christian mean with reference to myself, to others, and to God? What does being a Christian have to say about ethical living, with its failures and successes? Questions that we have discussed before lead naturally to the place of involvement, or the "experience" side of the religious question. Much of our previous discussion is theoretical but it is not without close connection to the practical. If one completely ignored what has been discussed in the previous ten chapters, there would be no basis for a chapter on the religious experience of the Christian.

When one attempts to dissect the Christian life, it will be found that there are certain experiences, attitudes, and hopes that are found in it. The New Testament has a number of terms that sound formidable to the uninitiated, but, like any other discipline, one has to learn some new vocabulary words. One must consider terms like faith, repentance, regeneration, sanctification, and others. The student needs the caution that while one must make what seems like tight distinctions between terms, it must not be concluded that separate religious experiences are being discussed. In reality *many* of these terms are vitally related and from the standpoint of religious experience come simultaneously.

Grace

The Christian life becomes possible because of God's grace. What does grace mean? All Christians speak of God's grace, but not all define it the same way. The Roman tradition speaks of sanctifying grace and actual grace. Sanctifying grace "enables our soul and its faculties to be in such a state that it can orientate itself towards God and our salvation." [1] The result of sanctifying grace is that one is cleansed from original sin as well as personal sin that may have been committed. Because of this grace also there takes place the radical transformation of the human nature and to it is restored what it lost in Adam's fall, the supernatural life.[2]

Actual grace in the Roman sense is "a force on man, continuous influence and help from God enabling us to live on the level to which He has raised us by sanctifying grace." [3] Actual grace helps the believer to perform some worthy service or avoid sin.

The focal point of grace is important in its distinction. Both types of grace are primarily received through the Church. Even where men

---

[1] *A Handbook of the Catholic Faith*, p. 213. (This term must not be confused with the idea of sanctification as understood in Protestant thought.)

[2] *Ibid.*, p. 211.

[3] George D. Smith, *The Teaching of the Catholic Church*, p. 588.

receive actual grace it is given that "they may be drawn to the Church." [4] Sanctifying grace is received in the waters of baptism initially and thereafter through the appropriate sacraments.[5]

Thus one can see that grace is a common factor in both Protestant and Catholic traditions. How do they agree and differ? Both agree that without the grace of God, man would not be redeemed. Roman thought recognizes that grace signifies something which is freely given.[6] But it speaks of it as a "positive reality superadded to the soul." [7] Protestant thought will stress the attitudinal definition of grace as benevolence, mercy, or love. Grace is not a "thing" or spiritual dynamic, or energy, or force. Grace for the Protestant is the motive of salvation. A criticism of the Roman view would be that it has never taken seriously the biblical ideas of the Holy Spirit concerning the religious life of the believer. Because God is gracious, the Holy Spirit indwells the life of the believer. If we are to speak accurately, grace as a substance does not exist. Grace is not added to the believer as a quantum, but what happens is that God's Spirit indwells him. Grace as a substance can neither give directions nor help to overcome sin, but God's Spirit can. Grace cannot illuminate the mind, but God's Spirit can. Grace cannot draw men to God, but it is the motive whereby God's Spirit works in human hearts.

The disagreement in concepts must be pushed further in regard to baptism or other sacraments. A substantive view of grace fits the sacramental system. When grace retains its biblical meaning of favor, there is nothing to impart. The Spirit of God operates in a more intimate fashion than through a sacramental system.

Grace, regarded as substantive, poses problems for the matter of the believer's persevering in the faith. If grace is so defined then one must have it within him at death, or he is condemned. In the Protestant sense of grace along with justification, spiritual life is not so precarious. This will be treated later in the discussion on justification. It will be seen that Roman thought has confused sanctification with justification and, in essence, has never understood the idea of justification by faith.

Protestants retain the biblical idea of grace, meaning "to be gra-

---

[4] *Ibid.*, p. 616.
[5] *Ibid.*, p. 567; cf. p. 606.
[6] *Ibid.*, p. 602.
[7] *Ibid.*, p. 552.

ciously disposed toward another." [8] This understanding of grace is behind the redemptive acts. The believer benefits because of God's life, but he benefits *by means of* the Holy Spirit, not grace. The Spirit is the Being in whom we have our existence. For convenience sake, one might say, "The grace of God abounded to me." But this is to say nothing else than that because of God's mercy the Spirit of God lives within my life.

The separation of the sacraments from the reception of the Spirit may seem strange to Roman ears, but it retains the personalistic dimensions of the New Testament. The Holy Spirit is not related to a sacramental system, but to faith.

Faith

The Christian life is a relationship to God based upon faith. The religious relationship in other world religions is not understood in terms of faith. "Paul was the first to use this word to describe the right relationship to God, and by so doing he gave it an absolutely dominating position in religious language." [9] At the same time, faith is misunderstood in the minds of many. Faith is often equated with believing something to be true. When a Christian recites the Apostles' Creed, "I believe in God. . . ," he is affirming the statement to be true. There is no meaning of the New Testament word "faith" in the opening phrases of the Creed. It amounts to saying that God is one in the same sense that I declare my belief in the fact that Napoleon lived. Believing in Napoleon and believing in the Apostles' Creed are on a par. To believe that both God and Napoleon exist requires nothing on my part.

By contrast, when the New Testament speaks of faith it means more than mere intellectual assent to a truth. What is faith? The Greek word for faith, *pistuo,* is defined as "a conviction, full of joyful trust, that Jesus is the Messiah—the divinely appointed author of salvation in the kingdom of God, conjoined with obedience to Christ." [10] To have faith in Christ is to give oneself to him. Faith speaks of obedience, acknowledgment, and confession. [11] Faith "is

---

[8] Rudolf Bultmann, *Theology of the New Testament* (New York: Charles Scribner's Sons, 1951), I, 284.

[9] Brunner, *Christian Doctrine of the Church, Faith, and the Consummation,* p. 140.

[10] Thayer, *op. cit.,* p. 511.

[11] Bultmann, *op. cit.,* pp. 318–19.

the condition for receiving salvation." [12] It means that I am no longer master of myself, but I "belong to another." [13] Faith means to give "an unconditional yes to that God who reveals himself." [14] Faith means dependence upon God. It means that independence is recognized as a sham, and real freedom begins in dependence.[15]

If faith is defined as trust some negative ideas must be rejected. Faith is not mere assent. Faith is not the cause of redemption. Faith is not a leap in the dark for which one has no reasons. Faith is not unwarranted optimism, the avoidance of skepticism, a façade for defeatism, or a despair of facing reality.

With the issue of faith as the beginning point, the question may be raised: Who has the faith? In the Roman Church the deposit of faith is in the church and may be represented by the parents or godparents when infants are baptized. In many Protestant churches, a similar parallel prevails until the time a child can consciously affirm his faith. Churches in the Baptist tradition insist upon faith that is personal. This means that one cannot have faith without awareness and personal responsibility. Faith, therefore, presupposes an age of awareness and involvement which cannot be true of infants.

While we have stressed faith as commitment in conformity to the New Testament, faith's relation to knowledge is important. Certainly it is true that believing the Apostles' Creed as true is different from commitment to Jesus Christ. But while commitment is stressed, it is not blind commitment. Faith and knowledge are related. Faith is dependent upon certain factual assertions. Faith cannot respond until it hears a gospel. The gospel includes a number of historical matters concerning the death and resurrection of Christ and its meaning for man. Aulén has stressed this in saying that "trust involves an 'assent' to the content and message of the divine revelation." [16] It seems difficult to suppose commitment to a person who is really dead and whose death has no real significance for our lives. Faith presupposes that Christ is trustworthy, that he is alive, that God exists, that God reveals himself, and that he is love.

---

[12] *Ibid.*, p. 316.
[13] Brunner, *Christian Doctrine of the Church, Faith and the Consummation*, p. 141.
[14] Aulén, *op. cit.*, p. 315.
[15] Brunner, *Christian Doctrine of the Church, Faith and the Consummation*, p. 286.
[16] *Op. cit.*, p. 315.

Faith is always related to the person of Christ. Knowledge of him alone makes one only a historian. Faith in him makes one a Christian. Calvin perceived this when he distinguished between what remains in one's brain and what is taken to the root of the heart.[17]

Because faith and knowledge are closely related, there is real value in teaching about Christ. In teaching there is the witness of Christ that brings the response of faith.[18]

Faith also involves a way of knowing. In commitment, which is based upon some knowledge, one also learns about Christ and experiences what he has done.[19] Further, one in faith acknowledges that Jesus Christ is the Saviour and in this acknowledgment, one learns for the first time what one really is. In faith I see myself as I really am—in rebellion, sin, and disobedience. In faith I learn of what Christ can do for me. By committing myself to Christ, I learn of what I will become; namely, conformed to his image.

Faith involves obedience. The same Lord who stands before man with the challenge to trust him also stands with the words *be* this or *do* this! But obedience cannot be separated from the Person and from faith *in* the Person.[20] Barth wrote, "Faith is not obedience, but as obedience is not obedience without faith, faith is not faith without obedience. They belong together, as do thunder and lightning in a thunderstorm."[21]

This leads naturally to the relation between faith and works. The stress on religious works, in Roman thought, as part of self-redemption is opposed by Protestants who insist on ethical transformation but not in the sense of self-redemption. The Protestant would insist on obedience as a meaning of commitment and faith, but he does not imply perfection in Christian growth in the term. The crucial issue in the matter is—if one is dependent upon personal salvatoric works for pleasing God—when has he done enough? Obviously, no one has loved God with all his heart, mind, and strength. Therefore, it is solely through God's grace that one can be redeemed. One re-

---

[17] *Op. cit.*, p. 510.

[18] Brunner, *Christian Doctrine of the Church, Faith, and the Consummation*, p. 241.

[19] Karl Barth, *Church Dogmatics* (Edinburgh: T. & T. Clark, 1956), IV-1, 766.

[20] Cf. Brunner, *Christian Doctrine of the Church, Faith, and the Consummation*, p. 297.

[21] *Church Dogmatics*, IV-2, 538.

ceives the full gift of God by faith. If faith is true faith, one will not find oneself wanting to rely upon works for redemption. If faith is receptive—which it is—it is not able to take an initiative in self-redemption.

Faith as the basis for the Christian life implies a choice. It is "a decision, a venture, perhaps a timid but at the same time a bold *yes* to God." [22] Sometimes faith is spoken of as a gift of God.[23] Faith can be said to be a gift of God in that God has the initiative that creates it. By his call to man, man then gives the response of faith, and in that sense it can be said to be caused by God.[24] But faith is foremost the personal response of the human heart to God's gracious gospel. There is no proxy faith, just as there is no proxy love.

In line with the personal dimension of faith for beginning the Christian life, faith is also related to confession. When one commits himself to the Master, it is for obedience. The command of confession is given by Jesus and the Christian must hold his banner high. The New Testament does not know anything of "undercover Christians." The Christian is to confess his faith in the language of the church as well as offer a translation of it to the world at large. Barth's words on confession are poignant:

"To someone who hesitates to confession of his faith, he would say, 'Dear friend, you may be a very spiritual man, but see to it that you are deemed worthy to be publicly responsible for your faith. And is your alleged shyness not shyness about emerging from your uncommitted private world? Ask yourself! One thing is certain, that where the Christian Church does not venture to confess in its own language, it usually does not confess at all.' " [25]

Faith, by its definition, means faith in someone and hence confession. Confessing and believing correspond to each other as in Romans 10:9.[26]

Faith in Christ asserts one's openness to God's Spirit who works in the believer's heart. Faith makes possible the redemptive event in

[22] Aulén, *op. cit.*, p. 320.

[23] So understood, it raises the question of whether all men are given this gift. Some theologians then speak of two types of grace: enabling grace or helping grace which makes it possible for one to have faith and thereby obtain saving grace.

[24] Cf. Brunner, *Christian Doctrine of the Church, Faith, and the Consummation*, p. 156.

[25] *Dogmatics in Outline*, p. 31.

[26] Bultmann, *Theology of the New Testament*, I, 317.

which one is renewed in the inner man, declared just, and begins growth in Christian maturity.

Repentance

The Christian life is initiated in repentance. A number of terms are used in the New Testament to describe repentance, but the most important is *metaneo*. It means "to change one's mind for the better, heartily to amend with abhorrence of one's past sins." [27] Repentance is thus "to turn away from sin and wickedness, and to God and righteousness." [28] Although many theologians who speak of repentance divide it into an intellectual, emotional, and volitional element, it is a "unitary act of man as a unitary being involving his mind, will, affections." [29]

Repentance must not be confused with being sorry that one is caught. Genuine repentance means regretfulness for sin although no one finds you out.

Repentance does not receive the same treatment on the modern scene as faith does. Tillich mistakenly compares it to the illumination of an idea [30] and it does not play a large enough role to merit a heading in the index of some theological literature. Yet repentance is a vital concept in the anatomy of the Christian life. Calvin spoke of its importance in connection with forgiveness of sins as being the sum of the gospel.[31] He distinguished it from faith but did not separate it from faith.[32] In order of discussion, repentance also followed faith in Calvin's thought.[33]

One reason theologians have not spoken at length concerning repentance is that it is presupposed in faith. It is impossible to think of God as holy and trust him in faith without involving a repudiation of sin. Yet repentance cannot stand alone. To repent without the turn toward the object of faith is meaningless. Repentance without faith only leads to despair. For this reason, repentance involves a turn from sin and a turn to God.

---

[27] Thayer, *op. cit.*, p. 405.
[28] Halverson and Cohen, p. 321.
[29] *Ibid.*, p. 322.
[30] Cf. *Systematic Theology*, III, 219.
[31] *Op. cit.*, p. 509.
[32] *Ibid.*
[33] *Ibid.*

Repentance is not to be confused with penance. Penance is a Roman Catholic sacrament involving contrition because of sin, confession of sin, satisfaction for it, and absolution of it. Penance thus involves—satisfaction—doing something. But repentance does not involve a "making up" for sin but a "forsaking" of sin.

Repentance may involve separation from wrongs or confession of sin, but these are the fruits of it.

Repentance is the negative side of faith, but neither stands without the other.

Conversion

Conversion is the end result of faith in Christ and the turn from sin to him. It is described as being necessary to enter into the kingdom of heaven (Matt. 18:3) by no less a person than Jesus.

What then is conversion? "It is just this turning in upon oneself, this turn right-about, this return to God."[34] Conversion is the "shattering of worldly standards," not in the sense of fleeing the world, but in the sense that one finds in God the true standard.[35] Conversion is "the beginning of the new life in fellowship with Christ"[36] because it is associated with faith and repentance. Conversion might be regarded as the human response, but from another perspective would be designated regeneration with its beginning spiritual life.

Conversion is in one way a once-for-all experience; and in another way it needs repetition. It is once for all, like that of birth. One does not continue being born again. It is repetitive in that after failures and sin one must always begin over, or reassert faith and repentance. This combined idea is expressed by Barth when he describes conversion as the "transition, the movement, in which man is still, in fact, wholly the old and already wholly the new man."[37]

Conversion is generally neglected where infant baptism is practiced. Obviously since everyone is a baptized Christian from birth, there is no place for conversion. Confirmation generally takes its

---

[34] Brunner, *Christian Doctrine of the Church, Faith, and the Consummation*, p. 289.

[35] *Ibid.*, p. 167.

[36] Friedrich Schleiermacher, *The Christian Faith* (New York: Harper & Row, 1956), II, 480.

[37] *Dogmatics in Outline*, IV-2, 572.

place and assent is given at an early age to the deposit of teaching held by the Church.[38]

Regeneration

We now turn to examine aspects of the Christian life that are more precisely termed the divine side of redemption. Although faith and repentance may be thought of as related to God's action upon us, yet regeneration is something that we cannot do ourselves. The word regeneration refers to God's work in the human heart that is compared to a birth—but spiritual—whereby a man once dead or nonexistent now comes alive to God. This change in the human heart is the result of the inward work of the Spirit. God's presence is like the wind but the results of the Divine Wind are felt and known. Regeneration means that one's life is linked with Christ, hence the term "being a new creature" is used. Of this doctrine, Brunner says, "Regeneration consists in this, that in this invisible core of personality the great, eternally decisive change takes place, that 'Christ is formed in us' through the death of the old man and the creation of the new, and that from this origin something new, even if only relatively new, comes into visible existence also." [39]

Regeneration is a term used to sum up the meaning of several words in the Bible. The word does occur in Titus 3:5, where the new spiritual life is meant. The idea of being born again occurs several times, mainly, but not exclusively, in the Johannine writings.[40] Another idea is that of being a new creation (Eph. 2:10) or a new creature (2 Cor. 5:17; Gal. 6:15) or a new man (Eph. 4:24). In addition to these, the idea of making alive (Eph. 2:5; 1 Cor. 2:12) is used. That which was alive to sin and dead to the rule of God now becomes alive to God and dead to the rule of sin.

The idea of regeneration means that man is not simply reformed in the hope of obeying God and winning his favor, but instead is transformed by the Spirit of God and is given his favor. Instead of viewing the Christian life in quantitative terms, it is seen in qualitative terms. Part of the burden of Kierkegaard was to declare that the

---

[38] Brunner, *Christian Doctrine of the Church, Faith, and the Consummation,* p. 276.

[39] *Ibid.,* pp. 273–74.

[40] John 1:13; 3:3–8; 1 Peter 1:23; 1 John 2:29; 3:9; 4:7; 5:1,4,18.

Christian is "infinitely qualitatively different" from the non-Christian. This is not to engender smugness on one's part, but to recognize that God is at work in the hearts where faith exists. It is the activity of God in the human heart that makes the difference and it is because pride has been spurned and faith affirmed that God is there.

Because of the new spiritual life within, which is the indwelling of Christ, there is a change in moral relations. We are to become renewed in righteousness and holiness of love (Eph. 4:23–24). Because one is regenerated and justified, he has access into the presence of God.

Regeneration is not the addition of some new element in the make-up of man's nature, but it is the making alive of the "old man." It is not a deposit of grace, a "created reality of an altogether higher order," [41] as held by Roman theologians. Regeneration is the "giving of a new direction or tendency to powers of affection which man possessed before." [42] Man possessed love in the unregenerate state, but turned it in upon himself. Regeneration means that his love is set supremely upon God. If one is to speak of a new element permeating man's existence, it is not a substance derived from a sacrament, but the living Spirit of God himself at work in him.

In experiencing regeneration, the believer is delivered from the rule of sin, but not from the confrontation with sin.[43] Regeneration must not be equated with sinlessness or confused with justification. The believer still must fight against sin even though he is no longer dominated by it. Regeneration is not nullified by virtue of his failure or lapse into sin. Instead, the fact that God's Spirit is at work in him makes it possible for him to start anew in his spiritual life. Failure on the part of a child does not mean he must be born anew to physical life. By the same token, because the believer possesses spiritual life, he can now grow in maturity and find victory over sin.

Regeneration is recognized as a necessity by most theologians, but the central issue is how it comes to pass. The two differing positions are basically through baptism (via infant baptism) or through faith alone. The advocates of baptism as the means of regeneration make their appeal to certain passages in the New Testament (Mark 16:16; John 3:5). Certain other passages in which the word "water"

[41] *A Handbook of the Catholic Faith*, p. 212.
[42] Strong, *op. cit.*, p. 823.
[43] Calvin, *op. cit.*, p. 516.

occurs are used to bolster the idea. Some words of caution are urged in using these verses.

The passage in Mark (16:16) is not a firm foundation to support a doctrine. Not only is it a questionable passage, not being recognized as an integral part of the early Greek manuscripts, but the passage continues to say that he that believeth not shall be condemned. Emphasis is placed upon the believing, not the role of baptism.

The other general comment is that a passage like John 3:5 and others really make no mention of baptism. It is inferred that "water" must refer to baptism. It would have been impossible for Nicodemus to understand it as such for the following reason. The principle of historical propriety in interpretation means that a passage must be understood from the standpoint of what the hearer could have understood by it. This means that it is illegitimate to force a sacramental view of baptism into the conversation of Nicodemus and Jesus. A sacramental view of baptism is alien to the New Testament. Hence, for these reasons and others, we must relate regeneration to faith alone. The conclusion of John 3:16, with reference to the conversation with Nicodemus, is that the believer's spiritual life depends upon believing in or committing oneself to Christ.

Although differences abound over the meaning of John 3:5, it still states—and almost all Christians agree—that regeneration, or being born anew, or from above, is necessary to enter the kingdom of God.

Justification

Justification is God's *declaration* to the man of faith that he is accepted in Christ. Justification means that the man of faith is forgiven. It is another way of talking about regeneration, but a difference persists between the two ideas. Regeneration speaks more of beginning, while justification or an accepted standing before God is related to the whole of the Christian life.

Because justification by faith stands as a key doctrine of the Reformation, two definitions will be useful.

The *Westminster Shorter Catechism,* following the Reformed tradition, says, "Justification is an act of God's free grace, wherein He pardoneth all our sins, and accepteth us as righteous in His sight, only for the righteousness of Christ imputed to us, and received by faith alone" (Q. 33). Calvin defined justification as "nothing else than to acquit from the charge of guilt, as if innocence were proved." [44] The acquittal motif is misleading, for it suggests that one is innocent; whereas in reality, in justification one is profoundly guilty. Thus justification is intimately related to forgiveness of sins.[45]

Justification has certain ambiguities about it. It made its way into early theology in the West in Latin, with the idea found in the legal system of a judge who rewards and punishes. In the same manner also the term "righteousness of God" has suggested a standard to which men must conform. The real meaning of these terms in the New Testament is removed from these traditional ideas. First, justification means to *declare* the sinner righteous.[46] It does not mean, as is sometimes stated, that God *makes* the sinner righteous. In this way, justification is not a quality of the soul but a relationship. Likewise, "it does not mean the ethical quality of a person." [47] Similarly, the righteousness of God is better understood with the preposition "from." It is the righteousness *from* God. It is not a standard to which man must conform but a gift of life in Jesus Christ. The righteousness from God means that God gives acceptance to man who is related in faith to Jesus Christ (Rom. 1:14–18).

A modern term used by Tillich expresses the meaning of justification as acceptance by God, "although being unacceptable according to the criteria of the law . . . and that we are asked to accept this acceptance." [48]

This leads us to consider the paradoxical nature of justification. At the same time that man is declared accepted, he is also unacceptable. How can this be? Because God created this new relationship. "What counts in 'God's sight' is for God alone and no one else to say. But he says: 'I assure you that, just as you are, you are right with me. I am the final authority that makes this decision. I love you, not because you are worthy of my love, but in spite of your unworthiness, simply because it is my will to do so.' " [49]

The paradoxical nature of justification must be stressed in all its

[44] *Ibid.*, p. 39.
[45] Aulén, *op. cit.*, p. 291.
[46] Brunner, *Christian Doctrine of the Church, Faith and the Consummation,* p. 200.
[47] Bultmann, *Theology of the New Testament,* I, 271–72.
[48] Tillich, *Systematic Theology,* III, 224–25.
[49] Brunner, *Christian Doctrine of the Church, Faith, and the Consummation,* p. 196.

fulness. Man the believer is not half sinner and half justified but simultaneously fully the sinner and fully the justified.[50] Not only is this true concerning justification, but the paradoxical nature extends to other areas.

The paradoxical nature of justification must not be interpreted to mean that God is only declaring man accepted and is not concerned with changing man and his way of life. Conversely, God not only declares man accepted but proceeds to work in man's life so that his eventual transformation (in the consummation) will conform to God's declaration.

This leads naturally to the discussion of justification and its relation to religious works or deeds. Is one accepted by God only on the basis of faith, or does one need to speak of faith-acceptance plus works, or the development of ethical religious deeds to augment justification by faith?

Roman theology affirms the latter. A fundamental principle in their theology is that Christ does what man cannot do, while on the other hand, man must do what is in his power to do. Traditional Roman theology seems to have misunderstood Luther by confusing justification with the idea of regeneration. This results in the necessary distinguishing of the types of sins into venial and mortal. If justification is regarded as the "interior renovation which blots out sin," then the return of sin in the believer leads to one of two alternatives: deny the seriousness of sin as in venial sins; or, accept its seriousness, admitting the realienation of the believer from God. Roman thought traditionally has done this. If one does not die in a state of inward grace free of mortal sin in the Roman sense, he is judged. On the other hand, venial sins are not serious enough to throw one out of the state of grace. The issue then becomes another question: Can the distinction between sins be valid? The New Testament does not warrant such a distinction. Jesus regarded lust equally as bad as adultery; hate as bad as murder.

The reason that justification by faith alone is so important is that only in it could one really have hope. If I must rely partly on my own works for salvation, three questions arise: could I ever do enough? when would I do enough? and how would I know when I had done it? Consequently, the place of personal merit and works was rejected as being contrary to the Scriptures. Calvin declared that

---

[50] Cf. Barth, *Church Dogmatics*, IV-1, 596.

"the Lord does not promise anything except to the perfect observers of the law; and none such are anywhere to be found." [51] Luther's despair reflects the result of a work's type redemption and hope only came when he saw clearly the real meaning of justification by faith alone.

It is to misunderstand the meaning of grace when additional human requirements are added. "Righteousness, then, cannot be won by human effort, nor does any human accomplishment establish a claim to it; it is sheer gift." [52] If faith is obedience, it can never be an accomplishment, for an accomplishment means that I assert my own will. Obedience means that I renounce my will for his.[53]

If man is to have hope in his religious life, it will come only through a proper understanding of justification by faith. Any other alternative leads to pessimism. Even the statement of Jesus in answering the question, What must I do to inherit eternal life? must be seen within the context of Judaism and not Christianity. To enjoin the fulfilling of the commandment—Thou shalt love God with all thy heart, soul, and mind—as the way to redemption is typically Jewish. It is an impossibility. But of course there was nothing else to say for he had not died nor had the new covenant been established. The new covenant is precisely what it says it is—new. It is a covenant of justification declaring forgiveness of sins not only at the point of regeneration but throughout the believer's life.

We spoke of justification with regard to forgiveness of sins. Forgiveness of sin is hard to believe and accept and it is for this reason that justification is hard to accept. For before forgiveness can come, pride must be surrendered and annihilated. The hesitancy to believe in forgiveness of sin makes one suspicious of whether there is full forgiveness. Much of human forgiveness is halfhearted and involves remembering the wrong. God forgives and remembers to forget.[54]

Justification is declared to be a once-for-all declaration, but its relation to forgiveness is continuing. Forgiveness is not an act that occurs once and then one must make up all deviations. Just the opposite—forgiveness belongs to the whole of one's spiritual life.

Justification and forgiveness of sins is not a barren experience. It

[51] Calvin, *op. cit.,* II, 105.
[52] Bultmann, *Theology of the New Testament,* I, 281.
[53] *Ibid.,* pp. 315–16.
[54] Cf. Aulén, *op. cit.,* p. 293.

involves the restoration of our broken relationship with God. Because we are justified and forgiven, we are invited to abide in him, to live and move and relate our lives to him.[55]

To sum up, justification involves two basic things: to be forgiven, which implies that deserved judgment has been remitted; and to be restored to fellowship with God.

Sanctification

As we turn to consider sanctification perhaps we should speak of its relationship to what has been considered. Justification is the declaration of God concerning the believer's new relationship. Regeneration is the work of God's Spirit in making alive the spiritually dead. Sanctification is God's work in nurturing the new being from its birth to its fulness of maturity in Christ, a nurturing that is not completed until after death. Sanctification without its beginning of regeneration is like trying to conceive of life without a birth. Sanctification without the standing in Christ as declared in justification would remove the fact of personal assurance from Christian faith.

But now what is sanctification? A historical definition is that it is "the work of God's free grace, whereby we are renewed in the whole man after the image of God, and are enabled more and more to die unto sin, and live unto righteousness." [56] Sanctification deals with the Christian's becoming Christlike. It recognizes the paradoxical truth of justification in being totally just and totally sinner, but sanctification involves the growing commitment to the direction of God's Spirit in making the believer the property and instrument of God.[57] Sanctification speaks of God's taking to himself that which stands against him, and in this claim upon the person he makes him serviceable to himself.

The work of God in the human heart spreads over the lifetime. He begins in the heart, the seat of human affections, by making it alive unto himself. Just as leaven permeates the loaf slowly, God presses out from the center of our lives slowly, taking captive our feelings, our thoughts, our desires, and ourselves. It is a paradoxical truth in the area of sanctification that the more one is controlled by God's Spirit

---

[55] *Ibid.*, p. 290.

[56] *Westminster Shorter Catechism*, Question 35.

[57] Cf. Brunner, *Christian Doctrine of the Church, Faith, and the Consummation*, pp. 295–96.

the more one is sensitive to the distance that separates him from God's nature.

It would be a mistake to identify sanctification with sinlessness. The ethical passages in the New Testament Epistles abound with warnings to the Christians not to sin. The truth of sanctification is that one is free from the rule and dominion of sin, but this is not to say that one is free from ever committing sins.[58] Sanctification must not be confused with moralism or the keeping of a prescribed set of rules. Adhering to rules solely is to overlook the inward change, which is the real meaning of sanctification.

Equally wrong is to think of sanctification in terms of negating the world or fleeing from it. The Christian becomes truly human in Christ—that is, he grows in approximation of what man should be. To be God's man is not something one is in isolation from society, but it means to be Christ's servant in community with mankind at large.[59] The influence of Greek philosophical dualism in the early centuries of Christianity made many flee from the world to be hermits and monks.

In spite of all the contributions of monasticism, it yet stands as a perversion of the Christian idea of sanctification. Likewise, the term "saint," used in the New Testament to speak of all who are set apart unto Christ, became corrupted to refer to a person who stands head and shoulders above other men in moral purity, or to mean a person who has little to do with the secular world. A saint in the New Testament is one committed to Christ and his will. The saint is Christ's man to his neighbor in need, and not the pious, indifferent person who is not concerned for his neighbor. The saint is not one who has renounced the pleasure of the world for a life of asceticism, but one who receives the good things of life from God and uses them in his service. While we speak of the use of the term "saint" in popular applications, it is yet true that no person singularly is designated such in the New Testament. Saints are only mentioned in plurality.[60]

With reference to sanctification, Paul Tillich describes it as the "New Being" in process. He gives four principles relating to the new life.

---

[58] Cf. Rom. 6–7; and Bultmann, *op. cit.*, p. 332.

[59] Cf. Brunner, *Christian Doctrine of the Church, Faith, and the Consummation*, p. 304.

[60] Cf. Barth, *Church Dogmatics*, IV, 512.

First, the believer has increased awareness regarding the struggles within and around him. The struggles relate to both demonic and divine. One becomes acutely aware as a Christian what one should be but disturbed in the slowness of progress and alarmed at the ease with which one can regress.

Second, the believer has increased freedom from the religious law as he lives in the commanding presence of the Spirit, and according to love.

Third, the believer experiences increased relatedness implying a triumph over seclusion of oneself and others too. Man, the believer, seeks matured relatedness. This is the experience in which the believer triumphs over loneliness "by providing for solitude and communion in interdependence." [61] Introversion is conquered by turning the person toward its help who is God.

Fourth, in sanctification the believer perceives self-transcendence. This means that awareness, freedom, and relatedness, cannot be achieved "without participation in the holy." [62] The last point calls for some program of action. Participation in the holy is related to some form of devotional life.

Spiritual growth comes when we *hear* God speaking *to us*. Meditation upon the sacred Scriptures plays a vital role in nurturing the Christian life. Without regularly listening to the word of God and meditating upon it, the believer will be living in a vacuum. By the same token, Christian life is nurtured as one *speaks to God*. Prayer is commanded in the Scriptures. Intercession is to be made for all men, especially the political leaders. The Model Prayer, commonly called the Lord's Prayer, teaches us to pray in gratitude, for our daily needs, both physical and spiritual. The Christian life is nurtured when one *speaks about God*. Sharing the good news is a tonic to the spiritual life. Not only is there the opportunity to help others, but in helping others, we grow ourselves.

Participation in the service of God includes many other things: the love of the neighbor; caring for the orphans, the widows, the sick; and many other deeds of mercy. However, the Christian life must not be reduced to mere activism which is not the same as participating in the holy. Self-transcendence does not come through sheer activism, but only as one is related to God through Christ.

---

[61] *Op. cit.,* III, 234.
[62] *Ibid.,* p. 235.

Sanctification can be discussed from another perspective. It is in one sense the work of God and in the other a work of man.

If we speak of it as the work of God, a parallel can be drawn to the doctrine of justification. In justification, the believer is a participant in the righteousness of Christ. In the same sense, we are declared righteous in him; we are declared sanctified in him.[63] Barth argues that much false teaching and many practical mistakes would have been avoided had this aspect of sanctification been emphasized.[64] After all, it is God who sanctifies us, not we ourselves. Christ did not die merely to justify us and leave the rest to us. Just as justification is achieved in our behalf, and accomplished, faith is called forth in response, so sanctification is accomplished in Christ and our obedience is commanded with our supreme love. Surely this emphasis leaves no room for despairing spiritual pessimism or a tedious legalism.

If we have sanctification in Christ, we come to the believer's response which involves the call to discipleship or obedience. To obey his call, "Follow me," is to submit to the transformation of self, which is eventually described as Christlikeness. Where there is disobedience to the call of Jesus, no progress can be made in being transformed to the image of Christ. When the call to obedience takes place, the follower of Christ is a disturbed sinner. The Master calls for the forsaking of the "old man," or the old way of life, and gives the presence of his Spirit to overcome. The call to obedience includes direction toward the goal of Christlikeness. Obedience to Christ's call produces the fruit of the Spirit as recorded in Galations 5:22–23. In the same breath that the believer is commanded to put to death the earthly—immorality, impurity, and so on, he is called to put on or to be alive to compassion, kindness, forgiveness, and love (Col. 3: 5–16).

In light of obedience to Christ's command, can we speak of a reward for our good works? Traditional Roman Catholic theology has argued that grace enables a man to do "good works" and thereby receive a reward. It is a recognized principle of society that rewards are the result of work and activity. In a case where work is volunteered, one may justly demand payment. "God respects this general human law, recognizing man's responsibility, rewards his fidelity in

---

[63] Cf. 1 Cor. 1:30.
[64] *Church Dogmatics,* IV-2, 511–33.

His service; only He raised the conception of reward for such service on to an altogether higher level." [65]

Protestants in general recognize no such principle of reward. God does not need volunteer laborers. Nor is he hiring laborers. Our labors in terms of good works are the result of a reward, not the basis for receiving one. We obey out of gratitude. If God has made us sons in Christ, joint-heirs in Christ, has given us the guarantee of his Spirit as the down-payment of everlasting life, what more can we desire? [66] If God then praises us for our faithfulness, it is not because we earned it, but because he is pleased in that his mercy has borne fruit in man's life.

One final matter in this doctrine is the teaching of some that the Christian attains perfection in this life. The biblical issue seems to center around passages like 1 John 3:6,9, which in the King James Version imply a state of sinlessness. The problem is one of translation and context. Williams gives the impact of the Greek tense in translating 1 John 3:6 as, "No one who continues to live in union with Him practices sin," and 3:9 as, "No one who is born of God makes a practice of sinning . . . because he is born of God." The word "practice" is the key to understanding. Christians do sin, but they do not practice sin as the guiding principle of life.

The context of 1 John indicates that sin is a problem to the believer. The writer included himself in the verse when he wrote, "If we say we have no sin, we deceive ourselves, and the truth is not in us" (1 John 1:8). It is because of sin that we have an advocate (1 John 2:1–2).

While we argue against a state of perfection in the Christian's life, equal emphasis must be placed upon the command of Christ to follow in discipleship. Remembering the apostle Paul's query in Romans 6:1–2, "Shall we continue in sin, that grace may abound? God forbid." Arnold of Rugby is supposed to have said, "Always strive for perfection: never believe you have reached it." [67]

Glorification

The Christian life begins now. The Gospel of John emphasized that everlasting life is a present possession. Everything that has been

---

[65] *A Handbook of the Catholic Faith*, p. 219.

[66] Schleiermacher, *op. cit.*, p. 521.

[67] Quoted in Strong, *op. cit.*, p. 880.

said so far is related to the Christian life in time. However, Christians are to live forever. This idea is summed up in the rather bulky word "glorification." Because Christians are citizens of two worlds, two dimensions, attention has been focused upon the Christian life in this world first, then on the next under the heading of glorification. This idea serves as a transition point to the next chapter on eschatology, the last things.

The term "glory" appears nebulous to us. In a general way, it relates to brilliance, splendor, or brightness. It refers to God in terms of magnificence and excellence. Our interest here is primarily concerning the believer. The word thus means the "glorious condition of blessedness into which it is appointed and promised that true Christians shall enter after their Saviour's return from heaven." [68] The idea appears in a number of different contexts. The present life in its sufferings is inconsequential in comparison to the glorious life to come (Rom. 8:18). The termination of life on earth is to experience the "glorious liberty" of the children of God (Rom. 8:21).

Life in the present may be lived in affliction and persecution, but everlasting life is glorious beyond all comparison. The future existence and fulfilment of the Christian's life is connected to Christ, the hope of glory (Col. 1:27). The return of Christ means the beginning of this new state of existence for the believer (Col. 3:4). Note should be made of the difference in the "state of the glorious life" and everlasting life. The believer has the second now and the first in the future. The future nature of the Christian's life is emphasized in 1 Peter 5:1, where the believer is a participant in the glory that is to be revealed.

The concept is related to the full nature of man. The physical nature of man will participate in the future existence of man's spiritual existence (1 Cor. 15:44). The most concrete conception of this change for the physical nature is the comparison made between Christ's resurrected existence and what we shall be like. His was a glorious body and so shall ours be (Phil. 3:21).

In conclusion, it must be stressed that the anatomy of the Christian life seems to suggest temporal sequence, whereas none is intended or can be made. At the same time one is converted, he is also glorified —for all of it takes place in Christ.

---

[68] Thayer, *op. cit.,* p. 156.

Addenda to the Christian Life and Glorification

We have purposely omitted a section on the doctrine of perseverance. Among many people, the issue of whether or not a person can fall from grace is discussed. Using the New Testament definition of grace as benevolent favor, falling from grace would be a contradiction in terms. As long as life still exists for man, God seeks his return to himself. The question should be better phrased as, "Can a person be 'saved' and then 'lost' again?" When the question is asked in this fashion, it then becomes a meaningless question. It is meaningless because the initial proposition cannot be established, namely, that a person was a genuine Christian. All that can ever be established is the statement that the person makes himself; namely, "I am a Christian," or one may say, "He says he is a Christian." It can never be proved whether there is genuine faith or not. If this could be proved beyond deception, then the argument would be meaningful. In reality, all one can say is that John Doe professed once to be a Christian but no longer makes such a profession. He was once active in Christian living but has now given it up.

Some passages of Scripture are used to suggest the possibility of apostasy. However, they are quite controversial and generally prove more than advocates of "falling from grace" really want to prove; namely, it is impossible to repent once one has committed apostasy. The passages in Hebrews, namely 6:4–6, should be interpreted in terms of a pastor who assesses the problems of his people. There are people today who *have been* "enlightened," "tasted of the heavenly gift," and it appears that the Spirit has been active in their lives, but they no longer meet in fellowship with God and his people. Their testimony is such that they crucify anew the Son of God and hold him in contempt. It appears impossible to restore them again to repentance. As a pastor works repeatedly to restore man to faithfulness, he appears always in defeat. However, these verses do not pronounce a theological decree from heaven that such people will never be restored to their fellowship in Christ. Only at the present can we make the statement, "It is impossible to restore again," not omitting the possibility that at some future time he may be restored.

The Christian life has its ups and downs. It is not a straight line growth—though it is sometimes so understood. There is yet a war being fought in the breast of man as God is at work in him. At a given time in the life of another person it might appear that God's side is not winning, but we can never conclude rightly.

The truth that is basic to the doctrine of perseverance, or the continued faithfulness of the believer, is that the believer *must trust the faithfulness of God*. The passages most often appealed to for support of the believer's perseverance are ones in which God's faithfulness is emphasized.[69] Our assurance in Christian life is found in God's acceptance of us.

---

[69] John 10:28–29; Rom. 11:29; 1 Cor. 13:7; Phil. 1:6; 2 Thess. 3:3; 1 Peter 1:5; Rev. 3:10.

XII. The Church, Part I

As we seek criteria for the definition of the fundamental principles and practices of church activity, to what source shall we look? Nothing is more important in the study of ecclesiology than to be clear on this point.

H. E. Dana, *A Manual of Ecclesiology*

It is in and through the Church that Jesus Christ has willed to effect the salvation of mankind.

The Teaching of the Catholic Church

Jesus did not "found" the Church; and Jesus unquestionably gathered around Himself a circle of disciples of such as were specially related to Him and whom He specially equipped and sent out in His service.

Brunner, *The Misunderstanding of the Church*

The unity of the churches similar to their holiness, has a paradoxical character. It is the divided church which is the united church.

Tillich, *Systematic Theology*

There is no justification theological, spiritual or biblical for the existence of a plurality of Churches genuinely separated in this way and mutually excluding one another internally and therefore externally. A plurality of Churches in this sense means a plurality of lords, a plurality of spirits, a plurality of gods.

Barth, *Church Dogmatics*

No true Ecclesia can be made out of twenty ecclesiastical institutions; Christian fellowship can spring only from spiritual knowledge of Christ, which implies the will to brotherhood in Christ.

Brunner, *Misunderstanding*

The third quarter of the twentieth century has seen the institutional church in deep ferment and turmoil. In spite of the use of statistics supporting nominal church membership and tacit support of the church, the church is increasingly forced to take an analytical look at itself. The shift in population to the city has forced the church to look at its centers of ministry. For instance, one denomination (Southern Baptists) has about 70 percent of its churches in towns of fifty thousand or less, while 70 percent of the population lives in cities above fifty thousand in population. On the other hand, the metropolitan areas are tending toward isolation from the church. The snug world of the apartment complex makes it possible for one to seal himself off from the traditional outreach of the church. The mobility of our society makes it increasingly difficult to promote a stabilized witness in a given area. A community of churches can be wiped out by one stroke when an industry, an air base, or some other complex is closed or moved.

Other complicating features include the revolutionary features of Vatican II, instituted by Pope John, bringing changes so that the Roman Catholic Church is accused of going Protestant, while the Protestant churches are accused of going Roman. Increasingly, the term "ecumenical" appears and the fever for church union of all types has run high.

The problems centering around the church as an institution have nowhere, perhaps, been analyzed as well as in the lucid work of Emil Brunner, *The Misunderstanding of the Church.*

The basic issue that Brunner sets forth is this: Is the church an institution or a fellowship? As an institution, the church is defined as a sacrament-dispensing organization which bestows grace through the sacraments to the faithful. A fellowship, on the other hand, has no sacramental grace to bestow. It has, however, a gospel to preach and ordinances that are observed, but not in the sacramental sense of the Roman Church. The misunderstanding centers around the institutional structure of the church, which is contrary to the New Testament. Because the term "church" is associated with a hierarchy of priests, sacraments, and generally a state-church relationship, Brunner prefers to jettison the term "church" for the term *ekklesia,* a transliteration of the New Testament word which is translated "church." But the English word "church" is "far removed from the meaning of *ekklesia* as used in the New Testament." [1] The issue is not a matter of poor translation but the association with an organizational structure. Brunner is not alone in objecting to the term. Luther, in spite of some affinities to Roman Catholicism, preferred not to use the term "church" and spoke of the *ekklesia* as the "community, the congregation, the company, or little company." [2] Still others have used the term "Spiritual Community" [3] or brotherhoods. Zinzendorf used this and is described by Karl Barth as the first genuine ecumenicist. [4]

The *ekklesia* in the New Testament is not an institution but a fellowship. "It is nothing other than men in fellowship, in fellowship with God and in fellowship with each other." [5] The fellowship is composed of those who have been reconciled and find their true selves in this reconciliation. The *ekklesia* is a "brotherly Christocracy," [6] that is, a community of people related to Christ by commitment and therefore, he is their Elder Brother.

It is in this area of difference, and thereby misunderstanding, that Brunner maintains the ecumenical movement is hung up. The tragic thing is not the continuing existence of pluralism on a denominational basis, but the "failure to acknowledge the Ekklesia as a spiritual brotherhood which is not an institution." [7]

The brotherhood can *have* laws and institutions but it can never regard these as belonging to its essence. But, above all, it can never *understand itself as an institution*. And precisely that is the essential thing. The Ekklesia's understanding of its own nature is not that of an institution. The nature of the Christian brotherhood is basically different from the nature of an institution, which is called the Church, and is indeed incompatible with it. [8]

How did the *ekklesia* in the New Testament degenerate into the institution of the church? This is difficult to answer. There is no

---

[1] H. E. Dana, *A Manual of Ecclesiology* (Kansas City: Central Seminary Press, 1944), p. 20.

[2] Barth, *Church Dogmatics*, IV-1, 651.

[3] Tillich, *Systematic Theology*, III, 163.

[4] *Church Dogmatics*, IV-1, 683.

[5] Brunner, *Christian Doctrine of the Church, Faith, and the Consummation*, p. 21.

[6] Barth, *Church Dogmatics*, IV, 680.

[7] *Christian Doctrine of the Church, Faith and Consummation*, p. 129.

[8] *Ibid.*, p. 30.

decisive point at which one can say the *ekklesia* has ceased, and the church as a new phenomenon begins.

The ecclesiastical development of the community of Jesus Christ is so difficult a conundrum precisely because the change takes place in tiny but continuous stages, and indeed at first in such a way that even the new institutional elements are not simple innovations but in actual fact—as Catholic theories assert—"develop" from obscure origins which are already partly latent in the New Testament *Ecclesia*.[9]

In its early adjustments and struggles against heresy and schism, the institutionalization of the fellowship took place. The fellowship was replaced by the institution, faith was transformed from a term meaning commitment to acceptance of a creed and a moral code, and the living Word was institutionalized in theology and dogma.[10]

What justification can be given for this transformation? This will be considered later in the matter of the norms governing the church, but at this juncture one can declare that no justification is possible from the perspective of the Scriptures. It can only be lamented. From the institutional standpoint, the Roman Church maintained for itself the role of the teaching church. Therefore, whatever now is, is right, for Christ has presumably directed the church to this present position. There are two basic assertions that the Roman Church has maintained which explain the transformation over the centuries. The first is the sacramental view of salvation which regards the church as the dispenser of grace requiring a priesthood. The second was the claim of temporal power which identified the church with the state. Both of these were contrary to the *ekklesia* in the New Testament.

The nature of the church is no mere academic question. The particular definition that one receives determines to a large extent his activity with reference to the church. Although the Reformation churches did not fully restore the *ekklesia,* they went far enough in that direction to change the pattern of culture in Europe and America from non-Reformed areas. Brunner acknowledges his indebtedness to the Free Churches [11] and declares that it is because of them "that there is in this part of the world personal freedom, social sense of responsibility, free criticism of the *status quo,* critical scholarship,

---

[9] Brunner, *The Misunderstanding of the Church,* p. 74.

[10] *Ibid.,* p. 53.

[11] The Free Church tradition is the nonsacramental, nonhierarchical, nonliturgical tradition within Protestantism.

even Biblical criticism, free science and an understanding of the dignity of the person and also a sense of the dignity of service." [12]

Thus, the question of the nature of the church or *ekklesia* will determine its direction in the world. At no other time since the Reformation has there been a need for a new Reformation to reclaim the *ekklesia* concept of the followers of Christ.

The Norm

What is the standard whereby such discussions can be judged? From what standpoint can one criticize the practices and activities as well as the organization of the church?

There are essentially three starting points for the discussion about the nature of the *ekklesia*.

Tradition.—A considerable portion of Christendom speaks of tradition as authoritative. Abandonment of the New Testament is not wholly done, but the changes in structure are justified on the basis of a germinal appearance in the New Testament. With the assumption that the church is the authoritative teacher and interpreter of the New Testament, there is little need to justify much from the Scriptures. The teaching function of the church includes the fact that the church is a learning church. As the Spirit of God is the soul of the church, then it progressively learns.

Tradition per se must be rejected because tradition gives support to many things that are contrary to the Scriptures. The Bible itself is the tacitly acknowledged source of tradition to something beyond itself. Tradition is a poor norm because traditions vary. Which tradition will one follow? Tradition is by no means a unanimous whole. The Church Fathers give quite a wide variety of opinions concerning both doctrinal and policy matters.

Tradition can be useful for the lessons it teaches, but not for the determination of the government and character of the church.

Expediency.—Advocates of expediency have maintained that no norm for the church has been given, but such matters have been left to human capacities and intelligence and that "those forms of church polity have been devised through the Christian centuries which were best adapted to the tastes and conditions of each successive age." [13]

---

[12] *Christian Doctrine of the Church, Faith, and the Consummation,* pp. 90–91.
[13] Dana, *op. cit.,* p. 199.

The church has made progress through the centuries in arriving at a useful form, but there is no absolute ideal which should serve as the standpoint of comparison.

Expediency is related to purposes, but the purposes of the church are declared in the Scriptures. While some things may be useful in accomplishing the purposes of the gospel, it remains that without the scriptural norm we are left without a knowledge of the church's purposes. Hence, expediency is left without a guide.

The Scriptures.—If we are to know anything about the *ekklesia,* it will have to come from the Scriptures. It is the Bible that gives rise to the church, and not the church viewed as the custodian of the Scriptures. It is true that the church was founded before the Bible was written, but there is no possibility of starting an *ekklesia* apart from the declaration of the gospel—written or unwritten.

Our argument is: if you want to know what the church should be, know what it was declared to be in the Scriptures.[14] This poses problems for the Roman tradition, for a church which believes itself infallible is, therefore, never genuinely open to the criticism of the Scriptures. It has closed its mind. But when the *ekklesia* accepts the Scriptures as the norm for its life and self-understanding, it stands under the criticism of its Lord. Self-criticism is the continual basis of self-reform.

The Definition of the Church

There are several definitions of the church. The three types parallel the broad differences of types of churches.

The body of Christ (corpus Christi).—The term "body of Christ" is used in one sense by Roman Catholic writers and in another sense by Protestant writers. The Roman tradition describes the Church as the outward institution possessing a priesthood which is authorized to administer sacraments and convey thereby the grace of God to the faithful. Separation from the Church is a *sacrilegium*. Separation or schism can come only because of a lack of love or pride. It is to be emphasized that the Church external is identified with the body of Christ.

Protestants use the term "body of Christ" to speak of the "invisible church" in which, apart from all external and spatial organi-

---

[14] See the refreshing treatment by the Roman Catholic theologian Hans Kung, on *The Church,* Sheed and Ward.

zations, the believer is related to Jesus Christ by faith. He is the church's head, and the church is the body. This is all conceived symbolically but intimately because of faith's relationship to Christ.

The church is the company of the elect.—Emphasized by Augustine, elaborated by Calvin, this view is summed up in the *Westminster Confession* which says, "The Catholic or universal Church, which is invisible, consists of the whole number of elect, that have been, are, or shall be gathered into one, under Christ the head thereof; and is the spouse, the body, the fullness of Him that filleth all in all." The church thus can include some who are beyond the bounds of the visible expression of the local church, as well as exclude some who are within its visible boundaries.

In a general way the Reformed churches stand in this tradition.

The church is the communion of the saints (communio sanctorum).—Arising out of the Reformed tradition but emphasizing the people who make up the church, rather than the decree of God's election, two confessions give historic expression of this concept. The *Belgic Confession* declares: "We believe and profess one catholic or universal church, which is a holy congregation of true Christian believers, all expecting their salvation in Jesus Christ, being washed by His blood, sanctified and sealed by the Holy Spirit." [15]

The *Second Helvetic Confession* declares similarly that the church is "a company of the faithful, called and gathered out of the world: a communion of all saints, that is, of them who truly know and rightly worship and serve the true God, in Jesus Christ the Saviour, by the word of the Holy Spirit, and who by faith are partakers of all those good graces which are freely offered through Christ." [16]

The communion of the saints places emphasis on the individual members united to Christ by faith through the Spirit of God. To the members individually are given the great promises. Belonging to the church does not refer to an outward institution, nor receiving the sacraments.

We may speak of the church or *ekklesia* in more simple terms. It is a group of people committed by faith to Christ, who in obedience to his command have been baptized (that is, who take the sign of his covenant for their lives), who are committed to obedience in their lives in seeking his purposes for mankind.

---

[15] *Belgic Confession*, Article XXVII.
[16] *Second Helvetic Confession*, Chapter XVII.

The third definition has broad parallels to the Free Church tradition. The personal category is opposed to the sacramental. "One of the most urgent requirements of a Church that wishes to be apostolic in the New Testament sense is that it should be freed from sacramental thinking." [17]

What judgment can we make about these three definitions? They are not compatible with one another. The visible structure of the Roman view has nothing in common with the church viewed as the company of the elect. Nor does the church viewed as a voluntary fellowship of the saints accord with either the first or second definition.

The third definition is the more biblical of the three. By the vantage point of our times it seems imperative to recover the concept of the *ekklesia* as opposed to the institutional-sacramental church. Man is interested in the problems of personality and the issues facing him. The brotherhood of Christ and the fellowship of God's people offer the means of meeting his needs. Jesus founded a people, not an institution. "A people has institutions, but it never understands itself as an institution." [18]

The Origin of the Church

To pinpoint the precise time the church became a reality is impossible. As a fellowship it began with the collection of the disciples by Jesus. As a fellowship, however, it had no good news to declare, nor even a mission to accomplish until after the resurrection of Jesus.

To talk of the church's origin from an institutional view is also difficult. The common source of appeal for the origin of the church during the ministry of Jesus is the confession of Peter, recorded in Matthew 16:16–18. The word "church" occurs only in two instances in the four Gospels—Matthew 16:18 and in Matthew 18:17. The appeal to Matthew 16:18 has been quite crucial for Roman Catholic theologians. [19]

Granting its genuineness, the more important question is the interpretation of the phrase, "I tell you, you are Peter, and on this rock I will build my church; and the powers of death shall not prevail

---

[17] Brunner, *Christian Doctrine of the Church, Faith, and the Consummation*, p. 125.

[18] *Ibid.*, p. 22.

[19] Some non-Roman writers reject the sayings as genuine on the grounds that Jesus did not speak of the church elsewhere.

against it." The traditional Roman view has appealed to these words to support the establishment of Peter as Christ's vicar on earth. In some cases an appeal is made to the Aramaic, in which case the word "Peter" and "rock" is the same (*kepha*). However, there are no Aramaic gospels. We have only the words in Greek, which draw an important distinction between the name of Peter (*Petros*) and the word rock (*petra*). Assuming the inspiration of the Scriptures, as does the Roman Church, one can rightly argue that it is not without significance that the play on words is used along with a different word. Jesus did not say to Peter that *on you* I will build, but on this *rock,* referring to something other than Peter, or something that Peter did.[20]

The better view, as we see it, is that Peter's confession of faith in Jesus as the Messiah is the "rock." The *ekklesia* is built upon the confession that Jesus is the Christ—for which reason Peter is described as blessed. Peter speaks for the group in confessing what Jesus had been subtly showing them all along. It is with reference to this confession that Jesus warns his disciples to tell "no man" at the moment (v. 20). The confession of faith is consonant with the requirement for confessing him before men (Matt. 10:32–37). However, the really important meaning of the text is the *one who is acknowledged,* not the one who is acknowledging. If one is inclined to emphasize the personal role of Peter as a foundation of the church, it must come in conjunction with the rest of the apostles and even prophets—but it is always Jesus who is the cornerstone (Eph. 2:20).

It is this confession—Jesus is the Christ, the appointed Messiah—that is the key to the kingdom of heaven. This perception of knowledge is unlike that of the religious lawyers whom Jesus criticized: "Woe to you, lawyers! for you have taken away the *key* of knowledge; you did not enter yourselves, and you hindered those who were entering" (Luke 11:52). Whoever confesses in faith, as Peter did, has the keys to the kingdom of God.

Having discussed some of the main problems in the passage, we must assess this as a proper place to speak of the church's origin. The passages give us little more than the "germ" of the church. The church proper is not an actuality until Pentecost, for it is not until

---

20 The play on words refers to different types of rocks. Peter is a *petros,* a stone, pebble; and *petra* is the ledge rock or foundation rock that is immovable.

then that it has the presence of the Spirit and a gospel to proclaim. Pentecost is the climax of the church's origination, for there the Lord *adds to the church*; that is, the fellowship of believers. Nothing at this point is said about officers, for officers are not a necessity to the church's origin. However, officers do have a contributory function in the *ekklesia*. Their role and origin will be discussed later.

We have not been consistent in our use of the term "origin of the church" from an institutional point of view. It is hard to be. One may speak of the origin of the church as Roman theologians do, but there is no final point where one may say, "This is the church." The developmental idea in Catholicism makes this impossible. Structurally the Roman Church has grown. It is not the same today as it was in the year A.D. 500. In all candor, the question, "When did the church (institutional) originate?" must be answered fairly with, "It is still originating."

Marks of the Ekklesia

Can we speak of the "true church"? Many will affirm this statement, but others are highly negative. Brunner regards the term "true church" as a self-contradictory statement. If the New Testament is the standard for deciding the question, then there is no "true church"; rather, there is a spiritual *ekklesia* or brotherhood that is not institutional in nature. The church is a new species that has arisen out of an old genus. Therefore, to discuss the question, one must remember the transformation that did take place in the history of the Christian community.

The transformation—the movement of the community into the world—continued apace until people were born into the church in the same way they were born into the state. The problems that arose when the church was coterminous with the state caused theologians to create a distinction in the church community. In a state-church situation, there are those who are members of the church in name only. On the other hand, there are those who manifest faith in Christ and walk in obedience. Because of the discrepancy between being Christian in name and faith, Augustine, along with others, spoke of a visible church in contrast to the invisible one. This distinction is yet current in theology. However, the distinction is rejected from two standpoints. It is rejected by the Roman Catholics who identify the visible church with its external institutional existence in its bishops. It is rejected from the other side by those who seek to recover the New Testament idea of the *ekklesia.*

The distinction is not meaningful because the invisible church does not appear in history, and thus it can never be a fellowship. Each person may be in the "invisible church" only on an individual basis. On the other hand, the visible church is no more a fellowship, "it is rather an institution, a collective, hence an external, means of help. Both the one and the other fail to tally with what was intended and realized in the New Testament: the communion of the fellowship with Christ which as such meant also the communion of the members one with another." [21] Moreover, the "invisible church" concept is completely foreign to the New Testament, "while the interpretation of the real visible Church as a merely external means of salvation is not only foreign to it but completely impossible." [22]

The evidence for the visible concept of the church as opposed to the invisible is the usage of the word in the New Testament. Eighty-one percent of the passages must be understood as a local group of believers.[23] The passages used to support an invisible church concept are drawn mainly from Ephesians, where the *ekklesia* is referred to spiritual Israel in an ideal sense, but not in a concrete sense. In these passages is stressed the blessing of union with Christ, which is common to all believers in all ages; and hence the spiritual relationship is meant. But this particular "spiritual conception of the *ekklesia* has no concrete expression in the form of objective existence, for the local *ekklesia* is a thing of different nature and function." [24]

Traditional "Marks" of the Church

The Unity of the Church

It is a truism that the church, or *ekklesia,* ought to be one, but the

---

[21] Brunner, *Misunderstanding of the Church,* p. 17.

[22] *Ibid.,* p. 9. Brunner elsewhere declares: "This double concept of the Church is wholly foreign to the New Testament. There is in it only the one Ekklesia, which is at the same time spiritual and invisible (intelligible to faith alone) and corporeal (recognizable and visible to all). No Apostle would ever have agreed that this visible entity, the Ekklesia, was only a support of faith, let alone an external support. For the disciples it was wholly impossible to distinguish between visible and invisible Ekklesia. . . . For them the Ekklesia which belongs to Christ through faith was at the same time the Ekklesia which everyone could see."—*The Christian Doctrine of the Church, Faith, and the Consummation,* p. 29.

[23] Dana, *Manual of Ecclesiology,* p. 67.

[24] *Ibid.,* p. 57.

real issue is, one what? One outward organization? A oneness of spirit? A unity of doctrine? A unity of purpose? There are generally two attitudes prevalent.

Oneness of organization.—The unity of the Roman Catholic Church is in its organization; therefore, it is not an ideal but is considered an actuality: "It was a mark of her constitution from the beginning. The unity promised by Christ was that proper to the society of his followers, to be manifested visibly in the unanimous profession of one faith, the performance of one act of worship, the acceptance of one system of government." [25] Historically, the unity has been stressed from the standpoint of being in union with the bishops of the Church.

Within the present ecumenical movement in Protestantism, there is amalgamation of denominations into larger units, whereby it is hoped that denominationalism will subside and structural unity will emerge.

Denominationalism does have its problems. It can lead to inefficiency, whereby efforts are duplicated by other groups; to pride and arrogance; to denominational exclusivism, whereby church life is stratified to economic class, and so on.

In contrast, it must not be supposed that a monolithic organization will guarantee unity. Even in the Roman Catholic tradition, one only has to know the history of the Jesuits, Dominicans, Franciscans, and Augustinians to know what violent differences of opinions have been held concerning major issues in doctrine. Even *de fide* declarations of faith do not guarantee unity. Many Roman Catholics reject some *de fide* statements, regardless of the authority of the church.

Organizational unity also has its problems. Church unionism presumes to say that denominational differences are in reality, trivial—which in many cases is true—but important doctrinal issues are often involved. Church unionism asks a person to give up ideas of faith that he holds to be important by virtue of his membership in a particular denomination. "Denominational prejudice is indeed unchristian, but not any more so than ecclesiastical dogmatism or repudiation of honest convictions." [26]

Church unionism cannot create a true *ekklesia,* regardless of how

---

[25] George D. Smith, *Teaching of the Catholic Church,* p. 703.
[26] Dana, *Manual of Ecclesiology,* pp. 167–68.

many ecclesiastical unions there may be. Spiritual knowledge of Christ produces Christian fellowship and brotherhood.

Oneness of fellowship.—The unity of the *ekklesia* is a spiritual unity. Because men are related to Christ by faith in him, they become aware of their spiritual identity with one another. The prayer of Jesus was that "they may all be one; even as thou, Father, art in me, and I in thee, that they also may be in us" (John 17:21). This hardly admits of an ecclesiastical structure.

Paradoxically, it is the leaders of the church who are working for church merger. The lay members recognize that when Christ is trusted as Saviour there is a spiritual unity among believers of all denominations. Oneness of fellowship implies the possibility of a diversity of appeal to diverse people. The Salvation Army brings together a fellowship of believers who would be alienated by a highly liturgical worship service. Yet, is not the same Lord present to both? Diversity of forms of worship does not exclude our spiritual unity in Christ. Strangely enough, it is the dying churches that are bent on uniting with the growing churches, and the more clerical in nature swallows the less clerical. In each case, some group is the loser.

In spite of the tendency to church unionism, the man in the pew often has a better understanding of the unity of the fellowship in Christ than the cleric. He understands that the unity of the churches is paradoxical. "It is the divided church which is the united church." [27]

The Holiness of the Church

The concept of the holiness of the church differs quite radically from Roman Catholicism to Protestantism.

Roman theory.—The Roman Catholic view is that the Church is made pure in actuality. "It implies freedom from sin and impurity and the possession of grace, whereby the whole direction of our lives is brought into harmony with the divine commandments." [28] "Moreover by means of her sacramental system, the Church effectively produces in her members the holiness which she preaches." [29]

Protestant theory.—The Protestant view is that the church is de-

---

[27] Tillich, *op. cit.*, III, 170.
[28] George D. Smith, *Teaching of the Catholic Church*, p. 703.
[29] *Ibid.*, p. 704.

clared to be holy in the sense that believers are declared to be just
in their position in Christ. Faith does not imply perfection in the
Christian life. By the same token, the church is holy in that it is
separated unto the service of God. It is not without sin. Yet it is a
forgiven church. The holiness of the church consists in its willingness
to hear the Word of Christ, believe and obey it, and respond in love
to mankind, because God has loved the *ekklesia.*

The church can only be declared holy because its Head is holy,
and its members have a connection with him.

To say that the church is holy is not to say that it is without sin.
The *ekklesia* is composed of those who confess they need God's
help. It is not a group of perfect people; it daily stands in need of
God's forgiveness. Holiness is not infallibility. The infallible church
is not existent. The church has made mistakes and the sooner it
acknowledges its sins and seeks God's forgiveness in humility, the
sooner it will recapture its vision of service to God and man.

The Catholicity of the Church

The term "Catholic Church" seems to have been used first by
Ignatius of Antioch (d. 117) in a letter to the Smyrnaeans: "Where-
soever Christ Jesus is, there is the Catholic Church." [30] The word is
Greek and means universal, general, or comprehensive. By the time
of the Apostles' Creed, the phrase apparently referred to an institutional structure.

Roman theory.—The catholicity of the church is defined in a
variety of senses with regard to its outward organization. It maintains: universality in place—it is diffused throughout the world;
time—it will always exist; people—it includes members from every
nation; conditions of men—all social structures; doctrine—it claims
the full teaching of Christ without change; and means of salvation—
it has the cure for men's spiritual illnesses.[31]

Protestant theory.—Many Protestants have spoken of the invisible
church as universal or catholic. The real catholic church is the one
including believers all over the earth at any one time. The *Heidelberg
Catechism* points up this view. Question 54 says, "What dost thou
believe concerning the holy, universal Christian Church?" The answer to be given is: "That from the beginning of the world to its end

[30] *Ibid.,* p. 705.
[31] *Ibid.*

the Son of God assembles out of the human race an elect community to eternal life by His Spirit and (His) Word in the unity of true faith, that He protects and upholds it, and that I am a living member of the same, and will continue to be so to all eternity."

It is obvious to many Protestants that one cannot identify the church invisible with the visible church. Moreover, catholicity originally referred to the universality of the church. Since many have never heard the Gospel, Protestants reinterpret the term and use it in a noninstitutional context. The church's universality must be understood in a teleological or purposive sense. The *ekklesia* is intended for the whole of humanity. This is the meaning of the Great Commission in which Jesus sent his disciples into *all* the world. This type of reinterpretation of universality is required also in the historical view of the church, when one may speak of a true church in the apostolic era, but certainly at a time when the church was not catholic or universal in outreach.

The Apostolicity of the Church

Roman theory.—The Roman Catholic Church seeks to maintain a continuity from the apostles unto the present day. One must look for a "legitimate, public and uninterrupted succession of pastors, heirs, as it were, of the Apostles, and in agreement with them in faith, worship and Church government." [32] It is admitted that a departure "from its original constitution would mean that the unity of the Mystical Body had been broken." [33]

Protestants have rejected the apostolic succession of the church for a number of reasons. First, one cannot read the New Testament and come up with the Roman Catholic system of government, or system of worship. The transformation of the *ekklesia* into the institutional church is a factor already discussed. Second, the list of Hegesippus on the line of bishops is more than doubtful, and it is also highly questionable whether the bishops have been preserved from error. This indicts the concept of bishops all the way up to some of the ancient popes.[34] Third, it is questionable whether historical continuity does guarantee purity of doctrine.

Protestant theory.—To say that the church is apostolic is to say

32 *Ibid.*, p. 705.
33 *Ibid.*, p. 706.
34 See *The Infallibility of the Pope* by Salmon.

that it is true to Christ. *Apostolic* means likewise to be under the "normative authority, instruction and direction of the apostles, in agreement with them . . . listening to them and accepting their message."[35] For the church to be apostolic also means for it to reject a formal hierarchy and to accept the *ekklesia* as the norm.[36]

Instead of a historical succession, Protestants have emphasized the spiritual succession or return to the norm of the New Testament. The apostolic church emphasized faith as commitment to Jesus Christ. Faith was not known as *assensus,* but *fiducia,* trust. The apostolic church was a genuine brotherhood. If there is any other kind of succession than spiritual continuity it would be a succession of service. "If the community is really to find itself and to act in line with Jesus Christ and His apostles, there is only one attitude, and that is the attitude of subjection and obedience."[37]

Other Approaches

The purpose of the "marks" as we have discussed them is to help men in recognizing the "true church." Some theologians speak of the foregoing discussion as "attributes" or characteristics of the church and define the "marks" as something else. When this is done the "marks" of the "true church" are defined variously from one to three. When only one mark is maintained, the other two are to be regarded as inherent in it.

The true preaching of the Word.—Calvin wrote, "Wherever we see the word of God sincerely preached and heard, wherever we see the sacraments administered according to the institution of Christ, there we cannot have any doubt that the Church of God has some existence, since his promise cannot fail."[38] The true preaching of the Word means that all the message and doctrine of the church is under the judgment of the Scriptures. It is not the Scriptures *and* tradition, or anything else, but *sola Scriptura.*

The right administration of the sacraments.—The comment by Calvin includes the sacraments which are integrally related to the Word and from which they derive their meaning. Sometimes called the "visible word," the sacraments are to be administered by "lawful

---

[35] Barth, *Church Dogmatics,* IV-1, 714.
[36] Brunner, *Christian Doctrine of the Church, Faith, and Consummation,* p. 119.
[37] Barth, *Church Dogmatics,* IV-1, 720.
[38] *Institutes of the Christian Religion,* p. 289.

ministers of the Word." [39] The sacraments will be discussed below.

The faithful exercise of discipline.—The exercise of discipline is necessary for maintaining pure doctrine and nonabuse of the sacraments. Discipline in morals and doctrine is the implication in this mark.

The Body of Christ

The church as the body of Christ deserves some detailed treatment, for the concept has great differences in Roman Catholicism and Protestantism. The Roman Catholic concept is defined as follows: "The Mystical Body of Christ—a body in which the members, living indeed their natural life individually, are supernaturally vivified and brought into harmony with the whole by the influence, the wondrous power and efficacious intervention of the Divine Head." [40] The vivification comes through the sacramental power of the Church which has become the repository of grace. As a corollary, the Church is the continued incarnation of Christ.[41]

Inasmuch as the Church is institutional and sacramental as well as incarnational, the Roman Catholic Church has been forced to defend its own ecclesiastical structure. In doing so, the real nature of the body of Christ has been subverted. The institutional church is a denial of the apostolic *ekklesia*. The Lord created for himself a communion of persons and not an institution. The indwelling of the Spirit is related directly to the person because of one's faith in Christ, rather than the Roman Catholic view that the Spirit is the soul of the Church in a sacramental context. When one speaks of faith in Christ, the indwelling of the Spirit is taken for granted (Eph. 1:13).

The body of Christ has another implication for Roman Catholics that it does not have for Protestants. The communion of saints is based upon the analogy of some parts of the body helping other parts. Therefore, those who are in the heavenly kingdom of God may be of help to the "faithful still wayfaring on earth." [42] The idea is based upon analogical reasoning rather than upon scriptural foundation.

Protestants have rejected the practice because the Spirit of Christ

---

39 Berkhof, *op. cit.,* p. 578.
40 George D. Smith, *Teaching of the Catholic Church,* p. 669.
41 *Ibid.,* p. 693.
42 *Ibid.,* p. 685.

is closer to us than anything else can be. There is no evidence that the departed can hear the prayers of the saints, along with the fact that no one loves us more than Christ. No one is more compassionate than he. To say that a saint, such as Mary, is compassionate and will be sympathetic to man's cry is to imply that Christ is not able to hear, or is not as compassionate as they. This attitude deprecates the person of Christ.

The communion of saints likewise rests upon another analogy for which there is no support in the Scriptures. The cell in the body is communicated to the attributes of the whole body and being of Christ. It becomes ubiquitous and can hear prayer just as Christ does. There is real danger in pushing analogies too far. But if one is inclined to build dogma on analogies, he must remember that the head only is Christ, and he alone is the ears of the *ekklesia*.

The Catholic veneration of the saints is defended against the charge of idolatry on the basis that reverence is not adulation. However, for many Protestants this is a matter of words that means nothing. If prayer is addressed to a saint, there is little difference in actuality, because the attributes of omnipresence, grace, and power are necessary on the part of the saint to hear the cry of the sinner.

What is legitimate in the role of intercession is that the living are to pray for the living. Christians are commanded to pray for one another, for rulers, and for all men (1 Tim. 2:1).

The body of Christ is promised the indwelling of the Spirit. The indwelling of the Spirit is within the person and not the church. (The gift of the Spirit has already been dealt with in an earlier chapter.) There can be no *ekklesia* without the Spirit; there can be a "church" without the Spirit.

Baptists and the Ekklesia

Martin Luther and John Calvin can be regarded as great leaders in the reform of the church. However, from the standpoint of the Anabaptists and the later Baptists, they did not go far enough. The Reformers retained the principle of Constantine and Theodosius that residents of a given territory must belong to the state church. The Anabaptists rejected the principle along with the expression of membership in the state church—infant baptism.

Neither Calvin nor Luther was consistent in his insistence upon faith on the one hand and infant baptism or state church on the other. In essence, the Baptist movement was an attempt, insofar as possible, to return to the *ekklesia* of the New Testament. The Baptists have been much maligned. The Reformers spoke of them as enthusiasts. Brunner, as a non-Baptist, maintains that they were caricatured out of all proportion to their sober faith in Christ and agreement with the New Testament as the single authority of faith. He asserts that the Baptist movement was premature but that its impact forced the churches eventually to adjust themselves to their own good.

The role of fellowship in the *ekklesia,* in contrast to the priestly hierarchical approach of the church, is seen in the Anabaptist response to the Great Commission. Franklin Littel describes the Anabaptist as the first group of people—since the time of the apostles—to make the Great Commission an imperative for every member of the *ekklesia*. For centuries, the Great Commission had been interpreted in terms of the apostles and their exploits for evangelism. The Anabaptist fellowship picked up anew and said to each member: "You must bear witness actively, openly, and vocally to the gospel of Christ."

It is the recovering of the *ekklesia* that is most needed in our day.

The Function of the Church

With the increasing secularization of the world and the church, the function of the church needs clarification. The churches have lost something of their participation in the world at large, thereby becoming at best a segment of life and at worst an isolated group. The *ekklesia* must again relate itself to society at large. It can do this in a number of ways.

First, the *ekklesia* may reemphasize the way of silent interpenetration.[43] This means that individual members of the *ekklesia* permeate society in the various groups related to themselves and, like a rose filling a room with fragrance, fill the group with the spiritual dynamic of the Christian life. This path seems difficult and overwhelming in light of the increasing secularization of the world. Yet to withdraw this type of influence would be to withdraw spiritual influence on a plane that would leave the world desolate by comparison.

Second, the *ekklesia* may assume the role of critic of society. Thus the church must declare the pagan way of life devoid of meaning and

---

[43] Tillich, *op. cit.,* III, 212 ff.

point the world back to its Creator. It is this type of approach, connected with other factors, that brought the early pagan society under the influence of the Christian gospel.

Third, it may take the way of political establishment. The first two ways fall within the religious sphere, while this one goes beyond it. Tillich wrote of this way: "Every church has a political function, from the local up to the international level. One task of the church leaders on all levels is to influence the leaders of the other social groups in such a way that the right of the church to exercise its priestly and prophetic function is acknowledged by them." [44]

As the church seeks to renew itself and work out avenues of approach, there are certain areas it cannot neglect.

First, it has a missionary function. The Commission of Christ implies a universal declaration of the gospel. The missionary expansion receives priority in the lineup of the functions of the church. A church that loses its feeling for evangelism is like a body that loses a vital organ. The means to a healthy life is gone.

Second, if the church is to continue without dying, it must fulfil its role of teaching—hence education. The crisis of this role is reflected in the sharp criticism of the Sunday school over the preceding years. The church's role in education must be more inclusive. The *ekklesia* must not only teach concerning the doctrinal ideas of the New Testament but it must also help its younger members, either in age or in religious experience, enter into the benefits of the fellowship. The young Christian must be taught and helped to pray, to share his faith with others, to study the Scriptures, and to defend his faith when necessary. The impartation of knowledge is only half the story—the experiences of "doing" is the other half.

Third, edification in love. The *ekklesia* must seek continually the renewal of itself in love. Love builds up the *ekklesia*, whereas knowledge does not do this. "In short, every Christian, the whole community, is the subject of edification." [45] In short, there is no edification that does not take into consideration the edification, or building up in love, of the whole *ekklesia*.

Fourth, service. There is a demand upon the *ekklesia* that it should serve. Its service includes a hand to the downtrodden, encouragement to the depressed, comfort for the bereaved, companionship to the

---

44 *Ibid.*, III, 214.
45 Barth, *Church Dogmatics*, IV-2, 635.

lonely, being a father to the fatherless and a mother to the mother-less. It seeks to bring meaning to the searching; peace where there is strife; and love where there is none. In a word, the *ekklesia* is to attempt to meet the redemptive needs of mankind, whatever they be.

Temptations of the Church

The *ekklesia,* being composed of people dedicated to Christ, is not without peculiar temptations. Some of the following temptations re-cur repeatedly in the life of the *ekklesia.*

First, one of its greatest temptations is to water down the message of the gospel for the sake of popularity. With the pollution of its message, the *ekklesia* loses its unique concepts such as sin and grace. With the demise of its message, it becomes naturalistic in ethics and religion. If the church becomes just another sociological group, it not only becomes inadequate but it "can be replaced by other groups not claiming to be churches; such a church has no justification for its existence." [46]

Second, the church has the temptation to become an end in itself. The church may regard its self-perpetuation as an adequate cause for self-assertion. The *ekklesia* was not founded for the purpose of having an institution that will persist. Its sole purpose for existence is in its Lord.

Third, there is the temptation of regarding its life as dependent upon something other than God's grace and power. If it seeks not its life in God, the sharp words of the world will make it take to itself philosophies alien to the Word of God. Its ethical standard will be-come dented without authority. Its message will become restricted by the momentary crisis of the environment without regard to the long view of history. Without looking to God for its survival it will turn to political alliances and economic forces which will dilute its influence for the gospel's sake. Unless it retains self-knowledge concerning its true nature, the church cannot transcend the mo-mentary.

Fourth, the danger of irrelevance. To many people the *ekklesia,* or the church, is irrelevant. It has become so involved with trivia that the great challenges are lost. Many a man, on becoming a Christian, has felt inspired to go forth and win the community for Christ, but

---

[46] Tillich, *op. cit.,* III, 166.

instead was sidetracked by being made the chairman of the flower committee.

Conclusion

In conclusion, the doctrine of the church is one of the most complex, as well as one of the most important, doctrines in Christian faith. It is primarily this doctrine that has divided much of Christendom. The sources of division are yet to be considered in the following chapter.

XIII. The Church, Part II

The last of all is marriage, which, while all admit it to be an institution of God, no man ever saw to be a sacrament, until the time of Gregory. And would it ever have occurred to the mind of any sober man?

Calvin, *Institutes*

It is for this reason that every Catholic is bound, under pain of mortal sin, unless there be legitimate excuse, to sanctify the Lord's holy day, Sunday, by assisting at Mass.

The Teaching of the Catholic Church

Therefore, the Last Supper is something very different from an institution: it is the performance of an act of fellowship— of the fellowship centred in Christ and grounded in the saving history of the past, present, and future.

Brunner, *Misunderstanding*

Wherever we see the word of God sincerely preached and heard, wherever we see the sacraments administered according to the institution of Christ, there we cannot have any doubt that the Church of God has some existence.

Calvin, *Institutes*

We have seen something of the diversity of viewpoint up to this juncture. The further we go in the doctrine of the *ekklesia*, the more diverse the opinion can become. There is a basic principle that underlies much of the difference between Protestants and Roman Catholics on the subject of the church.

The principle of the church as a teaching church means that the doctrines in "germ" in the Scriptures are fully developed under the teaching authority of the bishops of the church together and through their head, the Pope. It is impossible to connect the present highly organized, highly liturgical, and highly transformed structure of the modern Roman Church to the apostolic simplicity without this cardinal principle.

Likewise, a collateral line of development survives in much of Protestantism as it was inherited from the Roman Church. The Reformation did not by any means return to the apostolic norm of the *ekklesia* in everything. It recovered the doctrines of faith, grace, and authority of the Scriptures; but beyond that the reform was not sweeping and thorough. Therefore, because of the difference in degree in recovery of the apostolic form, there are differences in certain structures of the churches and practices.

Types of Polity

In dealing with the various types of polity, we will arbitrarily place them on a scale descending from the complex to the least complex.

Episcopal.—The episcopal system of government is based on the belief that the government or rule of the church was delivered by Christ to the bishops as successors of the apostles. There are different degrees of episcopacy. The House of Bishops of the Episcopal Church is one type in the United States in which there is equality of bishops. The Roman system is episcopal in nature but is ruled by a monarch, the Pope.

Ignatius is probably the earliest advocate of episcopacy. He speaks of the church "as having three grades of officers; namely, the bishop, the elders, and the deacons." [1] Along with the move toward episcopacy and growth of the powers of the bishopric there is the corresponding demise of power from the nonclerical members of the church. In the Roman system, the laity has no voice in the government of the Church.

Episcopacy in its early years of the second century grew in popularity as the problem of heresy increased. The need of a common faith, expressed in a church's having a continuity from the time of the apostles under a bishop who had succeeded, similarly was fulfilled and proved a powerful weapon against heresy. With a few generations, episcopacy grew to the extent that Cyprian declared, *"Ecclesia est in episcopo* [The Church is in the Bishop]." [2]

---

[1] H. E. Dana, *A Manual of Ecclesiology*, p. 103.
[2] *Ibid.*, p. 145.

The bishop is primary, but there are two officers under him—the priest (presbyter) and deacon.

The question of the legitimacy of this system will depend upon the standard adopted. Without a developmental principle, built upon circuitous inferences, one cannot derive the type of government from the New Testament. There is no transfer of authority to Peter and hence no evidence in the New Testament to support it. There is no biblical evidence that Peter appointed the bishops of Rome as his successors. The question concerning Peter's even being in Rome is yet debated.

Presbyterian.—In opposition to the episcopal system in which the power structure of the church resides in the bishops, the Presbyterian system locates the power and authority of the church in the session, or local congregation. From the session run lines of authority up to the General Assembly which meets once a year. In between are two areas of power: the presbytery, composed of proper representatives from the sessions of the area; and the synod, composed of a number of presbyteries of an area. A representative form of government seeks to safeguard the autonomy of the session as well as honor the cooperative aspects. There are three offices in the Presbyterian system: pastors, elders, and deacons.

Congregational.—The name of independency is sometimes given to this system. The individual congregation is the complete *ekklesia.* It does not derive its power or structure from another group. The authority for church action lies within the group. Officers are appointed by the church to serve various functions but have no power beyond that granted by the members of the church. A working relationship is often established with other churches of the same persuasion to promote various programs and boards; i.e., missions, education, and service. It might meet in annual conventions but the convention has no authority to impose its decisions upon the local congregation.

These are the diverse types. There are variations and degrees, but we will not speak of them here. The question that must be raised is: which type is right, if any at all?

In answer to this question, a number of approaches may be cataloged. There is the attitude summed up by John Macquarrie when he says, "Even if there had been an 'original' pattern of the ministry and one could discover what it was, this would not be specially important. It is clear that there must have been a formative period in which changes in the institutional forms would be required as the Church moved out from being a revolutionary movement in Judaism to become a settled, world-wide community." [3]

It seems to be a part of the thinking of many that it was not important what the nature of the structure of the apostolic church was, but it is vitally important that it remain what it is now. Macquarrie also declared that "alongside the New Testament, we have to recognize the living development within the Church. It is impossible to avoid the conclusion that from an early time the regular and universal pattern of the Christian ministry was the threefold one of bishops, priests, and deacons, and that this is a natural development from the New Testament picture itself." [4]

In spite of those in sympathy with Macquarrie, it is yet a legitimate question as to whether or not we can look to the New Testament for a pattern that is up-to-date in the twentieth century as well as having the endorsement of the apostolic norm. Did the development away from the simplicity of the apostles come because it was not working, or did it develop because of other reasons; namely, expediency, power politics, and political ambition from the area of religion?

Another attitude is that expressed by Berkhof concerning some of the Reformed churches today. "Reformed Churches," he writes, "do not claim that their system of Church government is determined in every detail by the Word of God, but do assert that its fundamental principles are directly derived from Scripture." [5] Berkhof maintains that the principles are consistent with the Scriptures but admits that the details are determined "by expediency and human wisdom." [6]

The third attitude is expressed in the desire to return to the New Testament pattern as far as it can be discerned. There is considerable description in the New Testament concerning the fellowship of the *ekklesia*. The following items point this up:

1. There were stated meeting times, generally on the Lord's day, or first day of the week (Acts 20:7; Heb. 10:25).

---

[3] *Principles of Christian Theology* (New York: Charles Scribner's Sons, 1966), p. 384.
[4] *Ibid.*
[5] Louis Berkhof, *Systematic Theology*, p. 581.
[6] *Ibid.*

2. The fact of election of certain members points out a form of democratic government in the churches. Matthias was chosen to succeed Judas and there were also elections of deacons.

3. The early church had leaders. In addressing the Philippi church, Paul delineated bishops and deacons. (Further discussion of the leaders will be presented below.) No mention is made of others.

4. The officers, or servants of the church, were designated such; and their appointment is linked to the Spirit, who had made them bishops or overseers.

5. There is a recognition of the authority of the church as a deciding body as well as the authority of the minister who is elected as pastor of the church (Matt. 18:17; 1 Peter 5:2).

6. The church had the power of discipline. This is also noted in Matthew 18:17, but Paul specifically, in writing to the church at Corinth, admonishes Corinthian Christians to exercise their right of discipline (1 Cor. 5:4,5,13).

7. The church had a financial record of some primitive arrangement. Even the twelve disciples had a treasurer in Judas who, among other things, got carried away with his role as treasurer; but the believers did store up money on the first day of the week for beneficent purposes (Rom. 15:26; 1 Cor. 16:12).

8. The early churches issued letters of commendation. In a world of charlatans and false teachers—both then and now—valid letters of communication are issued from church to church, commending or warning of people moving in their direction (Acts 18:27; 2 Cor. 3:1).

9. The benevolence program of the early church was developed enough to include a register of widows who needed aid (Acts 6:1; 1 Tim. 5:9).

10. The primitive church was uniform enough to warrant the apostle Paul to warn against certain practices and justify his warning on the basis that no such custom was practiced in the churches of God (1 Cor. 11:16).

11. The first churches observed certain religious ordinances. Of two we can be positive; namely, baptism and the Lord's Supper. Of any more there is debate among men of different denominations, depending on what they have at stake.

12. The proto-church seemingly had good order that was not only admonished but practiced also (1 Cor. 14:40; Col. 2:5).

13. A group normally requires certain qualifications for membership in it and the church in the scriptural accounts is no exception. The command of Jesus was to convert or make disciples, immerse, and teach them to observe what he had commanded (Matt. 28:19; Acts 2:47).

14. The early church seemed to be taken up with its work that was common to the whole body of Christ (Phil. 2:30). The common work is evidenced by the success of the church that wherever it went it bore witness to the gospel of Christ.

It is basically this type of fellowship that is presumed to be reproduced in the modern period. It is simple, and in its simplicity it made a phenomenal change in the world. Its flexibility of movement made it possible to invade the cities, to be a church on the move, to go where the people were. It is possible to deprecate the foregoing items by saying that there is "no system of government in the New Testament." Such a statement really means that if there is no more than the items listed above there is no pattern of church government in the New Testament.

At this point enters the question of other organizations in modern church life. What justification is there for such well used instruments as the Sunday school, ladies' missionary organizations, men's groups of various kinds, as well as subsidiary organizations? These things can be presumed on the basis of the *ekklesia's* ministry of self-education, mission outreach, and cooperative stewardship. As far as the functions of these organizations go, they are traveling under non-New Testament names to fulfil what the early church was most concerned to do—share the message as well as teach it.

Leaders of the Ekklesia

Within the *ekklesia* there were a number of leaders who were the servants of the people. They may be divided into two general categories—temporary and permanent.

Temporary Leaders

Undoubtedly the first group, the apostles, ceased with the death of the last of the twelve. Those directly called by Jesus became witnesses of his ministry and especially of the resurrection. Some of them performed distinct contributions by way of their writings which form the basis of the New Testament. Included within this group is the apostle Paul who was called after the resurrection of Jesus.

A second group of unique leaders were called prophets. The role of the prophet is seen in two ways. Occasionally there were prophets who spoke of future events. Such is seen in Agabus, who spoke of the famine that would come in Jerusalem, as recorded in Acts. The predictive role of the prophet is presumed lost since the apostolic period. The second role of the prophet is in the matter of spiritual building up or edification. Prophesying in this sense is tantamount to preaching (1 Cor. 14:32–33). This has been permanent in the *ekklesia.*

A third servant-type leader is seen in the evangelists. Not much is certain of them. Only about four are known: Philip, Timothy, Titus, and Mark. It is doubtful whether one can identify the evangelists in the New Testament with the concept of today. The modern evangelist is often a pastor who has greater success in the recruitment of converts than other pastors. The pastorate is the spawning ground of most modern evangelists.

Permanent Leaders or Officers

Bishop, overseer, pastor, elder, presbyter.—The bishop or overseer was the chief servant and leader of the *ekklesia.* A number of terms are used synonymously for that role. The following breakdown of the terms may help in understanding:

Bishop: an old Middle English word used as a translation of the Greek term *episcopos.*

Overseer: an alternate translation of the Greek term *episcopos.*

Pastor: a translation of the Greek word meaning "shepherd."

Elder: a translation of the Greek word *presbyter.*

Presbyter: a transliteration of the Greek word *presbyter* which means "elder."

Some form of these terms, except bishop, occurs in the book of Acts. In Acts 20:17, the leaders from Ephesus are called "presbyters," or as it is translated, "elders," while the same group is encouraged to "pastor" the flock over which they are overseers (*episcopos,* hence bishops) in 20:28.

A parallel example can be seen in our modern practice of speaking of one as pastor, minister, preacher, or "brother." It would be unfortunate to conclude that all four terms speak of four different offices. Basically, this misunderstanding has been imposed on the New Testament usages of these terms. Consequently, many denominations have different orders of ministry.

It may be of interest to note the disuse of the title of bishop among some Protestants. The term bishop occurs in several prominent places in the New Testament, especially when the qualifications of that person are outlined in 1 Timothy 3. Likewise, the term "elder" occurs most frequently in the New Testament and it is used very infrequently in today's church terminology. In some cases it is used today to designate an office lower than bishop.

The qualifications for the bishopric are listed in 1 Timothy as well as hinted at in other places. Certain of the qualifications relate to his moral life. The aspiring bishop must be irreproachable, or blameless, sober, temperate, not a drunkard, or a brawler. At the same time he must not be governed by the pursuit of money. In addition, he must have civil or social abilities to be courteous, hospitable, avoid quarrels, and have a forbearing disposition. Third, he must have certain capabilities. He must be a good teacher, he must manifest qualities of administration—first with his own family and then the congregation. Without the first, doubt is cast on his being able to qualify in the other.

Along with the capabilities, one can speak of spiritual maturity. A new convert is not firmly established and may fall into subtle sins such as conceit and pride. Fourth, there are marital qualifications. He must be the husband of one wife. The latter qualification is interesting in light of the widespread rejection of it in large segments of Christendom. Canon law of the Roman Church has forbidden a married clergy for centuries. Even where permitted, it is often limited to the lower ranks of clergy. But here in the New Testament it is connected with the office of bishop. Calvin inveighed against this alien practice and spoke of the dignity bestowed upon marriage by requiring that a bishop be the husband of one wife.[7] It is true that some men would prefer to be single for the work of the gospel, but it is not true for the large majority. Marriage is a wholesome

---

[7] John Calvin, *Institutes of the Christian Religion* (Grand Rapids: Eerdmans, 1957), II, 469.

relationship and a happily married bishop or pastor could do much to show the troubled marriages of today how marriage can be fulfilled.

The bishop is admonished certain roles of servitude. We have avoided as far as possible the term authority or power. The only authority one can speak of is geared to persuasion and leadership (1 Peter 5:2,3). The bishop is a servant of the people and as such he is a spiritual leader and teacher. The bishop has no rank, no command of power, and no demand of obedience. He is a leader by virtue of his devotion to God, wisdom, spiritual insight, and persuasiveness. The believers are urged to remember their leaders and "follow the example of their faith" (Heb. 13:7).[8]

The pastor or bishop has the role of preaching the Word of God for the upbuilding of the *ekklesia*. He is committed to preaching the Scriptures in a balanced way. His primary responsibility from Sunday to Sunday will be in the midst of believers who need to be lifted up and encouraged. All preaching has evangelical aims, but not all preaching is to be evangelistic preaching. The pastor must attempt to avoid preaching to people who are not in the audience.

A second role of service is leading the church to observe the ordinances. However, the pastor is not a priest in the usual sense and therefore is not indispensable. But for the sake of order, he is the leader when the ordinances are observed.

A third role of service centers around the matter of church discipline. The pastor must counsel those who have chosen to walk their Christian lives at a distance from the Saviour. Others must be kindly rebuked in love—speaking the truth in love—to keep them from bringing shame to themselves and to the name of Christ. The pastor has no power of expulsion from the church. Only the *ekklesia* can do this. He may lead it to initiate action, but without the *ekklesia* he can do nothing.

Deacon.—The second servant-type leader of the *ekklesia* is the deacon. This office is not mentioned as often as that of bishop. However, considerable detail is given about qualifications. There are character traits, such as "not indulging in double talk, given neither to excessive drinking nor to money-grubbing" (1 Tim. 3:8, NEB). In a word, they must not be scandalous. He, like the bishop, must be the husband of one wife, governing his household with discretion.

---

[8] Cf. Heb. 13:17, NEB; Acts 20:20,23,35; 1 Thess. 5:12.

The marital question is often misunderstood. Some moderns have understood the matter by saying a deacon should not be a person who has been divorced. A man may have messed up his life before becoming a Christian. Yet according to the rule, as it is understood, he cannot ever be a deacon; but it is possible that through the transforming power of Christ he may be better qualified than one who has never been divorced. The limitations here should be understood in light of the prohibition against polygamy rather than the past situation of a man's life before conversion.

Third, there are spiritual qualifications. The deacon must be a man of faith with a pure conscience. A firm hold "on the deep truths of our faith" is necessary (1 Tim 3:9). The deacon should be able to speak in behalf of the Christian faith in the same manner that the early deacons did. It was because of this aspect of his service that Stephen was martyred.

The *duties* of the deacon are not defined extensively. If the office of deacon originated in Acts 6:1–6, and some question this, then part of their work was in reference to benevolence and charity. If this is the case, one can say that the deaconate originated before bishops. The deacons were to relieve the apostles in the ministry of benevolence so that the latter could continue in preaching. In essence, they served both the bishop and the people. To the pastor they gave relief for preaching the Word of God; to the people relief from hardship.

Tradition has placed the serving of the Lord's Supper into the hands of the deacons in some churches. As a matter of order this is fine, but the deacon should also be directed toward more substantial acts of Christian service.

Other Leaders

The two officers mentioned above constitute the extent of the New Testament offices.[9] Nothing can be said to support archbishops, cardinals, or popes. There are some church offices that have come

---

[9] The limitation to two offices in the *ekklesia* is borne out by the *Didache,* which speaks of only two officers, bishop and deacons (15:1). Thus at about A.D. 150 the structure of the *ekklesia* had not departed far from the early prototype. By the time of Irenaeus one can see three orders of church officials. At the same time, because of his fight against heresy, he believed in the apostolic succession of the bishops. Under the bishops were the elders and the deacons. Dana, *Manual of Ecclesiology,* p. 109.

into existence purely on the basis of expediency. The role of the church clerk could be reflected in the fact that the churches issue letters of commendation but in the modern sense the clerk records the decisions of the church body from time to time. Even if this is expedient, it is an elective office without authority or rule. One office in the modern church is required by law; that is, the trustees. They are necessary for holding property in the name of the group. The same function could be achieved by the deacons, but a different group is often chosen.

Ordination

Ordination is the official act of recognition by a church that a man is called by God to fulfil the work of the ministry. Differences of opinion about ordination come in sacramental churches where a communication of grace and priestly power supposedly takes place in the act of ordination. Nonsacramental churches speak of ordination as merely the recognition and authorization to fulfil the ministry. Protestants, as a rule, profess no indelibility of character which is transmitted in ordination. The Roman view, however, implies a change of character. This may be expressed in the statement, "Once a priest, always a priest."

No ceremony is given in the New Testament with the exception of the phrase "the laying on of hands." And the meaning of this term is subject to debate. The New Testament knows nothing of a sacramental view of ordination. There is general misunderstanding concerning the idea of the laying on of hands. In the New Testament the Greek word has the meaning of stretching out the hand, as in voting; or to appoint, rather than touching of the hands to someone. The term does not refer to a ceremonial induction to office.[10] The nature of the appointment idea can be seen in the instance of Barnabas and Saul. They were designated to a new field of service, not ordained.

The right of ordination belongs to the church, whether ordaining one to the pastorate or sending him forth to minister.

Church Councils

There is a precedent in the book of Acts for a council to discuss certain issues bothering the churches. The issue of faith without

---

[10] Cf. Brunner, *The Misunderstanding of the Church*, p. 80.

legalism was the cause of the first meeting. In the history of the church other councils have met. Can councils be justified?

The first council, as recorded in Acts, was in reality the coming together of the mother church at Jerusalem. Instead of being ecumenical, it was little more than a church meeting. The proximity of the first church to Judaism, along with the presence of the apostles, made it the natural place for considering the problem of the Judaizers.

The more interesting aspect of the meeting was that it enjoined nothing upon the Christians in the affected areas than what they had already received in the gospel as it was preached to them. This precedent has not been kept.

Having said this by way of criticism, there is a useful device in councils. A council can discuss problems that are common to the Christian communities at large. It can bring to light certain trouble-makers, both in the realm of morals and doctrine. It can bring together some of the best minds for the solving of difficult, complex problems. In all of this, however, it must be remembered that a council is purely advisory and that it always is judged by the standard of the Scriptures.

Membership in Ekklesia

The requirements for membership in the early church were very simple, yet profound. The first requirement was conversion and faith in Jesus as the Christ (Acts 2:47). Second, one must be baptized (Acts 2:41); and third, to remain in the fellowship as an active member, one must maintain a consistent life in accord with the ethic of love.

From the standpoint of the necessity for fellowship and the makeup of the early *ekklesia*, the individual who shrugged off membership in the group would be an abnormal phenomenon. Fellowship in Christ implies fellowship with his followers.

Ordinances of the Ekklesia

The religious rites of the early *ekklesia* were described in unifying terms: one baptism and the unity of the one loaf and one cup. Ironically, Christendom is split the greatest over the meaning of these observances. A number of questions must be answered before a discussion of any of the observances can take place.

First, what is the origin of the rites?

It seems quite evident that Jesus originated two of the rites: baptism and the Lord's Supper. About this there is little question. Concerning other rites: confirmation, marriage, ordination, and so forth, there is more debate. The Roman Catholic opinion is that "all the Sacraments can be connected up with something that Christ said; and a foundation for the assertion that he instituted them can be found in his own words: the general behavior and temperament of the Apostles bear out that herein they acted on some sort of mandate received from Christ in person: precisely in what way he gave it, save in the case of Baptism and the Eucharist, we cannot ever know." [11]

This is to infer that because the Roman Catholic Church observes seven sacraments, because the apostles were so conservative that they would not have done anything without a mandate from Christ, therefore, Christ must have instituted them. A great part of the sacramental system of the Roman Church is built upon inference.

E. J. Mahoney has written, "In the case of some of the sacraments there is explicit reference in the New Testament establishing their institution by Christ. Others, like Matrimony, are not so explicitly mentioned, but the doctrine with regard to them is contained in tradition and rests ultimately on the infallible authority of the Church." [12] He readily admits, with the Council of Trent, that the doctrine of matrimony is *"inferred* from the New Testament on the basis of the 'indissolubility of marriage' as Jesus spoke of it." [13] Much is based on tradition and the "infallible authority of the Church." [14]

Recognizing the inability of the Roman Church to substantiate more than two rites by the words of Jesus, Protestants have firmly maintained that Jesus alone can establish a religious rite. Certainly without drawing questionable inferences it is possible to see only two rites that Jesus clearly instituted.

Second, how many? Two or Seven?

If one adopts the standards of the New Testament in its presentation, there are only two. If the tradition of the church, developing

---

[11] Smith, *Teaching of the Catholic Church*, p. 751.

[12] *Ibid.,* p. 1064.

[13] *Ibid.,* p. 1065.

[14] *Ibid.,* p. 1064.

and growing over the centuries, is accepted, then there are seven. On the latter view, it must be understood that the development was slow and it took a full one thousand years before a writer definitely spoke of seven sacraments.[15]

The Reformation returned to the position of two rites. It refused to set up other rites, because a religious rite must have met the following criteria:

1. A rite must be instituted by Christ. In the case of baptism and the Lord's Supper, there is undoubtedly a basis in the Scriptures. There is much more than questionable inferential evidence concerning them. Origin of the Lord's Supper is recorded in parallel in the three Synoptics and also in 1 Corinthians. The Great Commission completes the witness of the Scriptures concerning baptism as it stands under the approval of Jesus from the time of his own baptism.

2. A rite must be enjoined by Christ upon his followers. This is true for both of these rites. On the other hand, not all followers can receive the seven sacraments. It is an either/or case with marriage and holy orders.

3. A rite must exhibit a divine act and thought. The first two rites do this. Baptism depicts the act of the death, burial, and resurrection of Jesus. The Lord's Supper also exhibited the divine act of the death of Christ. Baptism commences the ministry of Jesus and the Lord's Supper is the termination of it. Baptism expresses his identification with mankind and the Lord's Supper speaks of his atonement for it. Baptism expresses the initiation of man into God's covenant; the Lord's Supper expresses the occasional renewal of his covenant with man.

Along with the first two criteria—which rule out the five additional rites adopted by the Roman Church—this standard not only has application there but in another supposed rite. There is no act of God symbolized in penance, marriage, extreme unction, confirmation or holy orders. At the same time, the matter of washing the feet of the disciples expresses something that they must do; not what God did. There is no evidence that the apostolic church thought differently or practiced such.

Third, what are these rites in nature?

The rites are sometimes called sacraments and sometimes ordi-

---

[15] Peter Lombard was the first writer to definitely catalog the sacraments as seven. This was done about A.D. 1150.

nances. The word sacrament does not occur in the New Testament. It is the Latin translation of the Greek word for mystery, and the Greek word occurs in a number of places (Eph. 1:9; 3:2; Col. 1:26; 1 Tim. 3:16). The term developed in meaning from an oath of allegiance to a commander to a distinctively religious use. Eventually the word's currency in Roman Catholic thought was defined as a religious rite using materials that are signs or symbols and the sign conveys the grace it signifies. Following Peter Lombard, it can be said, "A Sacrament is properly so called because it is the sign of the grace of God, and the expression of invisible grace, in such a way as to be not only its image, but its cause." [16]

As a means of conveying grace, Roman thought speaks of the rites by means of the term *ex opere operato;* that is, by virtue of performance of the sacraments. It appears to me that some Roman Catholic expositions on the subject are fuzzy. On the one hand, one can read statements like the following: "If you had to find one word in which to crystallize the Catholic sacramental tradition, I think it would be 'Efficacy.' The Sacraments are, as we see, efficacious of themselves." [17] On the other hand, the necessity of the right intention is set over against the efficacious nature of the sacraments. The intention does not have to be too conscious—in fact one might be quite distracted in the process—as long as it is latent in consciousness.[18]

Again, some of the sacraments—baptism, confirmation, and holy orders—are supposed to produce a sacramental character, an indelible character, so that one is forever a "baptised, confirmed, ordained person." [19] But on the other hand, it is possible to commit mortal sin and be forever condemned. A mortal sin "carries with it the forfeiture of God's friendship, loss of grace, spiritual death." [20] What happened to the indelible character?

Another fuzzy approach is seen in the matter of intention versus obstacles to receiving grace. Roman thought claims, on the one hand, that grace is conveyed through the sacraments where there are no obstacles to the channel. It is clearly maintained that an infant cannot

---

[16] Smith, *The Teachings of the Catholic Church*, p. 748.

[17] *Ibid.*, p. 763.

[18] *Ibid.*, pp. 754–5.

[19] *Ibid.*, p. 756.

[20] *Ibid.*, p. 926.

place such an obstacle to the efficacy of baptism.[21] But what about the intention? Obviously the infant knows nothing of faith, baptism, or the church. Proxy intention is then designated to the parents, or godparents, who have faith for it.

The Reformation view of the rites is such that the word sacrament is used with a different meaning. Calvin wrote:

> First, we must attend to what a sacrament is. It seems to me, then, a simple and appropriate definition to say, that it is an external sign, by which the Lord seals on our consciences his promises of goodwill toward us, in order to sustain the weakness of our faith, and we in our turn testify our piety towards him. . . . We may also define more briefly by calling it a testimony of the divine favor toward us, confirmed by an external sign, with a corresponding attestation of our faith towards Him.[22]

The Reformed position differs from the Roman view in several ways.

Generally speaking, the requirement of faith is necessary, with the exception of baptism, wherein infant baptism is practiced. In contrast to the Roman view, infant baptism is not a necessity. When the sacrament is received in faith, the grace of God accompanies it: "The external sign becomes a means employed by the Holy Spirit in the communication of divine grace." [23]

The Reformed view is not far enough removed from the Roman view to suit many others. People who seek a radical return to the New Testament speak of the religious rites that Jesus instituted as ordinances.

An ordinance is an outward rite or a visible sign of the saving truth of the gospel. The ordinances are "signs, in that they vividly express this truth and conform it to the believer." [24] An ordinance is also a rite speaking of a covenant or divine promise. In this sense they do not convey grace. To be more precise, grace is the cause of God's redemption. Faith does not bring grace; it responds to it. Faith in Christ brings the gift of God's Spirit, who works internally in the life of man to transform him, lift him up, make a new being of him. An ordinance is therefore a *reminder* of God's grace.

---

21 *Ibid.*, p. 795.
22 Calvin, *Institutes*, pp. 491–92.
23 Berkhof, *Systematic Theology*, p. 618. Cf. Calvin, *Institutes*, II, 497.
24 Strong, *Systematic Theology*, p. 930.

We never outgrow the reminder of our baptism; namely, that we confessed ourselves dead to sin and alive in Christ. We never outgrow the reminder of the Lord's Supper; namely, that in it God promises and guarantees the forgiveness of our sins because of our faith in Christ. These rites do not strengthen grace in the heart of man; they speak of faith and commitment on man's part and thereby the enlargement of the Spirit's control and direction of his life becomes possible.

The history of the church shows how men have bounced from one extreme to the other concerning the meaning of the rites. Men have emphasized the objectivity of the sacraments on the one extreme and rejected the personal qualifications of the administrator on the other. At the same time they have turned away in horror at the subjectivity of the rites.

The true view of the New Testament is the requirement of faith on the part of the recipient. This is tacitly admitted in the sacramental discussions on everything but baptism. But here is where it is most crucial. The requirement of faith, in essence, abrogates all sacramental systems, particularly the sacrament of infant baptism. More will be said of this in the discussion of the individual rites.

Baptism

Since the publication of *Die Kirchliche Lehre von der Taufe* (*The Teaching of the Church Regarding Baptism*) by Karl Barth in 1944, a theological storm has been raised over the question of baptism. As a Reformed theologian who usually defended infant baptism, Barth came to conclude that infant baptism was incorrect as well as meaningless apart from faith. Only a discerning person has faith; therefore, baptism must be limited to those of faith. Rejoinders in defense of infant baptism have been offered by Oscar Cullman, Joachim Jeremias, and others. Because of the evident requirement of faith for the candidate and the desire to retain infant baptism, there are theologians who have attempted to defend faith in the infant candidate. Attempts are then made to prove scripturally that infants have faith.[25]

There is more interest in the subject of baptism today than has been shown for generations. Stalemated positions now have erupted

---

[25] David P. Scaer, "The Conflict over Baptism," *Christianity Today*, April 14. 1967, XI, No. 14, p. 8 (688).

into open controversy. In an endeavor to treat the issue we will attempt to deal with a number of questions related to it.

What is baptism?—The word baptize is a transliteration of the Greek word *baptizo*. It has carried over into English because the translation of it into English seems to decide the question concerning the mode of baptism; namely, its translation by the term immersion. Barth writes, "The Greek word *Baptizein* and the German word *taufen* (from *Tiefe,* depth) originally and properly describe the process by which a man or an object is completely immersed in water and then withdrawn from it again." [26]

In churches where immersion is not practiced, baptism is not translated but interpreted to mean a rite involving the sprinkling or pouring of water upon the candidate. In either case, the "baptismal formula" is spoken: "I baptize thee in the name of the Father, Son, and Holy Spirit."

It is difficult to define baptism without a relationship to a number of questions, and the definition implies the answer to the questions. Strong wrote, "Christian Baptism is the immersion of a believer in water, in token of his previous entrance into the communion of Christ's death and resurrection—or in other words, in token of his regeneration through union with Christ." [27] One should wait for a definition of baptism until the other issues are settled. Then it is possible to incorporate these facts into the definition.

What is the meaning of baptism?—This question is one way of asking another question, "What does baptism do?" If the latter question is answered in the negative, that is, baptism does not wash away original sin, it does not convey grace, etc., then the meaning of baptism must be discussed. We will discuss the power of baptism next.

The meaning of baptism can be expressed in a number of ways. First, it is the "representation (Abbid) of a man's renewal through his participation by means of the power of the Holy Spirit in the death and resurrection of Jesus Christ, and therewith the representation of man's association with Christ, with the covenant of grace which is concluded and realized in Him, and with the fellowship of

[26] Karl Barth, *The Teaching of the Church Regarding Baptism,* trans. Ernest A. Payne (London: SCM Press, ET. 1948), p. 9.
[27] Strong, *op. cit.,* p. 931.

His Church." [28] Note the threefold association; with Christ, his covenant, his *ekklesia.*

Second, baptism is a pledge of God to man, which pledge God maintains through all circumstances. "It testifies to him that God has directed all His words and works toward him and does not cease so to do." [29]

Third, baptism serves as the entrance gate to the *ekklesia* and "stands at the beginning of every believer's life." [30]

Fourth, the intention of baptism is "the glorifying of God in the building up of the Church of Jesus Christ through the pledge given to a man, with divine certainty, of grace directed towards him." [31]

Fifth, baptism implies that the believer is "commissioned for special duty." [32]

Sixth, baptism is the visible means of expressing what has already happened "invisibly through the word and faith." [33] On this point Calvin concurs that baptism is a confession before the world. "That as we are to be ranked among the people of God . . . in short, we publicly assert our faith." [34]

Seventh, baptism portrays the fact that the believer is alive in a new spiritual life but dead to the old way of life in sin. This is true because of the link of faith to Christ, and what happened to him thereby happened to us (Rom. 6:3).

Eighth, it can be inferred that the word "baptize" symbolizes purification, not because of water and purity, but because the believer is linked to Christ by faith and therefore he has a new life, a new creation, hence he has put to death the old and put on the "new man" (Col. 3:5 ff.).

There are other possibilities for discussion. Is a part of the meaning of baptism the continuity between it and the Jewish rite of circumcision? Some, like Oscar Cullmann, argue that it is. Cullmann maintains that it is the successor to circumcision. He appeals to

---

[28] Barth, *The Teaching of the Church Regarding Baptism,* p. 9.

[29] *Ibid.,* p. 14.

[30] *Ibid.,* p. 15.

[31] *Ibid.,* p. 25.

[32] Oscar Cullmann, *Baptism in the New Testament* (Chicago: Allenson, 1950), p. 36.

[33] Brunner, *The Christian Doctrine of the Church, Faith, and the Consummation,* p. 42.

[34] *Institutes,* p. 520.

certain passages in the New Testament (Rom. 2:25 ff.; 4:1 ff.; Gal. 3:6 ff.; Eph. 2:11; Col. 2:11). The last passage alone is linked with any contextual mention of baptism. If continuity is important, and *some* continuity seems to be, then it is faith, not institution for institution or rite for rite.

It is quite easy to argue that the promise of God was a *new* covenant, which implies a degree of difference. The problem of the old covenant was that the outward sign of circumcision did not bring forth faith in the individual. Likewise, faith is a necessity before the covenant becomes applicable to the individual. The internal nature of the witness of the Spirit as spoken by Jeremiah limits the use of any covenant until the person has come to faith. The old covenant began with an adult (Abraham) and continued in its sign with infants. The merit of the new covenant is that it begins and continues with the same sign and status of person.

Clearly circumcision as a parallel has implications for infant baptism—which will be discussed below—and one of them is to substantiate by analogy the validity of infant baptism. It is argued that in a missionary church like the early one was, adult baptism was generally practiced; but as their children came along, it was correct to baptize the infants. In reaction to this, it can be said that the practice of infant baptism is the one sure way for a church to lose its missionary enthusiasm. When the second and third generations do not have the same experience of faith, they naturalize their faith to intellectual forms. At the same time, a church that is not missionary oriented is not an *ekklesia*.

What does baptism do?—In the above section we said that baptism does not *do* anything. This is rejected by those of a sacramental bent for whom baptism is said to *effect* something.

From the Roman perspective, baptism "exonerates us completely before God, since there is neither guilt nor debt of punishment in the souls of the baptised. More explicitly, whether it be a question of original sin or actual sin, baptism not only delivers us from eternal loss, but also remits all temporal punishment due to actual sin, and entitles us to eternal life." [35] In essence, baptism produces the regeneration of the soul, a new birth, the Christian life. Thus baptism is a

---

[35] Smith, *The Teaching of the Catholic Church*, p. 774.

necessity for salvation: "Without it, it is impossible to go to Heaven."[36]

Certain loopholes are found in this statement, however. Roman theologians admit martyrdom for the faith before baptism as the equivalent of baptism. In the case of one's being baptized by some heretical group, as long as it is done correctly, it is valid baptism. If it is not performed correctly, it is not. Baptism by desire is also permitted. Where one loves God, it could not be without a sorrow for sin. Loving God means that one must explicitly or implicitly desire the sacrament of baptism.

Such extenuating circumstances in theology are essential when baptism is regarded as a necessity.

Reformed theology regards baptism as a means of grace but does not conclude that it is necessary for salvation. Reformed thought seems to work its way into a corner when it deals with the question of infants. If it is supposed to strengthen, what is there to work on? There is no faith. If it does not regenerate, what does it do? The best answer that Berkhof gives—and it is not too good—is that the operation of baptism and its power is not limited to the time of performance but may strengthen later in augmenting the individual's faith. Obviously, it is a short step to saying, why not wait until later on when the child is aware and has faith?

The issue of baptism's power is a serious one. Does it bring forgiveness? Is it the means of the Spirit's reception? Is it necessary for eternal life?

The scriptural support for sacramental power of baptism rests upon inference, misinterpretation, and poor textual support.

With reference to inference, an example is seen in John 3:5: "Except a man be born of water and of the Spirit, he cannot enter into the kingdom of God." It is an inference that "water" refers to baptism. The term may refer to "water birth," as the context implies in the discussion of birth; or, it may refer merely symbolically to cleansing. Nothing is said of baptism in the passage. The same is true for Titus 3:5. The "washing of regeneration" can very well be a simile for the precise work of the Spirit without reference to real water at all.

---

[36] *Ibid.*, p. 776.

Poor textual support is seen when men quote Mark 16:16 to prove that baptism as a sacrament is necessary for salvation. The passage belongs to the longer ending of Mark which is not among the most ancient manuscripts. To build a doctrine upon such a shaky foundation is wrong.

Misinterpretation fits another category of passages like Acts 2:38, in which the King James Version says, "Repent, and be baptized every one of you in the name of Jesus Christ for the remission of sins, and ye shall receive the gift of the Holy Ghost." The crux of the passage rests upon the Greek preposition *eis,* which can mean for, with reference to, in token of, on the basis of, and because of. In this case the usage of "for" is used to support a sacramental line, while the use of "because of" the remission of sins is the non-sacramental approach to baptism. This is the meaning of the statement in Matthew 3:11, where John says, "I indeed baptize you [*eis*]"—because of repentance. This occurs similarly elsewhere.

Supporting this nonsacramental line of thinking, Emil Brunner wrote: "There is no question of Paul thinking that this sign itself effects something which had not previously been effected by the Word. Baptism is not itself a factor in salvation except in so far as it is the making visible of an invisible event. . . . The baptized person says 'I now belong to Christ and wish also to confess my faith before the whole world.' The preacher says, 'Through your confession you show that you really belong to Christ.' " [37]

What is the mode of baptism?—Strangely enough, this is often regarded as the most important question whereas it is really the least important. Baptists are often misunderstood when they insist on immersion. The argument over the mode is often confused with the meaning. Baptists insist on immersion secondarily, and the meaning primarily.

Concerning the mode, one can begin from the ground of general agreement. All parties agree that immersion was a form of administering the rite called baptism. Not all parties agree that it was the only one. Further, there is a difference of opinion on how early departures from immersion came. Can one infer that John the Baptist poured rather than immersed?

If the issue is decided on the basis of the meaning of the Greek

<hr>

[37] *The Christian Doctrine of the Church, Faith, and the Consummation,* p. 42.

word, there can be little doubt that it is correctly translated by our words immerse, dip, or sink into water. This is its usual meaning in the New Testament.

Various objections are raised on circumstantial grounds. Was there enough water in Jerusalem to baptize 3,000 after the Pentecost sermon? One must certainly allow some time for preparation, and there were certainly enough pools in Jerusalem to do so. In mission history, it is recorded that 2,222 Telugu Christians were immersed in 9 hours by 2 administrators. One need only think in terms of 12 apostles to easily accommodate 3,000.

Would the jailer have followed his prisoners outside the city of Philippi to be baptized? The jailer was so thankful for his life that he would have done almost any rash act, and baptism is not beyond the bounds of his reason.

Other circumstantial arguments have adequate answers. There is reason to look for such arguments only on the presupposition that infant baptism is true. Undoubtedly, immersion was the practice into the Middle Ages, as is shown from the great baptistries that have been uncovered.

In spite of our line of reasoning here, the question of the mode is not significant in comparison to the question of the meaning of baptism.

What are the requirements of baptism?—Here again one can set forth a proposition that all may agree on initially. Most camps agree that baptism requires faith. The division comes in saying "faith on the part of whom." Roman writers insist on faith as a prerequisite for baptism: "That these dispositions of faith and repentance are necessary for adult sinners is shown to us in the Sacred Scriptures." [38] As for infants, faith is required either in the parent or the god-parent. The requirement boils down, for the adult, to his intention of receiving the sacrament. He may not have repented of his sins, but the "character" of baptism is placed upon him. He is still validly baptized.[39]

On the Reformed line, faith is likewise required of the adult before baptism, but not from the infant. Faith is transferred to the congregation. "If faith were lacking in the congregation assembled for the Baptism, it would not be a congregation. . . . But where the

38 Smith, *The Teaching of the Catholic Church,* p. 792.
39 *Ibid.,* p. 791.

believing congregation is, there the Holy Spirit, operating within it
and knowing no limitations, has the power to draw an infant into his
sphere." [40]

In support of his reasoning, Cullmann argues that in Christ the
"essential act of Baptism was carried out, entirely without our co-
operation, and even without our faith." [41] In so arguing, Cullmann is
teetering on the verge of universal salvation. On this analogy, one
may say that all men are redeemed in Christ without regard to having
faith or not having faith. This would prove much more than the
Scriptures warrant. Again, if faith is a necessity, then it is limited to
an age of discernment. If baptism does not effect a change, why have
infant baptism? If it is solely a matter of the covenantal sign, why
not wait until it means something to the child?

The last line of reasoning is that of Karl Barth and the Baptists
who have long supported the requirement of faith as a conscious,
responsible act. Barth declares: "If it is to be natural, the candidate,
instead of being a passive object of baptism, must become once more
the free partner of Jesus Christ, that is, freely deciding, freely confessing, declaring on his part his willingness and readiness." [42] He
goes further to characterize as a "half-baptism" any rite that does not
call for a conscious knowledge of faith and regeneration.[43] In another place he speaks of baptism without faith and readiness as a
"clouded" baptism.[44]

Who may be baptized?—This question implies part of the foregoing. The question here deals more specifically with the issue of infant baptism or baptism only of the discerning; hence, more generally,
adult baptism.

Infant baptism has as its rationale presuppositions it must maintain
to be legitimate. First, that it can be sustained in the Scriptures as a
practice. Second, that it is a successor to circumcision which was
administered to infants. Third, that baptism washes away original sin
and is the means for regeneration of the person to insure his entrance into heaven. Fourth, the desire to retain some form of a national church (Volkskirche), whereby the church is coterminous
with the state. One is born into the church by baptism as one is born

[40] Cullmann, *Baptism in the New Testament,* p. 430.
[41] *Ibid.,* p. 23.
[42] *The Teaching of the Church Regarding Baptism,* p. 54.
[43] *Ibid.,* pp. 47–48.
[44] *Ibid.,* p. 40.

into the state by birth: both events come about without the consent of the individual.[45]

All of these presuppositions are disputed. All of them militate against the apostolic requirement of faith and repentance. Barth is rather decisive on the matter: "From the standpoint of a doctrine of baptism, infant-baptism can hardly be preserved without exegetical and practical artifices and sophism—the proof to the contrary has yet to be supplied." [46] Brunner is in agreement in saying, "It is impossible to harmonize Paul's teaching about faith and in particular his explicit teaching about Baptism with the thought of Infant Baptism." [47]

Supporters of infant baptism should not reason, as Calvin did, by using the words of Jesus concerning children, "Of such is the kingdom of heaven." It is their childlikeness in faith and commitment that is commended to adults to emulate. The kingdom of heaven is not theirs because they are little or even infants, but because of a trusting, childlike faith in God.

Who may baptize?—The Roman Catholic view is the most lenient: "All that has to be said about the minister of baptism can be summed up in these two statements: First, anyone, man or woman, baptised or unbaptised, can validly administer the Sacrament of Baptism. Secondly, while all can administer this Sacrament validly, only priests (and bishops, of course) are the ordinary lawful ministers of it; others being lawful ministers only in the case of necessity." [48] The lack of limitations is due to the sacramental nature of baptism. Emergency baptism is necessary sometimes when an infant is born and dies without the presence of a priest.

Calvin, on the other hand, without the burden of the sacramental approach to salvation, asserts that it is "improper for private individuals to take upon themselves the administration of baptism; for it, as well as the dispensation of the Supper, is part of the ministerial office." [49] He reinforces his reason by the command of Christ to the appointed apostles. He prohibited a woman from doing it.

At the other end are those in agreement with Baptists who, for

---

[45] *Ibid.*, pp. 52–53.

[46] *Ibid.*, p. 49.

[47] *The Christian Doctrine of the Church, Faith, and the Consummation,* p. 54.

[48] *The Teachings of the Catholic Church,* p. 785.

[49] *Institutes,* p. 524.

the sake of order, think in terms of the pastor's administering baptism but would have no objection if the *ekklesia* itself, without a leader, should appoint someone to officiate. The important question for the Baptist is not who is baptizing, but who is being baptized? When baptism is not regarded as sacramental in nature, the important question is whether the candidate has committed himself in faith to Christ.

In conclusion, one may define Christian baptism, according to the New Testament, as the immersion of a person who has faith in Christ and wishes to be initiated by immersion into the fellowship of his followers, and receive from him in baptism the sign of his promise that not even death can deter the surety of his covenant.

The Lord's Supper

It seems strange that there should be such a difference of opinion concerning the meaning and implication of the four little words, "This is my body." Ironically, a rite that was to symbolize unity has fractured the Christian church into many pieces. About the only common ground left is the words of Jesus, to which all make an appeal.

Here too, as in baptism, a definition would be better at the end, after answering certain relevant questions. For the sake of order, a preliminary definition will be given here and a final one to conclude the discussion.

What is the Lord's Supper?—The Lord's Supper is a religious rite instituted by Jesus the evening before he was crucified. He took bread and wine in turn and blessed both of them. Concerning the bread, he said to his disciples in the upper room, "Take, eat; this is my body." Then the cup of wine was passed with the words, "Drink of it; all of you; for this is my blood of the covenant, which is poured out for many for the forgiveness of sins" (Matt. 26:26–28). This is the rite in its simplicity.

This simple rite was enjoined upon the disciples to be observed in remembrance of him. From these simple statements many conclusions have been drawn.

The Lord's Supper is sometimes called the eucharist, an ancient name for it which implies a ceremony of thanksgiving. Another term which is nonbiblical is the Mass, a Latin word meaning "to dismiss."

What is the meaning of the Lord's Supper?—The first source of understanding comes from the Bible accounts which speak of certain things by way of Jesus' interpretation of the meaning of the simple rite. First, it is an act of remembrance (Luke 22:19; 1 Cor. 11:24). By observing it, the disciples were to look back to that night and the following events to recall that his body was broken and his blood spilled in their behalf.

Second, it is representative of the new covenant. All four Gospels incorporate this assertion which stand out as very important. A covenant was established by the ancient Hebrews in killing an animal and sprinkling its blood. In essence, Jesus is saying that the promises I have made are now to be ratified in covenant by my own blood. The basis of the covenant is now quite different from the past. In contrast to the use of animals for covenantal initiations, now Jesus, the Son of God, sets forth a new covenant founded upon his life's blood as the Son of God incarnate.

Because God has deigned to forgive sin, and because this is difficult to believe, he makes a new covenant whereby this is guaranteed to men of faith. Thus, as the Lord's Supper is observed from time to time, one is to remember God's covenant with him. This is part of its present reality.

Third, it is prophetic of his return. Two accounts speak of this fact. He will not share in this rite personally until the day when he drinks it new in his Father's kingdom. Paul's account to the Corinthians speaks of the rite as the continual announcement of the Lord's death until he comes.

The Lord's Supper can be admitted to be all of this by almost every professing Christian. But is it any more that that? Can one go from the simple Last Supper rite, in which Jesus holds up a piece of bread in the presence of his disciples, to the view that a simple piece of bread now literally becomes the body of Christ? Roman thinkers attempt to do this. In other words, once a symbol embodied a person, whereas now in the Roman Catholic idea of transubstantiation the person is embodied in the symbol. Instead of saying that the verb "is" in the sentence "represents" something, Roman Catholic writers insist that the verb "is" means that a transformation has taken place (transubstantiation) and now the elements contain the true body of Christ. On this has been erected an elaborate system. Thus, one can justify worship of the Eucharist, because of the living Christ is contained in the elements.[50]

The Mass is then regarded as a "bloodless sacrifice" which is re-enacted. Moreover, Christ is the "offerer" with his church in corporate worship as well as the one who is offered.[51] The Mass becomes a prayer on the part of the "offerers." [52] More important, it is regarded as a vital channel of grace. The Eucharist is supreme among the sacraments, "the sacrament par excellence of the Mystical Body, whereby we are continually nourished and united ever more closely with its Head." [53]

The starting point for the Roman understanding of the Eucharist is the Gospel of John, chapter 6, rather than the decidedly clear explanation of Christ himself in the Synoptic Gospels and 1 Corinthians.

John 6 deals with the feeding of the multitude and a description of Jesus as the Bread of life. The Roman Catholic conclusion from the chapter is summed up in the following words: "How does Jesus give eternal, everlasting life to men? How can bread give this life? And it is Christ himself who answers: 'I myself am the living bread that has come down from heaven. If anyone eats of this bread, he shall live forever. And now, what is this bread which I am to give? It is my flesh, given for the life of the world.' The bread is His flesh of which we must eat, and with the eating is bound up eternal life for all mankind." [54]

From this is concluded that the disciples must eat his literal flesh. The recollection of these words of Jesus, in their minds, is the basis of their understanding the Last Supper—a difficult thing to prove.

The Council of Trent gave the following definition of the matter: "Because Christ declared that which he offered under the species of bread to be truly his own body, therefore has it ever been a firm belief in the Church of God, and this holy Synod doth now declare it anew, that by the consecration of the bread and of the wine a con-

[50] Cf. Smith, The Teachings of the Catholic Church, pp. 869–70. "The practice of the Church of paying to the Eucharist the worship which is due to God alone is but a logical consequence of her belief that therein is permanently present the living Christ, true God and true man."

[51] Henri Daniel-Rops, This Is the Mass (Garden City: Image, 1959), p. 16. Such is Bishop Sheen's statement in the preface.

[52] Smith, The Teachings of the Catholic Church, p. 910.

[53] Ibid., p. 700.

[54] A Handbook of the Catholic Faith, p. 295.

version is made of the whole substance of the bread into the substance of the body of Christ our Lord, and of the whole substance of the wine into the substance of his blood; which conversion is by the Holy Catholic Church suitably and properly called Transubstantiation." [55] The act of consecration is the utterance of the words of Jesus, "This is my body."

Does John 6 support a sacramental view of the Lord's Supper? This may be answered with an emphatic no. Jesus frankly declares to his disciples that the flesh is of no avail, but it is the Spirit that gives life. He furthered this by saying, "The words I have spoken to you are spirit and life" (John 6:60–63).

One may conclude from these verses that the whole discourse has a deeper meaning than the surface understanding of the hearers who rebelled against the sayings. The deeper or symbolic meaning uses the metaphor of feeding upon Jesus to indicate believing and trusting. It seems strange that so much argumentation is used to literalize "this is my body" into a sacrament, while nothing is done to make sacramental meaning out of "I am the door. . . . I am the light. . . . I am the truth. . . . I am the way. . . . I am the good Shepherd. . . ." There are no good reasons for doing the first and neglecting the latter.

We may conclude this section with a reference to Brunner, who wrote: "Is the Lord's Supper celebrated by the Pauline community symbolic? Yes, certainly, for it is the same as that first Supper where Jesus was still bodily present, and where consequently there could as yet be no talk of a transubstantiation of 'elements' in a miraculous sense. With bread and wine, Jesus said something. He underlined what He was saying in His words, and Oriental man had no difficulty in understanding such sign-language." [56] He concedes that a miracle did take place the night of the the Lord's Supper, but it was a miracle involving the institution of the new covenant and not the "prodigy of the transubstantiation of the elements." [57]

What does the Lord's Supper do?—The answer to this question depends upon the church background.

The Roman Catholic answer is that the Eucharist conveys grace to the believer. It furnishes the spiritual food for daily growth in

---

[55] Smith, *The Teachings of the Catholic Church*, p. 857.
[56] *The Christian Doctrine of the Church, Faith, and the Consummation*, p. 62.
[57] *Ibid.*

Christ and is the channel of this grace. Conversely, "the Mass brings us no new merits, no new atonement, no new reunion between God and men. Mass is only the means by which the fruits of Christ's suffering and death are applied to men in particular." [58] The Mass is important enough that the Roman Church declares everyone of her members are bound—under pain of mortal sin—to observe the Lord's Day "by assisting at Mass." [59] Without the reception of the sacrament the individual cuts himself off from the source of God's grace.

The Reformed view is that the Lord's Supper is regarded as a sign and seal. Calvin wrote, "That sacred communion of flesh and blood by which Christ transfuses his life into us . . . he testifies and seals in the Supper, and that not by presenting a vain or empty sign, but by there exerting an efficacy of the Spirit by which he fulfills what he promises." [60] While denying a "real presence" in the Roman meaning of the term, because the body of Christ is localized in heaven, the elements nevertheless serve as instruments of God's grace.

This same truth was declared by Charles Hodge, who taught that "the sacraments are real means of grace, that is, means appointed and employed by Christ for conveying the benefits of his redemption to his people." [61]

There is a third view associated with the name of Baptists and others. The Lord's Supper does not transmit any mysterious spiritual power. The Lord's Supper does not bring Christ any closer to the believer than he was before. The believer may feel existentially, but not geographically, nearer to God. The Lord's Supper thus regarded is a memorial, convenantal, and prophetic symbol. As a memorial it reminds the believer of the death of Jesus Christ at a point in history. The believer continues to observe the memorial to his Lord. But unlike other memorials in which the person is yet dead, this memorial centers around one who died and is yet living and sharing in the memory of the believing in a living way. Because the living Saviour indwells the believing, the Lord's Supper does not increase any quantitative grace content in his life.

This covenantal aspect of the Lord's Supper is his promise of con-

---

[58] *A Handbook of the Catholic Faith,* p. 310.

[59] *The Teachings of the Catholic Church,* p. 909.

[60] *Institutes,* II, 563.

[61] Charles Hodge, *Systematic Theology* (Grand Rapids: Eerdmans, 1952), III, 499.

tinued forgiveness of sin. In observing the Lord's Supper the believer renews the sign of the covenant in his life and indicates his own dedication as well as cherishing God's promise of forgiveness over his own failing life.

The prophetic role of the symbol relates to Christ's promise of return. It speaks of a future supper. The prophetic meaning tells us that life is fleeting and unwhole. The convenantal and prophetic elements keep the rite from becoming a return to the past. Life is to be lived in the present with an eye to the future.

Who may receive it?—This question too must be answered from the vantage point of the tradition.

The Roman answer is for the person to be in a state of grace. This means one has been baptized, has examined the conscience with the possibility of having been absolved from sin through confession.

The Reformed church has similar demands. Faith in Christ is a requirement along with repentance of sin and a desire to grow in the Christian life. In addition, the recipient must have an understanding of the meaning of the Lord's Supper as opposed to a common meal. Children, who are not able to examine themselves, as well as unbelievers are excluded.

The Baptist tradition requires the recipient to have a conscious experience of conversion. This is followed by the requirement of immersion according to the command of Christ. The third usual requirement is to be a member of the *ekklesia*. The rite is not a private matter but is to be observed in the family of the *ekklesia*. The last requirement is obedience in the Christian life. Grounds for exclusion include immoral conduct, disobedience to the commands of Christ, and heresy or false doctrine.

Some Baptists are divided in opinion over whether the Lord's Supper should be observed by the members of the local church only or whether it is a general rite observed by members of the same faith but not necessarily of the same local group.

Who may administer it?—The administrators vary. By analogy, the people in the priesthood institute the Mass in the Roman Church, but in reality it is the priest alone who has the control of the elements. The Reformed churches are similar in their position on baptism. The administering of it belongs to the office of pastor. Churches related to the Baptist tradition declare that anyone whom the church appoints may administer the Lord's Supper.

How frequently should it be observed?—The logic of the Roman definition of the sacrament is this: if it is a means of grace, frequent communion is the conclusion. Daily communion would be ideal.

If one rejects the premise of a sacrament, some other answer is forthcoming. The denomination of the Churches of Christ observe the Lord's Supper weekly. This is not commanded, however. If the attitude of Jesus toward binding tradition is taken seriously, one must reject any arbitrary decision that makes a religious rite a routine event. For the sake of regularity some rule is needed, but room must be allowed for spontaneity and spiritual discernment. Freedom must dictate additional observance beyond regularity as well as omitting the regular when necessary.

To conclude the discussion, we may say that the New Testament describes the Last Supper as a simple memorial which has convenantal and prophetic meaning. To go beyond this means to go beyond the authority of the New Testament.

XIV. The New Beginning

*"Most of them," said Ransom, "have ceased to think of such
things at all. Some of us still have the knowledge but I did not
at once see what you were talking of, because what you call
the beginning we are accustomed to call the Last Things."*

*"I do not call it the beginning," said Tor the King. "It is
but the wiping out of a false start in order that the world may
then begin."*

C. S. Lewis, Perelandra

*It is unwise for Christians to claim any knowledge of either
the furniture of heaven or the temperature of hell; or to be
too certain about any details of the Kingdom of God in which
history is consummated. But it is prudent to accept the testimony of the heart, which affirms the fear of judgment.*

Niebuhr, Nature and Destiny

*If out of pity and humanity we admit the necessity, i.e., the
inevitability of universal salvation, we must deny the freedom
of the creature.*

Nicolas Berdyaev, The Destiny of Man

*No one would reject Christ's apocalyptic on the ground that
apocalyptic was common in first-century Palestine unless he
had already decided that the thought of the first-century
Palestine was in that respect mistaken. But to have so decided
is surely to have begged the question; for the question is
whether the expectation of a catastrophic and Divinely ordered
end of the present universe is true or false.*

Lewis, World's Last Night

The Meaning of Eschatology

The idea of eschatology is not properly related to the wild-eyed
fanatic who is carrying a sign that the world is coming to an end.

Eschatology, the doctrine of the last things, has been in disrepute because of such extremes since the Montanists in the early centuries of the church to the modern sensationalists like William Miller, the Jehovah's Witnesses, and others who have set dates and places for the return of Christ. After the date expires, some ingenious explanation is then given to explain the nonvisible appearance of Christ. Thus, modern man often cares little about eschatology and has grave suspicion about what he does know about it.

Only in recent times has the subject of eschatology been recovering from neglect and suspicion. At the turn of the century Johannes Weiss and Albert Schweitzer gave renewed importance to the doctrine. Although both men maintained that Jesus expected the kingdom of God to come in his own lifetime, and even though their views have not commanded wide acceptance, yet they rightly maintained that eschatology was firmly a part of Jesus' message.

Much of modern theology is written on the premise that eschatology *pervades* the thought of the New Testament. One may read Rudolf Bultmann's *Theology of the New Testament,* and other works of his; Reinhold Niebuhr's *The Nature and Destiny of Man*; C. H. Dodd's *The Parables of the Kingdom*; and the more recent works of Wolfhart Pennenberg and Jürgen Moltmann, to see how deeply theology must be viewed from the standpoint of eschatology.

If eschatology is to be reevaluated and enlarged in our thinking, what does it mean? What does it have to say about the present religious life? About man and his present existence in a secular world? About the meaning of history, and of right and wrong?

The definition must come first. "Eschatology" literally means the doctrine of last things. It refers customarily to the end of the world and suggests the termination of life as we know it. This is a part of it, but only a part. This definition is too narrow, negative, and futuristic. Eschatology has to do with the present also. It emphasizes a quality of life that is positive; hence it is an attitude toward life, too. It is in this vein that Jesus declared, "I come that they may have life, and have it abundantly" (John 10:10).

There is much to warrant a new name for eschatology. Taking the cue of C. S. Lewis, in his novel *Perelandra,* we might speak of it as a "new beginning." If we do this, the term may include several types of beginnings. If we accept a new beginning for something, it usually means that the old way stands under someone's judgment and is terminal and incomplete. We will attempt to show this in trying to give full meaning to the traditional concept of eschatology.

The following ideas are implied in the new beginning.

1. We begin with God's act in the past, the appearance of the Messiah—Jesus, the Christ—as the decisive eschatological event in history. This ushers in the new age, a new covenant, and a new beginning of God's dealings with man.

2. The believer's present relationship to Christ by faith, based on the historic cross and resurrection, is an eschatological relationship. God—the outsider to man—confronts man in his life, and when man responds by faith he enters into a new life; paradoxically, he experiences eternal life *now* (John 3:36). The life of faith in Christ is a new life, a "qualitatively different life," as Kierkegaard terms it.

3. Eschatology focuses attention on a new meaning in history. The Bible does not refer to history as a series of isolated facts. History is the arena of God's activity. The first eschatological event was a fact in history—the birth of Jesus in the reign of Caesar Augustus. The Old Testament repeatedly intimates that God is ruler and Lord of history. In the New Testament, viewed from the vantage point of eschatology, history is moving toward a goal, a consummation, and a new beginning.

The alternatives to a Christian view of history are basically two. In the first, history becomes a meaningless process of continuous events without ultimate fulfilment. Without God, man is a fortuitous accident who may experience minor fulfilment and purpose in the things that he does, but he is still without relation to cosmic purpose. The minor purposes man sees for himself are reducible to emptiness when unrelated to God.

The second alternative to a Christian view of history is seen in some Oriental thought forms which describe ultimate reality as timeless. Such a concept is often related to a "World Soul," or a pantheistic view of God. In this case, history is an illusion because only the World Soul has reality. Illusory history also becomes endless. Life is cyclical and repeats itself without termination.

Contrary to these alternatives, Christian faith declares that God *is* involved in history. In the sphere of history the incarnation took place. The cross was a historical event wherein centers man's redemption. Present religious experience is the encounter of God with man in history. Faith therefore grows strong and optimistic as it trusts God for the future. Faith becomes confident that God has not deserted mankind but that he is ever in the shadows, keeping watch over his own.

4. A corollary truth is that when history moves toward a goal it also ends under judgment. With a new beginning in the future, assessment of the old takes place. The judge of history has already placed an evaluation on man's activities in history. This reckoning points up the inability of man to be his own redeemer. It is evident that man cannot emancipate himself from the guilt of his sin or free himself from judgment.[1]

In the termination of history, three basic functions of life will come to an end: morality, culture, and religion. By the same token, they will be transcended by a new beginning. Morality will end, for I shall become what I should be. Thus the transformed life in Christ will close the gap between what I ought to be and what I am. Culture, with its mixture of good and evil and its creativity motivated by selfish motives, will be superseded by spiritual creativity. Religion shall end, for the believer will know God with true vision rather than seeing through a glass darkly.[2]

5. The new beginning in the consummated kingdom of God will reflect a judgment on what man has regarded as good and evil. This includes man's social order as well as man's social habits. Concerning the social order, the new beginning in the kingdom of God future means that life will not be utopian now. Certainly life can and should be made better and more tolerable. But the pervasive influence of man's selfish motives prevents society from being utopian. Thus man and his society stand in judgment. The future judgment means that divine love will bring supremacy over the forces of self-love.[3]

Man's social habits, or more properly man's ethical standards, will stand judgment. The judgment idea will declare what should be rather than what is. A growing amount of ethical theory and advice is based on results of sociological and anthropological studies of what people are doing or have done. Although one may show a head-count statistic that 60 percent of the college girls of 1953 had engaged in premarital sex relations, this says nothing about the rightness of their actions. Too many people conclude for moral relativity

---

[1] Niebuhr, *The Nature and Destiny of Man*, II, 293.

[2] Tillich, *Systematic Theology*, III, 402.

[3] Niebuhr, *op. cit.*, p. 290.

on the basis of what people are doing. The judgment, terminating the old way of life, deals with norms of what should be rather than with statistics of what has been done. The judgment idea means that distinctions between good and evil are real, not illusory or pragmatic.

Consequently, the Christian life never separates eschatology from ethics. The source book of faith, the Bible, speaks of the future, the new beginning, the judgment, and ethical living in the present—all in the same breath.

6. The new beginning in Christ means a new style of living for the Christian concerning the relativities of our existence, when evil appears to be victorious over good. Although evil still exists in our present world, judgment means that evil will be overcome. Christian faith asserts that judgment has *in principle* taken place on the cross, but in the final judgment evil *in practice* will cease. When the Christian suffers "for righteousness sake" he is not surprised. He takes heart in his Lord's warning that this would happen, and he takes comfort in his future vindication (Matt. 5:11–12). This is to view life eschatologically.

7. The new beginning refers to what man will be after he is redeemed and ultimately transformed. The new being that he has become in Christ *now* will be culminated *then*. Man's liberation from sin's rule began with Christ: then he is in true liberty from sin's presence. The Christian *then,* as a complete new being,[4] experiences individuality in the fullest sense. Christian faith, unlike Hindu thought with absorption of the individual into the World Soul, regards Christian individualism as a good, not an evil hope. The resurrection bears this out, for man is raised as a total being before God. Fellowship can be meaningful only as individuals confront one another. Being swallowed up by a World Soul negates fellowship.

8. Because the consummated new beginning may take place at anytime, there is an existential impact in eschatology, both for man in general and the believer in particular. The question of John Donne—"What if this present were the world's last night?"—becomes a continuing question through life.[5] Although men live as though the present form of existence shall continue forever, eschatol-

---

[4] Tillich speaks of the fall of man as the passing from essence to existence, and eschatology as passing from existence to essence. *Systematic Theology,* III, 395.

[5] C. S. Lewis, *The World's Last Night* (New York: Harcourt, Brace & World, Inc., 1959), p. 109.

ogy declares a halt to it. The present world is not man's blessed hope. Men have power to destroy civilizations but lack the power to produce or create a new age. Eschatology recognizes man's inability without God to carve out a meaningful and permanent existence. Therefore, a generation which has come to know the hydrogen bomb, space travel, and the curvature of space should not boggle at the possibility of a divine consummation unless its picture of God is too small.

9. Last, the new beginning deals in hope. Hope is based upon what God has done in the past. It is borne out of meeting with him in the present, and looks to the fulfilment of the Old and starting of the New. Hope rests upon God's promise of the kingdom of God. Without hope, life becomes unbearable. With hope, life, with its problems, doubts, and failures, can be endured, redeemed, and made new.

Thus eschatology is a wider, more inclusive idea than the last days. It is not simply futuristic, but it is that also.

Problems in Eschatology

Eschatology became shattered and fragmented over these questions: Did Jesus expect the kingdom of heaven to be established in his own lifetime, or was the kingdom postponed? Is it possible that the kingdom of heaven was present in Jesus' time as well as being a future event?

Several positions are held with regard to these questions.

First, argue as Schweitzer did, that the kingdom of heaven was to be inagurated within Jesus' lifetime. This creates grave problems. Jesus must be interpreted as a "deluded fanatic, a man who died because his faith was set upon wild apocalyptic dreams." [6] Moreover, passages in which Jesus speaks of the "kingdom among them" in his own person must be excised or explained away.

Second, argue that the kingdom of heaven and its coming must be related to the person of Jesus. The kingdom is not a future reality but a present one in him. This means that passages which speak of a future kingdom must be interpreted symbolically rather than literally. A criticism of this view centers in its freedom with passages in which an obvious future is meant.

---

[6] George Ladd, *Crucial Questions About the Kingdom of God* (Grand Rapids: Eerdmans, 1954), p. 30.

Third, argue that the kingdom is both present and future. The kingdom has begun in the person of Jesus, but it will not be consummated until he returns. This position appears to be the soundest approach by giving scriptural credence to both emphases.

Another set of problems center in the beginning point of interpreting eschatology. If one starts with the Old Testament, it seems evident that some form of millennialism will be formulated. It will then be argued that certain prophecies have not been literally fulfilled. Thus many millenarians look for the rebuilding of the Temple, reinstitution of sacrifice, and other aspects of Old Testament prophecies. However, if one begins in the New Testament and interprets Old Testament prophecies in the same free way that the New Testament writers did, then it is seriously questionable whether a form of millennialism will emerge. An example of the apostle's use of prophecy is seen in Paul's statement about the Christian's being the true Israel, the true seed of Abraham because of faith.[7]

If Christian faith is to be consistent with itself, it must begin with the New Covenant. The Old Covenant is incomplete and must be viewed from the standpoint of its fulfilment.

Types of Eschatology

Millennialism

The word "millennium" does not occur in the New Testament; it is Latin, meaning one thousand years. Associated with Revelation 20, millennial systems of eschatology have been widely held from the early centuries on. It is maintained that before the time of Origen (b.185) no one opposed the millenarian interpretation.[8] Millennialism is still an influence in fundamentalism and in certain conservative circles.

There are three types of millennialism: postmillennialism, premillennialism, nonmillennialism.

Postmillennialism.—No longer regarded as a viable option, postmillennialism held that a golden age or millennium would take place in the future. However, the millennium would be the result of the church's preaching of the gospel, which would spread like leavening

---

[7] Cf. Gal. 3:7,29; Rom. 4:16; Heb. 12:28. Another example can be seen in comparing Acts 2 with Joel 2.
[8] Ladd, *op. cit.,* p. 23.

through bread dough. This form of millennialism was popular in an era when a sense of progress was aligned with the concept of evolution. Postmillennialism stresses growth in the church in which God conquers the world. Following this golden age, Christ will return.[9]

The events following the golden age are the resurgence of evil, the sudden appearance of Christ who overcomes evil, the general resurrection, and the great judgment.

Postmillennialism had its difficulties, among which were its unbiblical conclusions that the world would be converted, evil would disappear, and the kingdom of God would come in an uncatastrophic way. Further, two world wars with minor side wars, the rise of nationalism with its attending conflicts, and the continuing surge of evil made it difficult to speak of our world as getting better.

Premillennialism.—This view asserts that Christ will return to earth before a millennium or a thousand-year-period of his rule. There are two general varieties of premillennial systems.

Historic premillennialism.—This system can be sketched as follows concerning the event to take place in the future.

1. A great apostasy will take place before the coming of Christ. This will be joined with persecution of the church.

2. Christ then comes to "rapture" or take out the church from the world. The dead in Christ are raised at this time, and the living are transformed to be like him.

3. Following this, Christ comes to the earth to destroy the Antichrist. This is followed by the judgment described in Matthew 25 (sheep and goats), whereby the destinies of the righteous and the unrighteous are pronounced.

4. The millennial kingdom is inaugurated, during which Satan is bound and the yet unrighteous nations are ruled with a "rod of iron."

5. As the millennium draws to a close, Satan is permitted to be free, whereby he gathers in peoples of the earth to wage war against the saints, but the forces of evil are destroyed by fire.

6. Then a second resurrection takes place, the raising of the wicked from death, and the white throne judgment is to follow (Rev. 20:11–15).

7. The end of all things is for a new beginning. A new heaven and

---

[9] Augustus Strong was typical of the men who held to postmillennialism.

a new earth are brought into being and the eternal kingdom of God begins (Rev. 21).[10]

Dispensational premillennialism.—This is a variation of the historic premillennial position. A popular source of this variety is the Scofield Reference Bible. Dispensational premillennialism could be said to have the following variations:

1. The second coming of Christ is in two stages: a coming for the church before the tribulation begins, and a coming with his church after the tribulation. (The tribulation is a period of terrible persecution and harrassment upon the earth.) Some speak of a secret coming for the church, in which the believers are taken out of the world (secretly) before Christ comes visibly *to* the world.

2. When Christ comes for the church the Holy Spirit will cease his activity in the world.

3. A second resurrection takes place after the tribulation for those who have come to believe during it and were martyred for their belief.

4. When Christ comes with his church, many Jews will believe and live in the millennium.

5. The kingdom is predominantly Jewish in nature. Temple worship will be established in Jerusalem.

Some problems attendant to dispensationalism are: its Jewish emphasis on the restoration of the Temple in the presence of Christ who is the end of sacrifice, the conversion of people without the presence of the Holy Spirit, and the question of whether a future millennium is legitimate.

The assessment may be made that without Revelation 20, the question of a future millennium would never come up. Most of the references in the New Testament speak of the consummation of the age without any indication of a long period of time required for a thousand-year reign of Christ. For many critics of the different forms of millennialism it appears that a towering theological structure has been built upon a highly symbolic passage in a book whose symbolism is intense. Can one justify a system of thought that is built upon a book so obscure in meaning?

Nonmillennialism.—For the sake of completeness, we will list the

---

10 Floyd E. Hamilton, *The Basis of Millennial Faith* (Grand Rapids: Eerdmans, 1952), pp. 22–23.

various types of nonmillenial systems, although we have referred to some of them briefly before.

Consistent eschatology is the view of Johannes Weiss and Albert Schweitzer that Jesus' teaching was entirely eschatological. The kingdom of God was to appear in his lifetime. Men were to prepare for it immediately and the radical ethic taught by Jesus was valid only for that short interim before the messianic age was to dawn.

Although the conclusions of Weiss and Schweitzer are not valid, they did have merit in drawing serious attention to the pervading emphasis on eschatology in the New Testament.

Realized eschatology, associated with the names of C. H. Dodd and Rudolf Bultmann, places strong emphasis on those passages suggesting that the kingdom of God has already come. Note the example from Luke 11:20: "If it is by the finger of God that I cast out demons, then the kingdom of God has come upon you." The doctrine of last things now becomes the doctrine of first things. No longer futuristic, the entire concept of eschatology is geared to the present life in Christ. References to the future end of the age must be interpreted symbolically, but the early church mistook it literally.

The ethical passages of Jesus are not rejected as an interim ethic as in consistent eschatology. The ethics of Jesus are for the "now" of all generations.[11] The kingdom of God that comes now to every man is God's deliverance for man. "It is the *eschatological* deliverance which ends everything earthly." [12] Bultmann speaks of Jesus' rejection of "the whole content of apocalyptic speculation" concerning the future, and men are forbidden to make any "picture of the future life." [13] In realized eschatology, "every hour is the last hour." [14] Bultmann explains eschatological existence as having already come for the believer. Man is desecularized; that is, the center of his life is faith, not society. One is in the world but not of it (John 17:11,14, 16). The committed already *has* life (John 3:36; 6:47; 1 John 5:12).[15]

Realized eschatology is not without its critics. Reinhold Niebuhr

[11] Bultmann, *Jesus and the Word* (New York: Charles Scribner's Sons, 1958), p. 129.
[12] *Ibid.,* p. 35.
[13] *Ibid.,* p. 39.
[14] *Ibid.,* p. 52.
[15] Bultmann, *Theology of the New Testament* (New York: Charles Scribner's Sons, 1955), II, 78.

has rejected the reductionism involved in its treatment of the second coming. Further, he maintains that the hope of the second coming of Christ is "indispensable for the Christian interpretation of history and for a true understanding of New Testament thought." [16]

The issue on which a futuristic eschatology is rejected seems to be the matter of mythology. Bultmann wrote, "The mythical eschatology is untenable for the simple reason that the parousia of Christ never took place as the New Testament expected." [17] Thus, if a reader is to follow Bultmann, he must learn to "demythologize" the Scripture by deleting the mythical elements "through a process of subjective judgement so that what remains is acceptable to his thinking." [18]

In assessing the position of Bultmann and others like him, it appears they stumble at certain things in the Bible which modern scientifically oriented man cannot accept. In making the twentieth-century secular mind the standard of rejecting the New Testament thought forms, it is implied that all "truth" must be judged from our standpoint. This is theological folly. With knowledge advancing so rapidly we must hesitate to reject the past on the basis of the specious present.

However, this is not the most serious charge against demythologizing. More serious is: what is to be demythologized and what is not? This is serious when one views the basic concept of the Bible that God has revealed himself in history. From the scientific viewpoint of our age, this must be regarded as mythic or nonsense. If our scientific sensitivities set the standard of what must be rejected or retained there is no end to what may be regarded as mythological. Forgiveness of sin by God is as offensive to our modern ears as it was to the cynic Celsus in the third century. Little will be left when we finish our excising of passages because they offend us.

The danger of regarding Scripture passages as mythic implies that the story is nonhistorical. It may convey a religious truth, but it is not a factual historical event. When eschatology is understood as mythic it means that God comes to every man, but not in a unique way in the historical past as asserted in the traditional idea of the incarnation. The cross understood mythically means that every man should

---

16 *The Nature and Destiny of Man*, II, 48.
17 *Kergyma and Myth* (New York: Harper & Brothers, 1961), p. 5.
18 Henry M. Shires, *The Eschatology of Paul in the Light of Modern Scholarship* (Philadelphia: Westminster Press, 1965), pp. 217-18.

sacrifice himself as the normal way of life. When the Bible is relegated to myth, Christian faith is reduced to a religious *principle* rather than an *historical fact*. Mythology bypasses the "once-for-allness" of the incarnation event as well as the historical salvation act of the cross. If Christian faith is transformed into a *religious principle* it means that man is in chief control of his destiny. If Christian faith stands upon *historical fact* it confesses that God is the Redeemer of mankind.

One may freely admit difficulty with biblical terminology in contrast to our modern viewpoint, but substitute terms frequently turn in the direction of abstraction. Seemingly, the more abstract one becomes, the more spiritual he is regarded. But when the personal is replaced by the impersonal, and the historical appeal to facts is replaced by the timeless principle, then Christian faith has turned about-face. It has become *another* faith.

Symbolic eschatology, advocated by Reinhold Niebuhr and Paul Tillich, maintains that the New Testament must be taken seriously and symbolically, but not literally. This is regarded as a superficial adjustment in the traditional meaning of eschatology. In Niebuhr's reconstruction, history is an "interim" between the first and second coming of Christ which illumines man's existence. The final judgment means that man will be emancipated from poor attempts at good and the power of evil. The final judgment means that the corner will be turned toward fulfilment of life. The symbol of the second coming expresses man's hastening toward death. It also shows our lack of understanding concerning history and life. The second coming points up the truth that happiness is beyond history, but it is a real happiness and fulfilment. Nonetheless, the second coming of Christ is not understood in literal terms of the New Testament apocalypse.

The reason for adopting this reconstruction arises out of certain passages. Niebuhr accepts the premise that Jesus thought the time between the first and second advents, or comings, would be short.[19] Passages such as Matthew 10:23, 16:28, and 24:34 seem to indicate an immediate return of the triumphant Messiah. One must be driven to accept some form of the Niebuhrian approach *unless* plausible, unforced explanations can be given to these passages. If this is not forthcoming it would be useless to go on to discuss eschatology that

---

[19] *The Nature and Destiny of Man,* II, 49.

accepts the passages literally. If it is possible to understand the passages without resorting to allegory or symbolism then symbolic eschatology must be rejected. Some consideration will be given to these critical passages later.

Inaugurated eschatology is a term used by Bernard Ramm to indicate a synthesis of a future as well as a present or realized eschatology.[20] Redemption may be described as an eschatological experience, or the breakthrough of God into the realm of human experience. This does not exhaust the full scope of eschatology. Some of the eschatological events cannot be presently experienced, such as the return of Christ and the resurrection from the dead. These remain as future fulfilments.

Inaugurated eschatology is a nonmillenarian,[21] or amillennial, approach. The first nonmillenarian seems to have been Origen,[22] but it was Augustine who introduced an alternate interpretation of Revelation 20.

Augustine argued that the "resurrection" in Revelation 20 symbolizes the experience of rebirth, being made alive in Christ, being raised from the dead, or the spiritual reign with Christ. The thousand-year symbol is not a future period of time but an indefinite symbol to indicate the time between the two advents of Christ. Therefore, we are living in the millennium, or the interim period between the two comings of the Son of God. Old Testament prophecy is understood as having been fulfilled in the church (see Eph. 2:12–22 for an example of this). Amillennialism has much in common with premillennialism concerning certain expectations in the future, except for a future millennium. The following outline is suggestive of future eschatological events.

1. At the close of the era a great apostasy will take place. This will lead to growing and intense persecution of the church.

2. Christ then returns to defeat the forces of evil incarnate in Satan, the dead are raised and transformed.

---

[20] Bernard Ramm, *A Handbook of Contemporary Theology* (Grand Rapids: Eerdmans, 1966), p. 44.

[21] To help avoid confusion, remember that premillennialism could be described as an inaugurated eschatology, for it poses the beginning of the kingdom of God in Jesus' day with a future millennium. However, under the heading of nonmillennial systems we will consider only the amillennial system, since we have already treated premillennialism in the millennial systems.

[22] Ladd, *op. cit.*, p. 24.

3. Following the resurrection, and the defeat of Satan, judgment will take place for all peoples.

4. Following the judgment, the eternal kingdom of God will be established.

In this system the broad outline is evident: the kingdom begins with Jesus, it continues with his reign in the human heart, it speaks of a future return, the resurrection, and the last judgment.[23]

Can the kingdom be both present and future? This question arises out of the previous discussion. Certainly Jesus spoke of the kingdom of God as beginning in his lifetime. His message, "Repent, for the kingdom of heaven is at hand" (Matt. 4:17) can hardly be understood otherwise. But what about the future? There are sayings of Jesus which indicate that the kingdom is future also. Jesus spoke of a day in the future when the true followers of Christ will enter into the kingdom (Matt. 7:21–23). The kingdom of heaven is repeatedly regarded as a future event in the Sermon on the Mount. Six of the eight Beatitudes are couched in a setting of the future. Other passages speaking of a future (Matt. 8:11–12; 19:28; 13:38–43; 13:47–50; 26:29; Luke 19:11–27) can be examined.

How may the idea refer to the present as well as the future? The answer lies in the meaning of the word kingdom, *basileia*. The basic meaning of *basileia* is "reign," not people or realm or region. "The kingdom of God is the sovereign rule of God, manifested in the person and work of Christ, creating a people over whom he reigns, and issuing in a realm or realms in which the power of his reign is realized." [24] This means that the kingdom begins in the person of Christ. Kingly authority has appeared. In opposing his enemies, Jesus declared that "the kingdom of God has come upon you" (Matt. 12:28). The kingdom of Satan has been invaded by the kingdom of God. One can recognize the full force of these passages and others like them. The fruits of the present kingdom of God are forgiveness of sins and the judgment on evil. However, this is not the fulness of the kingdom. What is now only a reign over the hearts of his followers will one day become a reign with his presence.

It is now time to consider the crucial question as it is raised by Reinhold Niebuhr. He declares that Jesus expected the interim

---

[23] Shires, *op. cit.*, pp. 63–64.

[24] Ladd, *op. cit.*, p. 80.

period between the first and second events to be short. He quotes Matthew 10:23 and 16:28 as proof texts. This serves as the basis for his reinterpretation of the biblical terms as symbols rather than a literal statement.[25]

What may we conclude from these problem passages?

Matthew 10:23.—"You will not have gone through all the towns of Israel, before the Son of man comes." It is quite possible that this refers to the second coming, but it is also equally possible that it does not. It might be much safer to confess ignorance on the passage than to read into it something that may not be there. Some have related the passage to the destruction of Jerusalem, or the coming of the Spirit at Pentecost. But it could refer to the coming of Jesus to overtake them as they journey from one place to another, or a spiritual comforting of all persecuted disciples throughout the Christian era. The latter fact has certainly been true, but hardly meets the context of the passage. However, must it be insisted that it speaks of the second coming when the phrase is too enigmatic to warrant dogmatism?

Matthew 16:28.—The passage declares that some of Jesus' contemporaries would not taste death "before they see the Son of man coming in his kingdom." A number of interpretations have been proposed for solving this passage, such as referring it to the passage immediately following it and the transfiguration. This seems more plausible than referring it to the destruction of Jerusalem, or the founding of the church at Pentecost. It might be more meaningful to refer it to the resurrection event, when all the disciples but Judas saw the glory of the resurrected Lord. The resurrection is the watermark of the kingdom and makes possible his reign in the hearts of men.

To understand the meaning of this passage in connection with the resurrection poses a problem only if one understands the kingdom as a political entity with a visible ruler. It is certain that no messianic political unity existed, and it is even more certain that Jesus did not expect a personal restoration of David's kingdom. If one can show that eschatology has a future fulfilment from other Scripture sources, then this passage may be related to the beginning of Christ's reign in the hearts of men.

---

[25] Cf. Niebuhr, *The Nature and Destiny of Man,* II, 50.

Matthew 24:1–36.—This passage is not easy. A. B. Bruce wrote of it, "What is said thereon is so perplexing as to tempt a modern expositor to wish it had not been there, or to have recourse to critical expedients to eliminate it from the text." [26] The key passage is 24:34, "Truly, I say to you, this generation will not pass away till all these things take place." The natural meaning of the word "generation" must be maintained.

The following breakdown is suggested in the passage: Verses 1–14 refer to the discussion as a whole. Verses 15–35 refer to the destruction of Jerusalem. Verse 23 is crucial for the section of 23–31. These verses are a "parenthetical correction" related to the warning when Jerusalem is destroyed. The idea is as follows: when Jerusalem is destroyed be warned against false messiahs who will come; reject them, for they do not come in the manner that the true Messiah will come. When the true Messiah comes, it will be according to the description of verses 23–31. The backdrop of these verses is the appearance of false messiahs claiming to deliver Jerusalem from destruction. These verses describe the second coming but only in relating the *manner* of his coming. They tell *how* but not *when*. The time of his coming is discussed in Matthew 24:36–51.

This proposal for the passage above may or may not be the true meaning, but it is not a stretch of plausibility to interpret it so. It can be seen as rising out of the context and warranted by it.

One other issue on the return of Christ needs discussion. Certain people did not expect Jesus to return immediately. Jude, 2 Peter, and 2 Thessalonians show this. What is the reason for this? Various proposals have been made. One is that Jesus taught an early return and was mistaken. Another is that Jesus did not teach it and his followers were mistaken. If the latter is the case, how can the idea be accounted for? A reasonable answer may be found in the messianic expectations in Judaism, and these could have carried over into Christianity. Certainly the thinking of the disciples in the days before the crucifixion was patterned in this direction. The question was raised in Acts 1:6 whether the kingdom of Israel would be restored or not. The answer of Jesus suggests that it would not be an immediate experience. The significance of this statement can only be minimized and undercut by regarding the story as a composition of

---

[26] A. B. Bruce, *The Expositor's Greek Testament* (New York: Dodd, Mead & Co., 1902), p. 294.

the early church, and not genuinely the words of Jesus, as Bultmann does.[27]

We have argued that the kingdom of God is both present and future. What place, if any, does a future millennium have? The following reasons give basis for rejecting a future millennium after Christ's return.

1. The bulk of the book of Revelation must be understood in terms of the readers of the first century. Therefore, it is difficult to see how a future millennium so far removed from the dangers of the present would give comfort to the reader's present peril.

2. The writer speaks of things that must come to pass very soon (1:10). Therefore its symbolism must be related predominately to the first century.

3. Inasmuch as intense symbolism runs through the book, it seems artificial to begin interpreting the twentieth chapter in a literal way. Without this switch in methods of interpretation, the problems posed by a millennium would not arise.

4. Not only is there no reference to a millennium in other New Testament passages, but the general resurrection is spoken of in a way that a millennium has to be *forced* into other passages if one insists on holding that doctrine. A millennium requires a number of resurrections—before, during, and after the millennium—which will not square with other passages concerning the resurrection.[28]

The Parousia, or Return of Our Lord

The future return of Christ is a relevant question only for certain types of eschatological systems. Where Jesus is not expected to return but is made known by his presence in contemporary religious experience, the following matters will not be germane. A future return of Jesus Christ is linked to what the Bible says about the ultimate transformation of the believer. Certain facts are deduced from the Scriptures.

1. No one knows the time of Jesus' return (Matt. 24:36).

2. His return is described as personal rather than impersonal. Any

---

27 *Theology of the New Testament* (New York: Charles Scribner's Sons, 1951), I, 45.

28 For a survey of other arguments on the millennium, see George E. Ladd, *Crucial Questions About the Kingdom of God*, pp. 135–83, and Floyd E. Hamilton, *The Basis of Millennial Faith*, pp. 126–40.

appraisal of the New Testament statements will lead to the conclusion that the writers believed in a real *parousia* in the future.

3. The coming of Jesus will be visible. We prefer to incorporate here the usual meaning implied in the statement that Jesus' return will be a physical one. But considerable ambiguity abounds in the discussion of whether Jesus will return physically. Some theologians reject what is designated as a "physical" appearance or return of Jesus, because it implies that the same body structure—molecules, etc.—that died was then raised again. Instead, they contrast the "resurrection body" to the resurrection of the "flesh." This distinction means that the resurrection body was a transformed being no longer the flesh.[29] The basis for such a distinction is Paul's discourse in 1 Corinthians 15:42–50. The misunderstood term is "spiritual body" (v. 44). Without serious thought one might conclude that a "spiritual body" is a nebulous entity bordering on nothingness. This is not Paul's thought. The spiritual body refers to the transformed state of existence due to God's power in which man becomes truly whole, truly individual. Thus the spiritual body of Christ was visible to his disciples and at his return he will be visible to mankind.[30]

4. His return is described as sudden but triumphant. His first coming was lowly and then only little by little was he recognized as the Messiah. His return will be sudden and all will know of his position.

Death

The leveler of mankind, death, is the final ominous fact in man's future. Yet modern man, for the most part, attempts to forget about it. To ignore or forget about death has been man's tendency for ages. The Greek heritage furnishes us with two diverse attitudes toward death. Greek classical naturalism views death as a purely natural phenomenon.[31] Death is the experience of all men, and beyond death there is no need of fear, for no judgment exists. Anxiety about death is useless when one is not dying. Likewise, fear of death

---

[29] Emil Brunner, *The Christian Doctrine of Creation and Redemption,* p. 372.

[30] Check Matt. 24:30, 26:64; Mark 13:26; Acts 1:11; Col. 3:4; Titus 2:13 for descriptions of the visibility of Christ's return.

[31] Rudolf Bultmann, *Primitive Christianity,* trans. R. H. Fuller (New York: World Publishing Co., 1956), p. 132.

is needless when one is dying, for one cannot do anything about it, and after death one will remember it no more.

The other heritage of Greece is in Platonism in which death becomes the crown of life when one is liberated from the bondage of the body. Real life is not in the body but in the rational nature of man. The liberation of the soul from the body makes possible the reunion of the soul with the Divine. Idealism, in the Platonic tradition, affirms the immortality of the soul but rejects the resurrection of the body in the future. In affirming natural immortality of the soul, death is denied in essence, for death becomes the liberator of man's slavery to the material world.

Contrast the calm experience of Socrates meeting death with the anxiety of Jesus in Gethsemane to see the different attitudes toward death. The difference in attitudes shows death as a tragedy in Hebrew thought, while death is viewed as a liberation in Greek thought.

What is death? The answer cannot be full, for none of us has been through it and back. Death is certainly a biological fact in which an organism will not sustain itself, but it is more than that. It is also a spiritual fact. Berdyaev wrote, "The meaning of death is that there can be no eternity in time and that an endless temporal series would be meaningless."[32] Life itself is full of dying and struggling to live. We die a little at a time and are never reconciled to death. But eternal life can be reached only by death. In this, man's final hope rests through death.

When we fail to take death seriously we concede that man is after all merely an animal. To banish death from our thoughts is to ignore personality which transcends the purely biological nature of man. It is tragic that personality should die.

Christian faith deals with death head-on. Jesus Christ destroys death by his death. Death is not the last word on man's existence, but the beginning point for all things anew, a transition to everlasting life. Neither philosophy or science can teach us how to die, but faith does. Trust in the resurrected Christ gives assurance in death. Only Christian faith speaks of man's resurrection with Christ who is the means of it. Christian faith stresses redemption of man in his helplessness; where the resurrection is taught in non-Christian religions

---

[32] Nicolas Berdyaev, *The Destiny of Man* (New York: Harper Torchbooks, 1960), p. 251.

it is a reward of human achievement. In Christian faith death is swallowed up in the victory of the Redeemer (1 Cor. 15).

Life After Death

Christian faith has affirmed that life is not terminated at death. Life in Christ means that life continues and Christians will live forever. Several issues are to be considered.

First, life after death will mean individual existence. Life will not be swallowed up or blotted out by eternity. A mystical union with the Divine, or World-Soul, is not what the Bible sets forth. Individual existence means also that there is continuity in personality beyond death. It will not be another self than mine which will be raised at the resurrection. Only a person is a subject and God will address each as such. Just as personal existence involves us here in fellowship with people and with God, so life after death means the same. If we begin on the proposition that God created to bestow his fellowship, so life after death only makes the relationship more intimate.

Second, life after death in the biblical sense demands the resurrection concept rather than the immortality of the soul concept. The Bible does not speak of the immortality of the soul. It does teach the resurrection of the body. The immortality of the soul idea was made popular by Greek philosophers and "suggests that a soul carries on apart from the body." [33] This Greek doctrine implies that the body itself is evil and is a prison house for the soul because of some evil the soul did in a preexistent state and was subjected to a body as punishment. No such idea appears in the New Testament. The immortality of the soul is really a sophisticated version of the animistic view of death in which there is a shadowy survival of the creature. In this there is little comfort.[34]

By contrast, the resurrection of the body means that man will take on a new transformed existence as a spiritual body, that is, "a body which expresses the Spiritually transformed total personality of man." [35] Body and flesh are contrasted in the New Testament. Man will be raised a transformed body.

We are limited in our description of the future state of the spiritual

---

[33] John Macquarrie, *Principles of Christian Theology*, p. 324.
[34] Cf. Niebuhr, *The Nature and Destiny of Man*, II, 295.
[35] Tillich, *Systematic Theology*, II, 412.

body of man, for the Bible is not interested in a chemical analysis of the substance of it, but the functioning. "The spiritual body must be such that it will be able to meet the demands of the spirit and transmit its life-giving energies, but the composition necessary to achieve these ends is determined by God alone." [36]

To this point our attention has been focused primarily on man's post-resurrection existence. What is his state of existence between death and the resurrection? Statements from the Bible relating to this question deal with the believing primarily, not the unbelieving. To die is to be ushered into the presence of Christ, of course, without our bodies, or in a state of incompleteness. Paul confesses this to the Philippians (1:20–26). Certain other passages imply this time to be temporary while man awaits the resurrection. The resurrection statements in 1 Thessalonians (4:13–18) speak of the Lord's "bringing with him" those who had died *and* then "the dead in Christ will rise first." This points to a reunion of the spiritual nature with a transformed body. Totality of existence comes only at the resurrection. Having been already with Christ until the resurrection may denote that the resurrection is anticlimactic. But the resurrection only emphasizes the more that man's existence is not complete without his "spiritual body."

Other proposals have been offered to the foregoing scriptural assessment. *Reincarnation* is not a biblical idea, but it affirms that life enters into a new form of existence—either up or down the scale of life—depending upon one's previous goodness or evil. Yet if reincarnation is true, there is no way "to experience the subject's identity in the different incarnations." [37]

Soul-sleeping has been advocated by others, such as Jehovah's Witnesses. This means that the conscious existence ceases at death into a state of nonexistence. The resurrection really becomes a new creation. While the Bible sometimes speaks of death as "sleep," it does so only poetically. The believer enjoys the presence of Christ immediately after death.[38]

Purgatory is the conclusion from a premise that only those departing this life entirely free from venial sins will enter immediately

---

[36] Shires, *The Eschatology of Paul in the Light of Modern Scholarship,* p. 99.
[37] Tillich, *Systematic Theology,* III, 417.
[38] Cf. Luke 16:19–31; 23:43; Acts 7:59; 2 Cor. 5:8; Phil. 1:23; Rev. 6:9 and 20:4.

into heaven. Every sin must be "forgiven and expiated" before one can attain heaven.[39] The departed soul must be purified. Although one will ultimately be released from purgatory, according to Roman teaching, it is perhaps the lot of most of the redeemed. Purgatory is admittedly not a biblical doctrine.

The biblical answer is that the believer's present life does not cease at death, but becomes more intimate with God. Paul's conviction was that neither death nor anything else could separate us from the love of God in Christ (Rom. 8:38). To depart this life is to be with Christ.

Before passing to the next issue in eschatology, we can note the psychological problem of believing in life after death. It is paradoxical. Believing in life after death is not the comfort it is supposed to be. There is perhaps more comfort in not believing in life after death, for no thought of personal judgment enters this position. The believer in life after death may find that he is overwhelmed by the prospect of judgment. The unbeliever makes it easy for himself, but his unbelief is suspect "just because it is so easy and comforting."[40]

Hell

Hell as an eschatological concept has fallen on deaf ears in modern times. It is usually consigned to fundamentalists and sectarians. Others have turned it into a purgatory or yet air-conditioned it. Reevaluation of the idea is needed.

Language about hell needs overhauling, or cautious use. If one speaks of hell literally as a place of fire, questions like the following may be raised: what will be left when the body burns and how does fire affect the spiritual nature of man? Tillich questions the "psychological impossibility of imagining uninterrupted periods of mere suffering." [41]

On the other hand, to speak of hell in symbolic terms signifies for many that hell is emptied of all its traditional meaning. This is patently false, for the symbol does designate an ominous fact—alienation from God's presence. Frequent Scripture references indicate the serious nature of this.[42]

---

[39] *A Handbook of the Catholic Faith,* p. 461.
[40] Berdyaev, *The Destiny of Man,* p. 264.
[41] Tillich, *Systematic Theology,* III, 417.
[42] Matt. 8:12; 13:50; Mark 9:43–44; 9:47–48; Luke 16:23,28; Rev. 14:10; 21:8; Matt. 18:8; 2 Thess. 1:9.

Opponents of hell usually follow three lines of argument.

First, the religious rationalist argues that God in his justice would surely not send people to hell. He is too good for that. Such a position does not seriously consider the meaningful concept of God's holiness or the nature of man's sin.

Second, the biblical universalist argues that hell would be a defeat of the love of Christ and his death for all men. If one is governed by the authority of the Scriptures, one must excise or rationalize the biblical passages on hell. The idea of hell as judgment may offend one's sensitivities, but it is not only there but mentioned more frequently by Jesus than any other single voice in the New Testament.

Third, some argue for conditional immortality. Following the judgment the righteous go into eternal life, but the unjust are annihilated and will live no more. The arguments based on certain Scripture passages are mostly negative in form, being based on the fact that much less is said about the future existence of the unjust as opposed to the future of the redeemed.

Hell must be considered seriously because of the biblical authority in Christian faith. If one can rationalize hell, then what stops one from doing the same to the rest of the New Testament where it offends one? The heart of the Christian message—the incarnation, the death and resurrection of Christ—is offensive to some. Why stop with rationalizing hell?

Hell must receive serious consideration if freedom is accepted. "Paradoxical as it sounds, hell is the moral postulate of man's spiritual freedom. Hell is necessary not to ensure the triumph of justice and retribution to the wicked, but to save man from being forced to be good and compulsorily installed in heaven. In a certain sense, man has a moral right to hell—the right freely to prefer hell to heaven." [43]

Hell gives man the right to continually rebel against God. In this sense it can be said that God does not send men to hell; he merely permits them to continue in their evil ways in isolation from him. The wrath of God in this sense is reflected in Romans 1:18–32. The wrath of God is his giving up man to follow his own lusts, passions, lies, and corrupted intent.[44] Hell becomes the continued self-centered existence of man in absolute isolation from God. It is erroneous to

---

[43] Berdyaev, *The Destiny of Man*, p. 267.

[44] Bultmann, *Theology of the New Testament*, I, 288.

speak of "fellowship in hell"; this is meaningful only in relation to
God. Part of the horror of hell is "to have my fate left in my own
hands. It is not what God will do to me that is terrible, but what I
will do to myself." [45] The contradictory nature of universal salvation,
or *apocatastasis,* is that it denies the freedom of man to continue in
rebellion against God.

Heaven

Heaven does not receive due consideration in much modern
thought. Heaven is regarded as a projection of man's wishes and desires; it is regarded as an escape from the difficulties of life; and it is
designated as a myth. In rejecting heaven, men secularize its qualities, and communism may be regarded as a secularized version of
man's attempt to build a heaven on earth. Heaven cannot be dismissed as mere mythology, for pagan mythologies relate to the past,
while the kingdom of God, or heaven, is futuristic.

Heaven as a biblical concept is the kingdom of God come in its
fulness. The new beginning now reaches its fulness. Heaven as a
concept stands for fulness of being, fulness of life, and the inaugura-
tion of man's everlasting life.

Only a few comments are given in the Scriptures about heaven.
Phrases like "the restitution of all things" (Acts 3:21, KJV); a "new
heaven and a new earth" (cf. 2 Peter 3:13; Rev. 21:1), and the
"new Jerusalem" (Rev. 21:2) indicate the new quality in existence.

Heaven has received a poor press. To many it sounds dull, monot-
onous, and lifeless. Mark Twain's description of heaven—where men
who hate to sing, not only sing all day but play a rusty harp, too—is
a caricature—an untrue view of heaven.

Heaven must be conceived in words of meaning and fulfilment of
God's creation. Creativity will be a part of heaven in opposition to
idleness. One might speak of ecstasy as a foretaste of it. The quality
of existence is often defined by negation—no night, no sickness, no
sin—because of the lack of an analogy for comparison. Heaven may
be described also as liberation, "because the creation itself will be
set free from its bondage to decay and obtain the glorious liberty of
the children of God" (Rom. 8:21).

---

[45] Berdyaev, *The Destiny of Man,* p. 277.

Appendix

The Holy Spirit
and the
Charismatic Movement

The modern-day charismatic movement has an unusual doctrine of the Holy Spirit. A basic assumption of the movement is that the baptism of the Spirit is a postconversion experience. In a widely circulated booklet titled *Baptists and the Baptism of the Holy Spirit*, one pastor declares:

To tell a born-again Christian that he does not have the Spirit is to show ignorance because we must have the Spirit to be children of God. But there is a difference in having the Spirit in regeneration, and having the Baptism of the Holy Ghost and Fire. . . .[1]

A similar distinction is made by Robert C. Frost in his widely circulated book, *Aglow with the Spirit:*

It is essential that you know Jesus Christ as your Saviour before you can meet Him as your Baptizer.[2]

The Scripture teaches differently. Peter's response to the multitude at Pentecost was "Repent, and be baptized everyone of you in the name of Jesus Christ for the forgiveness of your sins; and you shall receive the gift of the Holy Spirit" (Acts 2:38). Conversion and the baptism of the Holy Spirit are linked in Acts not only in Peter's sermon, but a surprising relation is seen in Acts 19

---

[1] John H. Osteen, *Baptists and the Baptism of the Holy Spirit*, Los Angeles: Full Gospel Businessmen's Fellowship International, 1963, p. 8.

[2] Robert C. Frost, *Aglow with the Spirit*, Plainfield, New Jersey: Logos International, p. 111.

where Paul asks the disciples of John the Baptist: "Did you receive the Holy Spirit when you believed?" Other books of the New Testament link the baptism of the Spirit and conversion just as Paul did in Acts 19. See how the promised Holy Spirit is linked with believing in Ephesians 1:13. The same relation is seen in Romans 5:1-5 and in Acts 11:17. There is an exception to this relationship in Acts 8:1-24 which relates to the hostility problem between the Samaritans and the Jews. A probable reason for this exception is that God did an exceptional thing to incorporate the hybrid Samaritans into the household of God. A special apostolic mission took place for their receiving of the Spirit.

The charismatic movement errs in its use of the term "baptism of the Spirit." The charismatics regard baptism of the Spirit as a second blessing, and the filling of the Spirit as a conversion gift. This reverses the use in the New Testament. The baptism of the Spirit is related to conversion, the filling of the Spirit is a term related to testimony and witness for Christ. When the disciples prayed for boldness to witness, God answered by empowering them, which is symbolized in the phrase "filled with the Spirit" (Acts 4:31). This occurs several times in Acts and reflects the highs and lows of service. If it be called a second blessing, one must continue to the third, fifth, and hundredth blessing.

The charismatic movement has another unusual emphasis. It maintains that the unique model for explaining how the Spirit works is preeminently seen in the Book of Acts. Consider the following:

No one would deny that our criteria for all our church work is found in the Book of Acts. Nobody who knows anything about the Bible denies that our primary example is the Book of Acts. We must go back to the Book of Acts, because that is where God told us the kind of Church He wanted.[3]

This argument is suspect for two reasons: (1) The Book of Acts makes no claim like the above, and (2) we must accept the whole of the New Testament as the basis of faith and practice. A standard of "Acts only" is the partial revival of an Early Church heresy propagated by Marcion who picked out the books of the New Testament that supported his doctrine and rejected the rest of them along with the Old Testament

---

[3] Osteen, *Baptists and the Baptism of the Holy Spirit*, p. 10.

Even if "Acts only" were accepted as a norm, does the charismatic movement abide by its norm? What about communal living? Do they follow the example of Acts? If Acts is the norm, must we also become Jews before we become Christians? Must we assume the early pattern of witnessing in the synagogue before going to the Gentile? Other questions could be raised. But we must conclude that every Scripture inspired by God gives us the adequate foundation for the church in its doctrine and practical outlook and not a single book separated out for promoting a particular doctrine.

A third and more controversial element of the charismatic movement is the idea that speaking in tongues is the only sure evidence that you have been baptized by the Holy Spirit. Think of the implications of the following statements:

The Scriptural evidence of the Baptism of the Holy Spirit is speaking in tongues.[4]

David J. Du Plessis, the theologian and recognized leader in the movement, wrote,

People in Pentecostal movements are very fond of the expression, "Tongues is the *initial* evidence of the baptism in the Holy Spirit." This is not found in Scripture, but it is nevertheless the truth according to the record in the Acts, from the day of Pentecost onward.[5]

The Bible does not give a basis for saying that speaking in tongues is the evidence of the Spirit's presence. There are only three instances in Acts where speaking in tongues is noted. These instances are connected with conversion stories of a unique kind and are only three of more than seventeen conversion stories in Acts. The first is in Acts 2 when the church, the New Israel, the New Covenant community is founded. Only the apostles communicated in languages to the multitude. Then three thousand people were converted and Peter's promise was fulfilled. Nothing is said about the converts speaking in tongues or that they were supposed to. The second glossolalia story is connected with the Jewish issue of fellowship with non-Jews, and the dramatic conversion of Cornelius and his family. Moreover, Peter and his friends were surprised that God gave His

---

[4] Osteen, *Baptists and the Baptism of the Holy Spirit*, p. 5.

[5] David J. Du Plessis, *The Spirit Bade Me Go*, Plainfield, New Jersey: Logos International, 1970, p. 89.

Spirit to the Gentiles as well as their speaking in tongues. This was the official turning point in which Christ's gospel is seen for all people. It may be seen as a second Pentecost.

The third glossolalia story appears in Acts 19. The context in Acts 18:24—19:7 indicates the problem of the relation of John the Baptist's followers to Christ. The story indicates that John's baptism was not related to the Spirit and was incomplete and non-Christian. These twelve men were converted to Christ (19:4-5), were baptized, and then spoke in tongues.

Thus there are three examples or parables telling the basic truths about the uniqueness of the Christian church. It is the New Israel, it is open to Gentiles and Jews, and the movement of John the Baptist finds its fulfillment in the Christian church.

The other conversion stories say nothing about tongues. Is it not strange that they are absent in those stories?

But there is another dimension to the statement that speaking in tongues is an evidence of the Spirit's presence. What about non-Christian glossolalia? Scholars have described this phenomena among primitive religions, Islam, and other world religions. Does this mean they too have the Spirit of God? This would prove more than even the charismatics would want to conclude.

What, then, is the proper evidence given to the believer whereby he can know he has the Spirit of God? Scripture is clear that this is based upon a promise and a sign. The promise relates to being baptized (Acts 2:38) and water baptism is the sign of it. This must not be viewed mechanically, for Simon was baptized but unconverted (Acts 8). Instead, the promised Holy Spirit which Jesus talked about indwells *any* who believe and He does this *when* one believes (Eph. 1:13). No better assurance can be given than God's promise.

We must now look at a facet of the movement that is frequently overlooked. The charismatic movement has a methodology. In other words, there are conditions or steps for coming to speak in tongues. A sample list would include "separation from sin, repentance and baptism, hearing of faith, obedience, intense desire, asking of God."[6]

Frost tells how he counseled people to begin speaking in tongues:

---

[6] Frederick D. Bruner, *A Theology of the Holy Spirit,* Grand Rapids: Eerdmans, 1971, p. 92.

We encouraged her to move her lips and tongue so as to form syllables, realizing in faith that these would be the prompting of God's Spirit.[7]

Du Plessis notes,

The moment you believe His word, His promises, you dare to speak, and the Spirit gives utterances.[8]

Again, Frost says,

I suggested he lift his voice and move his lips and tongue in faith realizing that in this way he would be cooperating with the Holy Spirit's desire to direct his praise.[9]

Many of the charismatic testimonies describe a discontent in their faith, an intense desire for something deeper, a struggle with the meaning of their existence, and then a pursuit of the gift of tongues. Following this procedure, glossolalia in the modern charismatic movement may be the fruit of an intense longing and self-suggestion that brings fulfillment.

In evaluating the matter, we believe that the Bible, even the Book of Acts, gives no methodology for speaking in tongues. In the three passages in Acts (2; 10—11; 19) there was no seeking. In Acts 2 the apostles were sitting, not seeking; in Acts 10—11 they were surprised it happened, which is not intense longing; and in Acts 19 the Spirit's presence is connected with baptism as in Acts 2:38.

We must conclude that there are no conditions offered in Acts whereby the apostles were to strive, yearn, struggle, act, or move their lips to initiate the Spirit's presence. The Spirit came as promised, not as won. If there is a methodology for gaining the second blessing, as the charismatics see it, then Christian faith has become corrupted to the requirements of the Judaizers of the Book of Acts and the Epistle to the Galatians. The Judaizers followed Paul around saying that something more than Christ was needed, that Christ was not adequate—one needed to obey the law of Moses also. The charismatics may be a modern variation of the Judaizers in saying that conversion to Christ is not enough—one must be second-blessed.

If there is any truth at all in Galatians, Colossians, Romans,

---

[7] Frost, *Aglow with the Spirit*, p. 94.

[8] Du Plessis, *The Spirit Bade Me Go*, p. 72.

[9] Frost, *Aglow with the Spirit*, p. 91

Hebrews, and other New Testament books, it is that when a man receives Christ as Savior he receives the Spirit as God's first and last gift of Himself.

The charismatic movement has theological problems at its core. Yet many do testify to their spiritual growth in the movement. How can one criticize something that makes for spiritual growth? Any evaluation must be on biblical rather than on other grounds. Our chief criticism is that the movement is not honest with its use of Scripture. We must not begin with experience and try to fit the New Testament to it. We must begin rather with the New Testament and seek to evaluate our experiences. There is no religious authority in experience. The real question, then, is: Is there biblical authority for this particular modern religious experience? Is it the same as the experience described in the New Testament? A fair examination of the New Testament brings us to a negative answer to both questions. The literature points to self-suggestion that can be emotionally lifting. But psychological lifts must not be confused with biblical theology.

GENERAL INDEX

Abelard, Peter, 149, 151-53, 154, 157, 159, 172
Abraham, 51, 90, 107, 152, 164, 167, 169-70, 181, 292
Abrahamic Covenant, 164, 167, 169-70
Adam, 46, 51, 169, 179-80, 181, 182, 195, 200-08, 214, 215, 216
  as covenant head, 202-03
  "Everyman," 179-80, 182, 204
  historical being, 179-80, 181-82
Adler, Mortimer J., 188-89
Adoptionism, 128, 131
Age of accountability," 206-07, 232
Ambrose, 196
Amillennialism. See Nonmillennialism
Anabaptists, 268, 269
Animism, 80, 324
Annihilation, 327
Annunciation, 106
Anselm of Canterbury, 9-10, 105, 149, 150-52, 153, 154, 157-58, 172
Anthropocentric religion, 3
Anthropology, 175-76, 194. See also Man, doctrine of
Antichrist, 312
Apollinarianism, 129-30, 131
Apostacy, 317
Apostle's Creed, 120, 232, 264
Aquinas, Thomas, 4, 6, 7, 47, 205
Arianism, 115, 131
Ascension, 38, 106
Assurance of salvation, 142-43, 164, 171, 243, 250, 291, 296, 298
Athanasian Creed, 109
Athanasius, 108, 205
Atheism/Atheist, 4, 5, 13, 16, 58, 98, 212. See also Belief in God, naturalistic
Atonement, 136, 147-73, 286
  central motif of, 160-68
  methodology, 159-60
  motivation for, 148, 152, 154
  necessity of, 83, 150
  presupposition of, 157-59
  self-, 224

  significance of, 85, 91
  theories of
    classical, 148-50, 157, 170, 172
    commercial, 150-52
    concept of honor, 150-52, 157, 158, 172
    example, 152-53, 157, 159
    Latin, 150-52
    new covenant, 160-73
      implications of, 168-73
    "no atonement," 155-57
    penal, 153-55, 157, 172
    ransom, 148-50
    satisfaction, 150-52, 172
Atonement, Day of, 161
Augustine, 24, 25, 103, 108, 111-12, 196, 201, 202, 204, 257, 260
Augustinianism, 202-03, 205
Aulén, Gustaf, 76, 85, 94, 95, 149, 211, 212, 215, 216, 217, 220, 232, 232, 234, 240, 242, 243
Authoritarianism, 71
Authority in religion, 52-75. See also Bible, authenticity, authority
  definition, 72-74
  ideal, 53
  pattern, 67-68
  problem, 52-75
  types, 53-72
    Bible, 68-70, 73, 75
    Christ, 68-70, 71-72
    church, 58-63, 67-68, 70-71, 262, 271, 275, 277, 285. See also Church government
    conscience, 54-56, 64
    experience, 71-72
    religious, 56-57
    Holy Spirit, 68-70, 71
    inner light, 53-54, 64
    reason, 57-58, 64, 71-72
    Scripture, 63-67, 274
Ayers, A. J., 77

Baptism, 87-88, 117, 123, 136, 152, 230, 232, 257, 277, 285 286-98, 303, 332. See also Sacraments
Christ's, 106, 122-23, 135, 286

335

SCRIPTURE INDEX